PRAISE FOR
FROM ABRAHAM TO PAUL:

Andrew Steinmann has placed biblical scholarship in his debt by this meticulous and magnificent addition to (indeed, replacement of) such magisterial works on biblical chronology as those by Edwin Thiele and Jack Finegan, the former limited to Israel's United Monarchy and the latter embracive of the full canon. Grounded in primary texts, Steinmann lays out here a foundation that doubtless will provide the basis for all subsequent discussions of biblical chronology, an indispensable preliminary to a proper understanding of the biblical narrative.

—Eugene H. Merrill, PhD
Distinguished Professor of Old Testament Studies
Dallas Theological Seminary
Distinguished Professor of Old Testament Interpretation
The Southern Baptist Theological Seminary

I can see this work appealing to both specialists and non-experts in the field, and indeed even to interested laypeople. Its combination of detailed table of contents, well organized and straightforward presentation, and especially the abundance of charts and graphics suggests that it will serve well as a reference tool. I very much appreciate Dr. Steinmann's even-handed and respectful tone. I say this because, although Steinmann assumes an unabashedly conservative posture with respect to the Scriptures and the Church's traditional hermeneutic, he does not shy away from engaging scholarship that proceeds from different presuppositions. While arguing against opinions and conclusions with which he is at odds— for example those of higher critics—Steinmann does not belittle or condescend. . . . Where he synthesizes and explains the well-founded conclusions of previous scholarship, he does so clearly and effectively. On the other hand, in those places where he challenges consensus views and presents new proposals, he does so persuasively, on the basis of careful research and well-reasoned arguments.

—Robert A. Sorensen, PhD
Associate Professor of Greek and Theology
Concordia University Chicago

Readers familiar with standard works in this field such as Merrill's *Kingdom of Priests* will be pleased to find much new information in this volume. New insights into the Quirinius census, the matching of Jubilee/Sabbatical year cycles with the date of the Exodus, the timing of the Magis' visit, and the sequence of events of the Passion Week—including the moon "turning to blood" immediately after the death of the Messiah—are part of Dr. Steinmann's intensely interesting study. Laymen and scholars alike will find their faith strengthened by the precision and factuality of the Bible in historical matters.

—Rodger C. Young
Independent Historian and Chronologist
St. Louis, MO

Steinmann's approach at point after point confirms the veracity, historicity, and accuracy of what is recorded in the biblical text. He comes to the texts sympathetically and patiently sifts the evidence, seeking explanations that account for all the evidence. This is evangelical scholarship at its best.

—James M. Hamilton, PhD
Associate Professor of Biblical Theology
The Southern Baptist Theological Seminary

FROM ABRAHAM TO PAUL

FROM ABRAHAM TO PAUL

A BIBLICAL CHRONOLOGY

ANDREW E. STEINMANN

Peer Reviewed

CONCORDIA PUBLISHING HOUSE • SAINT LOUIS

Concordia
Publishing House

Peer Reviewed

Published by Concordia Publishing House
3558 S. Jefferson Ave., St. Louis, MO 63118-3968
1-800-325-3040 · www.cph.org

This work uses the SBL Greek and Hebrew Unicode fonts developed by the Font Foundation, under the leadership of the Society of Biblical Literature. For further information on this font or on becoming a Font Foundation member, see http://www.sbl-site.org/educational/biblicalfonts.aspx

Cover:
Photo 1: Ziggurat of Nanna at Ur © Michael S. Yamashita/Corbis
Photos 2, 4-6: © Shutterstock, Inc
Photo 3: Canaanite Idol from Late Bronze II © Dr. James C. Martin.
    Israel Museum, Jerusalem. Photographed by permission.

Manufactured in the United States of America

Library of Congress Cataloging-in-Publication Data

Steinmann, Andrew.
 From Abraham to Paul : a biblical chronology / Andrew E. Steinmann.
   p. cm.
 Includes bibliographic references and index.
 ISBN 978-0-7586-2799-5
 1. Bible--Chronology--Handbooks, manuals, etc. 2. Bible--Chronology--Charts, diagrams, etc.
I. Steinmann, Andrew E. II. Title.

 BS637.3.S74 2011
 220.9'5--dc22   2011005880

 6 7 8 9 10   22 21 20 19 18 17

TABLE OF CONTENTS

Table of Contents

LIST OF TABLES

LIST OF FIGURES

DETAILED REFERENCE CHARTS

Dr. Steinmann prepared a series of extensive chronological charts to supplement the material found in *From Abraham to Paul: A Biblical Chronology*. Purchasers of the book may download these charts by going to **www.cph.org/aescharts**.

The charts, which provide biblical chapter and verse references throughout, include:

- The main Old Testament and Apocrypha chart covering the years from Abraham to the birth of Jesus
- The main New Testament chart covering the years from Roman involvement in Judea to the destruction of the temple in AD 70
- A timeline covering the biblical era, including rulers in the wider ancient world (Egypt, Mesopotamia, Greece, and Rome for the OT one; Egypt and Rome for the NT).

Tabs of information connected with the charts include the following:

- Lists of specific dates (i.e., those that can be narrowed to a specific month or day)
- Dates and references for Judges and Samuel
- The Kings of Israel and Judah
- A post-exilic timeline
- Events of 458–475 BC
- Events of Tishri 445 BC
- Jesus' ministry
- Holy Week AD 33
- 14 Nisan AD 33
- Paul's 1st and 2nd missionary journeys
- Paul's 3rd missionary journey
- Paul's imprisonment and journey to Rome

FOREWORD

Ask any American high-school senior today to place into proper chronological order the Attack of 9/11, the Great Depression, the Vietnam War, and World War II, and I would guess that he or she would happily and fairly easily oblige. Quiz any English schoolboy as to the rough dates of William Gladstone, Winston Churchill, and Tony Blair—you would probably get a reasonably good answer. Ask a German schoolgirl the corresponding years of the Unification of Germany, the Berlin Blockade, and the fall of the Berlin wall, I would wager she would get her facts more or less straight. Never mind that so many people are lamenting the state of education these days. Most educated people know the rough outlines of their national history, just as they know that national history matters. The reason it matters is because one cannot really begin to reflect on one's personal self-identity without first reflecting on one's place in history. In order for us to make sense of ourselves, we need to make some sense of history. And history, we find out soon enough, makes absolutely no sense apart from some awareness of chronology, sequence, and causality. Without the ability to place figures and events on a kind of map, the study of history soon degenerates into an insipid exercise of rehearing assorted and seemingly meaningless facts.

Educated modern-day Christians seem to understand this point reasonably well enough (at least no less so than their peers who have no interest in the Bible or Christianity). This should come as no surprise. There is, so far as I can see, nothing about Christianity that should render its adherents less appreciative of history than any other religion or worldview. In fact, given Christianity's status as a *historical* religion, with roots deeply entwined in the recorded past, one would think that Christians would possess a relatively high degree of historical awareness. Certainly, one might expect that a

Christian, who looks for salvation in God's self-revelation in history, would place a relatively higher premium on getting history straight than, say, a Buddhist, who searches for salvation within a timeless sphere. One would think this . . . however, I don't think there is any evidence that such is the case. In my experience, Christians care about national and world history about as much or as little as their neighboring Buddhists or Hindus—no more, no less.

But then this observation makes it all the more strange when we also observe that Christians have curious double-mindedness when it comes to history. Sure, when it comes to sorting out the relative order of the Vietnam conflict and 9/11, so-called "secular events", Christians will likely want to get their facts right—and see the facts as important. But then why is that when it comes to "sacred events" (call it the "history of Israel" or the "human history of the kingdom of God"), it is almost a mark of piety *not* to know about precise dates and times? Why is it considered in so many circles almost a matter of true spirituality not only *not* to know the historical facts but also not to care?

It is an odd state of affairs but it is a dynamic which I think can hardly be denied in the contemporary church. It is a dynamic in which we tacitly agree on the necessity and value of pinning down "real history" with real dates, but somehow make a virtue of keeping biblical history vague, fuzzy and hopelessly muddled in our heads. Part of this, I think, has to do with the way in which we have been conditioned to think about the Bible: not as history, but more as story. Somehow, somewhere along the line, we became unconsciously convinced that the likes of Abraham, David, and Jesus are much closer to the likes of Bilbo Baggins and Luke Skywalker than to, say, Winston Churchill or Osama Bin Laden. Of course, for those of us whose image of the David and Goliath story conjures memories of Sunday School flannel-graph figures or brightly-colored children's storybooks, the slip is easy to make. The problem is that even though we grow up intellectually in how we think about things like law and economics and human psychology, we somehow cordon off the Bible from rigorous intellectual handling so that it in fact never grows up along with us. It remains more the stuff of storybook than real history.

Enter Andrew E. Steinmann's *From Abraham to Paul*. It is a book which should have been written decades ago. Here's why. Steinmann not only assumes—quite rightly—that history matters, but he also shows two things about biblical history. First, he shows that in many cases with a little scholarly spadework we can have a pretty good idea as to when key events took place, events like the life of Abraham, the Conquest of the Promised Land, the birth of Jesus, or Paul's Second Missionary Journey. These events are not the yarn of legend: on the contrary, there is every good intellectually-compelling reason to accept them as history, history that really happened in time and space. For the believing Bible reader, there is something faith-building about such assurances when they come; for the casual reader of the Bible (whatever his or her faith commitment), there is something fascinating about them. Every year droves of westerners spend countless millions of dollars on Holy Land trips, guided tours of the sacred space of the Abrahamic faiths. In this volume Steinmann gives a guided tour of sacred time: "Here's what we can know chronologically; here's how we can know it." In these pages both the curious mind and the worshipful soul will find themselves sated.

The second thing Steinmann shows about history—and this is no less important—is its complexity. Some of the questions which the book takes up are thorny questions indeed, having provoked lots of black ink and fiery debate along the way. The author's approach is never polemical, but always clear; the positions taken are not necessarily always the standard positions, but they are always defended from the evidence. Indeed, it is precisely this quality that makes the book such a delight to read. Whereas Bible handbooks and dictionaries have a tendency to settle on the dominant scholarly position of the day without much argumentation one way or another, and whereas so much scholarly writing coming off the press has to justify its existence by cutting against the grain of consensus, *From Abraham to Paul* strikes an elegant balance between the two extremes. It succeeds as a reference work, and thus should find its way onto the shelf of every pastor or Bible teacher; it succeeds too as a fresh scholarly contribution, and thus should make its way into the library of advanced students of the Bible who want to stay up-to-date. Some books try to speak to lay audiences and scholars only to fail to address either: this book has hit the two targets simultaneously and hit them well.

We should be grateful for books like this. We should be grateful, because God made history and history matters. Apart from the conviction that our faith is a historical faith, we are left only to cast about. But, when we are fully persuaded that sacred history meshes with the history in which we live and move and have our being, that is when biblical faith becomes a real possibility. Likewise, every intellectually serious reader of the Bible (pious or not so pious) will learn to think twice before allowing himself or herself to be bullied (happily or anxiously) by the skeptics. True, there is so much we don't know. But, by the same token, there is much we can know—and know with some confidence. Whether or not you remember all the detailed arguments of the book you are about to read (of course the best books need to be studied), the heart-and-mind value of re-connecting the biblical world with the "real world" can hardly be overstated. Somehow in our confused modern-day thinking, we have managed to put asunder what God has joined together. A book like this is an excellent and fascinating step towards our re-forging the broken link.

NICHOLAS PERRIN
Franklin S. Dyrness Chair of Biblical Studies
Wheaton College Graduate School

PREFACE

For many years now I have had an interest in biblical chronology. Knowing *when* some event in the Bible happened can often add to our understanding of its significance. Being able to place an event in its temporal context in relation to other events within the pages of Scripture as well as within its extra-biblical context is useful, enlightening, and important for understanding the event better and more fully. Knowing *when* a biblical event occurred is every bit as important as known *where* and *why* it occurred.

However, it is not always easy to determine when an event took place, even a biblical event that has been provided with chronological information by the biblical author. This is so, because ancient ways of recording chronological data varied over time and from place to place and do not often match modern ways of understanding time. This book is an attempt to provide a chronology for much of the Bible. It also attempts to explain in some detail how we know a particular dating is accurate. It offers a defense for a particular biblical chronology, often accepting some proposals that have been previously put forward and rejecting others. While some readers will find the discussion very detailed and technical, specialists may wish at times for more discussion. This work attempts to find a middle ground by explaining enough for those who come at these chronological issues fresh in order to offer them enough explanation so that they can understand the matter at hand and make their own judgment as to whether the present author has made a reasonable argument in each case. At the same time, for those who wish to explore some of the chronological issues more deeply, an extensive bibliography has been provided. In addition, I would also direct readers to the bibliographic sections of Jack Finegan's *Handbook of Biblical Chronology*.

A few words should also be said about what this book is not:

- This is not a book about when individual books of the Bible were written, though it certainly has implications for dating the composition of many biblical books. The date of the composition of some books is directly relevant to the discussion and will be treated (i.e., for certain OT prophetic books or for the letters of Paul). However, no attempt will be made to date the composition of every biblical book.

- This is not a book about other proposed chronologies or other Christian chronographers, though at times, when relevant, other chronologies or chronographers will be mentioned. For a survey of other Christian chronographers and chronologies, the appropriate sections in Finegan's *Handbook* can be consulted.

- This is not a book about historical events surrounding the biblical narrative, though at times it will be important to treat such extra-biblical events. Readers may have to consult other works on ancient history for further details on this score.

- Finally, this is not a book about the historiographic methods of ancient historians such as Josephus or Eusebius or the Greek historians that preceded them. At times detailed discussions of such works will be necessary and helpful. However, there are many competent treatments of ancient historiography in general and of the historiographic methods of particular ancient historians. That work will not be reproduced here.

One may also ask why the limits of this book were chosen. Why begin with Abraham and end with Paul? Several reasons led to this choice. First of all, these limits cover most biblical events from the most important person in Genesis to the most important one in the latter parts of the New Testament. That in itself recommends these limits. Second, the heavily intertwined chronological and theological issues surrounding the period in Genesis before Abraham would require a book at least as large as the present volume to treat adequately and would detract from an otherwise nearly complete and comprehensive overview of biblical chronology. Such a project is best put aside for a later time and, perhaps, a different author.[1]

The choice of ending with Paul is, perhaps, even more obvious. This is where the book of Acts ends, although there are some chronological statements in Paul's letters that allow us to extend the treatment of Paul's life a bit longer than Acts does. However, there is barely any chronological information in the New Testament itself to extend a biblical chronology any further. Certainly whichever James one identifies as the author of the letter of James, that author was martyred before Paul's death. Peter apparently was martyred about the time of Paul, so there is nothing beyond Paul's day in his letters. There are no sure chronological markers in Jude. That leaves only the Johannine letters and Revelation. While these are often placed at the end of the first century based on church tradition, there is no chronological information within them that can guide us to any sure dates for additional New Testament chronology (such as the year of John's exile to Patmos or his death). Thus, the decision to end with Paul is based on practical considerations—there are few events mentioned in the rest of the New Testament and no way to date these few events.

This book also has an apologetic aspect—many biblical scholars doubt the historicity of large parts of the Bible, such as the narratives in Genesis or Luke's portrayal of the church in Acts. This work is written in part to demonstrate that it is not unreasonable to accept the Bible's witness as historically accurate and that in doing so, one can reconstruct a chronology that coordinates well with reliable

---

[1] This should not be taken to mean that the present author has no interest in the chronological aspects of the first chapters of Genesis. For instance, see Steinmann, "אחד as an Ordinal Number and the Meaning of Genesis 1:5."

chronological information from extra-biblical sources. It is not necessary or even desirable to discount the narratives about Israel's patriarchs as unhistorical or to deny Paul's authorship of some letters attributed to him on the basis of scholarly theories that take for granted that the Scriptures are theologically and ideologically biased, and are, therefore, historically inaccurate and, at times, historically contrived. While the books of the Bible possess a theological viewpoint, that fact does not in-and-of-itself require them to be historically inaccurate.

Throughout this book are numerous citations of previous literature. For modern literature the last name of the author and the title of the work are always listed. Further information on these works can be found in the bibliography at the end of this book. For ancient literature, including the books of the Bible, the standard abbreviations are used as defined in *The SBL Handbook of Style for Ancient Near Eastern, Biblical, and Early Christian Studies.* Bible references are separated by ‖ to indicate that they are parallel passages. References to Josephus are given in two systems. The first is that of the Loeb Classical Library. The second, which follows in brackets, is that of William Whiston's English translation for those readers who do not have access to Josephus in Greek.

No work of this range could be written without the help and support of others. I am grateful to Concordia University Chicago for the sabbatical leave that enabled me to work on this book. I would like to express my gratitude to Rodger C. Young, who was generous in sharing his work on the chronology of the ancient kingdoms of Israel and Judah and who aided me tremendously through e-mail correspondence concerning many technical issues relating to that topic. I would also like to acknowledge my colleague John Rhoads who generously shared his work on Josephus' treatment of the census of Quirinius with me in addition to serving as a sounding board for my ideas. John, thank you for the hours of discussion in my office. They were greatly appreciated.

Two peer reviewers offered comments and suggestions for improvement to this book: Rodger C. Young and my colleague Robert Sorensen. To both I am greatly appreciative of their time spent in reviewing and offering helpful suggestions for improvements. My son Christopher read a preliminary copy of this work, checked all of the Scripture references for me, corrected a number of typographical errors, and suggested several improvements. His help was also much appreciated. Of course, any remaining errors are my responsibility and not those of the reviewers. Finally, and most importantly, I would like to thank my wife Rebecca who often inquired about my progress, never complained about my piles and files of materials in our shared home office, and even gave me wide berth when I needed to ruminate over any number of thorny issues. Of her it can truly be said: רָחֹק מִפְּנִינִים מִכְרָהּ.

STANDARD ABBREVIATIONS

|| Parallel biblical passage

LXX   Septuagint, the ancient family of Greek translations of the Old Testament

n   used after a year date to indicate that the year began in the spring month of Nisan (e.g., 754n began in spring of 754 BC and ended after winter in early 753 BC)

t   used after a year date to indicate that the year began in the fall month of Tishri (e.g., 754t began in fall of 754 BC and ended after summer in 753 BC)

RESOURCE ABBREVIATIONS

Note: Abbreviations for biblical books and for ancient literature are the standard abbreviations set forth in Patrick H. Alexander, et. al, eds. *The SBL Handbook of Style for Ancient Near Eastern, Biblical, and Early Christian Studies.* (Peabody, MA: Hendrickson, 1999).

AJSL	*American Journal of Semitic Languages and Literature*
AMI	*Archaeologische Mitteilungen aus Iran*
AnBib	Analecta biblica
Ag. Ap.	Josephus, *Against Apion*
ANET	*Ancient Near Eastern Texts Relating to the Old Testament.* Ed. J. B. Pritchard. Third ed. Princeton: Princeton University, 1969.
Ant.	Josephus, *Jewish Antiquities*
AUSS	*Andrews University Seminary Studies*
BA	*Biblical Archaeologist*
BAIAS	*Bulletin of the Anglo-Israel Archaeological Society*
BAR	*Biblical Archaeology Review*
b. 'Arak	Babylonian Talmud, tractate *'Arakin*
BASOR	*Bulletin of the American Schools of Oriental Research*
BDF	Blass, F., A. Debrunner, and R. W. Funk. *A Greek Grammar of the New Testament and Other Early Christian Literature.* Chicago: University of Chicago, 1961.

Bib	*Biblica*
BJRL	*Bulletin of the John Rylands University Library of Manchester*
BN	*Biblische Notizen*
BR	*Biblical Research*
b. Roš Haš	Babylonian Talmud, tractate *Roš Haššanah*
BSac	*Bibliotheca sacra*
b. Sanh.	Babylonian Talmud, tractate *Sanhedrin*
b. Ta 'an	Babylonian Talmud, tractate *T 'anit*
t. Ta'an	Tosefta, tractate *Ta'anit*
y. Ta'an	Jerusalem Talmud, tractate Ta'anit
CAH	*The Cambridge Ancient History*. Second Edition. Cambridge: Cambridge University, 1970–2005.
CBQ	*Catholic Biblical Quarterly*
CH	*Church History*
Chm	*Churchman*
CJ	*Concordia Journal*
CJT	*Canadian Journal of Theology*
CQ	*Classical Quarterly*
CTQ	*Concordia Theological Quarterly*
Did	*Didaskalia*
ETL	*Ephemerides theologicae Lovanienses*
EvQ	*Evangelical Quarterly*
ExpTim	*Expository Times*
Haer.	Irenaeus, *Haereses*
HALOT	Koehler, L., W. Baumgartner, and J. J. Stamm. *The Hebrew and Aramaic Lexicon of the Old*

	Testament. Trans. and ed. M. E. J. Richardson. 5 vols. Leiden: Brill, 1994–2000.
HAT	Handbuch zum Alten Testament
HTR	*Harvard Theological Review*
HUCA	*Hebrew Union College Annual*
IDBSup	*The Interpreter's Dictionary of the Bible, Supplementary Volume.* Edited by Keith Crim. Nashville: Abingdon, 1976.
IEJ	*Israel Exploration Journal*
IJT	*Indian Journal of Theology*
Int	*Interpretation*
JANESCU	*Journal of the Ancient Near Eastern Society of Columbia University*
JAOS	*Journal of the American Oriental Society*
JBL	*Journal of Biblical Literature*
JBQ	*Jewish Bible Quarterly*
JBR	*Journal of Bible and Religion*
JCS	*Journal of Cuneiform Studies*
JEA	*Journal of Egyptian Archaeology*
JETS	*Journal of the Evangelical Theological Society*
JNES	*Journal of Near Eastern Studies*
Joüon	Joüon, Paul and T. Muraoka. *A Grammar of Biblical Hebrew.* Second edition. Subsidia Biblica. Rome: Biblical Institute, 2006.
JQR	*Jewish Quarterly Review*
JSJ	*Journal for the Study of Judaism in the Persian, Hellenistic and Roman Periods*
JSNT	*Journal for the Study of the New Testament*

JSOT	*Journal for the Study of the Old Testament*
JSOTSup	Journal of the Study of the Old Testament: Supplement Series
JTS	*Journal of Theological Studies*
Judaism	*Judaism*
J.W.	Josephus, *The Jewish War*
Levant	*Levant*
LQ	*Lutheran Quarterly*
LXX	Septuagint
MSJ	*Master's Seminary Journal*
MT	Masoretic Text of the Hebrew Old Testament
NAC	New American Commentary
NASB	New American Standard Bible
NBD	Douglas, J. D. and N. Hillyer, eds. *New Bible Dictionary*. Third edition. Downers Grove: Intervarsity, 1996.
NedTT	*Nederlands theologisch tijdschrift*
NET Bible	New English Translation Bible
NETS	*New English Translation of the Septuagint*
NRSV	New Revised Standard Version
NTS	*New Testament Studies*
OBO	Orbis biblicus et orientalis
OTL	Old Testament Library
PEQ	*Palestine Exploration Quarterly*
PL	Patrologia latina [= Patrologiae cursus completus: Series latina]. Ed. J.-P. Migne. 217 vols. Paris 1844–1864
PRSt	*Perspectives in Religious Studies*

RB	*Revue biblique*
ResQ	*Restoration Quarterly*
RevExp	*Review & Expositor*
RevQ	*Revue de Qumran*
RSO	*Revista degli studi orientali*
RTR	*Reformed Theological Review*
SacEr	*Sacris Erudiri*
SAOC	Studies in Ancient Oriental Civilizations
SBLSP	Society of Biblical Literature Seminar Papers
SJLA	Studies in Judaism in Late Antiquity
SJOT	*Scandinavian Journal of the Old Testament*
S. *'Olam Rab.*	*Seder Olam Rabbah*
Spec. Laws	Philo, *On the Special Laws*
SR	*Studies in Religion/Sciences religieuses*
ST	*Studia theologica*
TAD	Porten, Bezalel and Ada Yardeni, *Textbook of Aramaic Documents from Ancient Egypt Newly Copied, Edited and Translated into Hebrew and English.* 4 vols. Jerusalem: Hebrew University, 1986–1999.
Them	*Themelios*
TS	*Theological Studies*
TTE	*The Theological Educator: A Journal of Theology and Ministry*
TWOT	Waltke, Bruce K., R. Laird Harris, and Gleason L. Archer, *Theological Wordbook of the Old Testament.* 2 vols. Chicago: Moody, 1980.
TynBul	*Tyndale Bulletin*

UF	*Ugarit-Forschungen*
VT	*Vetus Testamentum*
WBC	Word Biblical Commentary
WMANT	Wissenschaftliche Monographien zum Alten und Neuen Testament
W-O	Walkte, Bruce K. and M. O'Connor. *An Introduction to Biblical Hebrew Syntax.* Winona Lake, IN: Eisenbrauns, 1990.
WTJ	*Westminster Theological Journal*
ZA	*Zeitschrift für Assyriologie und vorderasiatische Archäologie*
ZAW	*Zeitschrift für die alttestamentliche Wissenschaft*
ZDMG	*Zeitschrift der Deutschen Morgenländischen Gesellschaft*

1

TIME AND THE CHRISTIAN FAITH

From בְּרֵאשִׁית ("in the *beginning*"; Gen 1:1; cf. John 1:1) to ναί, ἔρχομαι ταχύ ("Yes, I am coming *soon*"; Rev 22:20) the Bible is a book about God's work in time. The God who created the world and ordered it in time and space continues to work in time and throughout time to redeem sinners. Time is not secondary or an afterthought in God's economy, but is intimately related to his works of creation, redemption and sanctification.

TIME AND THE GOSPEL

> . . . the New Testament claim that we have eternal life because Jesus walked out of the tomb on the first day of a certain week is not an innovation; it is simply continuing on in the trajectory that was laid out in [the Old Testament].

So notes John Oswalt.[2] The Gospel is so intimately bound up with events in time that it is impossible to extricate it from them. Thus, Saint Paul speaks about God sending his Son "in the fullness of time":

> But when *the fullness of time* had come, God sent forth his Son, born of a woman, born under law, to redeem those who were under law, so that we might receive adoption as sons. (Gal 4:4–5)

> . . . he predestined us for adoption as sons through Jesus Christ, according to the good pleasure of his will, to the praise of his

---

[2] Oswalt, *The Bible among the Myths*, 16.

glorious grace, with which he has blessed us in the Beloved
One. In him we have redemption through his blood, the
forgiveness of our trespasses, according to the riches of his
grace, which he lavished upon us, in all wisdom and insight
making known to us the mystery of his good pleasure,
according to his purpose, which he set forth in Christ as a plan
for *the fullness of time*, to unite all things in him, things in
heaven and things on earth. (Eph 1:4–10)

Paul's phrase implies what Oswalt observes—that the Old Testament,
including its historical narratives, flow toward their inexorable goal
just as rivers flow toward the sea. That goal is the incarnation and
redemptive work of Christ in the first century.

Jesus himself taught that the entire Old Testament pointed to him
(John 5:39; Luke 24:25–27), and that included the extensive historical
narratives found in the Pentateuch, the historical books, and the
prophets. Moreover, Jesus made use of God's acts in history as
paradigmatic for his own acts (e.g., Matt 12:40–42; 24:36–42; Luke
11:30–32; 17:26–30). Jesus' acts would be accomplished in the flow
of time by actual historical events in which he would bring about the
fulfillment of God's promises.

This synergy of the Gospel with the acts of God in history is also
reflected in the teachings of Jesus' apostles (e.g., Acts 2:29–32; Rom
1:1–6; 2 Tim 2:8; 1 Pet 3:18–22). In doing this Christ's apostles were
doing nothing more than employing the same method used by the
prophets of old—declaring that God is determined to act in time and
space to redeem his people (e.g., Num 24:17–24; Jer 31:31–34; Amos
9:11–15; Hag 2:1–9).

However, the acts of God in history did not end with Jesus and his
ascension, but continue onward through what the prophets called "the
latter days" and apostles called "the last days"—the time between
Jesus' ministry and his promised return. Those days are times when
God continues to speak to his people in word and in actions, even
though they are also perilous times with false teachers (Num 24:14;

Deut 4:30; Isa 2:2; Jer 48:47; 49:39; Ezek 38:16; Dan 2:28; 10:14; Hos 3:5; Mic 4:1; Acts 2:17; 2 Tim 3:1; Heb 1:1–2; 2 Pet 3:3).

Since the acts of God are so inextricably connected to time and history, the study of *when* those acts took place—biblical chronology—is inescapable for Christians. This is so because if the Bible's historical claims about the acts of God at particular times and in particular places are false, then Christian faith is built on nothing but invented myth that vanishes like a vapor. But the Christian faith is not a collection of "cleverly devised myths" that have been given a false historical backdrop (2 Pet 1:16). On the contrary—the acts of God, and especially the acts of God in Christ Jesus, are historical. Moreover, they can be arranged in chronological order as a witness to the Gospel (cf. 1 Cor 15:1–8).

CHRONOLOGY AND NARRATIVE

One way in which the Bible reflects God's work in time is through the *historical review*, a largely chronological reflection on the great acts of God in history and in the life of his people Israel. These reviews remember God's works on behalf of his people, illustrate his loving patience with an often recalcitrant Israel, and celebrate his mercy and grace. Psalms 78, 105, 106, 135, and 136 all contain historical reviews. They take the historical narratives of the Old Testament—especially the narratives about the exodus, the wilderness wanderings, and the conquest of the Promised Land—and use them to create their own narratives about God's love and mercy toward Israel.

While the prophet Ezekiel could also use the historical review to explain God's coming wrath upon the nation of Judah (Ezek 20:5–29), the longest and most complete historical review in the Old Testament is found in the prayer of the Judeans led by the Levites in Nehemiah 9:6–37. Here, as the Judeans review God's historical acts, they are led to confess their sinfulness, admit that God's just wrath had befallen them, and plead for his continued mercy, knowing that in past history he was patient and merciful with their ancestors. The largely chronological arrangement of the historical review points to the theological import of God's acting in history in specific times and places. The God of Israel is a God who is simultaneously transcendent—above and beyond all time and space (1 Kgs 8:27; 2 Chr 2:6; 6:18)—and immanent, personally present and involved with his people in time and space.

The historical review also has reflections in the New Testament. Stephen reviews Israel's history immediately before his martyrdom (Acts 7:2–53). His review is arranged chronologically and peppered with chronological details from the life of Moses (Acts 7:20, 23, 30, 36). Paul also employs historical narrative. For Paul this was a way to relay the Gospel. In his case, the historical narrative is autobiographical (Acts 22:3–21; 26:9–23). The writer to the Hebrews also continued in this tradition in his discourse on faith (Heb 11:1–40). While faith may be "the assurance of things hoped for, the conviction of things not seen" (Heb 11:1), it is firmly rooted in the acts of God in history in the lives of his saints—things that were seen and served as a foretaste of unseen things to come. These acts of God assure us that "God has provided something better for us" (Heb 11:40).

The authors of the narratives of the Old and New Testaments firmly rooted their texts in history by including chronological notices that enable us to locate these events in past time. These notices not only serve as anchors in time for the narratives of God's work, but they also invite us to investigate the chronology of biblical events, thereby reassuring us of God's intimate involvement with our own lives. In this way we derive comfort in the knowledge that "all things [including the events of our times] work together for good to them who are called according to his purpose" (Rom 8:28).

GOD'S CONTROL OF TIME AND EVENTS

Finally, the Bible promises us that God is in control of time and the events that take place within it. That control is demonstrated in the

Scriptures by the way he brought about the events of the past at particular times as indicated by chronological markers contained in the biblical text itself. He worked within history to redeem fallen humankind, and no power or authority could thwart his design. Events which may seem at times to career out of control are never out of his control. All things happen in his time, as seen especially in his sending his Son into the world at the proper time, or as Saint Paul reminds us "while we were still weak, at the right time (κατὰ καιρὸν) Christ died for the ungodly" (Rom 5:6).

If God did all this, then we can rest assured that our times are in his hands (Ps 31:15). This assurance underscores much of what the Scriptures tell us about time in this life:[3]

> On God rests my salvation and my glory; my mighty rock, my refuge is God. Trust in him at all times, O people; pour out your heart before him; God is a refuge for us. (Ps 62:7–8)

> So teach us to number our days that we may get a heart of wisdom. (Ps 90:12)

> Therefore I tell you, do not be anxious about your life, what you will eat or what you will drink, nor about your body, what you will put on. Is not life more than food, and the body more than clothing? Look at the birds of the air: they neither sow nor reap nor gather into barns, and yet your heavenly Father feeds them. Are you not of more value than they? And which of you by being anxious can add a single hour to his span of life? And why are you anxious about clothing? Consider the lilies of the field, how they grow: they neither toil nor spin, yet I tell you, even Solomon in all his glory was not arrayed like one of these. But if God so clothes the grass of the field, which today is alive and tomorrow is thrown into the oven, will he not much more clothe you, O you of little faith? Therefore do not be anxious, saying, "What shall we eat?" or "What shall we drink?" or "What shall we wear?" For the Gentiles seek after

---

[3] Translations below are from the English Standard Version. Unless otherwise noted, throughout this book translations are the author's own.

all these things, and your heavenly Father knows that you need them all. But seek first the kingdom of God and his righteousness, and all these things will be added to you. (Matt 6:25–33)

For he says, "In a favorable time I listened to you, and in a day of salvation I have helped you." Behold, now is the favorable time; behold, now is the day of salvation. (2 Cor 6:2)

Now may the Lord of peace himself give you peace at all times in every way. (2 Thess 3:16)

Come now, you who say, "Today or tomorrow we will go into such and such a town and spend a year there and trade and make a profit"—yet you do not know what tomorrow will bring. What is your life? For you are a mist that appears for a little time and then vanishes. Instead you ought to say, "If the Lord wills, we will live and do this or that." (Jas 4:13–15)

Because God has worked and continues to work in human history, the study of biblical chronology is not a specialists' sidelight that holds little consequence for the Christian's life. It is, instead, integral to the Christian faith. That is why it has occupied Christians from Eusebius of Caesarea through Bishop Ussher and down to the present day.

2

TIME IN THE ANCIENT WORLD

While we take for granted that time is divided into units of minutes, hours, days, weeks, months and years as well as an annual calendar of twelve months, when considering biblical chronology we cannot assume that our understanding of the passage of time is the same as that of the biblical writers. Moreover, since the various books of the Bible were written over a number of centuries and in different places, we cannot assume that every biblical author was referring to units of time in the same way. Therefore, we must first familiarize ourselves with the reckoning of time at various times and places in the ancient world.

UNITS OF TIME

DAY

The unit of time we refer to as a day—that is a 24-hour period of light and darkness—is, perhaps, the most familiar and most easily observed passage of time. The Hebrew word יוֹם was often used to refer to such an astronomical day (Gen 1:5). However, יוֹם was also used to refer to the part of a day that was light as opposed to לַיְלָה, "night." In Greek the corresponding words have the same possible meanings, with ἡμέρα referring to an astronomical day (Acts 28:13) or to the period of daylight as opposed to nighttime, which is called νύξ (Matt 4:2). In addition, Greek can refer to an astronomical day as νυχθήμερον (= νύξ + ἡμέρα; 2 Cor 11:25).

The reckoning of the beginning of the day could come at dawn or sundown or some other arbitrarily chosen point, such as the modern practice of reckoning it at midnight. In Mesopotamia and in Greece the day began at sundown.[4] The Egyptians mostly likely reckoned dawn as the beginning of the day.[5] The Romans followed the modern practice of reckoning the day as beginning at midnight (cf. John 19:14).[6]

Ancient Israel reckoned the day as beginning at sundown (Gen 1:5, 8, 13, 19, 23, 31; Neh 13:19; 2 Macc 8:25–27). The purity laws of Leviticus make this clear, since a person who becomes ceremonially unclean often remains unclean for the rest of the day, but becomes clean again at sundown at the end of the day (Lev 11:24, 25, 27, 28, 31, 32, 39, 40; 14:46; 15:5, 6, 7, 8, 10, 11, 16, 17, 18, 19, 21, 22, 23, 27; 17:15; 22:6; 23:32; 24:3; cf. Luke 23:50–54; John 19:31–42). Thus, holy days, such as Passover, the Feast of Unleavened Bread or the Day of Atonement began in the evening (Exod 12:6, 18; Lev 23:32; Deut 16:6).[7]

---

[4] Parker and Dubberstein, *Babylonian Chronology*, 26; Whibley, *A Companion to Greek Studies*, 589.

[5] Parker, *The Calendars of Ancient Egypt*, 10.

[6] Gow, *A Companion to School Classics*, 147.

[7] The contention of Finegan, *Handbook of Biblical Chronology*, 8, that passages like Gen 19:34 demonstrate that in an earlier period the day was reckoned from sunrise is wrong. This passage refers to a conversation that took place on the previous day, and the intervening sundown began a new day, the "next day" referred to in this verse. Likewise, Finegan's contention that in the NT Jews might reckon the day as beginning at dawn (*Handbook*, 9) is also wrong. For instance the reference to the dawn of the first day of the week at Matt 28:1||Mark 16:1–2||Luke 24:1 does not prove that the day began at dawn. Instead the day had already begun at the previous sundown, and these verses say nothing about reckoning dawn as the beginning of the day.

PARTS OF A DAY

During the eras covered by the OT the daylight period was not generally divided into set hours. Midday (צָהֳרַיִם), occurred around noon with morning (בֹּקֶר) before this and evening (עֶרֶב) afterwards. The night was divided into watches (אַשְׁמֻרוֹת) for military purposes (Exod 14:24; Judg 7:19; 1 Sam 11:11; Ps 63:6; 90:4; 119:148; Lam 2:19; Jdt 12:5; Jub 49:10–12). Two of these are mentioned by name: the middle watch (הָאַשְׁמֹרֶת הַתִּיכוֹנָה; Judg 7:19) and the morning watch (הָאַשְׁמֹרֶת הַבֹּקֶר; Exod 14:24; 1 Sam 11:11). Since there is a middle watch, it appears that the night was normally divided into three watches. Beckwith has argued that the Hebrew phrase "between the evenings" (בֵּין הָעַרְבַּיִם) refers to the first watch of the evening.[8]

During the NT era daylight could be divided into twelve hours (ὥρα, singular; John 11:9) that were usually referenced using ordinal numbers. The Jewish practice, as followed in the Synoptic Gospels and Acts, was to measure these hours from daybreak (Matt 20:3, 5, 9, 12; 27:45, 46; Mark 15:25, 33, 34; Luke 23:44; Acts 2:15; 3:1; 10:3, 9, 30).[9] The Roman practice, as followed in John's Gospel, was to measure them from midnight (John 1:39; 4:6, 52; 19:14).[10]

Luke and Acts only mention daytime hours that correspond to quarter days: the third hour (Acts 2:15), the sixth hour (Luke 23:44; Acts 10:9), and the ninth hour (Luke 23:44; Acts 3:1; 10:3, 30). Mark also appears to follow this scheme (Mark 15:25, 33, 34). Most likely these are references to quarter days, with the second quarter of the day beginning with the third hour (i.e., about 9:00 am to noon), the third quarter of the day beginning with the sixth hour (about noon to

---

[8] See Exod 12:6; 16:12; 29:39, 41; 30:8; Lev 23:5; Num 9:3, 5, 11; 28:4, 8. Beckwith, "The Day, Its Divisions and It Limits, in Biblical Thought," 219.

[9] Note, however, "the hour of incense" at Luke 1:10 (τῇ ὥρᾳ τοῦ θυμιάματος; about 3 p.m.).

[10] For further discussion see footnote 463 on page 293.

3:00 pm), and the fourth quarter beginning with the ninth hour (about 3:00 pm to 6:00 pm).[11]

Nighttime was divided into four watches called "evening" (ὀψέ), "midnight" (μεσονύκτιον), "cockcrow" (ἀλεκτοροφωνία) and "early morning" (πρωΐ; Mark 13:35; cf. Matt 14:25; Mark 6:48). It appears that the watches could also be referenced using a system of twelve nighttime hours, with nighttime watches referenced by one of the hours that occurred on a quarter of a night. Thus Acts 23:23 refers to "the third hour of the night" (τρίτης ὥρας τῆς νυκτός), which probably means the second watch (about 9:00 pm to midnight).

WEEK

A week is seven consecutive days. In Hebrew it is called שָׁבֻעַ (Gen 29:27, 28; Exod 34:22; Lev 12:5; Num 28:26; Deut 16:9, 10, 16; 2 Chr 8:13; Jer 5:24; Ezek 45:21; Dan 9:24, 25, 26, 27; 10:2, 3), and the seventh day is called Sabbath (שַׁבָּת).

In Greek the word σάββατον, a borrowing of the Hebrew word *Sabbath*, can signify either a Sabbath day or an entire week (singular: Mark 16:9; Luke 18:12; 1 Cor 16:2 or plural: Matt 28:1; Mark 16:2; Luke 24:1; John 20:1, 19; Acts 20:7).

Since the Sabbath was considered the last day of the week, the day God ceased (Hebrew שבת) from creating (Gen 2:2–3; Heb 4:4), the days of the week were numbered beginning with Sunday as the first day (Matt 28:1; Mark 16:2, 9; Luke 24:1; John 20:1, 19; Acts 20:7; 1 Cor 16:2).

In Greece and Rome the days were eventually named after the gods of the sun, moon and five visible planets, as evidenced in wall inscriptions at Pompeii:[12]

---

[11] Cadbury, "Some Luke Expressions of Time," 277–278.
[12] Finegan, *Handbook of Biblical Chronology*, 13.

Table 1
Greek, Latin and English Days of the Week

Greek Day	Latin Day	God	English Day
Ηλιου	Solis	Sun	Sunday
Σεληνης	Lunae	Moon	Monday
Αρεως	Martis	Mars	Tuesday
Ερμου	Mercurii	Mercury	Wednesday
Διος	Jovis	Jupiter	Thursday
[Αφρο]δειτης	Veneris	Venus	Friday
Κρονου	Saturni	Saturn	Saturday

Modern English day names are derived from the Latin name or its English equivalent (Sun: Sunday; Moon: Monday; Saturn: Saturday) or derive from Norse or Anglo-Saxon gods who were viewed as equivalent of the Roman gods (Tiw/Tyr: Tuesday; Woden: Wednesday; Thor: Thursday; Frigg: Friday).

MONTH

Months originally were reckoned from one new moon to the next.[13] This can be seen in the Hebrew word חֹדֶשׁ which can mean "new moon" (e.g., 1 Sam 20:5) or "month" (e.g., Gen 7:11). Similarly, one of the Greek words for moon, μήνη, is related to the word for month, μήν.

This period, known in modern astronomy as a synodic month, is about 29½ days.[14] Thus, there are just over twelve synodic months in a year.[15]

YEAR

The earth completes one orbit around the sun in about 365¼ days.[16] The word that approximately corresponds to this period of time in

---

[13] Finegan, *Handbook of Biblical Chronology*, 15.

[14] 29.530589 days.

[15] There are 12.134 months in a tropical year (365.24218967 days).

which the seasons also complete one cycle is called שָׁנָה in Hebrew. Greek calls this period ἔτος or ἐνιαυτός.

CALENDARS

SOLILUNAR CALENDAR

Because twelve lunar months are about eleven days short of a solar year, many ancient cultures used a solilunar calendar.[17] That is, they reckoned twelve months in most years, but occasionally adjusted the year by adding a thirteen month. This additional or *intercalary* month would align the solar and lunar cycles and keep the seasons from drifting through the months.

THE CALENDAR IN MESOPOTAMIA

The Mesopotamian calendar consisted of twelve months beginning in spring.[18] Alternating months of 29 and 30 days made up a year. An intercalary (thirteenth) month could be added before the first month of spring (the month in which the vernal equinox fell) or the first month of autumn (the month in which the autumnal equinox fell). The determination of when to add a month was done empirically—by observing the heavens. Eventually, the Babylonians determined that 235 lunar months were almost exactly equal to 19 solar years. This was seven more months than would have occurred in nineteen twelve-month years (228 months). Thus, they knew that seven years out of

---

[16] A mean tropical year, the average time between vernal equinoxes, is 365.24218967 days.

[17] Solilunar calendars were in use in early times in Mesopotamia (Parker and Dubberstein, *Babylonian Chronology*, 3–9) as well as Greece and Rome (Finegan, *Handbook of Biblical Chronology*, 50–51, 65). A notable exception was Egypt where three solar-based calendars were in use (Finegan, *Handbook of Biblical Chronology*, 18–25).

[18] This discussion is based on the observations about the Babylonian calendar in Parker and Dubberstein, *Babylonian Chronology*, 3–9.

every nineteen needed to have an additional month. Sometime in the fourth century BC the addition of the intercalary months became standardized.

The Babylonian months were:

Table 2
Babylonian Months

	Month	Modern Equivalent[19]
1	Nisanu	March/April
2	Aiaru	April/May
3	Simanu	May/June
4	Duzu	June/July
5	Abu	July/August
6	Ululu	August/September
7	Tashrinu	September/October
8	Arahsamnu	October/November
9	Kislimu	November/December
10	Tebetu	December/January
11	Shabatu	January/February
12	Addaru	February/March

THE CALENDAR IN PALESTINE

The Israelites appear to have followed a similar solilunar calendar.[20] Months began with a new moon festival, attesting to a lunar based

---

[19] The Babylonian months could begin late in one of the modern months or early in the following month. Thus, Nisanu could begin in late March or early April.

[20] Some studies have proposed calendar schemes different than what is discussed here. However, the large majority of scholars agree that the Israelites, the Canaanites, and other surrounding peoples followed a solilunar calendar. As will be seen in the discussion below, this is the clear implication of the biblical text and is supported by extra-biblical evidence. For a discussion of

calendar (1 Sam 20:5; 2 Kgs 4:23; Amos 8:5; Hos 2:11; Isa 1:13–14; Ezra 3:5).

Initially, the Israelite names for the months appear to be the same or similar to the Canaanite names.[21] The first month in the religious calendar (Exod 12:2) began in spring and was the month of the ripening ears of grain, from whence came its name, *Aviv*, (אָבִיב) which means "a ripe ear of grain" (compare Exod 12:2 with Exod 13:4; 23:15; 34:18; Deut 16:9). In order to keep this month at the beginning of spring a regular intercalation of an extra month would have been needed. Thus, Israel must have followed a solilunar calendar.

The other months named in the OT support this. The second month was *Ziv*[22] (זִו; 1 Kgs 6:1, 37), which probably means "bloom," referring to the spring flowers. The seventh month was *The Ethanim* (הָאֵתָנִים; 1 Kgs 8:2), "the constant streams," referring to the late summer when only a few constantly-flowing streams would have water in them. The eighth month was *Bul* (1 Kgs 6:38), probably related to the word מַבּוּל, which is used in Genesis to describe the great flood brought on by rain.[23] Cognate words in other Semitic languages signify heavy rains.[24] This month was the month of the beginning of the autumn rains. None of the names of these months

---

other proposals see Amadon, "Ancient Jewish Calendation"; Larsson, "Ancient Calendars Indicated in the OT"; Morgenstern, "Additional Notes on 'The Three Calendars of Ancient Israel,'" and "Supplementary Studies on the Calendars of Ancient Israel"; Parker, "Ancient Jewish Calendation: A Criticism."

[21] Months named *Ethanim* (1 Kgs 8:2) and *Bul* (1 Kgs 6:38) have been found in Northwest Semitic inscriptions as names of months. (Lizbarski, *Handbuch der nordsemitischen Epigraphik*, 1:231, 236, 412.)

[22] In modern Hebrew this is pronounced *Ziv*, but in ancient times it would have been pronounced *Ziw*.

[23] Gen 6:17; 7:6, 7, 10, 17; 9:11, 15, 28; 10:1, 32; 11:10.

[24] cf. *HALOT* s.v. מַבּוּל.

would have retained their meanings for long unless there were intercalary months regularly inserted into the Israelite calendar.[25]

Interestingly, the names of the four months preserved in the OT are the first two months of spring and the first two months of autumn. These were important months in both the agricultural cycle as well as in Israel's sacred year.[26] Perhaps they also indicate that in Palestine, as in Mesopotamia, intercalary months could be added before the vernal or autumnal equinox.[27]

THE JUDEAN CALENDAR AFTER THE BABYLONIAN EXILE

Though we have the name of four months used in Israel before the Babylonian exile, it was much more common to simply number the months, always beginning with Nisan/Aviv (e.g., 1 Chr 27:1–15).[28] During the Babylonian exile the Judeans apparently adopted the Babylonian names for the months into Hebrew. These Hebraized

---

[25] Segal, "Intercalation and the Hebrew Calendar," 256.

[26] Barley and wheat harvests began in the spring months, sowing took place in the autumn months. Passover was held in the month of Aviv and the Day of Atonement in the month of Ethanim.

[27] Segal noted that the Passover preparations were to begin on the tenth day of the first month of spring (Exod 12:3) and that the Day of Atonement was on the tenth day of the first month of autumn (Lev 23:27–32; Num 29:7–11). He proposed that these dates were chosen to allow for intercalation by observation of the heavens. One merely had to observe the heliacal rising or setting of a fixed star in the spring or autumn near the equinox. If the rising or setting occurred during the end of the sixth or twelfth month or during the first nine days of the following month, than the month following the sixth or twelfth month would be an intercalary month (a second sixth or twelfth month), and the first or seventh month would be delayed. Over a nineteen year period this would place an intercalary month in the first, fourth, seventh, ninth, twelfth, fifteenth, and eighteenth years—seven times in nineteen years, as in the Mesopotamian calendar. (Segal, "Intercalation and the Hebrew Calendar," 269–274.)

[28] Finegan, *Handbook of Biblical Chronology*, 79; Talmud *Roš. Haš.* 7a.

names are occasionally used in the post-exilic books of the OT and are common in later Hebrew:

[Note: Readers may wish to photocopy Table 3 and then trim the copy to the appropriate size for a bookmark, since the names of these months will be used extensively throughout the remainder of this book.]

Table 3
Hebrew Months

	Pre-exilic	*Post-exilic*	*Modern Equivalent*
1	Aviv[29]	Nisan[30]	March/April
2	Ziv[31]	Iyyar	April/May
3		Sivan[32]	May/June
4		Tammuz	June/July
5		Ab	July/August
6		Elul	August/September
7	Ethanim[33]	Tishri	September/October
8	Bul[34]	Marcheshvan	October/November
9		Kislev[35]	November/December
10		Tebeth[36]	December/January
11		Shebat[37]	January/February
12		Adar[38]	February/March

[29] Exod 13:4; 23:15; 34:18; Deut 16:1.
[30] Neh 2:1; Esth 3:7.
[31] 1 Kgs 6:1, 37.
[32] Esth 8:9.
[33] 1 Kgs 8:2.
[34] 1 Kgs 6:38.
[35] Neh 1:1.
[36] Esth 2:16.
[37] Zech 1:7.
[38] Ezra 6:15; Esth 3:7, 13; 8:12; 9:1, 15, 17, 19.

THE BEGINNING OF THE YEAR IN PALESTINE

Israel's sacred year begin in the spring with the first month, the month of Aviv (Nisan), according to Exod 12:2; 13:4; 23:15; 34:18; Deut 16:1. For this reason the numbering of the months in the Bible appears always to have used the spring as the beginning of the year.

However, there are indications that the year could also be reckoned to begin in autumn with the month of Ethanim (Tishri). This appears to be the case with the Gezer Calendar, a small inscribed limestone tablet discovered during an archaeological excavation at Gezer in 1908.[39] Paleographical studies indicate that the inscription is from the tenth century BC, which accords well with the history of Gezer, which was given to Solomon after being conquered by his Egyptian father-in-law (1 Kgs 9:15–17) and destroyed by Pharaoh Shoshenq I (Biblical Shishak) in the spring or summer of 926 BC. Thus, the Gezer Calendar dates between the 971 and 926 BC. The calendar reads:

His two months: ingathering	ירחו אסף ירחו ז
His two months: sow-	
ing His two months: late sowing	רע ירחו לקש
His month: cutting flax	ירח עצד פשת
His month: harvest of barley	ירח קצר שערם
His month: (wheat) harvest and measuring	ירח קצר וכל
His two months: vine harvest	ירחו זמר
His month: summer fruit (harvest)	ירח קץ
Abi[jah?]	אבי]

Thus, it would appear that this calendar begins in the autumn with the ingathering, which is associated with the autumnal Festival of Ingathering (Exod 23:16; 34:22). Interestingly, Exod 34:22 refers to this as "the turning of the year" (תְּקוּפַת הַשָּׁנָה), indicating that the year

---

[39] *ANET* 320; Ahituv, *Echoes from the Past*, 252–257. Josephus (*Ant.* 1.80 [1.3.3]) and *b. Roš Haš.* 11b also refer to Tishri-based years being observed during the Old Testament era.

could also be reckoned as beginning at this time. In modern Jewish reckoning the first month of the year is Tishri and the first day of the year is Rosh Hashanah on 1 Tishri. Autumn could also be called the "going out" of the year (צֵאת הַשָּׁנָה; Exod 23:16), as the year begins its journey. The spring, the traditional time to begin military campaigns, likewise could be called "the return of the year" (תְּשׁוּבַת הַשָּׁנָה; 2 Sam 11:1‖1 Chr 20:1; 1 Kgs 20:22, 26; 2 Chr 36:10). As the year would have been half over, it was now returning to its beginning in the autumn.[40]

In the united kingdom of Israel before the splitting of the kingdom after Solomon's death a king's regnal years were reckoned on an autumn-to-autumn basis. The same was done in the kingdom of Judah after Solomon's death.[41] First we should note that when counting periods of time, the usual method in Israel was to count *inclusively*, that is, the first period and the last period and all periods in between were counted. This can be seen by comparing Lev 12:3 with Gen 17:12. Both concern the day in which a newborn boy is to be circumcised. Lev 12:3 specifics this as "on the eighth day" (וּבַיּוֹם הַשְּׁמִינִי) from his birth. Thus, if he was born on a Monday, the eighth day from his birth would be the following Monday. However, Gen 17:12 says a boy is to be circumcised when he is "eight days old" (וּבֶן־שְׁמֹנַת יָמִים). While we would call the boy seven days old, by counting the day of birth and the day of circumcision and every day

---

[40] The objection of Clines, "The Evidence for an Autumnal New Year," 26–30 that this is only evidence of an agricultural year and not evidence of a calendar year is less than convincing for chronological purposes. It is akin to saying that an organization that uses a fiscal year for accounting purposes cannot thereby count years by its fiscal years even though those are not calendar years (January to January). However, an organization might have claimed to have made a profit five years in a row based on fiscal years. In a similar fashion, at times the authors of the Old Testament or their sources would count autumn-to-autumn years instead of spring-to-spring years.
[41] Thiele, *Mysterious Numbers*, 51–53.

between them the Israelites called him eight days old. In reality the child may have been alive a little over six days if he was born just before sundown at the end of a day and circumcised on the eighth day just after sundown.[42]

This inclusive reckoning was used at 1 Kgs 6:38 to arrive at the total of seven years for Solomon's building of the temple from the second month of his fourth year (1 Kgs 6:37) to the eighth month of his eleventh year (1 Kgs 6:38).[43] If Solomon's regnal years were reckoned as Nisan-to-Nisan years, this would total eight years.[44] However, if Solomon's regnal years were reckoned as Tishri-to-Tishri years, this would total seven years.[45]

---

[42] Therefore, there was no "rounding up" or "rounding down" around some break point, such as half of a day as is commonly done in contemporary reckoning. Other clear examples of inclusive counting in the Bible include counting fifty days to Pentecost from the day after a Sabbath to the day after seven Sabbaths later (Lev 23:15–16); Jesus' resurrection taking place on the third day, the Sunday after a Friday crucifixion (Matt 12:40; Mark 8:31); Jesus saying that he will perform miracles "today, tomorrow and *the third day*" (Luke 13:32), and the span from Hoshea's seventh to ninth years (= Hezekiah's forth to sixth years) counted as three years (2 Kgs 17:5; 18:10).

[43] Thiele, *Mysterious Numbers*, 51–52.

[44] From Nisan month 2 in year 4 to Nisan month 2 in year 11 (= seven years) + 6 months in Nisan year eleven = 8 years total by inclusive reckoning.

[45] According to a Tishri-based regnal year, Solomon's fourth year began in Tishri (Sept/Oct) of 968 BC (see discussion of Tishri-based years beginning on page 17 and the discussion of Solomon's reign beginning on page 37) and his eleventh year began in Tishri of 961 BC, with Temple completion in the following month, Bul/Marcheshvan (Oct/Nov). Since construction started in Ziv/Iyyar of Solomon's fourth year, i.e. in April/May of 967 BC, the total time of construction was six full years from April/May 967 to April/May 961 plus the six months to Oct/Nov of 961 = 7 years total by inclusive reckoning. Clines' objection that this seven years is combined with thirteen years for the building of Solomon's palace (7:1) to yield twenty years total (1 Kgs 9:10) cannot be correct since 7 inclusive years + 13 inclusive years = 19 years

This Tishri-to-Tishri year is confirmed by 2 Kgs 22:3; 23:23. Josiah began repairing the temple in his eighteenth year. After the passing of 1 Nisan, Josiah celebrated the Passover, but it was still his eighteenth year. This indicates that a new year did not begin in Nisan, but in Tishri.

Therefore, there are indications of two ways in which the year's beginning was reckoned: a sacred year beginning in spring with the month of Aviv (Nisan) and an agricultural/civil year beginning in autumn with the month of Ethanim (Tishri). Thus, when dating years mentioned in the OT, one must be careful to determine when the year was reckoned as beginning since these two ways of reckoning years are offset by six months.

When such precision is required for OT dates, I will use the system of indicating vernal or autumnal years developed by Rodger Young.[46] A vernal year that begins with the month of Nisan (Aviv) will be indicated with a trailing lower case "n." Thus 750n will indicate a year that began in Nisan of the Julian year 750 BC. This year would be approximately equal to the last nine months of 750 BC and the first three months of 749 BC. An autumnal year that begins with the month of Tishri (Ethanim) will be indicated with a lowercase

---

("The Evidence for an Autumnal New Year in Pre-Exilic Israel Reconsidered," 31). Clines' arithmetic is valid only if the last year of the building of the temple overlaps the first year of the building of the palace. However, Solomon did not necessarily begin his palace immediately after the completion of the temple. He may have used the intervening months to organize and hold the dedication of the temple in the seventh month of the year following the temple's completion. (1 Kgs 8:2—almost one year after the completion of construction!) He could have commenced the building of his palace in the year following the completion of the temple. In this way there would have been no overlap between the year of the temple's completion and the year of the beginning of the construction of the palace. In that case 7 inclusive years + 13 inclusive years = 20 years.
[46] Young, "When Did Jerusalem Fall?" 24–25.

"t." Thus, 750t will indicate a year that began in Tishri of the Julian year 750 BC. This year would be approximately equal to the last three months of 750 BC and the first nine months of 749 BC.

THE MACEDONIAN CALENDAR[47]

When Alexander the Great conquered the territory of the eastern Mediterranean basin, he also brought his native Macedonian calendar with him. This became the standard calendar in Palestine under Ptolemaic rule and later under Seleucid domination. The Macedonian calendar was also a solilunar calendar of twelve months, and the year began in the autumn. The names of the months were:

Table 4
Macedonian Months

	Month	Anglicized Name
1	Δίος	Dios
2	Ἀπελλαῖος	Apellaios
3	Αὐδυναῖος	Audynaos
4	Περίτιος	Peritios
5	Δύστρος	Dystros
6	Ξανθικός/Ξανδικός	Xanthikos/Xandikos
7	Ἀρτεμίσιος	Artemisios
8	Δαίσιος	Daisios
9	Πάνεμος	Panemos
10	Λῷος	Loos
11	Γορπιαῖος	Gorpiaios
12	Ὑπερβερεταῖος	Hyperberetaios

[47] For an extended discussion of this calendar, see Finegan, *Handbook of Biblical Chronology*, 51–64.

Though the Macedonian calendar was imposed on the conquered peoples, they adapted it to their own native calendar system. The official year began in autumn, but Jews at times continued to reckon their sacred year as beginning in spring.[48] In Syria (including Palestine) and Babylon the months were equated with the months in the traditional calendar, but the equating of months varied from time to time. In earlier centuries Tishri was equated with Dios.[49] Sometime in the first century AD, however, there was a shift of one month so that Tishri was equated with Hyperberetaios.[50] The equivalents would be:

Table 5
Hebrew and Macedonian Calendars before c. AD 40

	Month	Macedonian Month
1	Tishri	Dios
2	Marcheshvan	Apellaios
3	Kislev	Audynaos
4	Tebeth	Peritios
5	Shebat	Dystros
6	Adar	Xanthikos
7	Nisan	Artemisios
8	Iyyar	Daisios
9	Sivan	Panemos

---

[48] Josephus reckons the beginning of the year in the autumn in *Ant.* 1.80 [1.3.3] stating that Dios/Marcheshvan was the second month, but in *Ant.* 1.81 [1.3.3] reckons spring (Xanthikos/Nisan) as the beginning of the Jewish sacred year according to Moses. He also notes the Jewish year began in Xanthikos/Nisan at *Ant.* 3.248 [3.10.5].

[49] See Finegan, *Handbook of Biblical Chronology*, 54, table 19.

[50] Josephus, for instance, used this reckoning, since he equated Dios and Marcheshvan (*Ant.* 1:80 [1.3.3]), Xanthikos with Nisan (*Ant.* 1:81 [1.3.3]; 3.248 [3.10.5]), and Apellaios with Kislev (*Ant.* 11.148 [11.5.4]; 12.248 [12.5.4]; 12.319 [12.7.6]).

10	Tammuz	Loos
11	Ab	Gorpiaios
12	Elul	Hyperberetaios

Table 6
Hebrew and Macedonian Calendars after c. AD 40

	Month	Macedonian Month
1	Tishri	Hyperberetaios
2	Marcheshvan	Dios
3	Kislev	Apellaios
4	Tebeth	Audynaos
5	Shebat	Peritios
6	Adar	Dystros
7	Nisan	Xanthikos
8	Iyyar	Artemisios
9	Sivan	Daisios
10	Tammuz	Panemos
11	Ab	Loos
12	Elul	Gorpiaios

JULIAN CALENDAR

The Romans originally followed a solilunar calendar. However, late in the era of the Roman republic, the calendar was in a state of disorder mainly caused by problems of intercalation. In 45 BC, Julius Caesar proclaimed a new calendar, known as the Julian calendar. This calendar, following Roman custom that had already begun in 153 BC, transferred the beginning of the year from March in the spring to January in winter.[51] The year was expanded from the old solilunar

---

[51] This is why September, which means "seventh month," October, which means "eighth month," November, which means "ninth month," and Decem-

354 days to 365 days to approximate a solar year. Since this was still about a quarter-day short of a full solar year, an intercalary day was added to the end of February every fourth year. With slight modification used to produce the Gregorian calendar, this is the calendar in widespread use today. Dates before AD 1582 (the earliest adoption of the Gregorian calendar in Europe) are by standard convention given in Julian years.

GREGORIAN CALENDAR

The calendar that is the *de facto* international standard today is the Gregorian calendar, a modification of the Julian calendar. Since an average vernal equinox year is actually a small fraction of a day less than 365¼ days,[52] the Julian calendar overcorrects when it intercalates an extra day every four years. By 1582 this overcorrection amounted to ten days, moving the vernal equinox from March 21 to April 1. To correct this Pope Gregory XIII proclaimed that in 1582 the calendar would be modified. Ten days would be subtracted and intercalary days would only be added 97 times in 400 years. If a leap year was evenly divisible by 100 *but not by 400*, it would not have an intercalary day. Thus 1700, 1800, 1900 were not leap years, but 1600 and 2000 were.

Despite Gregory's proclamation, not all countries adopted the Gregorian calendar in 1582. A few Roman Catholic countries adopted it in 1582 or in the following years, but most Protestant countries simply ignored Gregory's proclamation. Eventually, however, most western countries adopted the Gregorian calendar. One of the last western European nations to adopt the Gregorian calendar was Great Britain and the British Empire (including what would become the United States), which made the switch in 1752.[53] By then there was

---

ber, which means "tenth month," are now the ninth through twelfth months.
[52] An average vernal equinox year is 365.2424 days.
[53] Greece was the last European nation to do so—in 1923.

an eleven-day difference between the Julian and Gregorian calendars. Russia did not adopt the Gregorian calendar until 1918.

The difference between the Julian and Gregorian calendars is a slight one, but is important when assigning dates to ancient events, which are always calculated using the Julian calendar. Thus, for instance, the tables of dates given in the widely used Babylonian chronology compiled by Parker and Dubberstein[54] are Julian dates and assume every fourth year is a leap year. This distinction is also important for determining the day of the week for an ancient event.[55]

SABBATICAL YEARS

The laws of the Pentateuch provide that every seventh year is to be a special year when the land was to lie fallow and Hebrew slaves were to be freed. Four passages in the Pentateuch require the Israelites to keep this special seventh year, called a Sabbatical year. The land was to rest, just as Israelites were to cease their work on the Sabbath, the seventh day of the week. For purposes of OT chronology, Sabbatical years can be used for confirming dates of a few events mentioned in the historical and prophetic books.

EXODUS 23:10–11

> For six years you shall sow your land and gather its produce, but in the seventh year you shall leave it to itself and let it lie fallow. Then the poor among your people may eat, and what they leave, the beasts of the field may eat. You will treat your vineyard and olive orchard in the same manner.

This passage legislates that Israelites may not sow crops or harvest them every seventh year, and it specifically includes vineyards and

---

[54] Parker and Dubberstein, *Babylonian Chronology 626 BC–AD 75*.

[55] Days of the week can be determined using the Julian Date Converter maintained by the United States Naval Observatory (http://aa.usno.navy.mil/data/docs/JulianDate.php). The remainder after dividing the Julian date minus 0.5 by seven is the number of days of the week after Tuesday.

olive orchards, in which plants are not sown yearly, but which must also remain untended. The poor and the wild animals could consume the land's produce during a Sabbatical year.

Since sowing took place in the autumn, this passage implies that there will be no harvest in the following year. That is, the Sabbatical year overlaps two years.[56] The sowing would not take place as normally done in Tishri and Marcheshvan, and there would be no harvest of crops in the following Nisan through Elul of the following year.

During Hezekiah's reign a year when the land was to voluntarily be left fallow is mentioned in 2 Kgs 19:29‖Isa 37:30, and we will see that this was a Sabbatical year (see the discussion beginning on page 148).

DEUTERONOMY 15:1–3

> At the end of seven years you shall forgive debts. Now this is the manner of the forgiveness of debts: Every creditor who has lent to his neighbor shall forgive debts. He shall not demand payment from his neighbor, his brother, because Yahweh's forgiveness of debts has been proclaimed. You may demand that a foreigner make payment, but whatever is yours with your brother you will let go.

This legislation requires that debts incurred by fellow Israelites must be forgiven in the seventh year. The Hebrew word for forgiveness of debts is *shemitah* (שְׁמִטָּה), and this word is often used as a designation for the Sabbatical year.

Since Israelites may have sold themselves into slavery to pay their debts, the Sabbatical year eventually became a year of release from slavery, since Israelites were only to serve six years in debt slavery, a regulation that follows closely upon the regulation for the Sabbatical year in these chapters (Deut 15:12; cf. Exod 21:2). Jer 34:8–10 notes

---

[56] The sacred year began in spring with the month of Aviv/Nisan (Exod 12:2; 13:4; 23:15; 34:18; Deut 16:1).

that Zedekiah proclaimed a release of slaves during his reign, and we will see that this occurred in a Sabbatical year (see the discussion beginning on page 148).

DEUTERONOMY 31:10–13

> Moses commanded them, "At the end of seven years, at the time of the year of the forgiveness of debts—at the Feast of Booths when all Israel comes to appear before Yahweh your God in the place that he will choose—you shall read this Law in front of all Israel as they listen. Assemble the people—men, women and little children—as well as the resident foreigners who are within your gates so that they may listen and learn and fear Yahweh your God and diligently keep the words of this Law."

An additional activity during the Sabbatical year is the public reading of the Pentateuch. It is to happen at the Feast of Booths, which takes place from the fifteenth to the twenty-first day of the seventh month (Ethanim/Tishri). This passage also notes that this is the time of the year when debts are to be forgiven.

The public reading of the Pentateuch is mentioned during the reign of two kings—during Jehoshaphat's third year (2 Chr 17:7–9) and during Josiah's eighteenth year (2 Kgs 23:1–2; cf. 2 Kgs 22:3). As will be seen below (discussions beginning on pages 50 and 148), these were both Sabbatical years.

LEVITICUS 25:1–6, 20–22

> The Lord spoke to Moses at Mount Sinai, "Speak to the Israelites and say to them, 'When you are coming into the land that I am giving you, the land shall observe a Sabbath to Yahweh. For six years you shall sow your field, and for six years you shall prune your vineyards and gather their produce. However, the seventh year shall be a special Sabbath for the land—a Sabbath to Yahweh. You shall not sow your fields, and you shall not prune your vineyards. What grows by itself from your reaping, you will not reap, and you will not harvest grapes that grow on their own. It will be a special Sabbath year

to Yahweh. The Sabbath of the land will be for you and your male and female slaves, your hired hands and the foreign inhabitants with you to eat. . . .

. . . 'And you might say, "What will we eat in the seventh year if we do not sow or harvest our produce?" I will command my blessing on you during the sixth year, and the land will make [enough] produce for three years. When you sow in the eighth year, you will eat some of the old produce. Until its produce comes, you will eat the old [produce].'"

Leviticus 25 contains regulations for celebration of both the sabbatical and Jubilee years (see page 30 below). Lev 25:1–7 contains the regulation for the Sabbatical year and its content is essentially the same as Exod 23:10–11. Lev 25:8–19 contains the regulation for the Jubilee year.

Since both sabbatical and Jubilee years required the land to lie fallow, Lev 25:20–22 further elaborates on a possible objection Israelites might have to foregoing a year's crops should they wonder how they will provide food for themselves and their families.[57]

The explanation is that God will bless the sixth year with enough produce to last three years. The Israelites were promised that if they did not sow in the seventh year, they would have plenty of food to eat

---

[57] That Lev 25:20–22 applies to the Jubilee is almost universally accepted, since it follows Lev 25:8–19 which is the regulation for the Jubilee, and it is followed by the rest of Lev 25, which contain regulations about the selling and redemption of landed property and its release in Jubilee years. What is often not recognized is that these verses also apply to Sabbatical years, as is evident in that they mention the seventh and eighth years, which are clear references to the Sabbatical cycle and not the forty-nine years or fiftieth year mentioned in the Jubilee cycle regulation. Thus, the outline of Lev 25 appears to be: 1. The Sabbatical year regulations (Lev 25:1–7); 2. The Jubilee year regulations (Lev 25:8–19); 3. A possible objection to Sabbatical and Jubilee regulations answered (Lev 25:20–22); 4. Regulations regarding selling land and its redemption (Lev 25:23–55).

in the eighth year. Since the sabbatical cycle is a seven-year cycle, the "eighth" year must be identical to the first year of the next cycle.

The promised three-year abundance would provide an excess of produce even though foregoing planting in the Sabbatical year would require two years of living off the last harvest. To understand this, let us examine how this would have worked in the ancient agricultural cycle of Palestine:

Table 7
The Sabbatical Cycle

Year (1st Cycle)	Year (2nd Cycle)	Month	Activity	Crop
7		Nisan	harvest	barley
		Iyyar	harvest	barley/wheat
		Sivan	harvest	wheat/grapes
		Tammuz	harvest	grapes/figs
		Ab	harvest	grapes/figs
		Elul	harvest	grapes/olives
Sabbatical year =		Tishri		olives
Tishri year 7 to Elul		Marcheshvan		
year 8		Kislev		
		Tebeth		
		Shebat		
		Adar		
8	1	Nisan		
		Iyyar		
		Sivan		
		Tammuz		
		Ab		
		Elul		
		Tishri	sowing	
		Marcheshvan	sowing	
		Kislev	sowing	
		Tebeth		

		Shebat		
		Adar		
9	2	Nisan	harvest	barley
		Iyyar	harvest	barley/wheat
		Sivan	harvest	wheat/grapes
		Tammuz	harvest	grapes/figs
		Ab	harvest	grapes/figs
		Elul	harvest	grapes/olives

Note that there would have been two years from the beginning of the last barley harvest before the Sabbatical year (the harvest in the spring of year 7) to the first harvest following the Sabbatical year (the harvest in year 2 of the new cycle). The harvest of other crops would also be separated by two years. Therefore, the promise to make the sixth year's planting yield three years of food in the harvest in the spring of year seven is a promise of surplus. This anticipates God's promised continual surplus of food that Israel would always have as long as it faithfully observed the statues and commands he gave them (Lev 26:10).

JUBILEE YEARS

The regulation for the Jubilee year is found at Lev 25:8–19. In addition the following verses, Lev 25:20–22 (examined above, page 27), gives the regulation governing both Jubilee and Sabbatical years. Furthermore, the Jubilee year is mentioned frequently in the ensuing regulations governing the right of redemption of land and people (Lev 25:23–55)[58] as well as at Lev 27:17, 18, 21, 23, 24; Num 36:4. Lev 25:8–19 says:

> You shall count seven weeks of years—seven years seven times—and they shall be for you seven weeks of years: forty-

---

[58] Lev 25:28, 30, 31, 33, 40, 50, 52, 54.

nine years. You shall sound a ram's horn signal in the seventh month on the tenth day of the month.

On the Day of Atonement you shall sound a ram's horn throughout your land. You shall consecrate the fiftieth year and proclaim liberty in the land to all its inhabitants. It will be a Jubilee for you. Each man will return to his property, and each man will return to his land. The Jubilee will be the fiftieth year for you. Do not sow and do not harvest what grows by itself, and do not pick its grapes, because it is a Jubilee. It shall be holy to you. You may eat its produce from the field. In this year of Jubilee each man shall return to his property.

If you sell to your neighbor or buy from your neighbor, do not take advantage of each other. You shall buy from your neighbor according to the number of years after the Jubilee. He shall sell to you the number of years of crops. If the years are many you shall increase the price. If the years are few you shall decrease the price, because he is selling you the number of crops. You shall not take advantage of each other, but you shall fear your God, because I, Yahweh, am your God.

Therefore, you shall do my statutes and keep my rules and do them. Then you will dwell in the land securely. The land will yield its fruit, and you will eat your fill and dwell in it securely.

While the Jubilee year is clearly tied to the cycle of Sabbatical years (Lev 25:8), there have been two widespread opinions as to whether the Jubilee year is simply another Sabbatical year with additional regulations (i.e., the Sabbatical and Jubilee years were concurrent) or whether it is an additional year, requiring two fallow years in a row (i.e., the Sabbatical and Jubilee years were consecutive and the fiftieth Jubilee year was also the first year of the next Sabbatical cycle).[59]

---

[59] Under either scheme, the Jubilees occurred every forty-nine years. Young, "The Talmud's Two Jubilees and Their Relevance to the Date of the Exodus," 75–76 presents evidence that the most ancient sources were unanimous in treating the jubilee cycle as a forty-nine year cycle. Other opinions have been offered but are generally rejected. Hoenig, "Sabbatical Years and the

According to the Talmud, the latter was the view of Rabbi Judah.[60] This has also been supported by a few modern scholars.[61] However, Rabbi Judah claimed that the Jubilee year "counted both ways." That is, it was both the fiftieth year of the old cycle and the first year of the new cycle.

The majority opinion of contemporary scholars is that the Jubilee year is concurrent with a Sabbatical year.[62] Under either scheme, however, successive Jubilee years are forty-nine years apart, since the fiftieth year mentioned in Lev 25:10–11 is also counted as the first year of the next cycle.

The majority opinion is almost certainly correct, and as we will see, has independent confirmation in the chronology of the kings of Judah. (See discussions beginning on pages 50 and 148.) Lev 25:20–22 most certainly applies to both the Sabbatical and Jubilee

---

Year of Jubilee," proposed that the Jubilee was a period of forty-nine intercalary days. Kaufman, "A Reconstruction of the Social Welfare System of Ancient Israel," 278, proposed that the Jubilee was simply a point in time. Kawashima, "The Jubilee, Every 49 or 50 Years?" proposed that the Jubilee was an entire year, but was on a fifty year cycle which would drift through the seven year cycles of Sabbatical years so that it would have to periodically be realigned with the Sabbatical cycle.

[60] *Roš. Haš.* 9a. According to this passage most rabbis held that the Jubilee Year was a separate fiftieth year and that the next sabbatical cycle began at the end of the Jubilee Year.

[61] Bergsma, *The Jubilee from Leviticus to Qumran*, 87–93; Bergsma, "Once Again, the Jubilee, Every 49 or 50 Years?"; Milgrom, *Leviticus*, 2183–2183, 2250; Zuckerman, *Treatise on the Sabbatical Cycle and the Jubilee*, 12–13.

[62] See, for example, Chirichigno, *Debt-Slavery in Israel and the Ancient Near East*, 1993; Elliger, *Leviticus*,352; Hartley, *Leviticus*, 434–436; Lefebvre, *Le Jubilé Biblique*, 154–166; North, *Sociology of the Biblical Jubilee*, 120–134; Noth, *Leviticus*, 186–187; Reventlow, *Das Heiligkeitsgesetz formgeschichtlich untersucht*, 125; Schenker, "The Biblical Legislation on the Release of Slaves," 25; van Selms, "Jubilee," *IDBSup*, 497; Wright, *God's People in God's Land*, 150.

regulations. It immediately follows the Jubilee year regulation, but numbers years seven and eight according to the Sabbatical cycle. This in itself suggests that the Jubilee year is a Sabbatical year. *However, it should also be noted that there is provision for only one fallow year, since sowing is allowed in the eighth year (Lev 25:22) for harvest in the ninth year.* Moreover as noted above in the discussion of the Sabbatical year (page 27ff.), God promised both a three-year yield in the year before the Sabbatical year (Lev 25:21) and a continual surplus for Israel no matter what the year (Lev 26:10). If the Jubilee had been a second successive fallow year, a three-year yield would have provided no surplus.

That the Jubilee begins in the autumn of the forty-ninth year is also evident from the command to sound the ram's horn on the Day of Atonement in the forty-ninth year in order to announce the beginning of the Jubilee (Lev 25:8–9).[63] This would make no sense if the Jubilee

---

[63] Bergsma argues that the years mentioned in the Sabbatical and Jubilee legislation are autumn-to-autumn agricultural years since Lev 25 repeatedly mentions sowing before reaping (Lev 25:4–5, 11, 20). However, this is contradicted by Lev 25:20–22, especially verse 22 which notes that the first sowing after the Sabbatical year will take place in the eighth year and the first harvest in the ninth year. This can only be true if Lev 25 is counting spring-to-spring sacred years. Bergsma further confuses matters by calling the autumn-to-autumn year "the cultic agricultural year" and the spring-to-spring year the "civil year" (Bergsma, *The Jubilee from Leviticus to Qumran*, 88, note 20). While the autumn-to-autumn year is agricultural, it is not cultic. The cultic/sacred year (not the civil year) is the spring-to-spring year, as noted in Exod 12:2–20 where the beginning of the year is specifically tied to the Passover and Feast of Unleavened Bread in the first month of the year (cp. Lev 23:5; Num 9:5; 28:16; 33:3; 2 Chr 35:1; Ezra 6:19; Ezek 45:21). Moreover, the autumn sacred festivals are always said to be in the seventh month, not the first month (Lev 16:29; 23:24, 27, 34, 39, 41; 25:9; Num 29:1, 7, 12; 1 Kgs 8:2; 2 Chr 5:3; Neh 8:14; Ezek 45:25). Bergsma apparently is confusing biblical practice with later Jewish practice of

were actually to begin twelve months later in the autumn of the next year.

So, how is the Jubilee year called the fiftieth year if it ran concurrently with every seventh Sabbatical year, and Sabbatical years began in the autumn of the forty-ninth year? The Jubilee year is a year when each Israelite is to "return to his property" (Lev 25:10). This is further explained in Lev 25:13–19, which takes up the return to property theme. There the Israelites were told that they could sell their land—but only until the Jubilee—and that what was actually being sold was not the land but the yearly crops (Lev 25:15–16). In the autumn after the end of the Jubilee year when the land had reverted to its permanent owner, it was once again sown for a new crop by its original owner or his heir. The land, that is, the crops, have now reverted to their permanent owner. The Jubilee celebrates God liberating the land from its "slavery," just as each Sabbatical year sees the liberation of Israelites who sold themselves into slavery. The focus is on the returning of the land and its crops to its original owner. That owner would sow the next crop in the autumn of the fiftieth year. Therefore, the Jubilee is called the fiftieth year, although the beginning of the fallow year takes place when the land is not sown in the forty-ninth year.

Note that in a similar way in Lev 25:20 the Sabbatical year is called "the seventh year" although it overlaps both the seventh and eighth years. There is no planting or reaping in this seventh year, although Lev 25:22 implies that the lack of reaping actually takes place in the eighth year. Thus, the Sabbatical year is called "the seventh year" because the emphasis is on the fallowing of the land. The autumn of that seventh year is the time when crops are not sown. In a similar way, the emphasis of the Jubilee year, which overlaps the forty-ninth and fiftieth years, is on owners returning to their land to begin sowing in the fiftieth year immediately after the end of the Jubilee, so the Jubilee is called "the fiftieth year."

---

celebrating a religious festival of *Rosh Hashanah* as the beginning of the High Holy Days in the autumn.

Another argument that is commonly advanced is that the Jubilee cycle of the fiftieth year is parallel to the counting of fifty days to determine the beginning of the Feast of Weeks (Pentecost) as set forth at Lev 23:15–16:[64]

> You shall count for yourselves from the day after the Sabbath, from the day you brought the sheaf of the wave offering: there shall be seven complete Sabbaths until the day after the seventh Sabbath. You shall count fifty days. Then bring an offering of new grain to Yahweh.

It is alleged that the Jubilee year must be a fallow year following a Sabbatical year just as the Feast of Weeks is the day after the seventh Sabbath. However, there are two problems with this logic. The first is that the Jubilee year is never compared to the Feast of Weeks anywhere in the OT. That comparison is only conjecture used to substantiate the claim that the Jubilee is a second consecutive fallow year. Secondly, the Jubilee is in some sense a celebration following the Sabbatical year, since it celebrates the return of the land to its permanent owners so that they can once again sow a crop following the fallow Sabbatical year.

Finally, it is claimed that the "main objection to counting the Jubilee as a successive sabbatical is the impossibility of two successive fallow years."[65] Israel, it is noted, at times withstood famines of up to three years (2 Sam 21:1; 1 Kgs 18:1; 2 Kgs 17:5; 18:10; 25:1–3),[66] so that two successive fallow years were within the realm of possibility. However, the question is not what was possible or impossible for ancient Israelites to endure, but what the text of Lev 25 commands. As already discussed, Lev 25:20–22 does not

---

[64] Bergsma, *The Jubilee from Leviticus to Qumran*, 89; Milgrom, *Leviticus 23–27*, 2163; Wellhausen, *Prolegomena to the History of Israel*, 119.

[65] Bergsma, *The Jubilee from Leviticus to Qumran*, 90.

[66] 2 Kgs 17:5; 18:10 mention artificial famines caused by sieges.

anticipate two consecutive fallow years, and provides for only one fallow year.[67]

Therefore, the Jubilee year occurred every forty-nine years and was coterminous with the Sabbatical year. The emphasis of the Sabbatical year was rest for the land which was allowed to remain fallow. The Sabbatical year began in the autumn of every seventh year. Thus, the Sabbatical year was called the "seventh year" after the spring-to-spring year in which it began. In contrast, the emphasis of the Jubilee year was on the end of the year in anticipation of the permanent owner of the land sowing the first crop following the fallow Sabbatical year. Thus, the Jubilee year was called the "fiftieth year" after the spring-to-spring year in which it ended.

The Jubilee was not only important historically for marking time—and made it possible for Israel to track its history over long periods of time—but also eventually became a way of imposing order on history and for interpreting prophetic time periods. This is seen in the intertestamental book of *Jubilees*, many copies of which were found at Qumran. *Jubilees* is a reworking of Genesis that divides world history into Jubilee periods of forty-nine years each. A document from the same era also found at Qumran, 11QMelch, interprets the seventy "weeks" in Dan 9:24 as 490 years made up of ten Jubilee periods.[68]

---

[67] In a curious concession to this point Fishbane, who holds that the Sabbatical and Jubilee years were two consecutive years allows that the Jubilee was not a fallow year, based on the clear statements made in Lev 25:20–22 (but in direct contradiction to Lev 25:11; Fishbane, *Biblical Interpretation in Ancient Israel*, 167–169).

[68] See the discussion in Finegan, *Handbook of Biblical Chronology*, 128–129.

3

ESTABLISHING BENCHMARKS FOR OLD TESTAMENT CHRONOLOGY

The OT contains so many chronological references that one has relatively few problems constructing a generally reliable *relative chronology*—a chronology that fixes events in order and distance in time from one another. However, fixing an *absolute chronology*—a chronology that fixes events with respect to a reference scale such as the modern numbering of years BC and AD—is much more difficult. However, there are two events in OT history that can be fixed to our modern reference system that will provide benchmarks for any investigation of OT chronology. One of these, the date of Solomon's reign, is comparatively uncontroversial. The other benchmark—the date of the Exodus—is extremely controversial. However, it is critical for dating earlier events in OT history.

THE REIGN OF SOLOMON (971T–932T)

The date of Solomon's death is generally accepted as 931 BC.[69] Assyrian historical records enable us to pinpoint this date, but to do so we must work backwards to Solomon's day from later kings of Israel.

---

[69] Finegan, *Handbook of Biblical Chronology*, 249; Kitchen, *On the Reliability of the Old Testament*, 83; Kitchen, "How We Know When Solomon Ruled," 33–37, 58; Mitchell, "Israel and Judah until the Revolt of Jehu (931–841 B.C.)," *CAH* 3.1, 445–446; Thiele, *Mysterious Numbers*, 67–78; Young, "Three Verifications," 168–173.

AHAB AND JEHU

The Black Obelisk of the Assyrian King Shalmaneser III (859–824) records that he received tribute from Israel's King Jehu.[70] His annals date this tribute to the eighteenth year of his reign, 841 BC.[71]

Twelve years earlier in the summer of 853 BC during the sixth year of his reign, Shalmaneser claimed victory over a Syrian-led coalition of kings at Qarqar on the Orontes River as commemorated in the Monolith Inscription.[72] Among the leaders of the forces opposed to Shalmaneser was King Ahab of Israel. Ahab must have died in the same year shortly afterward in the battle at Ramoth Gilead (1 Kgs 22:3, 35).

Two kings reigned between Ahab and Jehu—Ahaziah and Joram. According to 1 Kgs 22:51 Ahaziah reigned two years, and according to 2 Kgs 3:1 Joram reigned twelve years.

Thus, it would appear that the book of Kings records fourteen years between the reigns of Ahab and Jehu, but Assyrian records allow for only twelve years. However, the difference between the two sources is resolved by understanding how the kings of Israel reckoned the total years of their reign.

ACCESSION-YEAR VERSUS NON-ACCESSION YEAR RECKONING

Since a king would be unlikely to die on the exact day ending a particular year and his successor take the throne on the first day of the following year, it was likely that the last year of a king's reign was a partial year, and the rest of that year was served by the following king. Since both kings served part of a year, to whom was that year assigned? In some systems used in the ancient world, the year was assigned to the end of the reign of the previous king, and the partial year was not counted in the reign of the new king. Instead this was a sort of "year zero" for the new king, called his accession year. This

---

[70] *ANET* 281.

[71] *ANET* 280.

[72] *ANET* 278–279.

accession year system was typically used by the Assyrians and Babylonians.

The *non-accession year* system was used by the kings of Israel, whose first dynasty was founded by Jeroboam I.[73] Therefore, we must subtract two years from the fourteen years listed in the book of Kings for the two kings of Israel between Ahab and Jehu. This is because the last year of Ahab was also counted as the first year of his successor, and the first year of Jehu was also counted as the last year of his predecessor.

CALCULATING SOLOMON'S REIGN

We can now use the data given in the book of Kings to calculate the beginning of Jeroboam I's reign, which was the last year of Solomon's reign (1 Kgs 11:43–12:20). Kings provides us with the following information on the length of the reigns of the kings of Israel from the beginning of Jeroboam I's reign to the death of Ahab:

Table 8
Lengths of Reigns from Jeroboam I to Ahab

Jeroboam I	22 years	1 Kgs 14:20
Nadab	2 years	1 Kgs 15:25
Baasha	24 years	1 Kgs 15:28, 33
Elah	2 years	1 Kgs 16:8
Zimri	7 days	1 Kgs 16:10, 15
Omri	12 years	1 Kgs 16:23
Ahab	22 years	1 Kgs 16:29

The total of the reigns is 84 years. We must subtract six years for overlapping reigns, meaning that 78 actual years elapsed between Ahab's death and the death of Solomon. This places Solomon's death

---

[73] Non-accession year reckoning was used elsewhere in the ancient world. For instance, during some eras the Egyptians employed it.

in 931 BC, or the last year of his reign as 932t.[74] Since Solomon reigned forty years (1 Kgs 11:42; 2 Chr 9:30), his first year on the throne was 971t.

This is confirmed in the book of Kings by examining the information on the length of reigns from the beginning of Rehoboam's reign to the seventeenth year of Jehoshaphat's reign when Ahab died and was succeeded by Ahaziah (1 Kgs 22:51).

Table 9
Lengths of Reigns from Rehoboam to Jehoshaphat

Rehoboam	17 years	1 Kgs 14:21	2 Chr 12:13
Abijah	3 years	1 Kgs 15:1–2	2 Chr 13:1–2
Asa	41 years	1 Kgs 15:9–10	2 Chr 16:11–13
Jehoshaphat	17 years	1 Kgs 22:51	

The total is 78 years, once again making Solomon's last year 932t. (This also demonstrates that the early kings of Judah used the accession-year system to reckon the lengths of their reigns, since no years need to be subtracted to make this total the same as the reckoning of the non-accession year reigns of the kings of Israel.)

CONFIRMATION—SHOSHENQ'S INVASION

Several pieces of evidence confirm this dating of Solomon's reign. The first is the way in which the biblical data allow us to date the reign of the Egyptian Pharaoh Shoshenq I (Biblical Shishak). By counting backwards from the start of Egypt's twenty-fifth dynasty between 715 BC and 712 BC, it can be determined that Shoshenq began to reign no earlier than 945 BC and no later than 936 BC.[75] Kitchen has noted that Shoshenq must have invaded Judah about 925

---

[74] See the discussion on p. 133 showing that Solomon died before Tishri 1 of 931 BC, so that his final year was 932t by Judean Tishri-based reckoning.

[75] Kitchen, "Egypt and East Africa," 111.

BC near the end of his reign (943–923).[76] This date is derived from the biblical text and allows Egyptologists to date Shishak's reign.[77] The calculation is as follows: Since Shoshenq's invasion took place during the fifth year of the reign of Solomon's successor Rehoboam of Judah (1 Kgs 14:25; 2 Chr 12:2), the date derived above for Solomon's reign would make Rehoboam's fifth year 927t since Rehoboam's accession year began in 932t at the death of Solomon.

The general time for Shoshenq's reign that has been derived by Egyptologists is therefore consistent with the biblical dates of Solomon and Rehoboam. *However, it is important to note that the Egyptian data do not allow a precise chronology for this period.* It is only when Shoshenq's dates are correlated with the Bible's more precise chronological data that Egyptologists are able to refine Shoshenq's dates to 943–923 BC.

CONFIRMATION—SOLOMON'S FATHER-IN-LAW

Kitchen also notes that Siamun (986–c. 968) is most probably the Pharaoh who conquered Gezer and gave it to Solomon as a dowry for his daughter.[78] Siamun is the only Pharaoh of this era known to have campaigned in the Levant. This means that Solomon's reign had to have begun before the end of Siamun's reign, so a date of 971t for the beginning of Solomon's reign fits nicely within the latter years of Siamun's reign.

---

[76] Kitchen, "How We Know When Solomon Ruled," 35; Dates for Egyptian chronology are based on Hornung, Krauss and Warburton, *Ancient Egyptian Chronology*, 490–495; for alternate dates see Grimal, *A History of Ancient Israel*, 389–395. Kitchen dated Shoshenq's reign 945–924 BC.

[77] While there are a few Egyptologists who object to this dating and to equating Shoshenq I with Shishak, the overwhelming majority of Egyptologists accept the dating and the identification.

[78] Kitchen, "How We Know When Solomon Ruled," 35; Hornung, *Ancient Egyptian Chronology*, 474, 493. (Kitchen dated Siamun's reign as 979–960 BC.) This identification of Solomon's father-in-law was argued along the same lines by Horn, "Who Was Solomon's Egyptian Father-in-Law?" 3–17.

CONFIRMATION—THE TYRIAN KING LIST

The Tyrian king list also confirms that Solomon reigned from 971t to 932t.[79] The Tyrian king list is preserved by Josephus, quoting Menander of Ephesus.[80] While the lengths of reigns of individual Tyrian kings varies greatly among the extant manuscript traditions of Josephus, the traditions concerning the span from the beginning of the reign of Hiram to the founding of Carthage is much more certain, and clearly is 155 years and eight months:

> It should be emphasized that this exact figure of "155 years and 8 months" from the accession of Hiram (*Eirōmos*) to the founding of Carthage is attested in virtually all of the textual witnesses (in Syn[cellus] it is not explicit, but see below; Eus ex gr alone reads "155 years and 18 months," cf. above, note i). This textual unanimity is all the more striking when one considers that none of the original figures as now extant in the various texts adds up to this figure (all except Eus Arm fall short.)[81]

Moreover, there are two other important pieces of information given by Josephus: the temple in Jerusalem was built in Hiram's

---

[79] Young, "Three Verifications," 179–187. Young's work is based on the work of earlier scholars including Barnes, *Studies in the Chronology of the Divided Monarchy of Israel*; Cross, "An Interpretation of the Nora Stone," 17, n. 11; Lipiński, "Ba 'il-Ma'zer II and the Chronology of Tyre," 59–65; Liver, "The Chronology of Tyre at the Beginning of the First Millennium B.C.," 113–120.

[80] *Ag. Ap.* 1.107–126 [1.17–18].

[81] Barnes, *Studies in the Chronology of the Divided Monarchy of Israel*, 44, as quoted by Young, "Three Verifications of Thiele's Date for the Beginning of the Divided Kingdom," 181. The source that reads 155 years and 18 months corroborates the figure of 155 years and eight months, since this figure is obviously a mistake for 155 years and eight months. Otherwise 155 years and 18 months would have been written as 156 years and six months. See also the tables for the reigns of Tyrian kings in Galil, *The Chronology of the Kings of Israel and Judah*, 163–165.

twelfth year, and this was 143 years and eight months before the founding of Carthage.[82] Josephus, however, used Pompeius Trogus as his source for the date of Dido's departure from Tyre and her founding of Carthage. Pompeius Trogus clearly conflated the two events—Dido's departure from Tyre and her founding of Carthage. This led him to associate both events with the earlier one—the date of Dido's departure from Tyre in Pygmalion's seventh year as king, which can be securely dated to 825 BC. [83] (Dido founded Carthage eleven years later in 814 BC.) This means that there were 143 years from the construction of the temple to Pygmalion's seventh year.[84] From this information we can calculate Solomon's reign:

- 143 years before 825 BC yields 968 BC for the beginning of the construction of the temple in the month of Ziv during Solomon's fourth year (968t; 1 Kgs 6:1; 2 Chr 3:1–2).[85]

---

[82] *Ag. Ap.* 108, 126 [22, 26] . Young has an extended discussion of criticisms of the Tyrian king list and Barnes' reconstruction. Young demonstrates that the criticisms are misguided and that both Josephus and Barnes are reliable on this point (Young, "Three Verifications of Thiele's Date for the Beginning of the Divided Kingdom," 185).

[83] See the discussion in Young, "Three Verifications of Thiele's Date for the Beginning of the Divided Kingdom," 180, including note 42 as well as Barnes, *Studies in the Chronology of the Divided Monarchy of Israel*, 51–52.

[84] The additional eight months represents the reign of Phelles, four kings before Pygmalion. When Josephus made his summation he added this short reign in with the others. He should have either added a year to come to a total of 144 years or deleted a year, reckoning that Phelles' eight months overlapped the last year of his predecessor and/or the first year of his successor. Most likely the latter is the case. See the discussion in Young, "Three Verifications," 185, note 50.

[85] Though the official year begin in Tishri 968 BC, the actual construction began the following Ziv, which occurred in 967 BC (968t ≈ October 968– September 967 BC). This reconstruction assumes that the Tyrians, like Israel in Solomon's day and Judah thereafter, reckoned reigns from Tishri in an

- Solomon, therefore, acceded to the throne in 971t.

- Since Solomon reigned a total of 40 years, he would have died 36 years after 968t or in 932t.

- Hiram's reign began twelve years earlier in 980 BC during the latter part of David's reign. This, of course, agrees with the biblical information that Hiram was on friendly terms with both Solomon and David (2 Sam 5:11; 1 Kgs 5:1–12; 9:11–12, 27; 1 Chr 14:1).

---

autumn-to-autumn calendar. This is assumed based on an observation by Young. Young notes that the evidence indicates that the Tyrians, like the early kings of Judah, used accession year reckoning for the lengths of kings' reigns (Young, "Three Verifications," 186 note 54). Thus, it is also reasonable to assume that the Tyrians like Judah used an autumn-to-autumn calendar for the official years of their kings. That Judah and Tyre were using the same chronological system is also suggested by the Judean use of Phoenician month-names (*Ziv*, *Bul*, and *Ethanim*) in the time of Solomon. This is one of the many indications that the records of Solomon's reign given in Kings and Chronicles were taken from contemporaneous accounts and were not the invention of exilic and post-exilic redactors, since Babylonian month-names were used in the exilic and post-exilic period. An even more compelling argument against the "minimalist" position that the reign of Solomon is a fanciful invention from a later age is that a later writer, without access to the official court records of Solomon, could never have produced the rich chronological data found in the Bible that allow the precise dating of Solomon's reign. The correctness and precision of the dating from the biblical data have been demonstrated by the agreement with Solomon's dates that can be derived from the Tyrian King List, as discussed above, and, independently, with their exact agreement with the Jubilee data as tied to 1 Kgs 6:1 (see discussion beginning on page 48).

SOLOMON'S REIGN AS A CHRONOLOGICAL BENCHMARK

Thus, several lines of evidence point to Solomon's reign beginning in 971t and ending in 932t.[86] For this reason, the date of Solomon's reign can be used as an anchor to calculate the date of events as early as the reign of David and moving forward in time.

Unfortunately, the date of Solomon's reign cannot help us to fix dates for events before the reign of David because of a severe disruption in the text of 1 Sam 13:1. This verse tells us of the chronology of the reign of David's predecessor Saul. It reads:

בֶּן־שָׁנָה שָׁאוּל בְּמָלְכוֹ וּשְׁתֵּי שָׁנִים מָלַךְ עַל־יִשְׂרָאֵל

Saul was . . . years old when he became king. He ruled . . . and two years over Israel.

Apparently there was a serious disruption in the transmission of the text of 1 Sam 13:1. This disruption must have occurred early in the history of the transmission of the text, since none of the ancient versions offers any help in restoring the lost numbers. Clearly, from the account of Saul's reign in 1 Samuel, he reigned more than two years.

THE DATE OF THE EXODUS

1 KINGS 6:1

Because of the textual problem at 1 Sam 13:1, a second benchmark is needed that will allow us to date events before the reign of David. Fortunately, there is one chronological notice in the OT that enables us to skip backwards from Solomon's reign over the reign of Saul to a previous event.

---

[86] There is, in fact, another line of evidence first used by Coucke that derived the date for Solomon's reign from the Parian Marble and classical sources. Coucke, "Chronique biblique"; see also Young, "The Parian Marble and Other Surprises from Chronologist V. Coucke."

1 Kgs 6:1 states:

וַיְהִי בִשְׁמוֹנִים שָׁנָה וְאַרְבַּע מֵאוֹת שָׁנָה לְצֵאת בְּנֵי־יִשְׂרָאֵל
מֵאֶרֶץ־מִצְרַיִם בַּשָּׁנָה הָרְבִיעִית בְּחֹדֶשׁ זִו הוּא הַחֹדֶשׁ הַשֵּׁנִי
לִמְלֹךְ שְׁלֹמֹה עַל־יִשְׂרָאֵל וַיִּבֶן הַבַּיִת לַיהוָה:

In the four hundred eightieth year beginning with[87] the year
that the Israelites came out of the land of Egypt, in the fourth
year in the month of Ziv, that is, the second month, in the reign
of Solomon over Israel, he [began to] build a house for
Yahweh.

Solomon's fourth year was 968t. The second month occurred in
the following spring of 967 BC, which was 479 years after the
Exodus. This makes 1446 BC the year of the Exodus, and places the
Exodus in the month Nisan of that year (Exod 12:2; Num 33:3).

CONFIRMATION—JUDGES 11:26

There are two ways to confirm this date. The first is Judg 11:26 where
the judge Jephthah challenged the King of Ammon, who laid claim to
the Israelite territory in Gilead east of the Jordan River:

בְּשֶׁבֶת יִשְׂרָאֵל בְּחֶשְׁבּוֹן וּבִבְנוֹתֶיהָ וּבְעַרְעוֹר וּבִבְנוֹתֶיהָ
וּבְכָל־הֶעָרִים אֲשֶׁר עַל־יְדֵי אַרְנוֹן שְׁלֹשׁ מֵאוֹת שָׁנָה וּמַדּוּעַ
לֹא־הִצַּלְתֶּם בָּעֵת הַהִיא:

When Israel lived in Heshbon and its villages and in Aroer and
its villages and in all the cities which are beside the Arnon
River—three hundred years—why didn't you capture them
during that time?

Jephthah states that in his day Israel had occupied Gilead for 300
years. The tribes that received land east of the Jordan River were not
allowed to occupy it until after they had helped the rest of the tribes

---

[87] The Hebrew expression here indicates that Israel's Exodus initiated a
chronological era in which the Exodus itself occurred in year one of that era,
and Temple construction began in year 480 of that era, that is, 479 years after
the departure from Egypt.

gain a foothold on the land west of the Jordan (Num 32:20–28; Josh 1:12–15). Joshua's military campaigns began 40 years after the Exodus (Exod 16:35; Num 14:33–34; 32:13; Deut 2:7; 8:2, 4; 29:5; Neh 9:21; Ps. 95:10; Amos 2:10; 5:25; Acts 7:36, 42; 13:18; Heb 3:9, 17) and lasted seven years (1406–1400 BC assuming the date of 1446 for the Exodus). Therefore, 1400 BC is the earliest that Israel could have occupied Gilead. This implies that Jephthah's words were spoken around 1100 BC, assuming that in his message to the King of Ammon he is speaking in round numbers for rhetorical effect and not giving an exact chronological reference. That means there should be about 133 years between Jephthah and Solomon's building of the temple (1100–967 BC).

Jephthah was one of the last judges. Following him were Ibzan, Elon, Abdon, Samson and Samuel. Samson's judgeship could have overlapped any of the last judges, since all we are told about it chronologically is that it lasted 20 years during the days of the Philistine oppression (Judg 15:20; cf. Judg 16:31) that started in Jephthah's time (Judg 10:7–9) and continued at least until Saul became king. Therefore, it is of no help in establishing a chronology. However, we know the length of the judgeships of Jephthah (six years; Judg 12:7); Ibzan (seven years; Judg 12:8–10), Elon (10 years; Judg 12:11–12), and Abdon (eight years; Judg 12:13–15). We could assign at least a dozen years to Samuel's judgeship,[88] and perhaps as many as twenty (1 Sam 7:2), especially if his judgeship overlapped Abdon's. Saul's reign can be estimated at 40 years (Acts 13:21), and David's reign lasted 40 years (2 Sam 5:4). If we add these in a non-accession manner we obtain a total of 125 years. This is only 8 years less than the 133 years that there should be between Jephthah and the beginning of the construction of the temple if Jephthah was speaking in exact numbers. However, if Jephthah was not attempting to give the exact number of years but speaking in round numbers for rhetorical effect (much as we might when we say that Jesus was born

---

[88] Josephus, *Ant.* 6.249 [6.12.4].

2000 years ago), his figure of 300 years provides us with an approximation of the date of the Exodus that confirms the reliability of 1 Kgs 6:1 for calculating the date of the Exodus.

CONFIRMATION—JUBILEE YEARS

TRADITIONS PRESERVED IN JEWISH SOURCES

A second confirmation of the date of the Exodus comes from the Jubilee years.[89] The Babylonian Talmud notes the years of two Jubilees: the eighteenth year of King Josiah of Judah[90] and the twenty-fifth year of the exile as recorded by Ezekiel in Ezek 40:1.[91] Most scholars are agreed that the Talmud's chronological reckoning is based upon an older rabbinic work, the *Seder 'Olam Rabbah*. Tradition considers it to have been written about AD 160 by Rabbi Yose ben Halafta, a disciple of the famous Rabbi Akiba.[92] The *Seder 'Olam* also mentions these two Jubilee years.[93] Both the Talmud and the *Seder 'Olam* claim that the Jubilee in Ezekiel's day was the seventeenth jubilee.[94]

JEWISH SOURCES FOR THE JUBILEE YEARS

Before using this information to calculate the date of the Exodus, we should make four observations related to the use of Jewish sources about the jubilee years. The first is that there is no way to calculate the number of a particular Jubilee year simply from chronological information in the OT. One needs some extra-biblical information to fix an absolute date first, such as was done above for the date of

---

[89] This discussion is based on the work of Young. See Young, "The Talmud's Two Jubilees." Also see Young, "Ezekiel 40:1 as a Corrective for Seven Wrong Ideas in Biblical Interpretation."

[90] *b. Meg.* 14b.

[91] *b. 'Arak.* 12a.

[92] Guggenheimer, *Seder Olam*, x.

[93] *S. 'Olam Rab.* 11, 24 (see Guggenheimer, *Seder Olam*, 116, 211 note 4.)

[94] *S. 'Olam Rab.* 11; *b. 'Arak* 12b.

Solomon's reign (see the discussion beginning on page 37). Such extra-biblical synchronizations were not available in the second century when *Seder ʿOlam* was produced. Thus, *Seder ʿOlam*'s knowledge of which Jubilee was the seventeenth Jubilee must have come from Jewish tradition (i.e., an actual historical remembrance).

A second observation is that neither the Talmud nor *Seder ʿOlam* determined that Josiah's eighteenth regnal year was a Jubilee year by calculation from the Jubilee in Ezekiel's day. The Talmudic rabbis assumed that all mention of regnal years in the OT were to be understood as given in the non-accession method. This, however, would have meant that there were only 47 years between Josiah's eighteenth year and the one mentioned in Ezek 40:1.[95] Therefore, the knowledge that Josiah's eighteenth year was a Jubilee came from tradition, not from calculation from biblical data.

The third observation comes from the wording of Ezek 40:1. It indicates that this verse is referring to a Jubilee year.

בְּעֶשְׂרִים וְחָמֵשׁ שָׁנָה לְגָלוּתֵנוּ בְּרֹאשׁ הַשָּׁנָה בֶּעָשׂוֹר לַחֹדֶשׁ בְּאַרְבַּע עֶשְׂרֵה שָׁנָה אַחַר אֲשֶׁר הֻכְּתָה הָעִיר בְּעֶצֶם הַיּוֹם הַזֶּה הָיְתָה עָלַי יַד־יְהֹוָה וַיָּבֵא אֹתִי שָׁמָּה:

In the twenty-fifth year of our captivity, at the beginning of the year on the tenth day of the month in the fourteenth year after the city was struck on this very day, the hand of Yahweh was upon me and brought me there.

This verse dates Ezekiel's vision to the beginning of a year (Hebrew *rosh hashanah*) that takes place on the tenth day of a month. The only

---

[95] Young, "The Talmud's Two Jubilees," 77. The calculation would have subtracted one year from each king's reign as given in 2 Kings. Kings who reigned for less than a year would have been assigned no years. This yields 13 years remaining in Josiah's reign, zero years for Jehoahaz, 10 years for Jehoiakim, zero years for Jehoiachin, 10 years for Zedekiah and 14 years until Ezekiel's vision.

year that begins on the tenth day of a month is the jubilee year, which begins on 10 Tishri, the Day of Atonement (Lev 25:9).

The fourth and final observation is that the beginning of the first sabbatical cycle, and therefore, the first Jubilee cycle, was the entry into the land (Lev 25:2). The first Jubilee would have been the forty-ninth year after the entry into the land under Joshua's leadership, making the first year of the entry into the land 48 years earlier. The Exodus occurred 40 years before the entry into the land (Exod 16:35; Num 14:33–34; 32:13; Deut 2:7; 8:2, 4; 29:5; Neh 9:21; Ps. 95:10; Amos 2:10; 5:25; Acts 7:36, 42; 13:18; Heb 3:9, 17).

DATE OF THE EXODUS ACCORDING TO JUBILEE YEARS

The fourteenth year after Jerusalem's destruction by the Babylonians was 574t.[96] We can now calculate backward to the date of the Exodus:

Seventeenth Jubilee: 574t

First Jubilee: 574t + (16 x 49) = 1358t

Beginning of the first Jubilee cycle following the entry into the Land: 1358t + 48 = 1406t[97]

---

[96] Assuming that Jerusalem fell to Nebuchadnezzar on 9 Tammuz 587 BC, the first year after the city was struck would then be 587t. This agrees with the chronologies of Young, "When Did Jerusalem Fall?"; Wiseman and Kitchen, *NBD*, 217; Kitchen and Mitchell, "Chronology of the Old Testament." See also Kitchen, *On the Reliability of the Old Testament*, 67. Some scholars hold that Jerusalem fell a year later in Tammuz of 586. (Thiele, *Mysterious Numbers*, 191; McFall, "Has the Chronology of the Hebrew Kings Been Finally Settled?" 101; Galil, *The Chronology of the Kings of Israel and Judah*, 147). Young has demonstrated, however, that the only date that satisfies all the biblical passages that refer to the date of Jerusalem's final fall to Nebuchadnezzar is 9 Tammuz 587 BC (2 Kgs 25:1–3, Jer 1:3; 46:2 and Ezek 24:1; 40:1; see Young "When Did Jerusalem Fall?" and "Ezekiel 40:1 as a Corrective for Seven Wrong Ideas in Biblical Interpretation").

Year of the Exodus 1406t + 40 = 1446t + 6 months

Therefore, the Exodus took place on 14 Nisan in 1446 BC.

The same date is obtained counting backward from Josiah's eighteenth year, 623t.[98] Note that Josiah's sixteenth year is 49 years before the seventeenth jubilee in 574t, making it the sixteenth jubilee.

Sixteenth Jubilee: 623t

Year of the Exodus: 623t + (15 x 49) + 48 + 40 = 1446t + 6 months

Thus, the traditions about Jubilee years as preserved in the Talmud and in *Seder 'Olam Rabbah* agree with both 1 Kgs 6:1 and Judg 11:26 in dating the Exodus to 1446 BC.

Those who hold to any date other than 1446 BC for the Exodus, or who maintain that the Exodus never happened in any sense as described in the Pentateuch, and as remembered afterward throughout the Old Testament, have to contend that it is a strange coincidence that the date of the Exodus as calculated from the Jubilee cycles not only agrees, *but agrees exactly*, with the date of the Exodus as calculated from 1 Kgs 6:1. As mentioned previously, rabbinic chronological methods and calculations were unable to calculate correctly the 49 years from the twenty-fifth year of Ezekiel's captivity to Josiah's eighteenth year, much less the 872 years from Ezekiel's

---

[97] The entry into the land took place in the previous spring of 1406 BC (Josh 3:15).

[98] Josiah died in battle at Meggido opposing Pharaoh Neco when Neco was on his way to aid the Assyrians in the Battle of Carchemesh in Tammuz 609 BC (2 Kgs 23:29; 2 Chr 35:20–24). Since Tammuz 609 (which was in the latter part of 610t) occurred during Josiah's thirty-first year as king (2 Kgs 22:1‖2 Chr 34:1), Josiah's eighteenth year had to have been 623t (610t + 31 - 18 = 623t). For this reason almost all proposed chronologies of the kings of Judah agree that Josiah's eighteenth year began in 623 BC. These include those of Young, Thiele, McFall, Kitchen and Mitchell, and Galil. See *Table 31* on page 141.

vision back to the Exodus. The only credible explanation that has emerged so far for this supposed coincidence for the correct date of the Exodus as derived by two independent methods is that the Levitical priests had been faithfully counting the cycles of Sabbatical and Jubilee years over all the years since the entry into the land, as was their duty, even though the people in general were unwilling to observe the various stipulations associated in the Law of Moses with the Jubilee and Sabbatical years.

Other coincidences must be explained: Why did the two pre-exilic readings of the Law to the people happen to fall in a Sabbatical year, as was commanded in Deut 31:10? Why does the well-documented tradition that Jerusalem fell to the Babylonians in a Sabbatical year also fit this pattern? How is it that the Sabbatical year following the defeat of Sennacherib's army fit this pattern (see the discussion beginning on page 149)? Although these latter evidences are not, individually, as compelling as the mathematical demonstration that the time of the Exodus calculated from the Jubilee cycles matches the time derived, independently, from 1 Kgs 6:1,[99] they each lend their cumulative weight to the conclusion that Israel's priests knew the times of the Jubilee and Sabbatical cycles for all the time that Israel was in its land.

---

[99] The Law could have been read at any time, so there was one chance in seven that a given reading would happen in a Sabbatical year. The odds, however, that both readings (2 Chr 17:7–9; 2 Kgs 23:1–2) would be in a Sabbatical year is only one in 49. The probability that both readings were in a Sabbatical year and that the year of the land lying voluntarily fallow in Isaiah's day (2 Kgs 19:29‖Isa 37:30) is also a match for the Sabbatical-year calendar is one divided by seven to the third power (one in 343 or 0.29 percent). This makes it unlikely these events are inventions of exilic or post-exilic scribes. That all of them match the calendar of Jubilee and Sabbatical cycles testifies to the faithfulness of the priests in preserving the times of the cycles, and also to the authenticity of the historical events that are dated by them.

Not much attention has been given in scholarly literature to the usefulness of the Jubilee and Sabbatical cycles as a method of measuring the years over a long period of time (centuries), even though the Talmud states that they served that purpose in the time of the judges.[100] At the present time, however, the chronology of the monarchic period has been put on a sound basis by the work of Coucke, Thiele, and those who built on the chronological principles that they discovered underlying the biblical texts.[101] Because of their work it is possible to verify the accuracy of the Jubilee/Sabbatical year calendar that started in 1406 BC, based on the arguments presented just above.

This illustrates one of the principles stated in the preface to the present book: that some historical insights will remain obscured until the chronology of the period under discussion is determined properly. The Jubilee and Sabbatical cycles provide such historical insight. But they do more: they also offer theological insights on such important matters as the date and historicity of the Exodus and the origin of the Book of Leviticus. If, as has been argued, the times of the Jubilee and Sabbatical cycles were known all the time that Israel was in its land, and, further, that the only adequate explanation that has yet been given for Ezekiel's Jubilee being the seventeenth Jubilee is that the counting for these cycles actually started 832 years earlier, in 1406 BC, then it is logical to conclude that Lev 25–27, the texts that charter the Sabbatical years and the Jubilees, were in existence in the late fifteenth century BC.

---

[100] *b. Sanh.* 40a, b.

[101] See the discussion of the work of Thiele and others beginning on page 129.

THE LATE-DATE THEORY OF THE EXODUS

ADHERENTS TO THE LATE-DATE THEORY

However, despite the strong evidence for this date, some scholars hold that the Exodus actually took place sometime in the thirteenth century BC. This theory was popularized by William F. Albright in the 1930s.[102] The primary motive for Albright's theory was to harmonize the Exodus with archaeological evidence from Palestine. In the decades since Albright's death in 1971 most Palestinian archaeologists and most critical scholars have abandoned this theory in favor of denying the historicity of the Exodus and conquest. Virtually all of the remaining adherents of a thirteenth century Exodus are evangelical scholars.[103]

THE MERNEPTAH STELE

The late-date Exodus theory must place the Exodus sometime early in the thirteenth century. This is necessitated by the Merneptah Stele, a

---

[102] Wood, "The Rise and Fall of the 13th-Century Exodus-Conquest Theory," 475, including note 1. Some scholars before Albright proposed a thirteenth century date for the Exodus. Hoffmeier, "What Is the Biblical Date for the Exodus?," 231, notes 34 and 35 lists C. Richard Lepsius, *Briefe aus Aegytpen, Aethiopien und der Halbinsel des Sinai: Geschrieben in den Jahren 1842–1845 wärend des auf Befehl Sr. Majestät des Königs Friedrich Wilhelm IV von Preussen ausgeführten wissenschaftlichen Expedition, von Richard Lepsius.* (Berlin: W. Hertz, 1852) and A. H. Sayce, *"Higher Criticism" and the Verdict of the Monuments* (London: S.P.C.K., 1915).

[103] E.g., Alan Cole, *Exodus: An Introduction and Commentary* (Downers Grove: Intervarsity, 1973), 40–43; John Currid, *A Study Commentary on Exodus* (Auburn, MA: Evangelical, 2000), 27–29; Richard Hess, *Joshua: An Introduction and Commentary* (Downers Grove: Intervarsity, 1996), 139–143; Hoffmeier, "What Is the Biblical Date for the Exodus?" and *Israel in Egypt: The Evidence for the Authenticity of the Exodus Tradition* (New York: Oxford University, 1996); Kitchen, *On the Reliability of the Old Testament*, 283–289, 307–310.

victory inscription from the reign of the Egyptian pharaoh Merneptah discovered at Thebes in 1896. This stele contains the oldest extra-biblical mention of Israel as a people (not a city-state) living in Palestine. It dates to 1211 or 1210 BC.[104] Thus, the Exodus and the forty-year wilderness wanderings had to take place before about 1210. This would make 1250 BC the absolute latest date for the Exodus, if Merneptah's invasion took place in the first year of Joshua's conquest. However, it would appear from the inscription that Israel had been in Palestine for some time, making approximately 1270 BC the latest possible date for the Exodus.[105]

THE LATE-DATE THEORY AND 1 KINGS 6:1

Of course, the late-date Exodus theory must deal with 1 Kgs 6:1 and the claim that the Exodus took place 480 years earlier. The common explanation given is that the author of Kings actually understood there to be twelve generations between the Exodus and Solomon's day. He calculated 480 years by assuming that a generation spanned forty years, based on Num 32:13 (cf. Ps. 95:10). In actuality, however, one should most likely figure an average of about 25 years between generations, since this would place the birth of a son when is father was, on average, 25 years old. This would place the Exodus in the thirteenth century since 968 BC + (12 x 25) = 1268 BC.

There are several problems with this understanding of 1 Kgs 6:1, however. The most obvious is that there is no indication in the text of 1 Kgs 6:1 that the author understood there to be twelve generations from the Exodus to Solomon.

---

[104] For more details about this mention of Israel see Hasel, "Israel in the Merneptah Stela."

[105] Ahlström and Edelman, "Merneptah's Israel" argue that "Israel" is parallel to "Canaan" in the Merneptah stele. If they are correct, and Israel is a term used in the stele as a way of referring to Palestine in general, then Israel must have been occupying Canaan much earlier than even 1270 BC.

Another problem is that Num 32:13 does not state that a generation (i.e., the age of a father when his [first?] son is born) is forty years. It simply states that the "generation" of Israel who participated in the Exodus and rebelled against God wandered in the wilderness 40 years until all its members had died. The definition of generation in this sense was the remaining lifespan of the entire adult population of Israel at the Exodus (Num 14:26–35). Moreover, there were nineteen generations from the Exodus to Solomon.[106] 1 Chr 6:33–37 lists eighteen generations from Korah, who was an adult at the time of the Exodus (Exod 6:21, 24; Num 16:1, 5, 6, 8, 16, 19, 24, 27, 32, 40, 49; 26:9, 10, 11) to Heman, a temple musician in David's day (1 Chr 6:33; 15:17, 19; 16:41, 42; 25:1, 4, 5, 6; 2 Chr 5:12; 29:14; 35:15). Adding one more generation to Solomon makes 19 generations. If we assume about 25 years per generation, the Exodus took place 475 years before Solomon's day, in close agreement with 1 Kgs 6:1.

EXODUS 1:11 AND THE LATE-DATE THEORY

One biblical passage that is key to the late-date theory of the Exodus is Exod 1:11b.

וַיִּבֶן עָרֵי מִסְכְּנוֹת לְפַרְעֹה אֶת־פִּתֹם וְאֶת־רַעַמְסֵס

They built storage cities for Pharaoh: Pithom and Raamses.

This passage is held to indicate that the Exodus took place during the reign of Ramesses II (1279–1213), who rebuilt the Nile delta city of Avaris and renamed it Pi-Ramesses, "the house of Ramesses." Thus, among those who hold to the late-date theory of the Exodus, it is common to name Ramesses II as the Pharaoh of the Exodus.

There are several problems with using this passage, however. One is that it proves too much, since Joseph was said to have settled his father and brothers in "the land of Ramesses" (Gen 47:11) some 430 years before the Exodus (Exod 12:40–41). This had to have been long

---

[106] Wood, "The Rise and Fall of the 13th-Century Exodus-Conquest Theory," 486.

before the beginning of Rameside era in the early thirteenth century. Elsewhere Israel is said to have settled in the land of Goshen (Gen 45:10; 46:28, 29, 34; 47:1, 4, 6, 27; 50:8; Exod 8:22; 9:26). This region is called Ramesses only three times in the OT.[107]

Another problem is that Exod 1:11 characterizes Ramesses and Pithom as supply cities (מִסְכְּנוֹת), whereas Ramesses II built Pi-Ramesses as his capital city. Elsewhere in the OT supply cities are outlying cites built to store supplies and are never capital cities (1 Kgs 9:19; 2 Chr 8:4, 6; 16:4; 17:12; 32:28).

This evidence appears to suggest that the name *Ramesses* is a later scribal updating for what may have originally been *Avaris* in the text of Exod 1:11 and *Goshen* in the text of Gen 47:11. A later scribe may have updated the text to make it intelligible to the readers in his day, sometime during or after the reign of Ramesses II. If this is the case, Exod 1:11 cannot be an indication of a thirteenth century date for the Exodus.[108]

This type of later scribal updating is evident elsewhere in the Pentateuch, Joshua and Judges.[109] The most obvious of these scribal updatings is the city of Dan (Gen 14:14; Deut 34:1) which until the time of the Judges was named Laish (Judg 18:29). It would not have been possible for Moses to call it Dan.[110] Likewise, the city of

---

[107] Gen 47:11; Exod 12:37; Num 33:3, 5. These most probably refer to a region and not the city called Raamses at Exod 1:11, since the reference is to Israel leaving from this place. It was not likely that over two million people resided in the city of Pi-Rameses.

[108] See the discussion of the archaeology of Pithom and Rameses and their occupation during and before the fifteenth century BC in Wood, "From Ramesses to Shiloh," 258–262.

[109] See the discussion in Wood, "The Biblical Date for the Exodus is 1446 BC," 250–251, especially table 1.

[110] Therefore, evangelical scholars who hold to Mosaic authorship of the Pentateuch (cf. Hoffmeier, "What Is the Biblical Date for the Exodus?" 234, note 52) and to the late date theory cannot deny that such later scribal updat-

Hormah is always called by that name in the Pentateuch (Num 14:45; 21:3; Deut 1:44)[111] although it was called Zephath until the early days of the Judges (Judg 1:17). Other candidates for such post-Mosaic updating in the Pentateuch are Bethel, whose earlier name was Luz (Gen 12:8 [twice]; 13:3 [twice]) and Hebron (Gen 13:18; 23:19; 37:14; Num 13:22 [twice]), whose earlier name was Kiriath Arba (Gen 23:2; 35:27).[112]

ARCHAEOLOGY AND THE LATE-DATE THEORY

The primary impetus for the late-date theory of the exodus was archaeological.[113] Since there appeared to be widespread destruction of cities in Palestine in the mid-to-late thirteenth century, this destruction was attributed to the conquest of the land by Israel some forty years after the exodus (Exod 16:35; Num 14:33–34; 32:13; Deut

---

ing took place. Interestingly, Kitchen, who advocates the late-date theory, acknowledges such updating with Dan at Gen 14:14 and Rameses at Gen 47:11 (Kitchen, *On the Reliability of the Old Testament*, 335, 348, 354, 493).
[111] The same is true in Joshua (Josh 12:14; 15:30; 19:4).
[112] Luz was renamed Bethel by Jacob (Gen 28:19), so it is possible that Moses proleptically used the name Bethel for the city at Gen 12:8; 13:2. It is not known when Kiriath Arba was renamed. Wood suggests that it was re-named about 1094 BC based on Num 13:22, which states that Hebron was (re)built seven years before Zoan in Egypt. Zoan was built in the nineteenth year of Rameses XI, about 1087 BC (Wood, "The Biblical Date for the Exodus is 1446 BC: A Response to James Hoffmeier," 251, note 13). Wood does not note that for those who hold to the Mosaic authorship of the Pentateuch, this would imply that not only the name *Hebron* was a post-Mosaic scribal updating but also that the last seven words in Num 13:22 also would have to be a later scribal gloss (וְחֶבְרוֹן שֶׁבַע שָׁנִים נִבְנְתָה לִפְנֵי צֹעַן מִצְרָיִם), "Now Hebron was [re]built seven years before Zoan in Egypt").
[113] See the summary of Albright's arguments in Wood, "The Rise and Fall of the 13th-Century Exodus-Conquest Theory," 475–476, including notes 5–8.

2:7; 8:2, 4; 29:4; Josh 5:6; Neh 9:21; Ps 95:10; Amos 2:10; 5:25; Acts 7:36, 42; 13:18; Heb 3:9, 17).

A major problem with the late-date theory is that the book of Joshua does not depict a wholesale destruction of cities in Palestine.[114] Instead, it notes that only three cities were destroyed: Jericho, Ai, and Hazor. This is in keeping with Moses' words at Deut 6:10–12 which promised that Israel would occupy cities in the Promised Land which they did not build, a promise that was fulfilled under Joshua's leadership (Josh 24:13; cf. Josh 11:13; Neh 9:25). For this reason, the only archaeological evidence that is relevant for dating the conquest under Joshua would come from Jericho, Ai, and Hazor.

JERICHO

The archaeological evidence from Jericho shows no evidence of occupation in the thirteenth century, ruling out the late-date theory for the exodus. However, the evidence for the conquest of Jericho around 1400 BC is controversial.

Garstang, who excavated Jericho from 1930 to 1936, found evidence of collapsed walls, and he dated this destruction of the city to about 1400 BC at the time of Joshua.[115] Kenyon, who excavated at Jericho from 1952 to 1958, concluded that this destruction of the city occurred too early for Joshua's conquest, dating it to between 1580 and 1550 BC.[116] Wood subsequently argued that Garstang was correct, and Kenyon wrong.[117] Most recently, Bruins and van der Plicht

---

[114] This has been frequently noted. See e.g., Merrill, "Palestinian Archaeology and the Date of the Conquest"; Merrill F. Unger, *Archaeology and the Old Testament.* (Grand Rapids: Zondervan, 1954): 163–164; Waltke, "Palestinian Artifactual Evidence Supporting the Early Date of the Exodus," 35.

[115] Garstang and Garstang, *The Story of Jericho,* 121–127.

[116] Kenyon, "Some Notes on the History of Jericho," 113, 117; Kenyon, *Archaeology in the Holy Land,* 181–182.

[117] Wood, "Did the Israelites Conquer Jericho?"; Wood, "Dating Jericho's Destruction."

published carbon-14 dating results from six grain samples from Jericho associated with the disputed destruction layer at Jericho.[118] Their findings date these grains to the mid-sixteenth century, seemingly confirming Kenyon's dates.

However, there is a continuing controversy over the calibration of radiocarbon dating in the eastern Mediterranean basin for this period. Radiocarbon dating after the mid-second millennium BC agrees quite well with other chronological determinations used by historians and archaeologists. In contrast, radiocarbon-determined dates before this time, especially for the fifteenth century BC, disagree quite sharply with other chronological determinations, and there has been ongoing debate among scientists and archaeologists about the accuracy of the calibration scale for carbon-14 dating for this period.[119]

---

[118] Hendrick J. Bruins and Johannes van der Plicht, "Tell Es-Sultan (Jericho): Radiocarbom Results of Short-Lived Cereal and Multiyear Charcoal Samples from the End of the Middle Bronze Age," *Radiocarbon* 37.2 (1995): 213–220.

[119] For instance, see the discussion in Douglas J. Keenan, "Why Early-Historical Radiocarbon Dates Downwind from the Mediterranean Are Too Early," *Radiocarbon*, 44.1 (2002), 225–237. Also see Manfred Bietak, ed. *The Synchronisation of Civilisations in the Eastern Mediterranean in the Second Millennium B.C.: Proceedings of an International Symposium at Schloss Haindorf, 15th-17th of November 1996 and at the Austrian Academy, Vienna, 11th-12th of May 1998.* Vienna: Verlag der Österreichischen Akademie der Wissenschaften, 2000; Manfred Bietak, ed. *The Middle Bronze Age in the Levant: Proceedings of an International Conference on MB IIA Ceramic Material Vienna, 24th - 26th of January 2001.* Vienna: Verlag der Österreichischen Akademie der Wissenschaften, 2002; Manfred Bietak and F. Höflmayer, eds. *The Synchronisation of Civilisations in the Eastern Mediterranean in the Second Millenium B.C. III: Proceedings of the SCIEM 2000 - 2nd EuroConference, Vienna, 28th of May - 1st of June 2003.* Vienna: Verlag der Österreichischen Akademie der Wissenschaften, 2007.

For instance, Egyptologists date the reign of Thutmose III to the mid-fifteenth century, a dating tied quite closely to the subsequent pharaohs Amenhotep II, Thutmose IV, Amenhotep III and Amenhotep IV/Akhenaton, a sequence of father-to-son successions over five generations.[120] While radiocarbon dating confirms the reign of Akhenaton quite well to 1353–1336, it does not confirm the dates of Thutmose III, who must be dated to the mid-fifteenth century on the basis of Egyptian inscriptional evidence.[121] Instead, radiocarbon dating would appear to place Thutmose III about 170 years earlier.

This 170-year discrepancy corresponds quite well to the 170-year discrepancy in the dating of the fall of Jericho as determined by Bruins and van der Plicht's radiocarbon dating of the destruction of Jericho. Thus, if there is a problem with the carbon-14 dating from Jericho, and it should be lowered about 170 years from the mid-sixteenth century to the end of the fifteenth century, then the biblical date of the exodus at 1446 and the fall of Jericho forty years later in 1406 would be confirmed.

Only subsequent research and analysis will determine how to deal with the disparity between radiocarbon dating and other dating methods for this period. In the meantime we can conclude that there is no reason to absolutely reject the biblical dating of the fall of Jericho to 1406 BC and that Jericho provides no evidence for the late-date theory of the exodus.

AI

No site has been definitively identified as Ai. Many archaeologists and biblical scholars follow Albright's 1924 identification of et-Tell as Ai, since the Arabic name *et-Tell* is roughly equivalent in meaning

---

[120] E.g., Hornung, Krauss and Warburton's chronology dates Thutmose III to 1479–1425 and Akhenaten to 1353–1336. (*Ancient Egyptian Chronology*, 492.)

[121] For instance, see the discussion in Kenneth Kitchen, "The Historical Chronology of Ancient Egypt," *Acta Archaeologica* 67 (1996):1–13.

to Hebrew *Ai*, "ruin."[122] Excavations at et-Tell reveal no occupation around 1400 BC. Nor does et-Tell support the late-date theory, since there is no occupation in the thirteenth century either. As a consequence, many critical scholars have concluded that the account of the conquest of Ai in Joshua 7–8 is unhistorical. If et-Tell is Ai, then it offers no support for any date for Joshua's military activities or for the exodus.

While Albright's identification of et-Tell as Ai has influenced many scholars, it should be noted that nothing found in the various excavations at et-Tell has definitively proven it to be Ai, and some archaeologists have argued that it is not Ai.[123] Livingston identified Khirbet Nisya as Ai.[124] More recently, Wood has argued that Khirbet el-Maqatir is Ai, and that his excavations there support Joshua's conquest of the city around 1406 BC.[125] Both Livingston and Wood make a good case that Albright's identification of Ai (as well as his identifications for Bethel and Beth-Aven) was incorrect.

Given the doubt about the location of Ai, the worst we can conclude is that we have no archaeological evidence, since we cannot definitively identify any site as Ai. If Wood is correct in his identification of Ai, then the evidence favors a mid-fifteenth century exodus from Egypt and disproves the late-date theory.

HAZOR

The lower Canaanite city of Hazor has three primary strata, each ending in a destruction layer.[126] The second layer dates to about 1400

---

[122] See the discussion in Wood, "The Search for Joshua's Ai," 209.

[123] Livingston, "Location of Biblical Bethel and Ai Reconsidered"; Wood, "The Search for Joshua's Ai," 210–212. Both Livingston and Wood challenge Albright's identification of Beitin as Bethel. If Beitin is not Bethel, then the argument that et-Tell is Ai is severely weakened.

[124] Livingston, "Further Considerations," 159.

[125] Wood, "The Search for Joshua's Ai," 228–240.

[126] For the stratigraphy of the lower city see Yigael Yadin and Shimon

BC, the time of Joshua's campaign if the exodus took place in 1446 BC. The third destruction layer dates to about 1230 BC, and there is no subsequent urban occupation at Hazor until Solomon's time in the tenth century (1 Kgs 9:15).[127]

One might be tempted to assign the 1230 BC destruction to Joshua, thereby supporting the late-date theory for the exodus. However, Judg 4:24 implies that in the period following Barak's victory at the Wadi

---

Angress, eds. *Hazor II. The James A. de Rothschild Expedition at Hazor. An Account of the Second Season of Excavation.* Jerusalem: Magnes Press, 1960: 165.

[127] Doron Ben-Ami, "The Iron Age I at Tel Hazor in Light of the Renewed Excavations." Ben-Tor and Zuckerman are more cautious, stating only that "To date, no archaeological find or text enables us to determine the date of Hazor's destruction with any accuracy. All indications seem to point toward a date in the 13th century B.C.E., most probably sometime in the middle of that century, as also suggested by Finkelstein." (Ben-Tor and Zuckerman, "Hazor at the End of the Late Bronze Age," 2; See Finlelstein, "Hazor at the End of the Late Bronze Age," 345.) It is also significant the the official website devoted to the Hazor excavations states, "The first settlement of Hazor, in the third millennium BCE (Early Bronze Age), was confined to the upper city. The lower city was founded in approximately the 18th century BCE (Middle Bronze Age) and continued to be settled until the 13th century (the end of the Late Bronze Age) when both the upper and lower city were violently destroyed." (http://unixware.mscc.huji.ac.il/~hatsor/hazor.html; accessed June 28, 2010.) Petrovich, who worked with Ben Tor at Hazor, also dates this destruction to the late thirteenth century (Petrovich, "The dating of Hazor's Destruction," 490–492, 499). While there may be some indeterminacy concerning the date of Hazor's fall, it is significant that there is a consensus that it happened in the mid-to-late thirteenth century BC. The Late Bronze Age in Palestine extended to about 1200 BC. There is no evidence that Hazor was occupied after the end of the Late Bronze Age (i.e., in the twelfth or eleventh centuries) until Solomon rebuilt it in the tenth century except for a small Israelite settlement begun in early Iron IA Age (c. 1200–1150; Petrovich, "The dating of Hazor's Destruction," 510).

Kishon over the forces of King Jabin of Hazor, the Israelites conquered Hazor.[128] Therefore, the 1230 BC destruction layer cannot be assigned to Joshua, because this would leave no later conquest as depicted in Judges nor any city for Jabin to have ruled, since the city would not be occupied again until Solomon's reign.[129]

SUMMARY OF THE ARCHAEOLOGICAL EVIDENCE

Therefore, none of the archaeological evidence from Jericho, Ai or Hazor offers support for the late-date theory of the exodus. The evidence for a date of 1446 BC for the exodus is supported by

---

[128] Wood, "The Rise and Fall of the 13th-Century Exodus-Conquest Theory," 477. Kitchen, who supports the late date for the Exodus, attempts defend the late date of the exodus by positing that Jabin's description as "King of Hazor" (Judg 4:17) simply reflects his retention of a traditional title, though he ruled from elsewhere in Upper Galilee. Kitchen offers a few Near Eastern parallels in support of this hypothesis. (Kitchen, *On the Reliability of the Old Testament*, 213. Kitchen's theory, however, is invalidated by the fact the Judges not only gives Jabin the title "King of Hazor" but also specifically calls him "Jabin, King of Canaan, *who ruled in Hazor*" (Judg 4:2). The expression "ruled in" (the verbal root מלך + the preposition בְּ + a place name) is used extensively in the OT. When the place name is a city, it *always* signifies the actual capital city from which a king ruled (Gen 36:32; Josh 13:10, 12, 21; Judg 4:2; 2 Sam 5:5; 15:10; 1 Kgs 2:11; 11:24, 42; 14:21; 15:2, 10, 33; 16:8, 15, 23, 29; 22:42, 52; 2 Kgs 3:1; 8:17, 26; 10:36; 12:2; 13:1, 10; 14:2, 23; 15:2, 8, 13, 17, 23, 27, 33; 16:2; 17:1; 18:2; 21:1, 19; 22:1; 23:31, 33, 36; 24:8, 18; 1 Chr 3:4; 29:27; 2 Chr 9:30; 12:13; 13:2; 20:31; 21:5, 20; 22:2; 24:1; 25:1; 26:3; 27:1, 8; 28:1; 29:1; 33:1, 21; 34:1; 36:2, 5, 9, 11; Isa 24:23; Jer 52:1). See Wood, "The Rise and Fall of the 13th-Century Exodus Conquest Theory," 487–88, who notes that there is no evidence for occupation at or around Hazor or another suitable site for Jabin's capital in Upper Galilee from about 1230–1100 BC.

[129] Waltke, "Palestinian Artifactual Evidence Supporting the Early Date of the Exodus," 43–46; Wood, "The Biblical Date for the Exodus Is 1446 B.C.," 255–256.

archaeological finds at Hazor, and perhaps by evidence from Jericho and el-Maqatir, if it is to be identified as Ai.

CONCLUSION

We have two well-established anchor points for Old Testament chronology: Solomon reigned 971t–932t, and the exodus from Egypt took place in Nisan 1446 BC. From these two anchor points we can reconstruct a chronology of OT events from Abraham to the end of the post-exilic period.

4

ISRAEL'S PATRIARCHS

The chronology of Israel's patriarchs is relatively easy to establish once the date of the exodus is known.[130] Jacob and his family entered Egypt 430 years to the day before the exodus (Exod 12:40–41). Therefore, Jacob entered Egypt on 14 Nisan 1876 BC (1446 + 430). Jacob was 130 years old when he entered Egypt (Gen 47:9), so he was born in 2006 BC (1876 + 130).[131] Isaac was 60 when Jacob was born (Gen 25:26), so Isaac was born in 2066 BC. Abraham was 100 years old when Isaac was born (Gen 21:5), so Abraham was born in 2166 BC. Thus, the basic dates for this period are:

Table 10
Basic Dates in the Patriarchal Period

2166	Abraham born	Gen 21:5
2066	Isaac born	Gen 25:26
2006	Jacob born	Gen 47:9
1876	Jacob enters Egypt	Exod 12:40–41

---

[130] For earlier discussions of the chronology of this period see Merrill, "Fixed Dates in Patriarchal Chronology," and Finegan, *Handbook of Biblical Chronology*, 197–224.

[131] If Jacob was almost 131 years old, he could have been born in 2007. For the sake of simplicity, however, all birth and death dates will be listed by as single year instead of using some other notation such as 2007/2006.

From these dates the rest of the dated events in Genesis for the lives of Israel's patriarchs can be determined.

EXODUS 12:40–41

While the basic dates for Abraham, Isaac and Jacob seem assured, some scholars have challenged whether the 430 years for Israel's time in Egypt is correct.[132] The basis for this challenge is the LXX, where Exod 12:40 reads

ἡ δὲ κατοίκησις τῶν υἱῶν Ισραηλ ἦν κατῴκησαν ἐν γῇ Αἰγύπτῳ καὶ ἐν γῇ Χανααν ἔτη τετρακόσια τριάκοντα

The sojourning of the sons of Israel which they sojourned in Egypt *and in the land of Canaan* was 430 years.

LXX Exod 12:40 includes the time that Israel was in Canaan in the 430 years. Thus, it is claimed that Israel was in Egypt 215 years. This can be calculated by adding together Jacob's 130 years before entering Egypt (Gen 47:9), Isaac's 60 years before Jacob was born (Gen 25:26) and Abraham's 25 years in Canaan before Isaac was born (Gen 12:4; 21:5). This leaves 215 years for Israel's time in Egypt.

Advocates of this view support their assertion by noting that Abraham was told that his descendants would return from Egypt "in the fourth generation" (Gen 15:16). It is claimed that 215 years is a more reasonable time for four generations than is 430 years.

Moreover, advocates of a 215 year sojourn in Egypt claim that Paul in Gal 3:17 has the time from Abraham to the giving of the Law on Sinai in mind when he says the Law "happened 430 years afterward" (ὁ μετὰ τετρακόσια καὶ τριάκοντα ἔτη γεγονὼς νόμος). This would accommodate a 215 year sojourn in Egypt but not 430 years.

There are multiple problems with this theory, however. First of all, it should be noted that elsewhere in Scripture, Israel's time in Egypt is reckoned to be about 400 years in round numbers. Thus, God told

---

[132] See the discussion in Finegan, *Handbook of Biblical Chronology*, 203–207 and Hoehner, "The Duration of the Egyptian Bondage."

Abraham that for 400 years his descendants would be strangers in a land that was not theirs (Gen 15:13). This passage is quoted by Stephen in Acts 7:6.

Second, Israel grew from some seventy persons when Jacob entered Egypt (Exod 1:5) to over 600,000 men twenty years old or older at the Exodus (Num 1:46). This would hardly be possible in four generations over 215 years, but is entirely possible in 430 years.

Third, Paul's reference to 430 years in Gal 3:17 is not from the time Abraham entered Canaan to the time of the Exodus, but is clearly 430 years from the time that the covenant "previously had been ratified" (προκεκυρωμένην). Paul most likely had in mind the covenant to Abraham that contained the promise about Abraham's descendants' sojourn in Egypt as given by God in Gen 15. Note that Gen 15 previously mentioned a foreign sojourn as slaves for 400 years (Gen 15:13). Therefore, Paul probably considered Jacob's entry into Egypt as the ratification of the covenant. This would also make sense with Paul's statement in Acts 13:17–20 that Israel's time in Egypt, in the wilderness, and the time when Joshua apportioned the land among Israel's tribes was "about 450 years" (ὡς ἔτεσιν τετρακοσίοις καὶ πεντήκοντα).[133] The actual time was 477 years, which is reasonably approximated as "about 450 years."[134] Thus, Paul in

---

[133] At Acts 13:20 some manuscripts, especially those of the Byzantine Koine tradition, transpose the phrases "and after this" (καὶ μετὰ ταῦτα) and "430 years" with the result that the 430 years terminate with Samuel instead of the beginning of the period of the judges. This reading is reflected in the King James Version at Acts 13:20. However, this is clearly a secondary reading. The better reading, which places the 430 years before the judges, is also the reading of the Vulgate. It is impossible to place all of the events from Jacob's entry into Egypt to the time of Samuel into a 430 year period unless one almost completely discounts the chronological information in Judges as mistaken or fictional.

[134] 430 years in Egypt, 40 years in the wilderness and 7 years before the land was distributed. If Paul was using the 400 years of Gen 15:13, then the

Acts 13:20 and Gal 3:17 considered Israel's time in Egypt to be 430 years.

Fourth, the "fourth generation" of Gen 15:16 should be understood in context. The word דר, "generation," can reference a person's entire lifetime.[135] Since Abraham, Isaac and Jacob all lived well over 100 years, "in the fourth generation" may well be intended to indicate somewhat less than four complete lifetimes in terms understandable to Abraham.

Finally, Larsson notes that a comparison of Pentateuchal chronologies between MT and LXX reveals that LXX translators tended to alter the Hebrew text's chronology where the text is difficult to understand or was viewed as self-contradictory.[136] This appears to be the case at Exod 12:40, since LXX adds "and in the land of Canaan" *after* "in Egypt" when chronologically the Patriarchs' sojourn in Canaan came *before* Jacob's entry into Egypt. Moreover, both MT and LXX have "400 years" at Gen 15:13, making LXX Exod 12:40 likely a LXX alteration that thereby unwittingly created a conflict between LXX Exod 12:40 and LXX Gen 15:13.

Therefore, there is little to support the theory that Israel was in Egypt 215 years. Instead, the MT's 430 years should be accepted as accurate.

---

period is 400 + 40 + 7 = 447, even more reasonably an approximation of 450 years. The seven year period can be reckoned by noting that in Josh 14:6–12 Caleb requested his land 45 years after having been sent by Moses to spy out the land in 1444 BC, two years after the exodus from Egypt. Thus, there were 47 years from the exodus to the distribution of the land among the tribes of Israel.

[135] *TWOT* entry 418c.1.

[136] Larsson, "The Chronology of the Pentateuch." However, Larsson considers the time in Egypt to be "about 300 years," an estimate based on no explicit statement in the Pentateuch (Larsson, "The Chronology of the Pentateuch," 406).

ABRAHAM

Abraham lived to be 175 years old (Gen 25:7). Thus, the events of Abraham's life took place from 2166 to 1991 BC. This means that Abraham lived to see the birth of his grandsons Jacob and Esau (2006 BC) and died when they were fifteen years old.

Sarah was ten years younger than Abraham. This can be established from comparing Gen 17:17 with Gen 17:1, where we are told that God appeared to Abraham when he was 99. At that time God revealed to Abraham that Sarah would bear Isaac at the same time the next year (Gen 17:21). Since Sarah would be 90 when she bore Isaac (Gen 17:17), she would have been 89 when God's conversation with Abraham took place. Thus, Sarah was ten years younger than Abraham, and she was born in 2156 BC. Since Sarah lived 127 years, she died in 2029 BC. (Gen 23:1)

The first datable event in Abraham's life is his obedience to God's call to leave Haran, which happened in 2091 BC when he was 75 years old (Gen 12:4). After ten years in the land of Canaan (2081 BC) Abram married Hagar (Gen 16:3). Ishmael was born the next year (2080 BC) when Abram was 86 (Gen 16:16). Ishmael lived 137 years, dying in 1943 BC (Gen 25:17).

In 2067 BC when Abram was 99, God changed his name to Abraham and promised that Isaac would be born the next year (Gen 17:1, 21, 24). Ishmael was thirteen at the time, confirming that he was born in 2080 BC (Gen 17:25).

Between the time that Abram was renamed Abraham and the birth of Isaac, Sodom and Gomorrah were destroyed (Gen 18:16–19:29). Therefore, Sodom and Gomorrah were destroyed in 2067 or 2066 BC.

Therefore, the chronology of the events of Abraham's life is:

Table 11
Chronology of Abraham's Life

2166	Abram born	Gen 11:26; 21:5
2156	Sarai born	Gen 17:1, 17
2091	Abram leaves Haran	Gen 12:4
2081	Abram marries Hagar	Gen 16:3
2080	Ishmael born	Gen 16:16
2067	Renamed Abraham	Gen 17:1, 21, 24
2066	Isaac born	Gen 25:26
2029	Sarah dies	Gen 23:1
1991	Abraham dies	Gen 25:7

ISAAC

Genesis contains less narrative about Isaac than any other of Israel's patriarchs. Consequently, there are fewer datable events for Isaac's life than for the other patriarchs.

Isaac, who was born in 2066 BC, lived 180 years (Gen 35:28), dying in 1886 BC. As it turns out, this was the same year that Joseph entered the service of Pharaoh in Egypt (Gen 41:46, see the discussion on page 74 below).

When Isaac was 40 years old, Abraham arranged his marriage to Rebekah (2026 BC; Gen 25:20). This was three years after the death of Sarah, when Abraham was 140 years old. Thus, after three years of mourning over the death of his mother, Isaac found comfort in his marriage to Rebekah (Gen 24:67).

Rebekah and Isaac would wait twenty years before the birth of their twin sons Jacob and Esau in 2006 BC. At that time Isaac was 60 years old (Gen 25:26).

We do not know how long Rebekah lived. She certainly was alive to see Esau's marriages to the Hittite women Judith and Basemath in 1966 BC (Gen 26:34) and for Jacob's flight to Paddan Aram to escape Esau in 1930 BC (see the discussion beginning on page 74). Thus, Rebekah must have lived at least 96 years after her marriage to Isaac. However, she apparently had died by the time Jacob saw Isaac again at Mamre about 1900 BC (Gen 35:27). By that time Jacob had been back in Canaan about 10 years and had not seen his father during that time. This probably implies that Rachel had died before 1910 BC, since Jacob would have been motivated to see his mother who prized him as her favorite son. However, Jacob's delay of a decade before seeing his father may have been due to his having left his father's household after having tricked Isaac into granting him the blessing. He may have been reluctant to see his father without his mother present to advocate for him.

Therefore, the chronology of the events of Isaac's life are:

Table 12
Chronology of Isaac's Life

2066	Isaac born	Gen 25:26
2029	Sarah dies	Gen 23:1
2026	Isaac marries Rebekah	Gen 25:20
2006	Jacob and Esau born	Gen 25:26
1966	Esau marries	Gen 26:34
1943	Ishmael dies	Gen 25:17
1930	Jacob flees to Paddan Aram	Gen 29:15–30
1886	Isaac dies	Gen 35:28

JACOB

Jacob was born in 2006 BC and lived 147 years, dying in Egypt in 1859 BC (Gen 47:28). He migrated to Egypt in 1876 BC, 430 years before the Exodus (Exod 12:40–41). These are the basic dates for Jacob's life.

JACOB IN LABAN'S SERVICE IN PADDAN ARAM

The chronology of the remaining events during Jacob's life must be calculated by working backward from his migration to Egypt. When Jacob entered Egypt in Nisan of 1876 BC there were five years of famine remaining (Gen 41:1–36; 45:11). Therefore, the famine would not end until the harvest that began in Nisan 1871 BC. It would have begun with the failed harvest of Nisan 1878 BC. The famine was preceded by seven plentiful harvests from Nisan 1885 BC to Nisan 1879 BC. Since Joseph entered Pharaoh's service in time to begin storing grain from the seven successive plentiful harvests (Gen 41:47), he must have interpreted Pharaoh's dream sometime in 1886 BC (Gen 41:1–36). At that time Joseph was 30 years old (Gen 41:46). Joseph, therefore, was born in 1916 BC.

Joseph's birth apparently came near the end of the seven years of service Jacob owed Laban as a bride price for Rachel (Gen 29:27, 30), since immediately after Joseph's birth, Jacob proposed leaving Laban in Paddan Aram and returning to Canaan (Gen 30:25). Previous to his seven years of service in return for Rachel he had served seven years which were counted as the bride price for Leah (Gen 29:15–26). Thus, Jacob arrived in Paddan Aram fourteen years before Joseph's birth. This would have been in 1930 BC when he was already 76 years old. Seven years later in 1923 BC he married Leah and one week later, Rachel (Gen 29:27–28).

Although Jacob had proposed to leave Paddan Aram in 1916 BC after Joseph's birth, Laban convinced him to stay longer (Gen 30:25–36). Jacob continued in Laban's employ six more years for a total of twenty years (Gen 31:38, 41). So in 1910 BC Jacob returned to Canaan and settled at Shechem (Gen 33:18).

JACOB IN CANAAN

Jacob lived in four places after he returned to Canaan and before Joseph was sold into slavery: Shechem (Gen 33:18), Bethel (Gen 35:1–16), near the tower of Eder (Gen 35:21), and Mamre (i.e., Kiriath Arba/Hebron; Gen 35:27).

Little is recorded about Jacob's time in Shechem. The one event that is extensively recorded is the rape of Dinah and subsequent murder of the men of Shechem by Simeon and Levi (Gen 34:1–31). At this time Dinah must have reached puberty, but may have been only about 13 years old. Dinah was born to Leah sometime after Zebulun, probably after the birth of Joseph (Gen 30:21). Yet, she must have reached a minimum marriageable age before Jacob left Shechem (Gen 34:4). Thus, Dinah must have been born about 1915 BC, making her 13 in 1902 BC when she was raped by Shechem.

Apparently, Jacob left Shechem for Bethel on God's instruction immediately after this incident (Gen 35:1). This would place the death of Rebekah's nurse Deborah in 1902 BC.

Jacob must not have stayed long in Bethel, because by 1899 BC when Joseph was sold into slavery at the age of 17 (Gen 37:2), he was living in Mamre (Gen 35:27; 37:14). Thus, Rachel died and Benjamin was born near Bethlehem about 1901 BC (Gen 35:16–20). About that same time Reuben slept with Bilhah when Jacob was living near the tower of Eder (Gen 35:21–22). About 1900 BC Jacob must have settled in Mamre (Gen 35:27).

The chronology of the events of Jacob's life is:

Table 13
Chronology of Jacob's Life

2006	Jacob born	Gen 25:26
1966	Esau marries	Gen 26:34
1930	Jacob flees to Paddan Aram	Gen 29:15–30
1923	Marriage to Leah and Rachel	Gen 29:15–30
1916	Joseph born	Gen 41:46
c. 1915	Dinah born	Gen 30:21
1910	Jacob returns to Canaan	Gen 31:38, 41
c. 1902	Jacob goes to Bethel	Gen 35:1
c. 1901	Rachel dies/Benjamin born	Gen 35:16–20
c. 1900	Jacob settles in Mamre	Gen 35:27
1899	Joseph sold into slavery	Gen 37:2
1886	Joseph freed from prison	Gen 41:46
1885–1879	Years of plentiful harvest	Gen 41:47
1878–1871	Years of famine	Gen 45:11
1876	Jacob's family enters Egypt	Exod 12:40–41
1859	Jacob dies	Gen 47:28

JACOB'S CHILDREN

All of Jacob's children except Benjamin were born in Paddan Aram. His first eleven sons were born during the seven year period between his marriages to Leah and Rachel in 1923 BC and the birth of Joseph in 1916 BC. From this we are able to estimate the births of Jacob's first ten sons.

Leah bore six sons during this seven-year period.[137] Reuben, therefore, had to have been born in 1922 BC (Gen 29:32). Simeon followed in 1921 BC (Gen 29:33). The next year Levi was born (Gen 29:34), and Judah a year later in 1919 BC (Gen 29:35).

Jacob also had children by the two concubines Bilhah and Zilpah given him by Rachel and Leah. Most likely Bilhah was given to Jacob while Leah was pregnant with Judah so that her first son Dan was born about 1919 BC (Gen 30:1–6). Sometime later Bilhah bore Naphtali, who birth was probably in 1918 or 1917 BC (Gen 30:7–8).

Some months after bearing Judah, Leah noticed that she had not become pregnant again. This probably was during the first half of 1918 BC. In her competition with Rachel, she gave Zilpah to Jacob. Zilpah bore Gad. Gad's birth is probably to be dated early in the next year (Gen 30:9–11). Zilpah bore Jacob a second son sometime later, so Asher was probably born in early 1916 BC (Gen 30:12–13). He must have been born before Joseph, who was the youngest of the eleven sons born in Paddan Aram.

Leah, however, bore two more sons before Joseph's birth in 1916 BC. Therefore, the births of Issachar and Zebulun must have occurred early in 1917 BC and early in 1916 BC (Gen 30:14–20). Most likely, as we have seen, Dinah was born to her in 1915 BC (Gen 30:21).

The dates of the births of Jacob's children, therefore, can be summarized as:

---

[137] In order to address this tight schedule for Leah's bearing children, plus other issues involved with Jacob's sojourn in Paddan Aram, a few interpreters have suggested that the 20 years of Gen 31:38 are distinct from the 20 years of Gen 31:41. This would lead to the conclusion that Jacob spent a total of 40 years with Laban. Is is difficult—if not impossible—to interpret Gen 31:38 and 31:41 in this manner.

Table 14
Births of Jacob's Children

Year	Leah	Rachel	Bilhah	Zilpah
1922	Reuben			
1921	Simeon			
1920	Levi			
1919	Judah		Dan	
1918			Naphtali	
1917	Issachar			Gad
1916	Zebulun	Joseph		Asher
1915	Dinah			
1901		Benjamin		

JUDAH'S FAMILY

About the time Joseph was sold into slavery Judah married a Canaanite woman (Gen 38:1–2). Since Judah was about three years older than Joseph, he would have been about 20. By this Canaanite woman he had three sons: Er (Gen 38:3), Onan (Gen 38:4), and Shelah (Gen 38:5). If we estimate the date of Judah's marriage to about 1900 BC, then the marriage of Er to Tamar may have taken place about twenty years later in 1879 BC (Gen 38:6) when Er was 19 or 20 years old. Er died shortly after marrying Tamar (Gen 38:6–7), and Judah gave her Onan in a levirate marriage (Gen 38:8–10). Thus, Onan must have been born within a year or two of Er and was, perhaps, 18 or 19 years old at the time. Shelah, however, was too young to enter into a levirate marriage, but would have been old enough to fulfill this obligation in a few years (Gen 38:11). So Shelah may have been about 16 years old at the time.

After the deaths of Er and Onan, Judah's wife died (Gen 38:12). This led to his illicit assignation with Tamar and the births of Perez and Zerah (Gen 38:27–30). Since these boys were born in Canaan, they must have been born before Jacob took his family to Egypt sometime in 1876 BC. Therefore, Judah's wife must have died about 1878 BC and Perez and Zerah were born in 1877 or early 1876 BC.

The chronology for Judah's family is:

Table 15
Chronology of Judah's Family

c. 1900	Judah marries	Gen 38:1–2
c. 1899	Er born	Gen 38:3
c. 1897	Onan born	Gen 38:4
c. 1895	Shelah born	Gen 38:5
c. 1879	Er and Onan marry Tamar	Gen 38:6–10
c. 1878	Judah's wife dies	Gen 38:12
c. 1877	Perez and Zerah born	Gen 38:27–30

JOSEPH

We have already established most of the dates for Joseph's life (see the discussion on page 74 above). There are only a few dates left to establish.

Joseph was sold into slavery when he was 17 years old (1899 BC; Gen 37:2). He interpreted Pharaoh's dream in 1886 BC.[138] Since Joseph remained in prison for two entire years after interpreting the dreams of the cupbearer and baker (Gen 41:1), those dreams took place in 1888 BC. Joseph had been in prison for some time before this. He had been there long enough to have been found trustworthy to be placed in charge of the prison (Gen 39:20–23). Therefore, he probably was imprisoned a year or two before the cupbearer and baker had their dreams. That would imply that he was a slave in

---

[138] The Pharaoh that Joseph served was probably Sesotris I (1920–1875 BC).

Potiphar's household almost a decade from 1899 BC to about 1890 or 1889 BC.

Joseph lived 110 years (Gen 50:22). His death came in 1806 BC. The chronology of the events of Joseph's life are:

Table 16
Chronology of Joseph's Life

1916	Joseph born	Gen 41:46
1910	Jacob returns to Canaan	Gen 31:38, 41
c. 1902	Jacob goes to Bethel	Gen 35:1
c. 1901	Rachel dies/ Benjamin born	Gen 35:16–20
c. 1900	Jacob settles in Mamre	Gen 35:27
1899	Joseph sold into slavery	Gen 37:2
1899–c. 1889	Joseph serves Potiphar	Gen 37:36
c. 1889–1886	Joseph in prison	Gen 39:20
1888	Baker and cupbearer's dreams	Gen 41:1
1886	Joseph freed from prison	Gen 41:46
1885–1879	Years of plentiful harvest	Gen 41:47
1878–1871	Years of famine	Gen 45:11
1876	Jacob's family enters Egypt	Exod 12:40–41
1859	Jacob dies	Gen 47:28
1806	Joseph dies	Gen 50:22

5

MOSES

After 430 years of life in Egypt, God's chosen leader for Israel's deliverance would be 80-year-old Moses, the greatest OT prophet. Most of the events of Israel's history that are documented in the Pentateuch occurred during Moses' life but apply only to the last 40 years of his 120 year lifespan (Exodus 7:7; Deut 34:7). Nevertheless, the historical circumstances surrounding Moses' first 80 years are important for understanding the background to the Exodus.

EGYPTIAN HISTORY FROM JACOB TO MOSES

Joseph was sold into slavery during Egypt's twelfth dynasty at the end of the Middle Kingdom period. However, in the century after Joseph's death the twelfth dynasty would end and Egypt would descend into political uncertainty during the Second Intermediate Period (mid-eighteenth to mid-sixteenth centuries BC). This period was initiated by the rise of the Hyksos, an Asiatic people who invaded the Nile Delta.

During this period Egypt would see competing dynasties vie for control of the land. The Hyksos would eventually establish the fifteenth and sixteenth dynasties in Lower Egypt, though much of Upper Egypt would continue to be under control of native Egyptians. Some of the Hyksos rulers bore Semitic names, and it is often assumed that the Hyksos were of Canaanite origin.

In the mid-sixteenth century the last king of the seventeenth dynasty, Kamose (d. 1540), is traditionally credited with driving out the last of the Hyksos. His brother, Ahmose (1539–1515), founded the eighteenth dynasty and ushered in a new period of political stability in Egypt known as the New Kingdom period.

Since Moses was born 80 years before the Exodus in 1526 BC (Exod 7:7; cf. Deut 34:7) and Aaron was born three years earlier in 1529 BC (Exod 7:7; Num 33:39), they would have been born in the reign of Ahmose (1539–1515). Thus, Ahmose, the founder of the eighteenth dynasty is probably the "new king over Egypt who did not know Joseph" (Exod 1:8).

The memory of the Hyksos rulers combined with Israel sharing a common Semitic background with the Hyksos explains the Egyptian's fear that if war came to Egypt Israel would "join our enemies, fight against us, and escape from the land." (Exod 1:10). Thus, Ahmose most likely initiated the oppression of the Israelites that continued under Amenhotep I, and that was the setting for Moses' birth and childhood (Exod 1:8–2:10).

The OT does not tell us Moses' age at the next event of his life as related in Exodus—his murder of an Egyptian and flight to Midian (Exod 2:11–22). However, Acts 7:23 says that Moses was nearly forty years old at this time (Ὡς δὲ ἐπληροῦτο αὐτῷ τεσσερακονταετὴς χρόνος). This would place these events during the reign of Thutmose I (1493–1483 BC) in 1486 BC, about one year before the birth of Caleb.[139]

The chronology of events relating to Moses' early life is:

Table 17
Chronology of Moses' Early Life

1529	Aaron born	Exod 7:7; Num 33:39
1526	Moses born	Exod 7:7; Deut 34:7
c. 1486	Moses flees to Midian	Acts 7:23
1485	Caleb born	Josh 14:7

---

[139] Caleb was 85 years old in 1400 BC when Joshua's campaigns in Canaan ended (Josh 14:7).

THE EXODUS AND MOUNT SINAI

When Moses was nearly eighty years old, God spoke to him from the burning bush (Acts 7:30). This would have happened in late 1447 BC. In short order Moses returned to Egypt, met with Israel's elders, and confronted Pharaoh. The Pharaoh at that time was Thutmose III (1479–1425) according to the Low Chronology. If the High Chronology is accepted, then Amenhotep II would have been the Pharaoh (1454–1428).[140]

The ten plagues on Egypt ended with the death of the firstborn during the night of 14 Nisan 1446 BC. This would place the first plague some two or three months earlier in Shebat or early Adar (January or February) 1446 BC. The timing of the plagues is significant. The Nile turning to blood in the first plague would have taken place before the rising of the Nile in spring. The destruction of the crops that came with the seventh and eighth plagues (hail and locusts; Exod 9:13–10:20) would have occurred just before the grain harvests that would begin in Nisan and would have been seen as especially ill-timed by the Egyptians.

The announcement of the tenth plague (Exod 11:1–10) came in early Nisan, since it allowed time for the Israelites to choose their Passover lambs on 10 Nisan (Exod 12:3). The death of the firstborn came on the night of 14 Nisan during the first Passover (Exod 12:29–32), with the departure from Egypt occurring the next morning as the Egyptians were burying their dead (Num 33:3–4).

---

[140] Shea, "The Date of the Exodus," 245–248, proposes that there were two Pharaohs identified as Amenhotep II. The first drowned in the *Yam Suph* at the Exodus and was replaced by the second. Shea contends that Ps 136:15 states that the Exodus Pharaoh drowned in the *Yam Suph* ("The Date of the Exodus," 244). However, Ps 136:15 does not need to be read that way. See also Petrovich, "Amenhotep II and the Historicity of the Exodus-Pharaoh." Petrovich identifies Hatshepsut as Moses' adoptive mother ("Amenhotep II and the Historicity of the Exodus-Pharaoh," 106–110.)

The next month would see Israel journey from Ramesses to Succoth to Etham to Pi-hahiroth. Then they passed through the Red Sea and journeyed three days in the wilderness of Shur[141] to Marah. Then they journeyed to Elim, to a location to near the Red Sea, and finally to the Wilderness of Sin on 15 Ziv (Exod 13:17–16:1; Num 33:5–11). In the Wilderness of Sin God first graciously provided Israel with manna (Exod 16:1–36).

The following six or more weeks were eventful for Israel. They moved from Dophkah to Alush to Rephidim and finally came to the wilderness of Sinai on the first of the month of Sivan (Exod 17:1–16; 18:5; 19:1–2; Num 33:12–15).[142] At Rephidim God first provided water from the rock, and Israel defeated the Amalekites (Exod 17:1–15).

Israel would spend almost an entire year in the Wilderness of Sinai at the base of Mount Sinai, leaving on 20 Ziv the next year (Num 10:11). Thus, all of the events of Exod 18:1–Num 10:10 took place at Mount Sinai. However, only a few of the events are dated. The tabernacle's construction was completed by 1 Nisan 1445 BC when it was first set up (Exod 40:2, 17). 1–12 Nisan 1445 were the days when the tribes of Israel brought their offerings for the dedication of the altar (Num 7:1, 11–88). The second Passover took place at Sinai on 14 Nisan 1445 (Num 9:1). The first census of Israel was conducted on 1 Ziv 1445 (Num 1:1, 18).

---

[141] The wilderness of Shur is apparently called the wilderness of Etham at Num 33:8.

[142] It was the third month of the exodus trek (Exod 19:1: בַּחֹדֶשׁ הַשְּׁלִישִׁי לְצֵאת בְּנֵי־יִשְׂרָאֵל מֵאֶרֶץ מִצְרָיִם; cf. NASB, NET Bible; also LXX: τοῦ δὲ μηνὸς τοῦ τρίτου τῆς ἐξόδου τῶν υἱῶν Ισραηλ ἐκ γῆς Αἰγύπτου). This could be read as "on the third new moon" making the date 1 Tammuz (cf. ESV, NRSV). However, elsewhere in the OT בַּחֹדֶשׁ הַשְּׁלִישִׁי denotes the third month, Sivan (2 Chr 15:10; Esth 8:9), and nowhere else in the OT are new moons *per se* numbered.

Other events can be roughly dated during this period. God's speaking to Israel from Mount Sinai took place no earlier than 4 Sivan 1446 BC (Exod 19:11). The making of the golden calf must have taken place no earlier than mid-Ab 1446 (cf. Exod 24:18). The consecration of Aaron and his sons as priests must have happened in early Nisan 1445, and the death of Aaron's sons Nadab and Abihu appears to have occurred before 1 Ziv of the same year.

The datable events relating to the exodus and Mt. Sinai are:

Table 18
Chronology of Events Surrounding the Exodus

Late 1447	Moses at the burning bush	Acts 7:30
Shebat-Nisan 1446	Ten plagues	Exod 7:12–12:32
14 Nisan 1446	Israel leaves Egypt	Num 33:3–4
15 Ziv 1446	Arrival at the Wilderness of Sin	Exod 16:1
1 Sivan 1446	Arrival at Sinai	Exod 19:1
3 Sivan 1446	God speaks to Israel from Sinai	Exod 19:16ff.
Mid-Ab 1446 (?)	Israel worships the golden calf	Exod 24:18; Exod 34
1 Nisan 1445	Tabernacle erected	Exod 40:2, 17
1–12 Nisan 1445	Offerings for the dedication of the altar	Num 7:11–88
14 Nisan 1445	Second Passover	Num 9:1
1 Ziv 1445	Census taken	Num 1:1, 18

THE LAST YEAR OF MOSES' LIFE

The book of Numbers relates few incidents from the wilderness wandering between the first, aborted attempt to conquer Canaan (1445 BC; Num 13:1–14:45) and the last year of Moses' life. It appears that Korah's rebellion (Num 16:1–35) took place during this period between the early and late events of the wilderness wanderings.

Beginning with Num 20 the Pentateuch narrates events from the last year of Moses' life. In Nisan 1407 BC Israel arrived in the Wilderness of Zin at Kadesh, where Miriam died (Num 20:1). From there Israel would begin to move toward Edom, through which they were refused passage, and then to Moab. Along the way on 1 Av 1407 Aaron died (Num 33:38).

While Israel was on the plains of Moab, Balaam would prophecy God's blessing (Num 23–24). Also in Moab Israel would commit idolatry by worshiping Baal at Peor (Num 25), a new census would be taken (Num 26), and Israel would defeat the Midianites (Num 31).

Finally, on 1 Shebat in early 1406 Moses would address his final words to Israel (Deut 1:3). Shortly after this Moses would die on Mount Nebo (Deut 34). Leadership of Israel would pass to Joshua, who would lead Israel across the Jordan on 10 Nisan 1406 (Josh 4:19).

Datable events from the last year of Moses' life are:

Table 19
Chronology of the Last Year of Moses' Life

Nisan 1407	Arrival at Kadesh	Num 20:1
1 Av 1407	Aaron dies	Num 33:38
1 Shebat 1406	Moses addresses Israel	Deut 1:3
Early 1406	Moses dies	Deut 34

6

THE ERA OF JOSHUA AND THE JUDGES

The period from the death of Moses to the beginning of the reign of David is one of the most difficult to reconstruct chronologically. This is partly due to the corrupted nature of the text of 1 Sam 13:1 (see discussion on page 45). However, it is also due to lack of unambiguous chronological markers within the biblical text that can be used as anchor points for much of this period. Nevertheless, it is possible to construct a reasonable chronology for the period of Joshua and Israel's judges that can date most of the major events and figures with a reliability of about ±2 years. A few events, such as the beginning and ending of the conquest led by Joshua can be dated more accurately.

THE CONQUEST UNDER JOSHUA

THE BEGINNING OF JOSHUA'S CONQUEST (JOSHUA 1–6)

Since Moses died in early 1406 BC (see the discussion on page 86), Joshua's leadership also dates to early that year. Joshua 4:19 indicates that the Israelites crossed the Jordan River on 10 Nisan that year. This information enables us to reconstruct the chronology of the first six chapters of Joshua.[143]

Joshua's first major act was to tell the commanders to pass through the Israelite camp (Josh 1:10–11). The commanders were to have the troops prepare to cross the Jordan in three days. Apparently that same day he sent two spies to observe Jericho (Josh 2:1).

---

[143] This reconstruction is based on Howard, "'Three Days' in Joshua 1–9."

However, the king of Jericho learned of the spies' presence in Jericho, causing them to hide in the hills for three days, beginning with the evening of the day they left the Israelite camp and came to Jericho (Josh 2:21). Thus, Joshua's plan to cross the Jordan on the third day was delayed, since the spies did not return to report until that day (Josh 2:22).

The fourth day Joshua moved the troops from Shittim to the east bank of the Jordan River (Josh 3:1). At the end of three days at Shittim—that is, the sixth day overall—Joshua again sent the officers through the camp with instructions about crossing the Jordan (Josh 3:2–5). The next day Israel crossed the Jordan River (Josh 3:6–17). This enables us to reconstruct the events leading up to the crossing of the Jordan on 10 Nisan 1406 BC:

Table 20
Chronology of the Crossing of the Jordan River

4 Nisan	Officers sent through the camp; Spies sent to Jericho	Josh 1:10–11; Josh 2:1
6 Nisan	Spies report to Joshua	Josh 2:22–23
7 Nisan	From Shittim to the Jordan River	Josh 3:1
9 Nisan	Officers sent through the camp	Josh 3:2
10 Nisan	Israel crosses the Jordan River	Josh 4:19

Israel camped at Gilgal where the men were circumcised, perhaps on 11 Nisan (Josh 5:2–9). The Passover was celebrated on 14 Nisan (Josh 5:10). The Feast of Unleavened Bread followed (15–21 Nisan; Josh 5:11), with the manna ceasing on 16 Nisan (Josh 5:12).

The conquest of Jericho happened at least seven days after the beginning of the Feast of Unleavened Bread. If the events of Joshua 6 took place after the end of the Feast, then Jericho fell no earlier than

28 Nisan (Josh 6:15). This would place the seven days Israel marched around Jericho no earlier than 22–28 Nisan (Josh 6:3–14).

THE CONCLUSION OF JOSHUA'S CONQUEST (JOSHUA 14)

The remaining battles and activities of Joshua recounted in Joshua 7–13 have no firm chronological indicators that allow us to date them with any certainty. However, Caleb's speech at Gilgal does contain enough information to allow us to date the end of Joshua's military campaigns.

After giving the summary of Joshua's military activities (Josh 12:7–24), the book of Joshua recounts God's instruction to Joshua to distribute the land among Israel's tribes (Josh 13:1–7). The distribution begins with a recapping of Moses' distribution of land east of the Jordan River to Reuben, Gad and half of the tribe of Manasseh (Josh 13:8–33). Joshua 14:1–5 summarizes the allotment of land west of the Jordan River.

Beginning with Joshua 14:6 a particular incident is related: The tribe of Judah met with Joshua at Gilgal, and Caleb requested that he be given his portion of the land (Josh 14:6–15). Joshua apportioned to him the city of Hebron. During his request Caleb gives two pieces of information that allow us to date this incident and, thereby, to assign a latest possible date for the end of Joshua's military activity. Caleb stated that he was 85 years old at this time and that he was sent into Canaan by Moses as a spy 45 years earlier (cf. Num 13:1–24). Since the spies were sent to Canaan in 1445 BC sometime after the twenty-third day of the third month (Num 10:11, 33; 11:20, 33; 13:1), Caleb made his request to Joshua in 1400 BC. Thus, Joshua's military campaigns lasted no longer than about six years, from spring of 1406 BC to sometime in 1400 BC.

THE CHRONOLOGY OF THE JUDGES

The chronology of the book of Judges has always presented a challenge. Many have noted that simply adding up the various years of the judges and foreign oppressions as listed in the book yields 410 years, and this does not include the time for the deaths of Joshua and the elders who served with him (Judg 2:7–8).[144] From the end of Joshua's conquest in 1400 BC to the beginning of David's reign (1009 BC) there are only 389 years. This appears to allow inadequate time for the events in Judges to have taken place, much less account for the death of Joshua and the elders, the judgeships of Eli and Samuel, and the reign of Saul.

For this reason some have posited that the judges may have simply been local authorities and their reigns may have overlapped, while others simply discount the narratives in Judges as not historically accurate.[145] While some offer timelines or chronologies of the judges as rough guides,[146] the opinion expressed by Harrison over thirty

---

[144] Raymond B. Dillard and Tremper Longman, III, *An Introduction to the Old Testament* (Grand Rapids: Zondervan, 1955), 123; Frank Ely Gaebelein, J. D. Douglas, and Dick Polcyn, *Expositor's Bible Commentary* (Grand Rapids: Zondervan, 1992), 3.376; Andrew E. Hill and John H. Walton, *A Survey of the Old Testament* (Grand Rapids: Zondervan, 1991); William Sanford Lasor, David Allen Hubbard, and Frederica William Bush, *Old Testament Survey: The Message, Form, and Background of the Old Testament*, Second ed. (Grand Rapids, MI: Eerdmans, 1996), 160; *The New Interpreter's Bible*, (Nashville: Abingdon, 1998), 2.724.

[145] Dillard and Longman, *An Introduction to the Old Testament*, 123; Gaebelein, Douglas, and Polcyn, *Expositor's Bible Commentary*, 3.376; R. K. Harrison, *Introduction to the Old Testament* (Grand Rapids: Eerdmans, 1969), 330; Hill and Walton, *A Survey of the Old Testament;* Lasor, Hubbard, and Bush, *Old Testament Survey*, 160; James D. Martin, *The Book of Judges*, Cambridge Bible Commentary (Cambridge: Cambridge University, 1975), 3; *The New Interpreter's Bible*, 2.724. A common observation is that the periods of rest for the land are in multiples of forty. From this observation it is often argued that these are round numbers or inaccurate calculations based on the assumption that one generation equals about forty years. For example, see Daniel I. Block, *Judges, Ruth*, NAC 6 (Nashville: Broadman and Holman, 1999), 63.

[146] Dillard and Longman, *An Introduction to the Old Testament;* John H.

years ago still represents the consensus of scholars who do not discount the historicity of the judges altogether.[147]

> . . . it is obvious that the historical period in question presents difficulties both of chronology and of historical detail, and these cannot be resolved completely without fuller information.

For those who believe that the book of Judges does present accurate historical information, the chronological quagmire is compounded by the book itself, which seems to treat many of the judges' reigns as consecutive rather than overlapping, as when it is said that one judge died and another arose "after him" (e.g., Tola and Jair, Judg 10:2–3 or Jephthah and Ibzan, Judg 12:7–8).

Can simply following the information in the book itself unravel the chronology of the book of Judges? Several scholars have proposed that it can and that one can establish a relative chronology of the judges.[148] Furthermore, with the help of information from the books of Kings and Samuel as well as Josephus' *Antiquities*, one can establish an absolute chronology.

SIX CYCLES OF JUDGES

The book of Judges contains a prologue that sets the stage for the judges (Judg 1:1–3:6) and an epilogue that contains additional accounts of Israel's apostasy without any useful chronological notices (Judg 17:1–21:25). Between these are six cycles of judges. These cycles are in two groups of three cycles (1–3 and 4–6). At the end of the first three cycles we are told that the land had rest (the root שׁקט;

Walton, *Chronological Charts of the Old Testament* (Grand Rapids: Zondervan, 1978), 48.

[147] Harrison, *Introduction to the Old Testament*, 331.

[148] E.g., Merrill, *An Historical Survey of the Old Testament*, 181; Ray, "Another Look at the Period of the Judges,"; Steinmann, "The Mysterious Numbers of the Book of Judges,"; David L. Washburn, "The Chronology of Judges: Another Look."

Judg 3:11, 30; 5:31), whereas no such notice is given at the end of the second set of three cycles. This grouping of cycles is evident in the introduction to the first and fourth cycles

וַיַּעֲשׂוּ בְנֵי־יִשְׂרָאֵל אֶת־הָרַע בְּעֵינֵי יְהוָה

The sons of Israel did evil in the eyes of Yahweh (Judg 2:11; 6:1)

The second, third, fifth, and sixth cycles are introduced by the clause

וַיֹּסִפוּ בְּנֵי יִשְׂרָאֵל לַעֲשׂוֹת הָרַע בְּעֵינֵי יְהוָה

The sons of Israel *continued* to do evil in the eyes of Yahweh (Judg 3:12; 4:1; 10:6; 13:1)[149]

Each of these cycles recounts the exploits of one major judge who may be followed by one or more minor judges, whose acts are only briefly summarized.[150] The cycles are:

Table 21
Six Cycles in Judges

Cycle	Oppressor	Judges
1. 3:7–11	Cushan-Rishathaim	Othniel

---

[149] *Continued* for ויספו is better than the English versions *again* (see the entries in BDB and *HALOT* for the Hiphil use of יסף followed by an infinitive).

[150] Note that the minor judges are always introduced as coming after (אחר) a previous judge. This is never the case for the major judges. The distinction between major and minor judges was first made by Albrecht Alt, "The Origins of Israelite Law," Pages 101–171 in *Essays on Old Testament History and Religion*. Translated by R. A. Wilson. Garden City, NY: Doubleday, 1968. The concept was developed more fully by Martin Noth, "Das Amt des 'Richters Israels," Pages 404–417 in *Festschrift Alfred Bertholet*. Edited by Wilhelm Baumgartner. Tübingen: J. C. B. Mohr: 1950.

		Ehud
2. 3:12–31	Eglon	Shamgar
3. 4:1—5:31	Jabin	Deborah
		Gideon
4. 6:1—10:6	Midianites	Tola
		Jair
		Jephthah
5. 10:7—12:15	Ammonites and Philistines	Ibzan
		Elon
		Abdon
6. 13:1—16:31	Philistines	Samson

This raises the possibility that two types of chronological overlap may be present in judges. There may be overlap among judges, especially within a cycle. Alternatively, two or more cycles may overlap.

Before we begin to construct a chronology, we should note the manner in which chronological data were recorded in ancient times.[151] As is evident from the book of Kings, at times the partial years of a king's reign in Israel at the beginning or end of his reign were

---

[151] The earliest possible date for the composition of Judges is under David's reign. Not only do the several notices that in the days of the judges Israel had no king (Judg 18:1; 19:1; 21:25) point to a time after the establishment of the monarchy, but several other indications point to David's day as one possible date for the composition of the book. The Jebusites are said to "live in Jerusalem to this day" (Judg 1:21), indicating a time before David's conquest of the city. The continued presence of Canaanites in Gezer may indicate a time before the Egyptian Pharaoh captured it and gave it to Solomon as a dowry. However, even if the composition of Judges is much later (say in the captivity with the final editing of Kings), the observations here about the recording of chronological data in ancient Judah are still valid.

counted in the tally of total years.[152] Thus two kings who reigned in succession and were said each to reign ten years reigned a combined total of nineteen (not twenty) years on the throne, since the last year of the first king was the same as the first year of the second king. Since it was unlikely that the Judges were formally placed into office and unlikely that they had a formal line of succession, it is reasonable to assume that the time spans recorded in Judges are similarly reckoned as including both the beginning (partial) year and the ending (partial) year. Thus, if we are told that Judge A judged Israel ten years and Judge B seven years and then there was rest for twenty years, the total time is at most thirty-five years (10+6+19), not thirty-seven years (10+7+20).

CONSTRUCTING A RELATIVE CHRONOLOGY OF THE JUDGES

PROLOGUE: THE DEATH OF JOSHUA AND THE ELDERS

Before the first cycle begins, the prologue indicates a period of time elapsed between the wars conducted by Joshua and the rise of the first judge Othniel. We are told that the people served Yahweh during the lifetime of Joshua and the elders who outlived him and that Joshua died before Israel's apostasy and Othniel's reign as judge (Judg 2:7–8). Depending on the ages of the leaders relative to Joshua this period requires at least a decade or two.

---

[152] Following Edwin R. Thiele, *The Mysterious Numbers of the Hebrew Kings*, Third ed. (Grand Rapids: Zondervan, 1983), who notes that in Judah, the reigns of kings were recorded using the accession year method during most of its history (except from Jehoram through Joash). Israel used the accession year method except from Jeroboam I through Jehoahaz. Since the judges, unlike kings, were not publicly installed into office, it is unlikely that the accession year system would have been employed for recording the reigns of individual judges.

CYCLE 1: OTHNIEL

The chronological information in the first cycle appears to allow no overlap for the reigns of judges or other time periods. We are simply told that Cushan-Rishathaim subjugated Israel for eight years and that Othniel brought rest to the land for forty years before he died (Judg 3:8, 11).

CYCLE 2: EHUD AND SHAMGAR

Since the second cycle begins after the death of Othniel, and a new oppressor was stirred up by Yahweh, it appears that this cycle does not overlap with the previous one. Otherwise, the land did not have rest from oppressors. The chronological information given in this cycle is that Eglon oppressed Israel for eighteen years, and then Ehud established rest for the land for eighty years.

The first indication in Judges that one judge may have been active during the lifetime of another is found at 3:31. Here, after we are told that the land had eighty years rest as a result of Ehud's activity, the author tells us about Shamgar's exploits. No chronological data is given to us concerning Shamgar. We are simply told that he slew 600 Philistines, who are *not* said to be oppressors that Yahweh had raised up.[153] Only after Shamgar's judgeship is treated are we told that Ehud died. Thus, it is reasonable to assume that Shamgar was active during the eighty years of Ehud's peace, but probably not during Ehud's lifetime, since Shamgar's activity came "after him" (Judg 3:31).

CYCLE 3: DEBORAH

The third cycle begins with a notice of Ehud's death, eliminating any possibility that the third cycle overlaps the second. In this cycle we are told that Jabin oppressed Israel for twenty years and that as a result of the work of Deborah and Barak the land had rest for forty years.

---

[153] Note that we are not told that Yahweh gave Israel into the hand of the Philistines at this time (as we are later, Judg 10:7–8; 13:1).

CYCLE 4: GIDEON, TOLA AND JAIR

Since the fourth cycle, like the second cycle, began after a period of rest as Yahweh stirred up a new oppressor, it appears that this cycle does not overlap with the previous one. We are told that the Midianites oppressed Israel for seven years (Judg 6:1). Then Gideon brought peace for forty years before he died (Judg 8:28, 34). Abimelech's rule is said to have been three years after the death of his father. Then we are told that after Abimelech a new judge, Tola, reigned for twenty-three years (Judg 10:1–2). After Tola's death we are told that Jair arose to judge Israel for twenty-two years (Judg 10:3–5). There appears to be no overlap among these periods. While this cycle includes rest for the land during Gideon's lifetime, it does not end on a note of rest. This connects it to the next two cycles that also do not end with a notice of rest for the land.

CYCLES 5 AND 6: JEPHTHAH AND SAMSON

CYCLE 5: JEPHTHAH, IBZAN, ELON, AND ABDON

After the usual notice of Israel's continued apostasy, the fifth cycle notes a new oppression by the Philistines and the Ammonites.

וַיִּחַר־אַף יְהוָה בְּיִשְׂרָאֵל וַיִּמְכְּרֵם בְּיַד־פְּלִשְׁתִּים וּבְיַד בְּנֵי עַמּוֹן:
וַיִּרְעֲצוּ וַיְרֹצְצוּ אֶת־בְּנֵי יִשְׂרָאֵל בַּשָּׁנָה הַהִיא שְׁמֹנֶה עֶשְׂרֵה שָׁנָה
אֶת־כָּל־בְּנֵי יִשְׂרָאֵל אֲשֶׁר בְּעֵבֶר הַיַּרְדֵּן בְּאֶרֶץ הָאֱמֹרִי אֲשֶׁר
בַּגִּלְעָד: וַיַּעַבְרוּ בְנֵי־עַמּוֹן אֶת־הַיַּרְדֵּן לְהִלָּחֶם גַּם־בִּיהוּדָה וּבְבִנְיָמִין
וּבְבֵית אֶפְרָיִם וַתֵּצֶר לְיִשְׂרָאֵל מְאֹד:

And Yahweh became angry with Israel and sold them into the hand of the Philistines and into the hand of the sons of Ammon. They crushed and shattered the sons of Israel that year (eighteen years all the sons of Israel who were across the Jordan River in the land of the Amorites who were in Gilead). And the sons of Ammon crossed the Jordan River to attack even those in Judah and Benjamin and in the house of Ephraim. Israel was severely distressed. (Judg 10:7–9)

Two important pieces of information are given to us here. First, the notice to a particular year is intriguing ("that year" [בַּשָּׁנָה הַהִיא]). It could be a reference to the year that Yahweh sold Israel into the hands of the Philistines and Ammonites (Judg 10:7). However, this would be a rather strange notice. Since readers would have no special insight into God's deliberations, they would have no idea when that year was. More likely, it is a reference to the year of Jair's death (Judg 10:5).

This would mean that the Philistine and Ammonite oppressions were simultaneous (see the discussion below beginning on page 100). Moreover, starting in 10:8b this cycle is exclusively about the Ammonites. The Philistines are not mentioned again as oppressors until the sixth cycle. Thus, it appears that the fifth and sixth cycles overlap. The fifth cycle is mainly about affairs east of the Jordan River, whereas the sixth cycle is mainly about affairs west of the Jordan River. East of the Jordan River the oppression lasted eighteen years. (West of the Jordan it lasted forty years; cf. Judg 13:1.)

Secondly, chronological data in the fifth cycle includes the time of the oppression by the Ammonites (eighteen years for those tribes east of the Jordan River; Judg 10:8), and a report that, apparently in the first year (Judg 10:9), the Ammonites crossed the Jordan River to spread the oppression beyond the Israelites living in Gilead, to those in Judah, Benjamin, and Ephraim.

Note Judg 10:8b is a verbless clause (שְׁמֹנֶה עֶשְׂרֵה שָׁנָה . . .). This is a clear syntactic signal that this clause is not part of the main narrative. Past narratives like this one are told by a chain of preterite (*waw*-consecutive imperfect) verbs. An interruption in the preterite chain signals something outside the main narration is being inserted (quotations, parenthetical comments, authorial observations, etc.).[154] The main narrative then commences again with the next preterite verb—in this case at the beginning of Judg 10:9. In Judg 10:8 we have a parenthetical comment, which makes the verse mean something like this:

---

[154] Examples can be found at Gen 13:1–3; Num 12:2–4; 1 Sam 7:6.

"They crushed and oppressed the sons of Israel that year (eighteen years all the sons of Israel who were across the Jordan in the land of the Amorites which is in Gilead)."

The Ammonite oppression for Israel in general lasted one year overall, but eighteen for Gilead. This means that the main narrative of Judg 10–11 (the beginning of Jephthah's judgeship) takes place in the first year of the Ammonite oppression (Judg 10:8a) when they crossed the Jordan to attack even Benjamin and Ephraim (Judg 10:9). The verbless clause simply is an aside that tells us that their oppression of Israel in Gilead lasted longer than a single year.

This narrative sequence clearly places the beginning of Jephthah's judgeship at the beginning of the Ammonite oppression. This also explains the umbrage taken by the Ephraimites who had been attacked that first year of the oppression (Judg 12). It would have been unlikely that eighteen years after the Ammonites attacked them (but did not occupy their territory) they were offended by Jephthah's action and seeking some of the spoils from his campaign.

Nothing in the account of Jephthah's victory denotes permanence, and nothing signals the end of the Ammonite oppression. The phrase "give into the hand" (some form of נתן + בְּיַד; Judg 11:30; 12:3) does not necessarily signal a defeat with long-lasting consequences. It may signal only a victory in a particular battle or campaign (cf. 1 Sam 17:47; 23:4). The same can be said for "avenge from one's enemies" (cf. נְקָמֹת מֵאֹיְבֶיךָ; Judg 11:36). Nor does "humble someone" signal permanent end to hostilities (cf. וַיִּכָּנְעוּ; Judg 11:33). The fact that after Jephthah's death there is no peace is another good indication that he did not bring the Ammonite oppression to an end (Judg 12:7). Although we are told that the Ammonite threat lasted eighteen years, nowhere in this cycle are we told that the land had rest. This is because the Ammonites remained a force to be reckoned with in the reigns of Saul (1 Sam 11:1–11) and David (2 Sam 10:1–12:31) despite Jephthah's victories.

Nor can the extent of Jephthah's victories be used as an argument that he ended the Ammonite oppression. His Ammonite campaign is described as ". . . he struck them from Aroer to the neighborhood of Minnith, twenty cities, and as far as Abel-keramim, with a great blow. So the Ammonites were humbled before the people of Israel." (Judg 11:33). This sounds impressive in English. However, one must keep in mind that Hebrew עִיר, translated "city," refers to a permanent settlement of any size, and may even at times denote small villages. This must be the case here. Jephthah's military activity was initiated at Aroer on the southwest border of Ammon, which is the eastern border of the territory of Reuben and Gad. Aroer was just north of the Arnon River on the northern border of Moab. The exact location of Minnith and Abel-keramim are unknown, but Jephthah does not appear to have attacked the Ammonite capital of Rabbah (modern day Amman). Moreover, his attack appears to have remained along the border of Ammon with Reuben and Gad, and most likely did not penetrate into the interior of Ammon. The most likely location of Minnith is somewhere to the north and east of Heshbon, which would match its description in Ezek 27:17 as a supplier of wheat. The distance from Aroer northward to Minnith would, therefore, have been about 45 kilometers (28 miles). In this short distance Jephthah struck 20 cities. Some of them may have been more substantial communities such as Jahaz and Heshbon, but the rest were most probably only small villages. This would have been enough to "humble" the Ammonites, but it was certainly only a temporary setback for them. Jephthah did not come close to attacking the Ammonite capital of Rabbah (modern day Amman), and his attack does not appear even to have penetrated into the interior of Ammon. This would explain why the Ammonites would have continued to oppress Israel even after Jephthah's judgeship.

Moreover, the internecine warfare between Jephthah and the Ephraimites (Judg 12:1–6) does not mean that the Ammonite oppression was over. It simply means that in the aftermath of Jephthah's campaign, Ammon wasn't an immediate threat. In fact, this intra-Israel conflict probably was a good reason why Jephthah was unable to completely stanch the Ammonite oppression—he turned his attention westward and was unable to do anything other than check Ammonite aggression against Gilead for a short time.

Following the judgeship of Jephthah, which lasted six years until his death (Judg 12:7), Ibzan's reign as judge was seven years (Judg 12:8–10). Elon was judge for ten years after Ibzan's death (Judg 12:11–12). Finally, Abdon's reign lasted eight years after Elon's death (Judg 12:13–15).

CYCLE 6: SAMSON

The last cycle opens with the notice that the Philistines oppressed Israel for forty years. (Judg 13:1) Apparently the first eighteen of these years coincided with the Ammonite oppression (see discussion below beginning on page 100).

The only other chronological information we are given for Samson is that he judged Israel for twenty years. This is stated twice (Judg 15:20; 16:31). The first notice is the most helpful, since there we are told that he judged Israel twenty years *during the days of the Philistines*. Thus, Samson's judgeship happened sometime during the forty years of the Philistine oppression. This means that his judgeship may have overlapped with any of the judges in the fifth cycle, but at the very least must have overlapped with the judgeships of Elon and Abdon, as we will see.

Like the previous cycle, this last cycle did not end with rest for the land. As the book of Samuel records, the Philistines continued to be a menace to Israel throughout the reign of Saul and into the reign of David.

OVERLAPPING AMMONITE AND PHILISTINE OPPRESSIONS

Several literary features in the Jephthah and Samson cycles have a direct bearing on the chronology of Judges. The first of these is that after the Ammonite and Philistine oppression is introduced at Judg 10:7 the Philistines are curiously absent from the action until the beginning of the Samson cycle at 13:1.[155] Jephthah defeated the Ammonites, but he did not deliver Israel from the Philistines. This of itself argues that the Ammonite oppression and the Philistine oppression subsequently related in the Samson cycle were concurrent.[156]

Elsewhere in Judges, the formulaic statement 'the Israelites again did/continued to do evil' (cf. 13:1) marks the beginning of an era that follows chronologically upon the era that immediately precedes it. However, the verbal root יסף does not necessarily denote "do again" in the sense of "do anew," but may denote "do again" in the sense of "continue to do."[157] While some of the occurrences of clauses that begin this way in Judges may denote sequential events, there is nothing that inherently requires this clause to begin an episode that is sequential to the immediately previous one.

A prominent feature of the Ammonite and Philistine oppressions is that neither judge associated with them—Jephthah or Samson—brought rest to the land as all the other previous major judges did (Othniel—Judg 3:11; Ehud—3:30; Deborah—5:31; Gideon—8:28). This is a clear indication that the victories of Jephthah and Samson were not decisive and did not bring the oppressions to an end.

---

[155] The Philistines are mentioned by Yahweh at Judg 10:11 as one of the oppressors from whom he had delivered Israel in the past, but they are not part of the narrative's action at this point.

[156] Andrew E. Steinmann, "The Mysterious Numbers of the Book of Judges," *JETS* 48, 2005: 495–96. Others who had previously noted that the Ammonite and Philistine oppressions must have been simultaneous are: Daniel I. Block, *Judges, Ruth* (NAC 6; Nashville: Broadman and Holman, 1999), 35–36; C. F. Keil and F. Delitzsch, *Commentary on the Old Testament* Vol 2 (reprint Grand Rapids: Eerdmans, 1976), 373, 404; Eugene H. Merrill, "Paul's Use of 'About 450 Years' in Acts 13:20," 248; David L. Washburn, "The Chronology of Judges: Another Look," 424.

[157] *HALOT* s.v. יסף.

In the case of Jephthah, it is striking that Judg 11:33 states, "So the Ammonites were subdued (וַיִּכָּנְעוּ) before the Israelites" in language reminiscent of the victories over Moab, Jabin and Midian[158] but without any ensuing notice of rest for the land as in those cases (Judg 3:30, 5:31; 8:28). The implication is that Jephthah's victory brought temporary relief and did not end the oppression.

In Samson's case the author of Judges is even more direct in stating that Samson was not going to bring the end of the Philistine oppression. Instead, before Samson's conception his mother was told, ". . . he will *begin* to save Israel from the hand of the Philistines." (יָחֵל לְהוֹשִׁיעַ אֶת־יִשְׂרָאֵל מִיַּד פְּלִשְׁתִּים; Judg 13:5). Samson, the reader is told, is only the beginning of deliverance from the Philistine oppression.[159] God never intended that Samson should bring the end of the oppression. In fact, when one turns to the Book of Samuel, the Philistines continue to be the major threat at the opening of the book, and their oppression of Israel doesn't end until Samuel intercedes for Israel (1 Sam 7:3–14; esp. 7:13). Shortly thereafter God provided a king to ensure delivery from the Philistines (1 Sam 9:16). Samson's twenty-year judgeship most likely overlapped the work of Samuel (and Abdon) and ended shortly before Saul's anointing.[160]

---

[158] Judg 3:30; 4:23; 8:28, all of which use a form of the root כנע.

[159] This statement about Samson lends a certain irony to the question posed by the elders of Gilead as they search for the deliverer who will ultimately be Jephthah: "Who is the man who will *begin* to fight the Ammonites?" (Judg 10:18; מִי הָאִישׁ אֲשֶׁר יָחֵל לְהִלָּחֵם בִּבְנֵי עַמּוֹן) While this irony was not the intention of the elders, the author of Judges may well have intended the reader to see such irony. The reader is left to conclude that like Samson, Jephthah only *begins* the fight. He does not end it.

[160] I had previously listed Samson's judgeship as 1049–1030 (Steinmann, "Mysterious Numbers," 499). That was a mistake. It should have been 1068–1049, ending shortly before Saul's reign.

A RELATIVE CHRONOLOGY OF THE JUDGES

Now that we have examined the chronological data from Judges and noted periods of overlap, a relative chronology can be constructed:

Table 22
Relative Chronology of the Judges

	Event	Duration	Total Years
Cycle 1	Cushan-Rishathaim	8 years	8 years
	Othniel	40 years	47 years
Cycle 2	Eglon	18 years	64 years
	Ehud	80 years	143 years
	Shamgar		
Cycle 3	Jabin	20 years	162 years
	Deborah	40 years	201 years
Cycle 4	Midianites	7 years	207 years
	Gideon	40 years	246 years
	Abimelech	3 years	248 years
	Tola	23 years	270 years
	Jair	22 years	291 years
Cycles 5 & 6	Philistines	40 years	330 years

The chronology of Cycles 5 and 6 is:

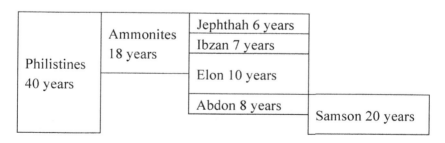

Since the combined reign of the judgeships of Jephthah, Ibzan, and Elon lasted twenty-one years, Samson's judgeship had to at least overlap the last year of Elon and the entire judgeship of Abdon if he was active during the last twenty years of the Philistine oppression. He could have begun his activity earlier and could have overlapped any three of the four judges in the fifth cycle. However, this is unlikely. Samson's birth occurred at the beginning of the forty-year Philistine oppression (Judg 13). He began his activities as judge who inflicts casualties on the Philistines with his marriage (Judg 14). Thus, Samson was of marriageable age—at least 18, but more likely 20—when he began his judgeship. This would place his 20 years as judge at the end of the Philistine oppression.

The 330 years needed for the judges is more than adequate to accommodate the time between the biblically indicated date of the conquest (1406 BC; forty years after the Exodus) and the beginning of the reign of Solomon (which has been firmly established as 971t).[161] This leaves 135 years to accommodate the conquest (seven years; Josh 14:10),[162] the deaths of Joshua and the elders before the oppression of Cushan-Rishathaim, and the reigns of Saul and David after the "days of the Philistines."

ESTABLISHING AN ABSOLUTE CHRONOLOGY FOR THE JUDGES

In order to establish an absolute chronology for the Judges, a starting point is needed to fix the date of one of the events. The most obvious are the beginning of the period of the Judges or the end. The beginning of Judges, however, cannot be established, since after the end of the conquest in 1400 BC there is an undefined time for the death of Joshua and the elders before the oppression by Cushan-Rishathaim.

---

[161] Young, "Tables of Reign Lengths," 227.

[162] At Josh 14:7–10 Caleb states that he was forty years old when he was sent out from Kadesh as a spy. He was eighty-five when he spoke these words. Israel arrived at Kadesh in the spring of 1445 BC (Num 20:1). Therefore, Caleb was eighty-five years old in 1400 BC when Joshua's conquest ended. (Thus, also, Caleb was born in 1485 BC).

If we determine the end of the "days of the Philistines," we could work backwards. The end of the 40-year Philistine oppression must be dated to their defeat when Samuel appealed to God in 1 Sam 7. 1 Sam 7:13 tells us that after this the Philistines did not enter Israel's territory—clearly implying that they did so (probably with impunity) before this. 1 Sam 7:14 tells us that as a result of the Philistine defeat, Israel regained its territory from the Philistines—an unmistakable sign that the oppression continued until this event. This must be the end of the Philistine oppression, and it takes place shortly before Saul was anointed king (1 Sam 8–10).

It is relatively easy to determine the beginning of David's reign, since we know the date of Solomon's assuming the throne (971 BC; see the discussion beginning on page 37). We are told that David reigned forty years. Since David shared the throne with Solomon for a while (1 Kgs 1:5–2:12), the most reasonable assumption is that David died shortly before the beginning of the construction of the temple.[163] Not only did David make extensive preparations for the construction during this coregency period before he died, but he also organized the duties of the priests and Levites and gave Israel and Solomon instructions concerning the temple's construction (1 Chr 22:2–29:30). Since Solomon commenced the building of the temple in the month of Ziv in 967 BC (1 Kgs 6:1, 37), it is reasonable to assume that David died shortly before this, probably sometime in 969 BC. This would make the first year of David's 40½ year reign 1009 BC.

However, we run into a difficultly in attempting to work backwards from David's reign to the beginning of Saul's reign. As is well known, the text of 1 Sam 13:1 which reports the length of Saul's reign is defective:

בֶּן־שָׁנָה שָׁאוּל בְּמָלְכוֹ וּשְׁתֵּי שָׁנִים מָלַךְ עַל־יִשְׂרָאֵל

---

[163] David's death before the start of construction was required because David was prohibited from building the temple (2 Sam 7:12–13; 1 Chr 17:11–12; 28:3).

Saul was . . . years old when he began to reign. He reigned over Israel . . . and two years.

Fortunately, two other sources indicate that Saul ruled for forty years. The first is Acts 13:21 where Paul states that Saul ruled forty years. Josephus' *Antiquities* also attributes a forty-year reign to Saul:[164]

ἐβασίλευσε δὲ Σαμουήλου ζῶντος ἔτη ὀκτὼ πρὸς τοῖς δέκα τελευτήσαντος δὲ δύο καὶ εἴκοσι καὶ Σαοῦλος μὲν οὕτω κατέστρεψε τὸν βίον

Now Saul reigned eighteen years while Samuel was alive and twenty-two years [after Samuel's] death. Then Saul took [his] life. (*Ant.* 6:378 [6.14.9])

Since Saul died in 1009 BC, he began to reign about 1049 BC.[165] This, in turn, allows us to establish an absolute chronology from the entrance of Israel into Canaan through the end of the "days of the Philistines."

Table 23
Chronology of the Judges

1406–1400 Joshua's conquest

1399–1379 Period for the deaths of Joshua and the elders

1378–1371 Oppression by Cushan-Rishathaim

---

[164] Josephus is consistent in stating that the first part of Saul's reign overlapped the last eighteen years of Samuel's life. Cf. *Ant.* 6:294 [6.13.5]. However, this is probably mistaken. The narrative of the last chapters of 1 Samuel strongly implies that Samuel died only two or three years before Saul's death. 1 Sam 25:1 notes Samuel's death, just six chapters before Saul's death at 1 Sam 31:8. More than sixteen months transpired between Samuel's death and Saul's death (1 Sam 27:7).

[165] It is possible that the 40 years of Acts 13:21 is a round number and that Josephus knew this same round number. If this is the case, then Saul's reign may have been as long as 42 years. (Since the 2 survived in the damaged text of 1 Sam 13:1, it may have originally read "42 years.")

1371–1332 Othniel/Rest for the land	
1332–1315 Oppression by Eglon	
1315–1236 Ehud/Rest for the land/Shamgar	
1236–1217 Oppression by Jabin	
1217–1178 Deborah	
1178–1172 Oppression by the Midianites	
1172–1133 Gideon/Rest for the land	
1133–1131 Abimelech	
1131–1109 Tola	
1109–1088 Jair	
1088–1071 Oppression by the Midianites 1088–1049 Oppression by the Philistines 1068–1049 Samson (?)	1088–1083 Jephthah 1083–1077 Ibzan 1077–1068 Elon 1068–1061 Abdon

This timeline for the judges is consistent with archaeological finds from this period.[166] Monumental building activity at Jericho, "the City of Palms," in the fourteenth or early thirteenth century is consistent with Eglon's occupation of that city (Judg 3:13). The destruction of Hazor about 1230 BC is consistent with the aftermath of Barak's victory (Judg 4:24). The destruction of Shechem about 1125 BC agrees with Abimelech's activity at that time (Judg 9:45).

It should be noted that the twenty-one year period for the death of Joshua and the elders is consistent with what one might expect.

---

[166] Wood, "From Ramesses to Shiloh," 269–280.

Moreover, it is well known that at Judg 11:26 Jephthah claims that Israel had occupied cities in the Trans-Jordan for 300 years. Since Jephthah was engaged in conversation and not writing a precise history, the 300 years may be a round number. But how close is it? We should keep in mind that the Trans-Jordan tribes were not allowed to occupy their land until after they had helped their fellow Israelites subdue the land of Canaan west of the Jordan River. So, the earliest they could have occupied cities like Aroer or Heshbon was 1400 BC at the end of Joshua's campaigns. Since Jephthah appears to have spoken his words in 1088 BC, the actual time was 312 years, making Jephthah's 300 years a reasonable approximation.

SAMUEL AND ELI AS JUDGES

In addition to the chronology of the judges, we can determine a few other dates using the information in Scripture and Josephus. If Josephus' information is correct that Samuel was a judge for twelve years (*Ant.* 6:294 [6.13.5]), Samuel's career as a judge lasted from 1060 BC to 1049 BC. Note that Samuel's judgeship closely follows the death of Abdon in 1061. Therefore, the indication that Samuel was a judge (1 Sam 7:6, 15, 16, 17) seems to fit with the chronology of the judges and provides for nearly uninterrupted leadership from Othniel until the institution of the monarchy, or nearly uninterrupted leadership from Moses to Joshua and the elders through the judges ending in Samuel.

1 Sam 7:2 states that twenty years passed between the time that the ark was returned to Israel and Samuel interceded for the people at Mizpah shortly before Saul was anointed king. This would place the return of the ark in 1068 BC. The season was spring, since it was the time of harvesting wheat (1 Sam 6:13). The death of Eli, seven months earlier (1 Sam 6:1), would have been in 1069 BC. Finally, given other information from 1 Samuel, we can reconstruct Eli's life:

Table 24
Chronology of Eli's Life

1167	Eli born (1 Sam 4:15)
1109–1069	Eli's priesthood/judgeship (1 Sam 4:18)
1069	Eli's death (1 Sam 4:15)

This dating also aligns well with the archaeology of Shiloh, which indicates that Shiloh was destroyed about 1050 BC. This would have been at the time of the ark's capture by the Philistines and the death of Eli (Ps 78:60; Jer 7:12–14; 26:6, 9).[167]

---

[167] Wood, "From Ramesses to Shiloh," 280–281.

7

SAUL, DAVID, AND SOLOMON

The period between the anointing of Saul and the death of Solomon is often characterized as Israel's "united monarchy" in contrast to the division of Israel into the kingdoms of Israel (north) and Judah (south) after Solomon's death. This characterization is accurate except for the first years of David's reign when David reigned over Judah alone, and Saul's son Eshbaal reigned over the rest of Israel (2 Sam 2:10).[168]

THE BASIC CHRONOLOGY OF THE UNITED MONARCHY

The reign of Solomon can be securely dated as 971t–932t (see the discussion of Solomon's reign beginning on page 37). David reigned 40 years (2 Sam 5:4; 1 Kgs 2:11). This was calculated by accession year reckoning, since in 1 Kgs 2:11 he is credited with 40 years: seven in Hebron, and 33 in Jerusalem. However, David was actually king in Hebron for seven years and six months (2 Sam 2:11; 5:5).

---

[168] Eshbaal (1 Chr. 8:33; 9:39) is called Ishbosheth in 2 Samuel. Ishbosheth ("man of shame") is most likely a purposeful scribal bowdlerization of his name, since his actual name Eshbaal ("man of the master"?) contained the word *baal* , "master" (perhaps as a reference to Israel's God Yahweh; cf. Hos 2:16). This could have been misunderstood as the name of the pagan storm god Baal, which some ancient scribe may have found unacceptable for someone from Israel's royal house. The same alteration appears to have been made with Jonathan's son Meribaal ("contender with Baal"; 1 Chr. 8:34; 9:40), whose name throughout 2 Samuel was purposely bowdlerized to Mephibosheth ("from the mouth of shame").

This means that his first six months in Hebron were reckoned as his accession year and not counted in the total. Thus, David began to reign during the month of Nisan, and his first regnal year was reckoned from Tishri of that same year.

As 1 Kgs 1:5–2:9 and 1 Chr 23–29 make clear, Solomon shared the throne of Israel with David for some time. David's preparations to build the temple as related in 1 Chr 23–29 require a period of at least a year or two. This co-regency period had ended by Ziv 967 when Solomon began to build the temple and David had died—since David was forbidden by God from building the temple (2 Sam 7:12–13; 1 Chr 17:11–12; 28:3). Thus, David's last year was 969t, and his death occurred no later than Nisan 967 BC. David's first year as king over Israel in Jerusalem, therefore, was 1002t (969t + 33). His first year as king over Judah in Hebron was 1009t (969t + 40), with his reign actually commencing in Nisan of 1009 BC.

Sometime during the period that David was king in Hebron, Eshbaal's great-uncle Abner made him king over the northern tribes of Israel. The narrative of 2 Sam 5:1–6 implies that shortly after Eshbaal's death David was acknowledged to be king over all Israel. This means that Eshbaal was king over the rest of Israel for two years beginning no earlier than 1009t, but no later than 1004t (2 Sam 2:10), two years before David conquered Jerusalem.

As for Saul's reign, as we have already seen, the text of 1 Sam 13:1 is corrupt, since the text as preserved credits Saul with a impossibly short reign of two years (see the discussions beginning on pages 45 and 106). However, Acts 13:21 and Josephus (*Ant.* 6:378 [6.14.9]) indicate that Saul reigned 40 years (see discussion on page 106). This may have been a round number, but is most likely close to the actual total.

One confirmation of this can be seen in the birth of Saul's youngest son, Eshbaal, who was 40 years old when he became king of most of the tribes of Israel (2 Sam 2:10). Throughout Saul's reign he had three sons: Jonathan, Ishvi and Malchishua (1 Sam 14:49;

31:2).[169] However, there is no mention of Saul's fourth son Eshbaal (1 Chr 8:33; 9:39). Thus, it would appear that Eshbaal was born after Saul began to reign about 1049 BC. Eshbaal was forty years old when he became king and reigned two years during David's seven years and six months in Hebron (2 Sam 2:10–11). The means that Eshbaal began to reign no earlier than Nisan 1009 and no later than 1004t. Therefore, he was born no earlier than sometime in 1049 or late 1050 BC and no later than 1044 BC. Eshbaal's age at his accession to the throne confirms that Saul reigned about 40 years, and certainly no less than 35 years.

Since Saul died in the spring of 1009 BC, his reign commenced about 1049 BC. We cannot know whether, like David's dynasty, Saul reckoned his regnal years from Tishri. If so, his official reign would have been c. 1050t–1010t. If, however, he reckoned his regnal years from Nisan, then his reign would have been c. 1049n–1009n. Since 1 Sam 13:1 credits Saul with two years on the throne, its original text may have read "42 years" with only the number two surviving in the now corrupted text. If this is the case, Saul could have taken the throne as early as 1052t or 1051n.

Thus, the basic chronology of the united monarchy is:

Table 25
Basic Chronology of the United Monarchy

c. 1049–1009	Reign of Saul
Nisan 1009–1002t	David's reign in Hebron
1002t–969t	David's reign in Jerusalem
971t–969t	Solomon's coregency with David
969t–932t	Solomon's sole reign

---

[169] Apparently, Ishvi is another name for Abinadab (cf. 1 Sam 31:2; 1 Chr. 8:33; 9:39; 10:2).

THE REIGN OF SAUL (C. 1049–1009)

There are few explicit chronological markers in the narrative of Saul's reign in 1 Sam 10–31.[170] Therefore, any reconstruction of the events during Saul's reign will contain some degree of uncertainty.

Before David is introduced in the narrative, Saul led a campaign against the Philistines (1 Sam 13–14) and a campaign against the Amalekites (1 Sam 15). In both instances Saul failed in some way to obey God, prompting Samuel to inform Saul that God had already chosen someone else as king (1 Sam 13:14; 15:28). These statements imply that David was already living. Since David was born thirty years before he became king (between mid-1040 and early 1039 BC), these statements imply that, apart from the acts of Saul at the very beginning of his reign (1 Sam 10–12), at least the first decade of Saul's reign is passed over in silence. More likely, David was approaching the age of 20—the normal age for military service (Num 1:3)—when Saul was informed that someone else had been chosen to be king. This would place the Philistine campaign no more than about two years before 1019 BC when David turned 20 (i.e., 1021 BC) and the Amalekite campaign about a year later than the Philistine campaign (i.e., c. 1020 BC)

David volunteered to confront Goliath (1 Sam 17:32), implying that he was at least 20 years old, but not much older, since he was a young man and despised by the older Goliath (1 Sam 17:33, 42). Moreover, David had no experience in armor or with a sword (1 Sam 17:38–39), which also implies that he was just over the age for military service. Therefore, David most likely killed Goliath about 1019 BC and was anointed by Samuel shortly before this (1 Sam 16).

Well into his reign David did not know of the existence of Jonathan's son Meribaal (Mephibosheth; 2 Sam 9:3). This implies

---

[170] The only useful notice for reconstructing the chronology of Saul's reign is that David spent the last 16 months of Saul's reign as a mercenary for the Philistine king Achish (1 Sam 27:7).

that he most likely fled from Saul's court before Meribaal's birth. Since Meribaal was five years old when Saul died, he was born in 1014 BC. David, therefore, fled Saul's court about 1015 BC. This places the events of 1 Sam 18 between c. 1019 BC and c. 1015 BC.

During the last sixteen months of Saul's reign (c. Tebeth 1011/10 BC to c. Nisan 1009 BC) David served as a mercenary for the Philistine king Achish (1 Sam 27:7). If we allow a year or two for the events between the death of Samuel and David entering Achish's service, Samuel's death can be dated to c. 1012 B.C (1 Sam 25:1). This, in turn places the events of 1 Sam 19–24 between c. 1015 and c. 1012 BC.

Major events during Saul's reign can be summarized as:

Table 26
Chronology of Saul's Reign

c. 1049	Saul made king (1 Sam 9–12)
c. 1045	Eshbaal (Ishbosheth) born
1039	David born
c. 1021	Saul's Philistine campaign (1 Sam 13–14)
c. 1020	Saul's Amalekite campaign (1 Sam 15)
c. 1019	David anointed/David kills Goliath (1 Sam 16–17)
c. 1016	David marries Michal (1 Sam 18:27)
c. 1015	David flees Saul's court (1 Sam 19–21)
1014	Meribaal (Mephibosheth) born
c. 1012	Samuel's death (1 Sam 25:1)
c. 1011	David marries Abigail and Ahinoam (1 Sam 25:42–43)
1010–1009	David in Achish's service for 16 months (1 Sam 27; 29–30)

THE REIGN OF DAVID (NISAN 1009–969T)

The narratives of David's reign are found in 2 Sam 2–24 and 1 Chr 11–29. In contrast to the narrative for Saul's reign, there are several notices in the narratives of David's reign that are useful in reconstructing a chronology of events during this period. However, even with this information, many of the dates for individual events will be approximate.

DAVID'S REIGN IN HEBRON (NISAN 1009–1002T)

The majority of the account of David's time in Hebron when he reigned over Judah (2 Sam 2–4) concerns the two years in which Eshbaal reigned over the rest of Israel (2 Sam 2:12–4:12). The narrative of 2 Sam 5 implies that David was made king over all Israel shortly after Eshbaal was assassinated. This, in turn, implies that for about four years after Judah acknowledged David as king, the rest of Israel had no acknowledged king until Saul's uncle Abner, who had been commander of Israel's army, made Saul's son Eshbaal king (2 Sam 2:8–9).

Confirmation of this can be found in Abner's later comment to the elders of Israel that for some time they had been considering acknowledging David as king (2 Sam 3:17). By placing Eshbaal on the throne, it would appear that Abner was attempting to stanch the erosion of the power he and his family had held during the previous four decades. Therefore, we can date Eshbaal's reign to about 1005t–1003t. This, in turn, allows us to construct the following chronology for David's reign over Judah in Hebron:

Table 27
Chronology of David's Reign in Hebron

Nisan 1009	David made king of Judah in Hebron (2 Sam 2:1–7)
Mid-1005	Abner makes Eshbaal king (2 Sam 2:8–11)
Early 1004	Joab defeats Abner at Gibeon (2 Sam 2:11–31)

Late 1003	Joab murders Abner (2 Sam 3)
Early 1002	Eshbaal assassinated (2 Sam 4)
Mid-1002	David made king of Israel/ Jerusalem conquered (2 Sam 5:1–8)

DAVID'S REIGN IN JERUSALEM (1002T–969T)

To the careful reader it quickly becomes obvious that the material about David's reign in 2 Sam 5–24 (||1 Chr 11–21) is not arranged in strict chronological order.[171] First, it is clear that 2 Sam 5:9–16 is a summary of David's activity in Jerusalem throughout his reign there. 2 Sam 5:11–12||1 Chr 14:1–2 notes that David's building activity was aided by Hiram of Tyre, whose reign began in 980t, almost twenty years after David conquered Jerusalem. Clearly, this notice, plus the summary of the sons born to David in 2 Sam 5:13–16||1 Chr 14:3–7 marks this section as a summary of David's 33 years in Jerusalem.

Another indication that the arrangement of events for David's reign in Jerusalem is out of chronological order is the Philistine war in 2 Sam 5:17–25||1 Chr 14:8–17. This clearly was initiated before David conquered Jerusalem in mid-1002 BC. 2 Sam 5:17 notes that the Philistines threatened to attack shortly after David was anointed king. In response, David went down to the "stronghold" (מְצָדָה), a term used earlier to describe Jerusalem (2 Sam 5:7, 9).[172] Heretofore the Philistines probably considered David their ally, since they both opposed the house of Saul. However, as soon as David became king

---

[171] Much of the following discussion is dependent on the observations of Merrill, "The 'Accession Year' and Davidic Chronology." However, Merrill's chronology is not adopted because of two problems. First, Merrill incorrectly considers 977t as Hiram's first year instead of the correct 980t. Second, Merrill does not correctly reckon David's coregency with Solomon, so he counts 1004t as David's first year in Jerusalem instead of 1002t.

[172] That David "went down" from Hebron to Jerusalem is geographically accurate, since Hebron is some 500 feet higher in elevation than Jerusalem.

over a united Israel, the Philistines attacked him, and he found a more secure capital in Jerusalem before retaliating and defeating the Philistines.

The very next event in the accounts of David's reign is David's bringing the ark to Jerusalem (2 Sam 6||1 Chr 13; 15–16). As 1 Chr 15:1 makes clear, the ark was brought to Jerusalem *after* David had built his palace—that is, after 980t when Hiram became king of Tyre (2 Sam 5:11).

Later, the Ammonite war is related (2 Sam 10:1–11:1; 12:29–31|| 1 Chr 19:1–20:3). There are two indications that this war took place *before* 980 BC. One is that the war was precipitated by the disrespect shown by the new Ammonite king Hanun to David's ambassadors (2 Sam 10:1–5||1 Chr 19:1–5). This had to have taken place early in David's reign before he had become powerful. Later in David's reign Hanun would not have dared to insult him. In addition, Hanun was the son of Nahash (2 Sam 10:2||1 Chr 19:2), who attacked Jabesh Gilead at the beginning of Saul's reign (1 Sam 11:1–11). If Hanun precipitated the Ammonite war sometime after 980t as required by a strict chronological arrangement of material in 2 Sam 5–24, then Nahash would have had to reign almost 80 years! If, however, the Ammonite war took place early in David's reign, Nahash would have had a very long—but not impossibly long—reign of 45 or 50 years.

A second indication that the Ammonite war happened early is the age of Solomon. Although we do not know exactly how old Solomon was when he became king, shortly after David's death he characterized himself as "a young child" (נַעַר קָטֹן; 1 Kgs 3:7; cp. 1 Chr 22:5). While this is most certainly hyperbole on Solomon's part, it is probable that Solomon was in his early twenties when he took the throne. His eldest son, Rehoboam was born in 973 BC, two years before Solomon's first regnal year (971t).[173] This, in turn requires that Solomon to have been at least in his middle teens, and

---

[173] Rehoboam ascended to the throne in 932 BC when he as was 41 years old (1 Kgs 14:21||2 Chr 12:13; 932 BC + 41= 973 BC).

more likely closer to twenty years old when his wife Naamah became pregnant (1 Kgs 14:21). Since Solomon's birth followed David's adultery with Bathsheba during the Ammonite war (2 Sam 11:1–12:23), Solomon, Bathsheba's second child, was most likely born within two or three years of the siege of Rabbah. Thus, if we assume that Hanun ascended to the Ammonite throne in 998t after a 50-year reign by his father, the outbreak of the Ammonite war can also be placed that year. The siege of Rabbah would then have been in the spring of 997 BC (2 Sam 11:1‖1 Chr 20:1) and the birth of Solomon about 994 BC (2 Sam 12:24). Solomon would have been 21 years old when Rehoboam was born and about 23 years old at the beginning of his first regnal year (971t).

All this demonstrates that the material for David's reign is not arranged in strict chronological order, and each incident in the narrative must be examined carefully to determine when it took place.[174] Sufficient clues exist, however, to estimate the dates of most major incidents in David's reign.

Key to determining the chronology of the remaining major events of David's reign is the narrative concerning Absalom (2 Sam 13–19). The sequence of the events is related as follows:

1. Amnon raped Absalom's sister Tamar (2 Sam 13:1–22). At this time Absalom was old enough to have his own household—at least 20 (2 Sam 13:20).

2. Two years later Absalom murdered Amnon (2 Sam 13:23–33; esp. 2 Sam 13:23) and fled to Geshur (2 Sam 13:34–39). Absalom remained in exile in Geshur for three years (2 Sam 13:38).

---

[174] A quick examination of 1 Chronicles in light of the discussion above will also reveal that its narrative for David's reign is also not arranged in chronological order. In both 2 Samuel and 1 Chronicles it appears as if the account of David's reign is primarily arranged topically, and chronological arrangement is a secondary concern.

3. Absalom's return from exile is facilitated by Joab (2 Sam 14:1–27).

4. Absalom is received by David two years after returning from exile (2 Sam 14:28–33).

5. Absalom spends four years preparing to overthrow David (2 Sam 15:1–11).[175]

6. Absalom leads a rebellion, is defeated, and is killed by Joab (2 Sam 15:13–19:43).

There are two indications that Absalom's rebellion took place after David built his palace and moved the ark to Jerusalem. First, Absalom's defiling of David's concubines took place on the roof of David's palace (2 Sam 16:22). Second, when David fled Jerusalem, Zadok attempted to take the ark from the city, only to have David order him to return it (2 Sam 15:24–29). Thus, Absalom's rebellion took place several years after 980t when Hiram became king of Tyre (2 Sam 5:11; 1 Chr 14:1). The most opportune time for Absalom to begin his political campaign to gain the support of the elders of Israel would have been while David was immersed in building his palace and moving the ark to Jerusalem. If we assume that Hiram made his first overture to David soon after assuming the throne of Tyre in 980t, then we can estimate that David began work on his palace in 979 BC.

About three years would have been a reasonable time to build a palace, placing the completion in 976 BC.[176] The ark would have been

---

[175] The Hebrew text of 2 Sam 15:7 reads "forty years," which is most certainly a scribal error. LXX, Syriac, Vulgate and Josephus (*Ant.* 7.196 [7.9.1]) read "four," a much more reasonable period, and a reading that is adopted in most English translations. The suggestion of Althann, "The Meaning of ארבעים שנה in 2 Sam 15,7" that the text originally read "forty days" would leave an unreasonably short time for Absalom to gather the needed political support for his rebellion.

[176] Solomon spent 13 years building his palace (1 Kgs 7:1‖2 Chr 8:1).

brought to Jerusalem the next year, 975 BC. Thus, a reasonable period for Absalom's four years spent undermining David's authority would have been from about 978 BC when David was in the midst of palace construction to about 974 BC when Absalom rebelled.

Working backward yields 980 BC when Absalom returned from exile, 983 BC when Absalom murdered Amnon and went into exile and 985 BC when Amnon raped Tamar. It should be noted that Amnon was David's eldest son, the first of David's six sons born during the seven and one-half years he ruled in Hebron (2 Sam 3:2–5‖1 Chr 3:1–4). Since David had been married to Ahinoam, Amnon's mother, some time before coming to Hebron (1 Sam 25:43; 27:3), it is possible that Amnon was born as early as 1009 BC. Absalom's birth probably came a year or two later in 1008 or 1007 BC. This would have made Amnon about 24 years old when he raped Tamar. Absalom would have been 22 or 23 years old at the time.

Following Absalom's rebellion, Sheba rebelled. This can be dated to about 973 BC. The census David ordered should probably be dated to most of 972 BC (2 Sam 24‖1 Chr 21).[177] It may have been a reaction to the two rebellions and based on David's desire to know how large an army he could raise in case of another revolt. This would explain God's anger, since David was relying on human might instead of God's power to retain his kingdom.[178]

The end of the narrative about the census tells of David buying the threshing floor of Araunah which would become the site of the temple (2 Sam 24:16–25‖1 Chr 21:15–22:1).[179] The remaining two or three years of David's reign were primarily spent with a renewed dedication to build the temple. David made preparations for the

---

However, Solomon's palace was clearly meant to be an extravagant building, and Solomon certainly had more resources than David (1 Kgs 4:20–34). That David's palace was much smaller and less imposing is implied by Solomon's construction of another palace.

[177] The census was conducted for nine months and twenty days (2 Sam 24:8).

[178] Taking a census *per se* was not sinful (Exod 30:11–16).

[179] Araunah is called Ornan in 1 Chronicles.

construction of the temple as he reigned with his coregent Solomon (1 Chr 22:2–29:25).

This leaves only two major events during David's reign undated: the avenging of the Gibeonites (2 Sam 21:1–14) and the later Philistine wars (2 Sam 21:15–22||1 Chr 20:4–8). The avenging of the Gibeonites took place at the end a three year famine "during the days of David." Since 2 Sam 21 also relates the Philistine wars that took place after the capture of Rabbah (1 Chr 20:4), it is most likely that the famine and the avenging of the Gibeonites also should be placed after the conquest of Rabbah. The best that can be estimated chronologically is that both the famine and the Philistine wars are to be dated between the capture of Rabbah about 996 BC and about 980 BC. A later date is not warranted, since by that time David had built his palace, and God had granted him peace from his enemies (2 Sam 7:1, 9, 11||1 Chr 17:8, 10).

Therefore, the approximate chronology of the events of David's reign in Jerusalem can be summarized as:

Table 28
Chronology of David's Reign in Jerusalem

1002	David conquers Jerusalem/defeats the Philistines (2 Sam 5||1 Chr 11:4–9; 1 Chr 14)
998	Ammonite war begins (2 Sam 10:1–11:1; 12:29–31||1 Chr 19:1–20:3)
997	Rabbah captured/David commits adultery (2 Sam 11–12)
994	Solomon born (2 Sam 12:24–25)
985	Amnon rapes Tamar (2 Sam 13:1–22)
983	Absalom murders Amnon/Absalom goes into exile (2 Sam 13:23–39)
980	Absalom returns from exile (2 Sam 14:1–27)

979–976	David builds his palace (2 Sam 5:11‖1 Chr 14:1)
978	Absalom received again by David (2 Sam 14:28–33)
975	Ark moved to Jerusalem (2 Sam 6‖1 Chr 13; 16); God's covenant with David (2 Sam 7‖1 Chr 17)
974	Absalom's rebellion (2 Sam 15:13–19:43)
973	Sheba's rebellion (2 Sam 20); Rehoboam born (1 Kgs 14:21‖2 Chr 12:13)
972	David orders a census taken (2 Sam 24‖1 Chr 21)
972–969	David makes preparations for the construction of the temple (1 Chr 22:2–29:25)
971	Solomon made coregent (1 Kgs 1; 1 Chr 23:1)
969	David dies (1 Kgs 2:10–12‖1 Chr 29:26–30)

THE REIGN OF SOLOMON (971T–932T)

While the reign of Solomon contains proportionally more dated events than either the reign of David or the reign of Saul, the narrative of Solomon's reign in 1 Kings/2 Chronicles is much shorter than the narratives of the reigns of his predecessors in 1–2 Samuel/ 1 Chronicles.

We have already established that Solomon's reign began in 971t and ended in 932t and that he began construction on the temple in the month of Ziv in 968t (that is, in April or May 967 BC; 1 Kgs 6:1‖ 2 Chr 3:2; 1 Kgs 6:37; see the discussion of dating Solomon's reign on pages 37–45 above).

Since David most likely died sometime in 969 BC, the events related in 1 Kgs 2:13–3:28 (cf. 2 Chr 1:1–13)—the executions of Adonijah and Joab, the banishment of Abiathar, the confinement of Shimei, and Solomon's prayer for wisdom at Gibeon—took place in late 969 BC or early 968 BC. Thus, the execution of Shimei took place in late 966 BC or early 965 BC (1 Kgs 2:39–46).

Solomon's marriage to Pharaoh's daughter appears to have taken place after David's death, but early in Solomon's reign, because Pharaoh's daughter lived in the City of David while the temple was being built (1 Kgs 3:1).

Solomon completed the temple in the month of Bul seven years later in his eleventh year (1 Kgs 6:38). Therefore, the temple was completed in October or November 961 BC. Shortly after the dedication of the temple Solomon must have begun construction of his palace, which took 13 years to complete and was finished in 948 BC (1 Kgs 7:1), with the entire time spent building both the temple and the palace totaling twenty years (1 Kgs 9:10; 2 Chr 8:1). Thus Solomon began construction on the palace in early 960 BC and completed it in 948 BC. That same year he gave Hiram 20 cities in Galilee (1 Kgs 9:10–14).

Sometime in the years that followed, Solomon conquered Hamath Zobah and rebuilt cities in his realm (2 Chr 8). Also sometime in the following years the Queen of Sheba visited Solomon (1 Kgs 10:1–13‖2 Chr 9:1–12). Unfortunately, we cannot date these events except to say that they occurred after 947 BC but probably before the rebellions against Solomon late in his reign (1 Kgs 11) which would have made both the travel of the Queen of Sheba and extensive construction projects difficult. A reasonable estimate of the date for the visit of the Queen of Sheba is about 940 BC after Solomon had completed the temple and his palace and his fame (including the magnificence of his building projects) had spread internationally.

Therefore the datable events of Solomon's reign are:

Table 29
Chronology of Solomon's Reign

971	Solomon made coregent (1 Kgs 1; 1 Chr 23:1)
969	David dies (1 Kgs 2:10–12‖1 Chr 29:26–30)
969 or 968	Solomon secures his throne (1 Kgs 2:13–38)
Ziv 967	Temple construction begun (1 Kgs 6:1‖2 Chr 13:2; 1 Kgs 6:37)
966 or 965	Shimei executed (1 Kgs 2:39–46)
Bul 961	Temple construction completed
960	Palace construction started
948	Palace construction completed
c. 940	Queen of Sheba visits Solomon (1 Kgs 10:1–13‖2 Chr 9:1–12)
932t	Solomon dies[180]

---

[180] Young, in "When Did Solomon Die?" had calculated that Solomon's death occurred sometime between Nisan and Tishri of 931 BC, but he offers the following clarification in his later "Tables of Reign Lengths" paper, p. 227, note 3: "Although my *Solomon* paper showed that Solomon died and Rehoboam began before Tishri of 931 BC, I was not justified in assuming that Jeroboam's reign also began before Tishri of that year. Some weeks or even months were necessary for the news of Solomon's death to reach Egypt and for Jeroboam to return from there and be installed as king of the breakaway tribes. Whether this time extended past Tishri 1 of 931 is not known. The Scriptural data only allows us to narrow the beginning of Jeroboam's reign to some time in 931n and the beginning of Rehoboam's to some time in 932t."

8

THE DIVIDED MONARCHY

The period of Israel's history from the death of Solomon to the fall of the kingdom of Judah to the Babylonians is generally called the era of the divided monarchy. For most of this period Israel was divided into two kingdoms. The kingdom that ruled northern ten tribes retained the name *Israel*. This kingdom saw a number of dynasties. The southern kingdom that ruled only the territory of the tribes of Judah and Benjamin was called *Judah*. This kingdom had only one dynasty, the continuation of the dynasty of David. These kingdoms existed side-by-side for just over two centuries. After the fall of Samaria to the Assyrians in 723 BC, only the kingdom of Judah survived until it was brought to an end with the conquest of Jerusalem in 587 BC.

DATA FOR THE REIGNS
OF THE KINGS OF JUDAH AND ISRAEL

The books of Kings and Chronicles supply a large amount of information about the monarchs of Judah and Israel. Often the length of a king's reign and a synchronism with the king in the other Israelite kingdom is given. For the kings of Judah other pieces of information are often given: the king's age when he assumed the throne and his mother's name.[181] For instance, the notice for Jehoshaphat says:

---

[181] Age at accession to the throne is given for all of Judah's kings except Abijah (1 Kgs 15:1–2||2 Chr 13:1–2) and Asa (1 Kgs 15:9–10||2 Chr 16:11–13).

Jehoshaphat, son of Asa reigned over Judah in the fourth year of King Ahab of Israel. Jehoshaphat was thirty-five years old when he reigned, and he reigned twenty-five years in Jerusalem. His mother's name was Azubah, daughter of Shilhi. (1 Kgs 22:41–42; cf. 2 Chr 20:31)

Since a large amount of chronological information is supplied in the books of Kings and Chronicles, one might expect that it would be relatively easy to determine the dates for the reigns of the monarchs of the divided kingdom. However, there are a number of factors that make determining the chronology of these kingdoms very complex: The official start of the new year was different in Judah (Tishri) than in Israel (Nisan).[182] Judah initially used accession year reckoning whereas Israel used non-accession year reckoning (see the discussion of reckoning of regnal years on pages 38–39). For a while Judah switched to non-accession year reckoning before switching back to accession year reckoning. Israel eventually changed to accession year reckoning. For Judah, there is the matter of coregencies.[183] Especially when the reigning king was unable to fulfill all of his duties (e.g. Uzziah; 2 Chr 26:21) or when there was an unstable political situation, the king's son may have been named coregent with his father. Thus, the years of their reigns may have overlapped.[184]

---

[182] That Tishri-based years were used in both Solomon's day for all Israel and in Josiah's day for Judah can be demonstrated by a careful analysis of the data for the construction of the temple by Solomon (see discussion above on page 42) and for the cleansing of the temple by Josiah (2 Kgs 22:3; 23:23). Josiah began repairing the temple in his eighteenth year. After the passing of 1 Nisan, Josiah celebrated the Passover, but it was still his eighteenth year. This indicates that a new year did not begin in Nisan. A careful analysis of the synchronisms of Shallum (2 Kgs 15:13), Menahem (2 Kgs 15:17), Pekahiah (2 Kgs 15:23), and Pekah (2 Kgs 15:27) with Uzziah demonstrates that Israel's calendar did not start in Tishri.

[183] There was only one coregency during Israel's history: Jeroboam II reigned for a while with his father Jehoash. See Table 32.

[184] There are two explicit references to coregencies in Kings. Solomon was

All of these factors necessitate a careful treatment of the data supplied by the books of Kings and Chronicles as well as an awareness of the way the ancient court records were kept and reigns were calculated.

THE REIGNS OF THE KINGS OF ISRAEL AND JUDAH

THE CHRONOLOGY OF EDWIN R. THIELE

Because of the complicated nature of the biblical data, the chronology of the reigns of the kings of the divided monarchy remained largely undetermined until the groundbreaking work of Edwin R. Thiele.[185] Thiele was able to demonstrate the basic observations about the ancient data preserved in Kings and Chronicles already discussed above. In reconstructing the chronology of this period, it was critical to recognize the use of Tishri or Nisan years, accession and non-accession dating, and coregencies. While he was working out these conclusions about the biblical data, Thiele was unaware of the work

---

coregent with his father David (1 Kgs 1:28–2:9; 1 Chr 22:2–29:30). Jotham was coregent with his father Uzziah (Azariah; 2 Kgs 15:5||2 Chr 26:21). There is another coregency that is clearly indicated: King Joram of Israel began to reign in the eighteenth year of Jehoshaphat (2 Kgs 3:1) and in the second (first) year of Jehoram (2 Kgs 1:17). This clearly indicates that Jehoram served a coregency with his father Jehoshaphat.

[185] Thiele, "The Chronology of the Kings of Judah and Israel"; "Comparison of the Chronological Data of Israel and Judah"; "The Synchronisms of the Hebrew Kings—a Re-Evaluation: I"; "The Synchronisms of the Hebrew Kings—a Re-Evaluation: II"; "Pekah to Hezekiah and the Azariah and Hezekiah Synchronisms"; "Coregencies and Overlapping Reigns among the Hebrew Kings"; "Additional Chronological Note on 'Yaw, Son of 'Omri'"; *The Mysterious Numbers of the Hebrew Kings. Mysterious Numbers* appeared in three editions. First edition—New York: Macmillian, 1951; Second edition—Grand Rapids: Eerdmans, 1965; New Revised (third) edition—Zondervan/Kregel, 1983. Unless otherwise specified, page numbers throughout this book refer to the third edition.

of an earlier twentieth century scholar—V. Coucke of the Grootseminarie Brugge.[186] Coucke had made these same basic observations, but his work had largely been forgotten.

The basic soundness of Thiele's reconstruction was eventually demonstrated by its ability to coordinate with already-dated events from the ancient Near East. In some instances, Thiele was able to correct erroneous dating of events.[187] For instance, as he was determining the sequence of reigns after the time of Ahab, Thiele found that his chronology provided a date of 702 BC for the fourteenth year of Hezekiah, the year in which Sennacherib besieged Jerusalem (2 Kgs 18:13; Isa 36:1). Assyrian texts, however, quite definitely date Sennacherib's siege to 701 BC. Thiele's chronology, based on biblical reign lengths and synchronisms, only allowed 152 years between the Battle of Qarqar and Sennacherib's siege, whereas the commonly accepted Assyrian chronology gave 153 years (854 BC to 701 BC) between the two events. On investigation, Thiele found that the date of 854 BC for the Battle of Qarqar that was accepted by most scholars had been challenged by a few European researchers who held instead to 853 BC. This led Thiele into a textual study of the sources of the Assyrian Eponym Canon. He was able to show that 853 BC was the correct date, and he published the corrected Eponym Canon in all three editions of *Mysterious Numbers*.[188] Thiele's study of these

---

[186] Couke, "Chronologie des rois de Juda et d'Israël," "Chronique biblique." Thiele eventually discovered Couke's work. See *Mysterious Numbers*, 59, note 17.

[187] This is because Thiele first worked out a relative chronology of the kings using the biblical data and only then checked to see if it fit the extra-biblical data. He did not attempt to fit the biblical data to absolute (BC) dates until after he had worked out the relative chronology based solely on biblical data. See Strand, "Thiele's Biblical Chronology as a Corrective for Extrabiblical Dates," esp. 314–315.

[188] See *Mysterious Numbers*, 221–225.

Assyrian sources is largely responsible for the fact that 853 BC is now commonly accepted as the date for the Battle of Qarqar.

In another instance Thiele predicted that when the full text of the extant portions of the Iran Stele of the Assyrian king Tiglath-Pileser III was published, it would reveal that the date favored by most Assyriologists for Menahem's tribute to Tiglath-Pileser, 738 BC, was based on an improper interpretation of the previously-deciphered text dealing with that tribute. In 1994, eight years after Thiele's death, Hayim Tadmor published the full text of the Iran Stele, verifying Thiele's conjecture that the texts listing Menahem's tribute were summary lists, and hence could not be used to establish 738 BC as the time of the tribute.[189] These texts, however, when compared with the activities described for Tiglath-Pileser in the Assyrian Eponym Canon, are consistent with Thiele's date of 743 or 742 BC for the tribute.[190]

The dates from extra-biblical sources that relate to the kings of Israel and Judah are important. They serve as a cross-check on any proposed chronology for the divided kingdom, and Thiele's chronology was able to satisfy all of them. These dates are:

Table 30
Extra-Biblical Synchronizations: Israel and Judah

853	The Battle of Qarqar (Ahab king)[191]
841	Jehu's tribute to Shalmaneser III[192]

---

[189] Tadmor, *The Inscriptions of Tiglath-Pileser III, King of Assyria*, 260–264.
[190] For further discussion see Mitchell, "Israel and Judah from the Coming of Assyrian Domination," 326, and Young, "Inductive and Deductive Methods," 113–115, where the significance of the Iran Stele in negating Tadmor's dates for Menahem's tribute is discussed in detail.
[191] From the Monolith Inscription of Shalmaneser (*ANET* 278–279). Shalmaneser lists "Ahab the Israelite" as one of his opponents at the battle. The battle took place in Shamaneser's sixth year.

743	Azariah's tribute to Tiglath-Pileser III[193]
731	Hoshea's tribute to Tiglath-Pileser III[194]
723	Samaria falls to Shalmaneser V (Hoshea king)[195]
Tammuz 609	Egyptians and Assyrians defeated at Haran (Josiah's death)
605	Nebuchadnezzar captures Jerusalem (1st time) (Jehoiakim king)
597	Nebuchadnezzar captures Jerusalem (2nd time) (Zedekiah made king)[196]

---

[192] From the inscription on the Black Obelisk of Shalmaneser III. The tribute was paid in Shalmaneser's eighteenth year (*ANET* 281). McCarter has argued that Joram, not Jehu, is the Israelite king in the inscription, but his suggestion has found little support (McCarter, "Yaw, Son of 'Omri').

[193] *ANET* 282. It was the third year (by non-accession reckoning) of Tiglath-pileser.

[194] Na'aman, "Historical and Chronological Notes on the Kingdoms of Israel and Judah in the Eighth Century B.C."

[195] Some chronologies propose that Samaria fell in 722 to Sargon II, since Sargon claims to have conquered Samaria in some of his late inscriptions. However, Assyrian records record no campaign of Sargon in the west in 722 or 721 BC (Tadmor, "The Campaigns of Sargon II of Assur," 38). Most likely Sargon was glorifying his reign by taking credit for the accomplishments of his predecessor. See the discussion in Finegan, *Handbook of Biblical Chronology*, 250–251, §426. Also note the thorough discussion of the matter in Young, "When Was Samaria Captured?", 583.

[196] BM 21946. See the summary of the contents of this tablet in Wiseman, *Chronicles of the Chaldaean Kings*, 48. See also the discussion in Finegan, *Handbook of Biblical Chronology*, 256, §437.

MODIFICATIONS TO THIELE'S CHRONOLOGY

Thiele handled the biblical material in a more consistent manner than did Coucke. As a result, Thiele's completed system required fewer emendations of the biblical text than did Coucke's. Eventually even these emendations were found unnecessary by those who built upon Thiele's work.

The most important correction to Thiele's work was in the chronology of Hezekiah's reign. Several scholars indicated that Thiele's problems with the years of Hezekiah could be solved by positing a coregency of Hezekiah with his father Ahaz, similar to the coregencies that Thiele derived from the biblical texts for the three generations before Ahaz and the next generation after Hezekiah.[197] By making this correction, Leslie McFall was able to work through the biblical data and produce a chronology that accounted for all the biblical texts and was consistent with several fixed dates from Assyrian and Babylonian history.[198]

Another important correction to Thiele's system was made by Rodger C. Young.[199] Thiele established that the divided monarchy began sometime in 931n. Thiele, without explanation, assumed that Solomon died in the latter half of this year—between the beginning of Tishri 931 BC and the end of Adar 930 BC. This assumption led to a one-year discrepancy in Thiele's chronology. When Thiele realized this, he attempted to fix this problem by making a one year

---

[197] Horn, "The Chronology of King Hezekiah's Reign"; Kitchen and Mitchell, "Chronology of the Old Testament," 217; McFall, "A Translation Guide to the Chronological Data in Kings and Chronicles," "Some Missing Coregencies in Thiele's Chronology," and "Did Thiele Overlook Hezekiah's Coregency?" Numerous reviewers of Thiele's *Mysterious Numbers* also noted that his suggested emendations for Hezekiah's reign were unnecessary if Hezekiah served a coregency period with his father Ahaz.
[198] McFall, "A Translation Guide to the Chronological Data in Kings and Chronicles."
[199] Young, "When Did Solomon Die?"

adjustment in his chronology for the reigns of Jehoshaphat through Athaliah.[200] However, Young demonstrated that Thiele's assumption was incorrect. Solomon died some time before the latter half of 931n (i.e., before Tishri 1 of 931 BC), but after Tishri 1 of 932 BC, so that his final year was 932t, not 931t as assumed by Thiele. This correction leads to moving the starting year for Athaliah and all the kings who preceded her in Judah back one year from those given in Thiele's chronology.

Those who have proposed chronologies for the reigns of the kings of Judah and Israel since the work of Thiele have tended to stray only in a few details from Thiele's chronology. These include the chronologies of Galil, Kitchen and Mitchell, McFall and Young.[201]

CHRONOLOGIES THAT REJECT THIELE'S WORK

Occasionally biblical scholars will propose chronologies that deny some of the observations made by Thiele. Examples of these are the chronologies proposed by Hayes and Hooker or Tetley.[202] These invariably prove to be unworkable given the requirements both of the biblical text and of extra-biblical sources.

Hayes and Hooker's chronology denies the existence of coregencies and proposes that Israel reckoned its years beginning with the month of Marcheshvan. It has numerous flaws including dating the end of Solomon's reign to 926 BC (see the discussion of

---

[200] Compare the chart in *Mysterious Numbers*, 101 which indicates the beginning of Athaliah's reign at 841t with the statement in *Mysterious Numbers*, 104 which puts the beginning of her reign in 842t. See also the discussion in Young, "When Did Solomon Die?" 589–599, especially note 10.

[201] Galil, *The Chronology of the Kings of Israel and Judah*; Kitchen and Mitchell, "Chronology of the Old Testament"; McFall, "A Translation Guide to the Chronological Data in Kings and Chronicles" and "Has the Chronology of the Hebrew Kings been finally settled?"; Young, "Tables of Reign Length from the Hebrew Court Recorders."

[202] E.g., Hayes and Hooker, *A New Chronology for the Kings of Israel and Judah*; Tetley, *The Reconstructed Chronology of the Divided Kingdom*.

Solomon's reign beginning on page 37).[203] Moreover, it clearly misdates Jehu's reign. According to Assyrian sources Jehu paid tribute to Shalmaneser III in 841 BC. However, according to the Hayes and Hooker chronology Jehu did not begin to reign until two years later in 839 BC. Also, it is clear from the biblical sources that Josiah died in battle at Megiddo against Egyptian forces that shortly thereafter were defeated by the Babylonians at Haran in Tammuz 609 BC. This makes Tammuz 609 BC the date of Josiah's death. According to Hayes and Hooker, Josiah died before Nisan 609 BC.

Tetley's chronology not only denies that there were any coregencies and radically redates the end of Solomon's reign, but it also substitutes questionable data from LXX when it conflicts with the Masoretic text. In addition, she proposes a radical realignment of well-established extra-biblical dates from Assyria and Egypt in order to make her system work. Reviews of Tetley's book have been almost uniformly negative.[204]

DECIDING AMONG COMPETING CHRONOLOGIES

Given that Thiele's work was basically correct, but had to be modified at several key points, which of the other major proposals that modify Thiele's chronology is to be preferred?[205] Let us examine two crucial dates that will allow us to determine which proposal

---

[203] The same flaw exists in the chronology proposed by Miller, "Another Look at the Chronology of the Early Divided Monarchy," 288.

[204] Stephen L. McKenzie, *JHS* [http://www.arts.ualberta.ca/cocoon/JHS/r209.html] (2005); Jennifer Singletary, *RBL* [http://www.bookreviews.org] (2005); Andrew Steinmann, *RBL* [http://www.bookreviews.org] (2005); Angelika Berlejung, *ZAW* 118 (2006): 319; Gershon Galil, *CBQ* 68 (2006): 131–133; Paul J. Kissling, *JBL* 50 (2007):177–179; David T. Lamb, *JSOT* 30 (2006): 50–51; Leslie McFall, *VT* 57 (2007): 575–575; Rodger C. Young, *AUSS* 45 (2007): 278–283; Ralph W. Klein, *JNES* 67 (2008): 221.

[205] The four major competing theories are those of Galil, Kitchen and Mitchell, McFall, and Young.

meets all the requirements, satisfying both the biblical data and the extra-biblical synchronizations.

The first date is the fall of Samaria. Some chronologies place the end of Hoshea's reign with Samaria's fall to the Assyrian king Shalmaneser V in 723 BC. Others place Samaria's fall a year later in 722 BC when Sargon II had become the Assyrian king. However, Assyrian records record no campaign of Sargon in the west in 722 or 721 BC, effectively ruling out 722 BC as the date of Samaria's fall.[206] Moreover, Young has produced a thorough study of the biblical data that demonstrates that the only date for the fall of Samaria that accounts for all the biblical references is 723 BC.[207] Since the chronologies of Galil and of Kitchen and Mitchell place the fall of Samaria in 722 BC, they can be eliminated.

The second date is the third fall of Jerusalem to Nebuchadnezzar. Some chronologies date this to 9 Tammuz 587 BC, while others date it a year later to 9 Tammuz 586 BC. There are several sources of biblical data relating to the fall of Jerusalem: 2 Kgs 25:1–3; 2 Chr 36:17–20; Jer 1:3; 52:3–27 and Ezek 24:1; 40:1. While the analysis of these texts is complicated, it should be noted that the only way all of them can be brought into harmony with each other is if Jerusalem fell in 587 BC.[208] Most importantly, the information supplied in Ezek 26:1–2 undercuts the theory of those who hold that Jerusalem fell in 586 BC.[209]

---

[206] Tadmor, "The Campaigns of Sargon II of Assur," 38.

[207] Young, "When Was Samaria Captured?"

[208] For the complete analysis that leads to this conclusion see Young, "When Did Jerusalem Fall?" and "Ezekiel 40:1 as a Corrective for Seven Wrong Ideas in Biblical Interpretation." See also the discussion of the summer of 587 BC as occurring during a Sabbatical year (page 150 below).

[209] The significance of these verses was brought to my attention by Rodger Young (private correspondence).

וַיְהִי בְּעַשְׁתֵּי־עֶשְׂרֵה שָׁנָה בְּאֶחָד לַחֹדֶשׁ הָיָה דְבַר־יְהוָה אֵלַי
לֵאמֹר: בֶּן־אָדָם יַעַן אֲשֶׁר־אָמְרָה צֹּר עַל־יְרוּשָׁלַ͏ִם הֶאָח נִשְׁבְּרָה
דַּלְתוֹת הָעַמִּים נָסֵבָּה אֵלָי אִמָּלְאָה הָחֳרָבָה:

In the eleventh year on the first day of the month, the word of
Yahweh came to me, "Son of Man, because Tyre has said
about Jerusalem, 'Aha! The gate of the peoples is broken. It
has been opened to me. I will be filled. It has been laid
waste.'. . . " (Ezek 26:1–2)

This oracle about Tyre's gloating over Jerusalem's fall came to
Ezekiel in the eleventh year of his exile on the first day of an
unspecified month. Since Tyre's schadenfreude could only have been
expressed *after* the fall of Jerusalem and it had been "laid waste,"
Ezekiel's oracle must have been delivered after 9 Tammuz 586 BC
(July 18) according to the chronologies that hold that Jerusalem fell in
586 BC. But the captivity of Ezekiel and Jehoiachin started in Adar of
597 BC according to Babylonian records (cf. 2 Kgs 24:10–12; 2 Chr
36:9, 10), so that the eleventh year of exile would be 588t (Tishri
reckoning) or 588n (Nisan reckoning), and with either reckoning the
year would have expired before Tammuz of 586 BC. Even Thiele's
device of using Nisan years and starting the first year of captivity one
month later, in Nisan of 597 BC, so that the eleventh year was 587n,
will not solve this. Galil attempted to resolve a similar problem with
Ezek 24:1 (he does not discuss 26:1–2) by holding that at times
without notice to the reader, Ezekiel switches from reckoning years
from his exile to years of the reign of Zedekiah. This allows Galil to
reconcile Ezek 24:1 (and, by inference, 26:1–2) with a supposed fall
of Jerusalem in 586 BC.[210] All chronologies that place the fall of

---

[210] Galil, "Chonronolgy of the Last Kings of Judah," 370. (See also Thiele,
Mysterious Numbers, 189, who makes this assumption without explanation.)
Such a procedure smacks of special pleading, however. On the other hand if
one simply understands Ezekiel as always reckoning his dates from his exile
using Tishri years, his dates always reconcile with a 587 BC date for the fall
of Jerusalem without resorting to some questionable scheme such as Galil's
attempt to make the dates harmonize.

Jerusalem in 586 BC must resort to artificial schemes such as this in order to reconcile Ezek 24:1 and 26:1, whereas no such strained exegesis is necessary when the correct date of 587 BC is given for Jerusalem's fall. Thus, the chronologies of Galil and McFall and others that date the fall of Jerusalem to 586 BC can be eliminated.[211]

Therefore, the only chronology that satisfies all of the biblical and extra-biblical data is that of Young.[212] His chronology of the kings of Judah and Israel is given in the tables on the following pages.[213]

READING THE TABLES: THE KINGS OF JUDAH AND ISRAEL

> Years ending in "n" indicate a calendar year beginning in the month of Nisan. Years ending in "t" indicate a calendar year beginning in the month of Tishri.

> A six-month span is indicated by two dates separated by a slash (e.g., 914n/914t = the six months from the beginning of Nisan to the beginning of Tishri in 914 BC).

---

[211] Galil's chronology has other difficulties which make it difficult to sustain, especially his rejection of Judah's use of Tishri-based years in favor of holding that both Judah used Nisan-based years in clear contradiction of 2 Kgs 22:3; 23:23. See the review of Galil by McFall, *VT* 49 (1999): 572–74. Moreover, Galil admits that his dating for Jerusalem's fall does not agree with the release of Jehoiachin by Amel-Marduk, and he attempts to explain this as only an approximation by the biblical author (2 Kgs 25:27; Jer 52:31; Galil, "The Babylonian Calendar and the Chronology of the Last Kings of Judah," 377).

[212] To be fair it should be noted that Young's chronology is simply a modification of Thiele's chronology and incorporates McFall's observations about Hezekiah's coregencies.

[213] From Young, "Tables of the Reign Lengths from the Hebrew Court Recorders," 245–248. For how individual reigns, coregencies, rival reigns, reckoning of reigns and other such matters are determined see Thiele, *Mysterious Numbers* and Young, "When Did Jerusalem Fall?"; "When Was Samaria Captured?"

When non-accession reckoning was used in the biblical text, the total years of reign are given twice. The number in parentheses is the number used in formulas when calculating spans of time.

Dates in the tables are given according to the Hebrew calendar. When the month and day are known, the dates can be converted to Julian calendar dates if they occur after April 5, 626 BC.[214] For *Table 31* the dates are:

> 21 Marcheshvan 598 is Saturday, 9 December 598 BC.[215]
>
> 2 Adar 597 is Saturday, 16 March 597 BC.
>
> 9 Tammuz 587 is Saturday, 29 July 587 BC.

Table 31: The end of Jotham's reign at (735n/735t) 732t—Jotham's sixteen (fifteen) years ended when his son Ahaz was installed by the pro-Assyrian faction in Judah, in 735n/735t, although some considered him the rightful ruler until his death in 732t, thus giving him the twenty years mentioned in 2 Kgs 15:30.

Table 32: The reign of Shallum—In the second edition of *Mysterious Numbers*, pp. 87–88, Thiele worked carefully through the scriptural data for the five kings of the northern kingdom, Jeroboam II through Pekahiah. For each of these kings there is a synchronism with the long reign of Uzziah. By recognizing that Uzziah's reign was reckoned according to Judah's Tishri-based year while the northern kingdom observed a Nisan-based year for its kings, what otherwise

---

[214] Using the tables in Parker and Dubberstein, *Babylonian Chronology 626 B.C–A.D.75*

[215] Days of the week can be determined using the U.S. Naval Observatory Julian Date Converter at http://aa.usno.navy.mil/data/docs/JulianDate.php. The remainder after dividing the Julian date minus 0.5 by seven is the number of days of the week after Tuesday.

seem to be occasional discordances in the synchronisms all fall into place. This six-month difference in when the year began then proved to be a useful aid in determining the half-year in which some of these kings terminated their reign, and in the cases of Jeroboam II through Shallum, the actual month of the king's death could be determined. Thus the scriptural data showed that Shallum began to reign in Adar of 752 BC, and his one-month reign ended in Nisan of the same BC year. During that time a new regnal year for Israel began on the first of Nisan. This is why his one-month reign is shown as occurring in 753n–752n in Table 32. Thiele's logic in all this is impeccable. The basic data that allowed this kind of precision in dating could never have been provided by a late-date editor; the data must have come from contemporary accounts, most probably from the official court records of these two kingdoms. Apparently Thiele eventually judged that the derivation of these precise dates was too complicated for the average or even the scholarly reader, so he omitted this discussion in the third edition of *Mysterious Numbers*, providing only less precise dates for these kings. For a presentation of this basic logic in a different format, thus preserving the precision, see Young, "When Was Samaria Captured?" pp. 583–584.

Table 31
Reigns of the Kings of Judah

King	Began Coregency	Began Sole Reign	End of Reign	Official Reign	Total Years
Rehoboam		932t	914n/914t	932t–915t	17
Abijah		914n/914t	912t/911n	915t-912t	3
Asa		912t/911n	871t/870n	912t–871t	41
Jehoshaphat	873t	871t/870n	848n/848t	873t–849t	25 (24)
Jehoram	854t	848n/848t	841n/841t	849t–842t	8 (7)
Ahaziah		841n/841t	841n/841t	842t	1 (0)
Athaliah		841n/841t	835n/835t	842t–836t	7 (6)
Joash		835n/835t	796n/796t	836t–797t	40 (39)
Amaziah		796n/796t	767n/767t	797t–768t	29
Uzziah	791t	767n/767t	740t	791t–740t	52 (51)
Jotham	750n/750t	740t	(735n/735t) 732t	751t–736t	16 (15)
Ahaz	735n/735t	732t	716t/715n	732t–716t	16
Hezekiah	729t/728n	716t/715n	687t	716t–687t	29
Manasseh	697t	687t	643t	697t–643t	55 (54)
Amon		643t	641t	643t–641t	2
Josiah		641t	Tammuz 609	641t–610t	31
Jehoahaz		Tammuz 609	Tishri 609	610t–609t	3 months
Jehoiakim		Tishri 609	21 Marcheshvan 598	609t–598t	11
Jehoiachin		21 Marcheshvan 598	2 Adar 597	598t	3 months 10 day
Zedekiah		2 Adar 597	9 Tammuz 587	598t–588t	11 (10)

Table 32
Reigns of the Kings of Israel

King	Overlapping Reign	Began Sole Reign	End of Reign	Official Reign	Total Years
Jeroboam I		931n	910t/909n	931n–910n	22 (21)
Nadab		910t/909n	909t/908n	910n–909n	2 (1)
Baasha		909t/908n	886t/885n	909n–886n	24 (23)
Elah		886t/885n	885t/884n	886n–885n	2 (1)
Zimri		885t/884n	885t/884n	885n	7 days
Tibni		885t/884n	880n/880t	885n–880n	
Omri	885t/884n	880n/880t	874t/873n	885n–874n	12 (11)
Ahab		874t/873n	853n/853t	874n–853n	22 (21)
Ahaziah		853n/853t	852n/852t	853n–852n	2 (1)
Joram		852n/852t	841n/841t	852n–841n	12 (11)
Jehu		841n/841t	814t/813n	841n–814n	28 (27)
Jehoahaz		814t/813n	798n/798t	814n–798n	17 (16)
Jehoash		798n/798t	782t/781n	798n–782n	16
Jeroboam II	793n	782t/781n	Elul 753	793n–753n	41 (40)
Zechariah		Elul 753	Adar 752	753n	6 months
Shallum		Adar 752	Nisan 752	753n–752n	1 month
Menahem		Nisan 752	742t/741n	752n–742n	10
Pekahiah		742t/741n	740t/739n	742n–740n	2
Pekah	Nisan 752	740t/739n	732t/731n	752n–732n	20
Hoshea		732t/731n	723n/723t	732n–723n	9

Table 33
Synchronisms: Israel to Judah

Reference	King	Began	in	Date
1 Kgs 15:25	Nadab	sole reign	2 Asa	910t/909n
1 Kgs 15:28, 33	Baasha	sole reign	3 Asa	909t/908n
1 Kgs 16:8	Elah	sole reign	26 Asa	886t/885n
1 Kgs 16:10,15	Zimri	sole reign	27 Asa	885t/884n
1 Kgs 16:21–23	Omri	sole reign	31 Asa	880n/880t
1 Kgs 16:29	Ahab	sole reign	38 Asa	874t/873n
1 Kgs 22:51	Ahaziah	sole reign	17 Jehoshaphat	853n/853t
2 Kgs 3:1	Joram	sole reign	18 Jehoshaphat	852n/852t
2 Kgs 1:17	Joram	sole reign	2 (1) Jehoram	852n/852t
2 Kgs 9‖2 Chr 22	Jehu	same time as	Athaliah	841n/841t
2 Kgs 13:1	Jehoahaz	sole reign	23 (22) Joash	814t/813n
2 Kgs 13:10	Jehoash	sole reign	37 Joash	798n/798t
2 Kgs 14:23	Jeroboam II	sole reign	15 Amaziah	782t/781n
2 Kgs 15:8	Zechariah	sole reign	38 (37) Uzziah	Elul 753
2 Kgs 15:13	Shallum	sole reign	39 (38) Uzziah	Adar 752
2 Kgs 15:17	Menahem	rival reign	39 (38) Uzziah	Nisan 752
2 Kgs 15:23	Pekahiah	rival reign	50 (49) Uzziah	742t/741n
2 Kgs 15:27	Pekah	sole reign	52 (51) Uzziah	740t/739n
2 Kgs 15:30	Hoshea	sole reign	20 (19) Jotham	732t/731n
2 Kgs 17:1	Hoshea	ended	12 Ahaz	723n/723t

By comparing column 4 in this table with Table 31 it can be seen that the scribes of ancient Israel always employed an official starting year from Judah (a Tishri year) for determining synchronisms.

Table 34
Synchronisms: Judah to Israel

Reference	King	Began	in	Date
1 Kgs 15:1‖2 Chr 13:1	Abijah	sole reign	18 (17) Jeroboam	914n/914t
1 Kgs 15:9	Asa	sole reign	20 (19) Jeroboam	912t/911n
1 Kgs 22:41	Jehoshaphat	sole reign	4 (3) Ahab	871t/870n
2 Kgs 8:16	Jehoram	sole reign	5 (4) Joram	848n/848t
2 Kgs 8:25	Ahaziah	sole reign	12 (11) Joram	841n/841t
2 Kgs 9:29	Ahaziah	sole reign	11 Joram	841n/841t
2 Kgs 9‖2 Chr 22	Athaliah	same time as	Jehu	841n/841t
2 Kgs 12:1	Joash	sole reign	7 (6) Jehu	835n/835t
2 Kgs 14:1	Amaziah	sole reign	2 Jehoash	796n/796t
2 Kgs 15:1	Uzziah	sole reign	27 (26) Jeroboam	767n/767t
2 Kgs 15:32	Jotham	coregency	2 Pekah	750n/750t
2 Kgs 16:1	Ahaz	coregency	17 Pekah	735n/735t
2 Kgs 18:1	Hezekiah	coregency	3 Hoshea	729t/728n
2 Kgs 18:9	Hezekiah 4 (3) = Hoshea 7			725n/725t
2 Kgs 18:10	Hezekiah 6 (5) = Hoshea 9			723n/723t
2 Kgs 14:17‖2 Chr 25:25	Amaziah outlived Jehoash 15 years			767n/767t

By comparing column 4 in this table with Table 32 it can be seen that the
scribes of ancient Judah always employed an official starting year from Israel
(a Nisan year) for determining synchronisms.

Birth Date and Ages of the Kings of Judah

Using the information from Table 31 as well as biblical information for the ages for the kings of Judah when they began to reign, it is possible to calculate a range of dates for their birth and other information. If a king acceded to the throne when he was 25 years old, he may in fact have been almost 26 years old. However, since his accession was before his twenty-sixth birthday, he is said to be 25 years old. Thus, a king who was 25 years old in 900t could have been born as late as 1 Tishri 925t or as early as 2 Tishri 926t. The date for his birth in Table 35 would then be listed as 926t–925t.

The month or exact day in which the last four kings of Judah began their reign is known. In Table 35 their birth dates are listed as a span from the exact month of the two possible years in which they were born.

In addition, the ages for the kings who served coregencies given for the kings of Judah in Kings and Chronicles may be either from the beginning of their coregency or from their sole reign and must be determined from a careful analysis of the biblical data. Such analysis reveals that some of the kings (e.g., Hezekiah) would have been too young at their accession as coregent to father a child. In Table 35 the age given in the biblical text for a king at his accession is in bold italics. Calculated ages are in standard type. When no firm determination can be made as to whether a king's age is given from his coregency or his sole reign (Jehoshaphat and Jehoram), both possibilities are listed.

Two scribal errors in the transmission of the text of 2 Chronicles should be noted. 2 Chr 22:2 says that Ahaziah was 42 years old at the beginning of his reign.[216] If this were so, Ahaziah would have had to have been born before his father. 2 Kgs 8:26 preserves the correct

---

[216] Many English translations disregard the MT of 2 Chr 22:2 and read "22 years old" instead, following the correct figure given in 2 Kgs 8:26.

figure: 22 years old. 2 Chr 36:9 says that Jehoiachin was eight years old when he was placed on the throne by Nebuchadnezzar.[217] The correct figure is 18 years old as preserved in 2 Kgs 24:8, as indicated by the fact that he had wives who were taken with him into captivity (2 Kgs 24:15).

---

[217] Many English translations disregard the MT of 2 Chr 36:9 and read "18 years old" instead, following the correct figure given in 2 Kgs 24:8.

Table 35
Birth and Ages of the Kings of Judah

King	Birth	Age at Accession as Coregent	Age at Beginning of Sole Reign	Age at Birth of Successor	Age at Accession of Son as Coregent	Age at Death
Rehoboam	974t–973t		*41*			59
Abijah						
Asa						
Jehoshaphat	909t–908t	*35*	37–38	21–23 or 27–29	52	59
	907t–905n	32–33	*35*	18–21 or 24–27	50	57
Jehoram	887t–886t	*32*	39	21–24		46
	881n–880t	24–25	*32*	16–18		39
Ahaziah	864n–863t		*22*	19–22		22
Athaliah						
Joash	843n–842t		*7*	18–21		46
Amaziah	823n–822t		*25*	13–16	31	54
Uzziah	808n–807t	*16*	39–40	30–33	57–58	67
Jotham	776n–775t	*25*	35–36	18–21	40–41	43
Ahaz	756n–755t	*20*	23–24	13–16	26–28	39
Hezekiah	742t–740n	12–13	*25*	30–33	44–45	54
Manasseh	710t–709t	*12*	22	43–45		66
Amon	666t–665t		*22*	15–17		24
Josiah	650t–649t		*8*	15–17/14–16/30–32		39
Jehoahaz	Tam. 633–Tam.632		*23*			
Jehoiakim	Tish. 635–Tish. 634		*25*	17–19		36
Jehoiachin	Mar. 617–Mar. 616		*18*			Over 55
Zedekiah	Adar 619–Adar 618		*21*			

As can be seen from Table 35, there was a general trend of encouraging young princes to produce offspring, with many of the kings having been born when their father was in his mid-teens.[218] This probably resulted from kings arranging a marriage for their sons at an early age to ensure that there would be heirs to the throne.

It is also not surprising to find that the average age of a king when his son was made coregent was 40 years old. The kings lived only to an average age of 47. Should a reigning king become infirm or there be another threat to his life or wellbeing, it would have been seen as prudent to install one of his sons to ensure a smooth succession.

Judah proved to be a remarkably stable kingdom for most of its history. The average reign for the kings from Rehoboam to Josiah was 20 years. In contrast, the average reign for the kings of Israel (excluding the abortive reign of Tibni) was only 11 years.

CELEBRATION OF SABBATICAL AND JUBILEE YEARS

We have already seen that 623t, the eighteenth year of Josiah, was a Jubilee year (see discussion beginning on pages 48–54). We have also argued that Jubilee years were concurrent with Sabbatical years (see the discussion beginning on page 30). In addition, we argued that Jubilee years occurred 49 years apart, since they were celebrated concurrently with every seventh Sabbatical year. This is confirmed in that the eighteenth year of Josiah (623t) and the twenty-fifth year of the Babylonian exile (574t; Ezek 40:1) were both Sabbatical years and were exactly 49 years apart (see the discussion on pages 48–54).

One test of whether the chronology of the kings of Judah as set forth in Table 31 is correct is whether the Sabbatical years observed during the reigns of Judah's kings fall in multiples of seven years from the Jubilee years 623t or 574t. While there are no events in the

---

[218] While in a couple of instances it was theoretically possible that a successor was born when his father was as young as 13 years of age, this is hardly likely. It is more probable that the successor was born at the later end of the range of years in those cases.

Old Testament that explicitly call a specific year a Sabbatical year, there are indications of three Sabbatical years celebrated under three different kings.

The first Sabbatical year mentioned was during Jehoshaphat's third year, 868t.[219] He sent officers throughout Judah to teach the Torah (2 Chr 17:7–9). Public reading and teaching of the Torah was a requirement in each Sabbatical year (Deut 31:10–13). Thus, it is very probable that 868t was a Sabbatical year, and a simple calculation demonstrates that it did occur in a multiple of seven years from 623t or 574t:

868t – 623t = 245 = 7 x 35

868t – 574t = 294 = 7 x 42

The second Sabbatical year mentioned was referenced by Isaiah in a prophecy during Sennacherib's siege of Jerusalem in the summer and fall of 701 BC.[220] The siege took place in Hezekiah's fourteenth year, 702t (2 Kgs 18:13; Isa 36:1). During that siege the prophet Isaiah came to Hezekiah with a promise that God would break the siege. He gave Hezekiah this word from God:

> And this shall be the sign for you: this year eat what grows on its own, and in the second year what springs from that. Then in the third year sow and reap and plant vineyards, and eat their fruit. (2 Kgs 19:29; cf. Isa 37:30)

Isaiah told Hezekiah that there would be two fallow years. The first one (701t, Hezekiah's fifteenth year) would begin in the autumn of that same year, and there would be no harvest because the Assyrian invasion prevented the people of Judah from planting crops. However, the second year would also be fallow—but not because of the Assyrians. By late autumn or early winter of 700 BC the Assyrians had been defeated by God and retreated from Judah. Instead, 700t (Hezekiah's sixteenth year) would be a second consecutive year when

---

[219] Reckoned from the beginning of his sole reign in 871t.
[220] *ANET* 288.

the land was left fallow—implying that the land would be left fallow for a different reason. That reason could only be because 700t was to be a Sabbatical year. Once again a simple calculation confirms this:

$$700t - 623t = 77 = 7 \times 11$$

$$700t - 574t = 126 = 7 \times 18$$

The third year was 588t when Zedekiah ordered the release of Hebrew slaves (Jer 34:8–10), one of the customs associated with Sabbatical years. Nahum Sarna has demonstrated that this was indeed a Sabbatical year.[221] Calculation once again confirms this:

$$623t - 588t = 35 = 7 \times 5$$

$$588t - 574t = 14 = 7 \times 2$$

Thus, the evidence of Sabbatical years confirms the chronology of the reign of Judah's kings in Table 31 (and, therefore, also the interlocked chronology of Israel's kings in *Table 32*).[222]

Finally, we should note that there is also a strong ancient Jewish tradition (i.e., Jewish historical remembrance) that the temple in Jerusalem was destroyed by the Babylonians in the month of Av (Jer 52:12) during the latter part of a Sabbatical year.[223] Since 588t was a

---

[221] Sarna, "Zedekiah's Emancipation of Slaves and the Sabbatical Year."

[222] It should be noted the chronology in *Table 31* is basically that of Thiele with a few corrections. In fact, Thiele's chronology and others based on it (e.g., Galil, Kitchen and Mitchell, McFall) also correctly fit the chronological requirements of these sabbatical years, except for the sabbatical year in the time of Jehoshaphat. McFall's latest chronology, however, now agrees with the chronology presented here for Jehoshaphat and the first kings of Judah, contra his earlier chronology (McFall, "Do the Sixty-nine Weeks of Daniel Date the Messianic Mission of Nehemiah or Jesus?" 695, n. 58). These other chronologies based on Thiele are less accurate, however, in that they incorrectly date either the fall of Samaria or the fall of Jerusalem or both.

[223] *S. 'Olam Rab.* 30; *t. Ta'an.* 3.9; *b. 'Arak.* 11b–12a; *b. Ta'an* 29a; *y. Ta'an* 4.5; see Young, "*Seder Olam* and the Sabbaticals Associated with the Two Destructions of Jerusalem: Part 1," 176–178.

Sabbatical year, Av 587 BC (which occurred at the end of 588t) is the correct date of the fall of Jerusalem (see the discussion above on page 136).

DATED EVENTS DURING THE DIVIDED MONARCHY

Apart from the information about the kings and their regnal years, the books of Kings and Chronicles and several prophetic books—Isaiah, Jeremiah, Ezekiel and Daniel—contain information that allows us to date quite a few events during this period. Any prophecy that gives information that is datable to a particular year will be treated below.

However, a number of prophets date their prophecies by noting which king was reigning at the time but without giving any specific information that would allow us to date their prophecies to particular years. For instance, Amos 1:1 tells us that Amos prophesied during the reigns of Uzziah (791t–740t; official sole reign 768t–740t) and Jeroboam II (793n–753n). If we assume that Amos meant that Uzziah was on the throne after his coregency period with Amaziah, we are still left with a range of more than a decade: 768t–753n. Amos' notice that his prophecy came two years before an earthquake is of little help in narrowing the date of his prophecies to a specific year, since we do not know the date of the earthquake. Because we cannot date prophets who give similar notices to a particular year, the dates of their prophecies will not be treated below.

In the discussions below it is often possible to categorize the events as falling during the reign of either a king of Israel or a king of Judah. For the sake of simplicity, the dates will be coordinated only with one king—the monarch whose reign is under discussion when a particular event is related in the books of Kings or Chronicles.

REHOBOAM OF JUDAH (932T–915T)

According to 1 Kgs 14:25||2 Chr 12:2, Pharaoh Shishak's (Shoshenq I) invasion of Judah took place in Rehoboam's fifth year (927t), probably during the spring or summer of 926 BC. Shemaiah's prophecies (2 Chr 12:5–8) also were delivered at this time.

ASA OF JUDAH (912T–871T)

Quite a few events are datable during Asa's reign. The first is the prophecy of Azariah (2 Chr 15:1–7), which took place early in the fifteenth year of Asa's reign (897t), probably in Tishri or Marcheshvan. Later in that same regnal year, in Sivan 896 BC, Asa and Judah entered into a new covenant with Yahweh (2 Chr 15:9–15; cf. 15:10). In this year he also removed his mother Maacah from her position as queen mother.

Since during Sivan 896 the spoils of war captured from Zerah the Cushite were sacrificed in Jerusalem, Zerah's invasion of Judah must have taken place earlier in the spring of 896 BC (2 Chr 14:9–15). This, in turn, means that the ten years of rest for the land during Asa's days had lasted from 905–896 BC (2 Chr 14:2).

After the invasion by Zerah, Baasha of Israel (909n–886n) began to fortify Ramah (2 Chr 16:1). This happened in 896t, probably in the fall (after 1 Tishri) of 896 BC (2 Chr 16:1). 2 Chr 16:1 calls this the thirty-sixth year of Asa, which appears to be a mistake, since Baasha died in Asa's twenty-sixth year (1 Kgs 16:8). By Asa's thirty-sixth year Omri (885n–874n) occupied Israel's throne. The solution, however, is that this was Asa's thirty-sixth year by dynastic reckoning in Judah. That is, the separate kingdom of Judah came into being with Asa's grandfather Rehoboam in 932t. Reckoning dynastically, the thirty-sixth year of the dynasty that Asa represented was 896t (932t − 36 = 896t). [224] In keeping with this, when 2 Chr 15:19 says that there

---

[224] Thiele recognized that 2 Chr 15:19 and 2 Chr 16:1 used dynastic reckoning (*Mysterious Numbers*, 84). However, he attributed the reference to Asa as a mistake by the Chronicler instead of recognizing that is was simply another method of reckoning a king's regnal years. The interpretation that the thirty-fifth year of 2 Kgs 15:19 and the thirty-sixth year of 2 Kgs 16:1 are to be reckoned from the division of the kingdom is at least as old as the second century AD (*Seder 'Olam*, 16).

was "no war" (not "no more war") until the thirty-fifth year, this refers to 897t, the year in which Zerah invaded the land and was defeated. Therefore, the statement that ends the period of peace in the "thirty-fifth year" (dynastic reckoning) of 2 Chr 15:19 agrees with the dating of the invasion of Zerah to the "fifteenth year" of Asa's reign (2 Chr 14:9–15:10). Both specify the year 897t. The agreement between these two methods of delineating when the ten years of peace came to an end reinforces the plausibility of the interpretation of 2 Chr 15:19 and 2 Chr 16:1 advocated here.

After Baasha began to fortify Ramah (2 Chr 16:1), Asa made a treaty with Aram (2 Chr 16:2–3), Ben-hadad of Aram attacked Israel (2 Chr 16:4–5), and Asa fortified Geba and Mizpah (2 Chr 14:6). That same year Hanani prophesied against Asa, who had the prophet imprisoned (2 Chr 15:7–10).

In Asa's thirty-ninth year, 873t, he developed a foot disease (2 Chr 16:11). This reference to Asa's thirty-ninth year is probably not by dynastic reckoning but by reckoning according to Asa's own reign, since his son Jehoshaphat was made coregent in 873t, apparently in reaction to Asa's disability.

JEHOSHAPHAT OF JUDAH (873T–849T; SOLE REIGN FROM 871T)

As we have already discussed, Jehoshaphat's third year, 868t, was a sabbatical year in which he sent teachers throughout Judah to instruct the populace in the Torah (see the discussion above on page 149).

In 853n after the death of Ahab of Israel, Jehu, son of Hanani prophesied to Jehoshaphat (2 Chr 19:1–3). Jehoshaphat probably appointed judges throughout Judah this same year (2 Chr 19:4–11). In this year also, it appears as if Moab and Ammon attacked Judah, perhaps sensing Judah's vulnerability in the wake of the defeat at Ramoth-Gilead where Ahab was killed (2 Chr 20:1).

This would also imply that Jehoshaphat's alliance with Ahaziah of Israel that sent the ill-fated fleet of ships to Ophir took place in late 853 BC or early 852 BC, with Eliezer's prophecy coming at that time (1 Kgs 22:48–49∥2 Chr 20:35–37).

AHAB OF ISRAEL (874N–853N)

The bulk of the ministry of the great prophet Elijah took place during Ahab's reign. Unfortunately, we cannot date the events during this portion of Elijah's ministry except to say that they appear to have occurred before 855n.

From 855n–853n there was peace between Aram and Israel (1 Kgs 22:1). At the end of this period Ahab allied himself with Jehoshaphat of Judah (1 Kgs 22:2||2 Chr 18:2), and Micaiah prophesied Ahab's death in battle (1 Kgs 22:3–28||2 Chr 18:3–27). Shortly thereafter Ahab was killed in battle at Ramoth-Gilead (1 Kgs 22:29–40||2 Chr 18:28–34).

AHAZIAH OF ISRAEL (853N–852N)

Since Ahaziah of Israel died between Nisan and Tishri of 852 BC, we can date Elijah's prophecy of Ahaziah's death to this period (2 Kgs 1:2–17). This, in turn also places Elijah's ascension to heaven and Elisha's first acts as a prophet to these months (2 Kgs 2:1–24).

JEHORAM OF JUDAH (854T–842T; SOLE REIGN FROM 849T)

Jehoram suffered from a bowel disease for the last two years of his reign, beginning in 843t (2 Chr 21:18–19).

JOASH OF JUDAH (836T–797T)

In 814t during the twenty-third year of his reign, Joash admonished Judah's priests for misappropriating the funds that were supposed to be used for repairing the temple (2 Kgs 12:4–16||2 Chr 24:4–14). Also this same year Joash paid tribute to Hazael of Aram (2 Kgs 12:17–18).

The events of the last year of Joash's life are related in some detail (2 Chr 24:20–27). Late in 797 BC or early in 796 BC, the high priest Zechariah prophesied against Joash, and the king had Zechariah assassinated (2 Chr 24:20–22). At the end of that year, that is in the late summer of 796 BC, Aram attacked Judah, severely wounding

Joash (2 Chr 24:23–24). Shortly thereafter (Jo)zabad and Jehozabad assassinated Joash (2 Chr 24:25–26‖2 Kgs 12:21–22).[225]

UZZIAH OF JUDAH (791T–740T; SOLE REIGN FROM 768T)

Uzziah, who is called Azariah in 2 Kings, enjoyed the longest reign of any Israelite king. 2 Chr 26:16–21 relates how Uzziah contracted leprosy when Yahweh afflicted him with this disease as he attempted to usurp the priests' prerogative of burning incense in the temple (cf. 2 Kgs 15:5–6). Since Uzziah's leprosy was the reason his son Jotham was made coregent sometime between Nisan and Tishri of 750 BC, Uzziah's sin can be dated to this same period.

Uzziah died in 740t. This was the year in which Isaiah received what apparently was his inaugural vision (Isa 6:1–13).

JOTHAM OF JUDAH (751T–736T; SOLE REIGN FROM 740T)

Both 2 Kgs 15:33 and 2 Chr 27:1, 8 report that Jotham reigned sixteen years. However, 2 Kgs 15:30 reports that Hoshea seized the throne of Israel in Jotham's twentieth year. This implies that Ahaz, Jotham's son, deposed his father in the last half of 736t (i.e., Nisan–Tishri 735 BC), but allowed Jotham to live. This, in turn, implies that Jotham was probably infirm, having suffered some malady that struck him in 736t.

This also aids us dating Jotham's victory over the Ammonites (2 Chr 27:5). Here we learn that as a result of his victory, the Ammonites paid Jotham tribute for three years. Sensing that Judah was no longer in a position to demand tribute, they most likely

---

[225] Jozabad (יוֹזָבָד; 2 Kgs 12:21) is called by the shorter form of this name, Zabad (זָבָד) at 2 Chr 24:26. At LXX 2 Kgs 12:22 he is called Jozacar (Ιεζιχαρ = יוֹזָכָר). Most English versions call him Jozacar at 2 Kgs 12:21, assuming that the LXX is reflecting the name accurately and that the names in the MT of both 2 Kings and 2 Chronicles reflect an early scribal error of double graphic confusion—an original כ accidently read and subsequently written as ב and an original ר accidently read and subsequently written as ד.

stopped paying tribute when Ahaz seized the throne.[226] Thus, Jotham's victory over Ammon should probably be dated to 738t.

HOSHEA OF ISRAEL (732N–723N)

During the last three years of Hoshea, Samaria was besieged by the Assyrian king Shalmaneser (2 Kgs 17:5). Therefore, the siege of Samaria began in 725n.

HEZEKIAH OF JUDAH (729T–687T; SOLE REIGN FROM 716T)

In the year that Ahaz died and Hezekiah came to the throne, 716t, Isaiah received the oracle against Philistia preserved in Isa 14:28–32.

In the month of Nisan during the first year of his reign (i.e., Nisan 715 BC) Hezekiah began repairing the temple (2 Chr 29:3). The events of Nisan and Ziv 715 BC are given in some detail in 2 Chr 29–30. They can be outlined as:

Table 36
Events of Nisan and Ziv 716 BC

1–7 Nisan	The Holy of Holies cleansed (2 Chr 29:16–17)
8–16 Nisan	The Holy Place cleansed (2 Chr 29:17)
After 16 Nisan	Temple, priests, Levites consecrated (2 Chr 29:18–36)
End of Nisan–Beginning of Ziv	All Israel invited to the Passover (2 Chr 30:1–12)
14 Ziv	Passover Celebrated (2 Chr 30:13–20)
15–21 Ziv	Feast of Unleavened Bread (2 Chr 30:21–22)
22–28 Ziv	Additional celebration of Unleavened Bread (2 Chr 30:23–27)

In the summer of 701 BC during Hezekiah's fourteenth year (702t), the Assyrian king Sennacherib besieged Jerusalem (2 Kgs 18:31–19:35||2 Chr 32:1–22||Isa 36:1–37:36).

---

[226] Thiele, *Mysterious Numbers*, 132.

That same year Hezekiah became deathly sick, but God granted his request not to die (2 Kgs 20:1–11‖Isa 38:1–22; cf. 2 Chr 32:24), and he ruled 15 more years (2 Kgs 20:6‖Isa 38:5). Apparently, shortly after this Hezekiah received envoys from Babylon, thereby bringing forth Isaiah's prophesy of the captivity of Judah (2 Kgs 20:12–19‖Isa 39:1–8; cf. 2 Chr 32:31).

Isaiah's oracle against Egypt and Cush (Isa 20:3–6) followed after three years in which the prophet was naked and barefooted (Isa 20:1–2). The beginning of this period was probably the Assyrian campaign against Philistia in 711 BC, placing the oracle in 709 BC.

JOSIAH OF JUDAH (641T–TAMMUZ 609)

Several events from Josiah's reign are dated in Kings and Chronicles. The first is in Josiah's eighth year (633t) when he began to "seek the Lord" (2 Chr 34:3).

Four years later in his twelfth year (629t) he began to purge idolatrous worship from Judah (2 Chr 34:3). Jeremiah began his ministry that same year, which he calls Josiah's thirteenth year (Jer 1:2), since Jeremiah used non-accession reckoning for the reigns of kings.[227] Therefore, Jeremiah's first visions (Jer 1:4–19) were received sometime in 629t. His prophecies in Jer 2:1–3:5 may also have been received at this time.

In the first half of Josiah's eighteenth year, Tishri 623 BC–Nisan 622 BC, Josiah ordered repairs on the temple during which time a copy of the Torah was discovered in the temple. This triggered further

---

[227] Young, "When Did Jerusalem Fall?" 33–37. This can be seen most clearly at Jer 46:2, which places the Egyptian Pharaoh Neco II's defeat at Carchemish during Jehoiakim's fourth year. The Battle of Carchemish took place in May or June of 605 BC (= 606t). Since Jehoiakim began to reign sometime in Tishri 609, his first official year by accession reckoning would have been 608t. This would have made 606t his *third* year (as at Dan 1:1). However, by using non-accession reckoning and counting all of 609t as Jehoiakim's first year, Jeremiah called 606t Jehoiakim's fourth year.

reforms by the king (2 Kgs 23:1–20||2 Chr 34:8–33). When he inquired of the prophetess Huldah, she prophesied Judah's downfall, but promised it would not be in Josiah's day (2 Kgs 22:14–20; 2 Chr 34:19–28). Later in that year on 14 Nisan the Passover was celebrated (2 Kgs 23:21||2 Chr 35:1–19).

JEHOIAKIM OF JUDAH (TISHRI 609–21 MARCHESHVAN 598)

Jeremiah's prophecy predicting the destruction of the temple (Jer 26:1–6) was delivered in the temple courtyard at the beginning of Jehoiakim's reign. Although Jeremiah was condemned to death by the priests and prophets in the temple, his life was spared (Jer 26:7–24).

During the summer of 605 BC, which was both Jehoiakim's fourth year and Nebuchadnezzar's first year by non-accession reckoning (Jer 25:1), Nebuchadnezzar attacked Jerusalem. Daniel, using accession year reckoning, called it Jehoiakim's third year (Dan 1:1). This year, 606t, was an active one for the prophet Jeremiah. He prophesied that the captivity would last 70 years (Jer 25), he dictated all his prophecies up to this point to Baruch (Jer 36:1–8), he prophesied to Baruch (Jer 45), and he uttered oracles against various nations (Jer 46–51).

In Kislev (December) 605 BC, Jehoiakim's fifth year, the king burned the scroll of Jeremiah's prophecy (Jer 36:9–26). As a result God commanded Jeremiah to dictate his prophecies once again to Baruch (Jer 36:27–32).

The Babylonian Chronicle tells us that Nebuchadnezzar's campaign in Syria and Palestine lasted until Shebat (early February), 604 BC.[228] At this time he returned to Babylon, taking captives with him. These captives most likely included Daniel, Hananiah, Mishael, and Azariah (Dan 1:6). Thus we can date Dan 1:3–19 to early 604 BC.

We are told that Daniel interpreted Nebuchadnezzar's dream (Dan 2) in Nebuchadnezzar's second year, 603n. This came after "three

---

[228] BM 21946, obverse, line 12 (Wiseman, *Chronicles of Chaldaean Kings,* 68–69).

years" of training (Dan 1:5, 18). The three years were reckoned inclusively and were counted as follows:

First year: the end of Nebuchadnezzar's accession year, early 604 through Adar 604.

Second year: Nebuchadnezzar's first official year, Nisan 604 through Adar 603 (= 604n).

Third year: most of Nebuchadnezzar's second official year, 603n.

Therefore, Nebuchadnezzar's dream most probably occurred in the last months of 603n, that is, at the end of 603 BC or the beginning of 602 BC.

Table 37
Prophetic Activity during Jehoiakim's Reign

Date	*Reference*
Late 609	Jer 26
606t	Jer 25; 45; 46–51
Summer/Autumn 605	Jer 36:1–8
Kislev 605	Jer 36:9–32
Early 604	Dan 1
Late 603/Early 602	Dan 2
Undated	Jer 35

ZEDEKIAH (2 ADAR 597–9 TAMMUZ 587)

DANIEL 3

Unlike most major sections of Daniel, Dan 3 contains no chronological notice for the setting of the events it recounts.[229] However, a careful reading of the book of Jeremiah and the chronicles of Nebuchadnezzar's reign suggests a date for the

---

[229] This section is based upon the discussion in Steinmann, *Daniel*, 167–169.

convocation to dedicate Nebuchadnezzar's golden statue of late December 594 BC or January 593 BC during the reign of Zedekiah.[230]

The Babylonian Chronicles states that a rebellion took place in Babylon from the month of Kislev (began December 15, 595 BC) to the month of Tebeth (ended February 11, 594 BC) in Nebuchadnezzar's tenth year.[231] Nebuchadnezzar suppressed the rebellion and purged his army of those he suspected of supporting the uprising.[232] At the end of that year (i.e., before April 11, 594 BC), Nebuchadnezzar made a trip to his western provinces to collect tribute from his vassals.[233] This trip may have been intended to enforce his authority in light of the rebellion that he had recently suppressed. He returned to those same western provinces with his army in the month of Kislev the next year (December 4, 594–January 1, 593 BC).[234]

During the first half of his fourth (non-accession) year as king (Tishri 595–Adar 594 BC), Zedekiah apparently made a trip to Babylon (Jer 51:59–64).[235] Perhaps this trip was demanded by

---

[230] The specific chronicle is preserved on tablet BM 21946. See Wiseman, *Chronicles of Chaldaean Kings,* 66–75. The identification of the chronicle sequence that includes the convocation was first proposed by Shea, "Daniel 3." It has been favored by Dyer, "The Musical Instruments in Daniel 3," 426–427. While some critical scholars have rejected Shea's work, none has given any reasoned argument for the rejection. More controversial and much less certain is Shea's identification of Shadrach, Meshach, and Abednego as three officials of Nebuchadnezzar listed on a clay prism (Shea, "Daniel 3," 37–41, 46–50).

[231] BM 21946, reverse, line 21.

[232] BM 21946, reverse, line 22.

[233] BM 21946, reverse, lines 23–24.

[234] BM 21946, reverse, line 25.

[235] The only mention of Zedekiah's trip to Babylon is in Jer 51:59 which states that a certain Seraiah went to Babylon "with King Zedekiah of Judah in the fourth year of his reign." LXX and Arabic versions of this text, however, say that Seraiah went "*from* King Zedekiah of Judah" instead of

Nebuchadnezzar to impress upon Zedekiah and other vassal kings that they were to be loyal Babylonian clients. However, it appears to have had the opposite effect, since later that year, before the end of the month of Av (August) 594 BC, Zedekiah, having returned to Jerusalem, plotted with the emissaries from Edom, Moab, Ammon, Tyre and Sidon to rebel against Nebuchadnezzar. Jeremiah advised against this rebellion (Jer 27).

This sequence of events yields a date of some time from Tishri (October) 595 BC to July 594 BC for Zedekiah's trip to Babylon and his return and, therefore, also for the events of Dan 3. The convocation in Dan 3 is a likely setting for the occasion of Zedekiah's trip, since the trip was probably for the purpose of securing Zedekiah's loyalty to Nebuchadnezzar (cf. Dan 3:3–7).

While we cannot be certain that this is the date for the events of Dan 3, it is the most probable of any known verifiable date. Therefore, a possible sequence of events surrounding the dedication of the golden statue in Dan 3 is:

Table 38
Sequence of Events Relating to Daniel 3

Date	Event
Tishri 595–Adar 594	Zedekiah travels to Babylon (Jer 51:59–64) for the dedication of the golden statue (Dan 3)
Kislev 595–Tebeth 594	Nebuchadnezzar suppresses a revolt in Babylon
Early 594	Nebuchadnezzar collects tribute from his western provinces
Kislev 594/593	Nebuchadnezzar marches west with his army

---

with him, a reading which is grammatically and contextually feasible (i.e., מֵאֵת instead of MT's אֶת־).

Tammuz or Ab 594	Zedekiah plots with his allies to rebel against Nebuchadnezzar (Jer 27)

DATING THE SIEGE OF JERUSALEM

After 594 BC no Babylonian records have been found dealing with the remainder of the reign of Nebuchadnezzar with the exception of a fragment apparently dealing with a campaign against Egypt in 568/567 BC. In the absence of such Babylonian records, all dates for the siege and fall of Jerusalem must be decided on the basis of the Scriptures. These must be tied to the surviving Babylonian records from early in Nebuchadnezzar's reign as well as to Amel-Marduk's accession year, the year in which Jehoiachin was released from prison (2 Kgs 25:27; Jer 52:31). In order to date the fall of Jerusalem accurately it is essential to determine the methods of dating used by Jeremiah, Ezekiel and the authors of 2 Kings and 2 Chronicles when dealing with the last days of Judah. One other datum is from Josephus, who states that Nebuchadnezzar's siege of Tyre lasted 13 years.[236] This is often used in conjunction with Ezek 29:17–18 to date the siege to approximately 586 to 576 BC, since Ezek 29:17–18 is dated to the first of Nisan of the twenty-seventh year of exile, April 8, 572 BC. Ezekiel's prophecy also says that after the hard and unrewarded labor of the Babylonians against Tyre, the Lord would provide them with abundant plunder in Egypt. This is consistent with the date of the Babylonian fragment that was mentioned earlier, some four years after Ezekiel's prophecy.

PROPHECIES OF JEREMIAH AND EZEKIEL

Two of Jeremiah's prophecies apparently can be dated to the first months of Zedekiah's reign, shortly after Jehoiachin (Jeconiah) was taken into captivity. These are Jer 24 and Jer 29.

Two other prophecies of Jeremiah are also dated to the "beginning" (בְּרֵאשִׁית) of Zedekiah's reign, but are clearly a reference

---

[236] *Ag. Ap.* 156 [32].

to one of the earlier years of his reign—his fourth year, 595t.[237] These are Jer 27 and Jer 28. The second of these prophecies involves Hananiah's confrontation of Jeremiah in Av 594 BC (Jer 28:1). Jeremiah prophesied Hananiah's death, which took place in Tishri 594 BC (Jer 28:17).

As Zedekiah was on the throne in Judah, Ezekiel began his prophetic ministry in exile. His inaugural vision (Ezek 1:1–3:14) is dated to 5 Tammuz in the fifth year of Jehoiachin's exile (Ezek 1:2). Since the first year of Jehoiachin's exile began when Nebuchadnezzar deposed him on 2 Adar 597 BC (Saturday, March 16), the fifth year of his exile would have begun on 1 Tishri 594. Thus, Ezekiel's vision was received on 5 Tammuz 593 BC (Monday, July 31). Ezekiel also calls this "the thirtieth year," probably a reference to his age, since Ezekiel was of priestly lineage. This would have made him old enough to serve as a priest if he were not in exile in Babylon. Thus, Ezekiel was most likely born in 623 BC.

Ezekiel's next prophecies (Ezek 3:15–5:12) were revealed to him after he had been with the exiles at Tel Abib on the Chebar canal for seven days, beginning with 5 Tammuz. Thus, the date was 11 Tammuz 593 BC (Sunday, August 6). Starting that day Ezekiel was to lie on his side for 390 days (Ezek 4:5), which would have ended on 17 Ab 592 BC (Friday, August 31). He then lay on his side for 40 days, ending 28 Elul 592 BC (Wednesday, October 10). Ezekiel dates his next set of prophecies to 5 Elul 592 BC (Monday, September 17).

---

[237] Sarna has argued that this is a reference to Zedekiah's accession year and that the "fourth year" (Jer 28:1) is a reference to the fourth year of a sabbatical cycle. (Sarna, "Zedekiah's Emancipation of Slaves and the Sabbatical Year," 149.) This is possible, since Zedekiah came to the throne in 598t which was four years after the last Sabbatical year, 602t. However, there is no unambiguous example of dating simply by sabbatical year cycles in the entire Old Testament, making this unlikely. It is more likely that the phrase "the beginning of Zedekiah's reign" (בְּרֵאשִׁית מַמְלֶכֶת צִדְקִיָּה) simply refers to his early years on the throne.

He calls this "the sixth year" (presumably of his exile; Ezek 8:1). It appears that these oracles (Ezek 8–19) were received on this day or shortly thereafter. While the oracles in Ezek 6–7 are not explicitly dated, they probably were received in 592 BC also, considering their placement in the prophet's book. Ezekiel received his next revelations from God (Ezek 20–23) during the following year on 10 Ab 591 BC (Wednesday, August 14; Ezek 20:1).

THE FINAL SIEGE AND DESTRUCTION OF JERUSALEM

Events related to the three Babylonian sieges of Jerusalem that marked the end of the Judean monarchic period, the destruction of the temple, and captivity of the Judeans in Babylon are shown in Table 40 below. The three Babylonian investitures of Jerusalem occurred in the days of Jehoiakim (2 Kgs 24:1; Jer 46:2–12; Dan 1:1–2), Jehoiachin (2 Kgs 24:10–17; 2 Chr 36:10), and Zedekiah (2 Kgs 25; 2 Chr 36:17–20; Jer 34, 35, 37–40, 52; Ezek 24:1–2; 30:20–21; 33:21; 40:1). As mentioned above, the final breaching of Jerusalem's wall occurred on 9 Tammuz (July 29) of 587 BC. A month later Nebuchadnezzar's official Nebuzaradan came to the city and its final destruction began

After two years of not prophesying Ezekiel received the prophecy of Ezek 24:1–14 (and probably 24:15–25:17) on the very day that Nebuchadnezzar began his final siege of Jerusalem, 10 Tebeth of the ninth year 590t (Tuesday, January 27, 589; Ezek 24:1; 2 Kgs 25:1; cf. Jer 39:1). A year later, on the twelfth day of Tebeth (Monday, Jan 17, 588 BC), he received his first oracle against Egypt (Ezek 29:1–16).

During the siege of Jerusalem Ezekiel continued to prophesy. His oracle against Pharaoh (Ezek 30:20–26) was delivered on 7 Nisan 587 BC (Saturday, April 29). The second oracle against Pharaoh (Ezek 31) was spoken on 1 Sivan 587 BC (Wednesday, June 21).

Jeremiah was also active during the siege. Jer 21:1 introduces a section of the prophet's words with an inquiry about whether God will act to deliver Judah from Nebuchadnezzar's attack. Thus, Jer 21–

23 most likely dates from the time of the siege (10 Tebeth 589 BC – 9 Tammuz 587 BC = January 27, 589 – July 29, 587).

Early in the siege, before Jeremiah was imprisoned, he was active in prophesying around Jerusalem (Jer 37:4). However, when the Babylonians were temporarily forced to lift the siege because of an Egyptian incursion into Judah, Jeremiah attempted to leave the city. For this he was imprisoned and persecuted. Since Ezekiel first prophesied against Egypt on 12 Tebeth 588 BC (Monday, January 17), it is likely that the Egyptian incursion took place during or before early Tebeth. This is confirmed by that fact that by late 588 BC Jeremiah was in prison (see below). Therefore, Jeremiah's prophetic activity as related in Jer 37–38 dates between 10 Tebeth 589 BC and early Tebeth 588 BC.

Although he was imprisoned, the prophet was instructed to buy a field in Anathoth (Jer 32). This happened in the tenth year of Zedekiah (589t) and the nineteenth year of Nebuchadnezzar (588n).[238] The overlap of these two years is the span from the beginning of Nisan 588 BC to the end of Elul 588 BC. Jeremiah 33 and 34 can be dated to sometime between the release of slaves in Tishri 588 and the defeat of the Egyptian army on or before Nisan 7, 587 BC (Ezek 30:20).

Following the defeat of the Egyptian army, Nebuchadnezzar's siege of Jerusalem resumed. The siege ended when Jerusalem's wall was breached on 9 Tammuz 587 BC (Saturday, July 29; 2 Kgs 25:3; Jer 39:2; 52:6).

The Babylonian official Nebuzaradan was sent to Jerusalem to oversee its pillaging. 2 Kgs 25:8 dates his arrival to 7 Ab (Friday, August 25). Commentators often ascribe the difference between this and the date of 10 Ab given in Jer 52:12 to a scribal error in one of

---

[238] Jeremiah reckoned every king's reign according to the non-accession year system. Therefore, this was Nebuchadnezzar's seventeenth year according to official Babylonian reckoning. The Babylonians used the accession year system.

these sources. There are extensive discussions in rabbinic literature of this apparent discrepancy. Perhaps the best known attempt at reconciliation is that of the Babylonian Talmud, where it is said that the heathens entered the Temple on the seventh of Ab, then continued to desecrate it on the eighth of Ab.[239] Towards dusk of the ninth they set it on fire, and then the major part of the conflagration occurred on the tenth.

Rodger C. Young offers another interpretation, based on the observation that it is unreasonable to expect that Nebuzaradan would have mustered his forces to carry out the extensive depredations in the city as described in Jer 52:13–23 and 2 Kgs 25:9–17 on the same day that he finished his long trip from Nebuchadnezzar's camp in the land of Hamath (2 Kgs 25:6; Jer 52:9).[240] There was surely a period of rest and planning with the commanders already in the field before the Babylonians began their looting of the city. A grammatical comparison of 2 Kgs 25:8 with Jer 52:12 lends support to this reconstruction of events. In the Kings passage Nebuzaradan came *to* Jerusalem (בָּא...יְרוּשָׁלָם)—that is, presumably to the Babylonian camp just outside the city—on the seventh day of the fifth month. This construction is similar to 2 Kgs 18:17b where Sennacherib came to Jerusalem without entering the city, and to Dan 1:1, where Nebuchadnezzar came to the city to begin his siege, but he had not taken the city. In Jer 52:12, the grammatical construction suggests that Nebuzaradan actually entered *into* Jerusalem (בָּא...בִּירוּשָׁלָם) on the tenth of the month, three days later. The construction of Jer 52:12 is similar to that of Jonah 3:4, where Jonah went *into* the city (לָבוֹא בָעִיר) of Nineveh, after arriving *at* the city on the previous day. In the days between the seventh and tenth of Ab, Nebuzaradan would have been consulting with the commanders already in the field and

[239] *b. Ta'an.* 29a.
[240] Rodger C. Young, "The Parian Marble and Other Surprises from Chronologist V. Coucke."

devising plans for the pillage and destruction of the city. The actual destructions would then have begun on the tenth day of the fifth month. Consistent with this, Josephus relates that the First and Second Temples were both burnt on the tenth of Ab.[241]

Table 39
Prophecies during the Reign of Zedekiah

Date	Prophecy
Early 597	Jer 24; 29
595t	Jer 27
Av 594	Jer 28
5 Tammuz 593	Ezek 1:1–3:14
11 Tammuz 593	Ezek 3:5–5:12
592	Ezek 6–7
5 Elul 592	Ezek 8–19
10 Av 591	Ezek 20–23
After 10 Tebeth 589	Jer 21–23
10 Tebeth 589	Jer 37–38
10 Tebeth 589	Ezek 24–25
12 Tebeth 588	Ezek 29:1–16
1 Elul 587	Ezek 26–28
Nisan 588/Elul 588	Jer 32
Tishri 588/Nisan 587	Jer 33–34
1 Nisan 587	Ezek 30:20–26
1 Sivan 587	Ezek 31
Undated	Jer 20

JUDAH AFTER THE FALL OF JERUSALEM

Later, in Tishri 587 BC some supporters of the Judean royal family assassinated Gedaliah, the governor appointed by Nebuchadnezzar, and fled to Egypt, forcing Jeremiah to go with them (2 Kgs 25:22–26;

---

[241] Josephus, *J.W.* 6.250 [6.4.5].

Jer 41:1– 43:13). There in Egypt Jeremiah uttered what was probably his final prophecy (Jer 44).

In the aftermath of the fall of Jerusalem, Ezekiel prophesied against Tyre (Ezek 26–28). This oracle against Tyre is dated to the eleventh year (i.e., 588t) on the first day of an unspecified month (Ezek 26:1). Since the oracle says that the Tyrians had received news of Jerusalem's fall (Ezek 26:2), which happened on 9 Tammuz, it is probably the month of Elul.[242] Thus, Ezek 26–28 was probably delivered by the prophet on 1 Elul 587 BC (Monday, September 18).

---

[242] The only months that could have had a first day in 588t after the fall of Jerusalem on 9 Tammuz would have been Ab and Elul. If word reached Tyre by 1 Ab (Saturday, August 19), only 21 days had passed since Jerusalem's fall.

Table 40
Events Related to the Babylonian Destruction of Jerusalem and the Temple

Hebrew Date	Julian Date	Sources
606t	Summer 605	Jer 46:2–12; 2 Kgs 24:1; Dan 1:1–2; *Ant.* 10.84 [10.6.1]; *Bab. Chron.* BM 22047
2 Adar 597	Tue 16 Apr 597	2 Kgs 24:10–17; 2 Chr 36:10; Ez 1:2; *Ant.* 10.96-97 [10.7.1]; *Bab. Chron.* BM 21946
Late fall/winter 595/94	Oct 595 to Jan 594	Jer 51:59
10 Tebeth 589	Tue 27 Jan 589	Ezek 24:1–2; 2 Kgs 25:1
1 Tishri 588	Thu 29 Sep 588	Jer 34:8–10
Between Tishi 588 & Nisan 587	Oct 588 to end of Apr 587	Jer 34:11–22; 37:5–16
7 Nisan 587	Sat 29 Apr 587	Jer 34:21–22; Ezek 30:20–21
9 Tammuz 587	Sat 29 Jul 587	2 Kgs 25:2–4; Jer 39:2; 52:7; Eze 33:21; 40:1; *Ant.* 10.135–140 [10.8.2]
7 Ab 587	Fri 25 Aug 587	2 Kgs 25:8
10 Ab 587	Mon 28 Aug 587	2 Kgs 25:9–19; 2 Chr 36:18–19; 52:12–25; *Ant.* 10.144–148 [10.8.5]; *J.W.* 6.250 [6.4.5]

9

THE BABYLONIAN EXILE
AND THE PERSIAN PERIOD

The fall of Judah to the Babylonian king Nebuchadnezzar in 587 BC marked not only the end of the Davidic dynasty as a territorial power, but also ushered in a era where biblical time would no longer be measured by the reigns of Israelite kings. In many ways this simplifies compiling a chronology of the later books of the Old Testament, since the reigns of the monarchs of the Babylonian and Persian empires are well documented. During this era whenever the biblical authors preserve the exact date of an event, it can be converted to dates in the Julian calendar.[243]

BIBLICAL EVENTS DURING THE BABYLONIAN EXILE

Babylon would become the home for the Judean exiles until Cyrus' conquest of that city in 539 BC. The kings of Babylon during this period were:

---

[243] The tables in Parker and Dubberstein, *Babylonian Chronology*, 27–36, provide a convenient reference for determining dates during this era. We can assume with a high degree of confidence that the intercalary months added periodically to the Babylonian calendar were used throughout both the Babylonian and Persian empires during this era. Days of the week can be easily determined using the Julian Date Converter maintained by the United States Naval Observatory (http://aa.usno.navy.mil/data/docs/JulianDate.php). See footnote 215, page 139.

Table 41
Kings of the Neo-Babylonian Empire

Date	King
605n–562n	Nebuchadnezzar
562n–560n	Amel-marduk
560n–556n	Neriglissar
556n	Labashi-marduk
556–539n	Nabonidus
553n or 550n–539n	Belshazzar (coregent)

NEBUCHADNEZZAR (605N–562N)

Ezekiel, who had been in exile in Babylon since 597 BC, continued to prophesy after the fall of Jerusalem in 587 BC. News of Jerusalem's fall reached Ezekiel on 5 Tebeth (Friday, January 19) 586 BC. In response to this news Ezekiel prophesied again (Ezek 33:21–39:29).

On 1 Adar (Thursday, March 15) 586 BC Ezekiel received his fourth oracle against Egypt, a lament over Pharaoh (Ezek 32:1–16). Just two weeks later on 15 Adar (Thursday, March 29), he received his fifth oracle against Egypt, a lament over Egypt (Ezek 32:17–32). Most probably the prophecies of Ezek 33–39 were also uttered at that time.

Some four years after Jerusalem's fall Babylon was still subduing Judah. Jer 52:30 reports that in 582 BC the Babylonian official Nebuzaradan took more captives from Judah to Babylon.

After almost a decade of prophetic silence, Ezekiel received his great vision of a restored Jerusalem on 10 Tishri 574 BC (Ezek 40–48). Ezekiel calls this "the fourteenth year after the city was struck" (בְּאַרְבַּע עֶשְׂרֵה שָׁנָה אַחַר אֲשֶׁר הֻכְּתָה הָעִיר; Ezek 40:1). Since Jerusalem fell on 9 Tammuz 587, the first year after the city was struck was 587t. Thus, 574t was the fourteenth year.

Ezekiel would utter his final prophecy two and one-half years later on 1 Nisan (Tuesday, April 26) 571 BC. It was his sixth oracle against Egypt (Ezek 29:17–30:19).

Daniel continued to serve Nebuchadnezzar after Jerusalem's fall.[244] Dan 4, however, contains no chronological notice of when Nebuchadnezzar suffered the insanity reported in that chapter. Nevertheless, there are clues in Dan 4 that enable us to determine a time span in which this incident took place. Nebuchadnezzar had his dream when he was at home in his palace and "at ease and flourishing" (Dan 4:4). Twelve months later he was struck with insanity (Dan 4:29–33). As a result he did not occupy the throne for a period of "seven times," a period that is usually understood to be seven years, but probably refers to a shorter period of time that was indeterminate, but clearly delimited.[245]

The Babylonian Chronicle for the reign of Nebuchadnezzar ends in his tenth year, Nisan 595 through Adar II 594 BC.[246] As mentioned above, Babylonian records have not been found for the years of Nebuchadnezzar following 594 BC, except for the fragmentary inscription referring to a campaign in Egypt in 568–567 BC to quash a revolt by a rebellious regent whom he had placed over that part of his empire.[247] From Ezek 29:17–18 and Josephus,[248] his siege of Tyre is usually dated from c. 586 BC to c. 573 BC. Thus, it would appear that Nebuchadnezzar had his dream sometime between 573 BC and his death in 562 BC. Nebuchadnezzar was "at ease" and "flourishing" (Dan 4:4) when he had his dream, and he was in Babylon twelve months later when his dream was fulfilled (Dan 4:29). Since he was insane for some period afterwards, he could not have had the dream during the years 570–565 BC, since in 568–567 BC he was in Egypt and sane enough to lead his troops in battle.

---

[244] This discussion is based on Steinmann, *Daniel*, 207–208.

[245] See the discussion in Steinmann, *Daniel*, 236–237.

[246] BM 21946. See Wiseman, *Chronicles of the Chaldaean Kings,* 72–75.

[247] See Wiseman, *Nebuchaddrezzar and Babylon*; Weisberg, *Texts from the Time of Nebuchadnezzar.*

[248] *Ag. Ap.* 156 [32].

This means there are only two spans of time for the events of Daniel 4: either 573–569 BC or 564–562 BC. There is hardly enough time for all these events to have taken place during the last two years of Nebuchadnezzar's reign. In addition, the Babylonian Chronicle states that he was at Tyre in 564 BC.[249] The most likely period during which Dan 4 was set is, therefore, 573–569 BC. Perhaps this explains the Egyptian rebellion that led Nebuchadnezzar to Egypt in 568 BC. Nebuchadnezzar's insanity could have been perceived as an opportune time by the regent of Egypt to rebel.

Table 42
Nebuchadnezzar's Reign: Biblical Events & Prophecies

7 Nisan 587	Ezek 30:20–26
1 Sivan 587	Ezek 31
5 Tebeth 586	Ezek 33:21–39:29
1 Adar 586	Ezek 32:1–16
15 Adar 586	Ezek 32:17–33:20
582n	Nebuzaradan takes Judean captives to Babylon (Jer 52:30)
10 Tishri 574	Ezek 40–48
1 Nisan 571	Ezek 29:17–30:19
Bet. 573 and 569	Nebuchadnezzar's insanity (Dan 4)

AMEL-MARDUK (562N–560N)

Nebuchadnezzar's successor, Amel-marduk, reigned only about two years. In the Bible he is called by the Hebrew reflection of his name, Evil-merodach (אֱוִיל מְרֹדַךְ). On 25 Adar (Wednesday, March 31) 561 BC Amel-marduk freed Jehoiachin from prison (Jer 52:31).[250]

---

[249] Wiseman, *Nebuchadrezzar and Babylon*, 28.

[250] 2 Kgs 25:27 dates this event two days later. There has been a scribal error

BELSHAZZAR (553N OR 550N–539N)

In 556 BC Nabonidus deposed Labashi-marduk, the last of Nebuchadnezzar's direct descendants to sit on the throne of Babylon. However, Nabonidus proved to be singularly unpopular in Babylon because of his devotion to the god Sin instead of Marduk, the patron god of Babylon. In response to this unpopularity, Nabonidus "entrusted the kingship"[251] to his son Belshazzar and voluntarily exiled himself to Tema in the Arabian Desert for about a decade. The commonly accepted date for the beginning of Belshazzar's coregency is 553 BC, although there is good evidence that it did not begin until 550 BC.[252]

Daniel dates two of his visions to Belshazzar's reign. Dan 7 comes from Belshazzar's first year, 550n (or possibly 553n). Dan 8 dates to Belshazzar's third year, 548n (or possibly 551n).

Daniel's reading of the handwriting on the wall to Belshazzar (Dan 5) took place on the evening before the fall of Babylon to the Persians on 16 Tishri (Monday, October 12) 539 BC (cf. Dan 5:30). Therefore, the events of Dan 5 date to the evening of 15 Tishri (Sunday, October 11) 539 BC.

BIBLICAL EVENTS DURING THE PERSIAN PERIOD

The fall of Babylon to the armies of Cyrus the Great ushered in the final period of Old Testament history. The Persian Empire would dominate the ancient Near East for about two centuries. During the first half of that empire the final events of the Old Testament transpired. The kings of Persia (i.e., the Achaemenid dynasty) were:

---

in the transmission of the text of either 2 Kings or Jeremiah, but it is impossible to determine which text is corrupt.

[251] The Persian Verse Account, *ANET*, 313.

[252] Shea, "The First and Third Years of Belshazzar (Dan 7:1; 8:1)"; Shea, "Nabonidus, Belshazzar, and the Book of Daniel," 135.

Table 43
Achaemenid Emperors

538–530	Cyrus (the Great)[253]
529–522	Cambyses
521–486	Darius I
485–465	Xerxes
464–424	Artaxerxes I
423–405	Darius II
404–359	Artaxerxes II
358–338	Artaxerxes III
337–336	Arses
335–331	Darius III

CYRUS THE GREAT (538–530)

To even the most casual reader, it appears that Dan 6, 9 and 10–12 are dated early in the reign of Cyrus. Dan 6 takes place shortly after the fall of Babylon and mentions Daniel's prosperity during the reign of Cyrus (Dan 6:28). The vision in Dan 10–12 was revealed to Daniel in Cyrus' third year (Dan 10:1). The previous vision, Dan 9, was revealed during the first year of "Darius the Mede," (Dan 9:1), the same ruler mentioned in Dan 6 at the beginning of Cyrus' reign (Dan 6:1, 6, 9, 25, 28; cf. Dan 5:31; 11:1). The problem of the identity of Darius the Mede has been much discussed in studies of Daniel. However, the most likely solution to the problem is that Darius the Mede is another name for Cyrus, whose mother was a Median princess.[254]

---

[253] Cyrus officially became king of Babylon in Nisan 538 BC, after having conquered the city in 539 BC. The beginning date given for each ruler is the date of his first official regnal year, which began in the spring month of Nisan (see Parker and Dubberstein, *Babylonian Chronology 626 B.C.–A.D. 75*, 29–36).

[254] For a fuller discussion of this issue see Steinmann, *Daniel*, 290–296.

THE EARLY YEARS OF CYRUS' REIGN

The evidence for the identification of Cyrus as Darius the Mede is considerable. Darius was about 62 years of age when Babylon was conquered (Dan 5:31). Cyrus died at the age of 70 in 530 BC. This would have made him about 62 in 539 BC when Babylon was conquered. Herodotus twice notes that Cyrus was not the great Persian ruler's original name but that his mother, a Median, had given him a different name at birth.[255] Darius appointed 120 satraps (Dan 6:1), issued a letter to "all the peoples, nations, and languages that dwell in the entire earth" (Dan 6:25–27), and restricted prayer so that it could only be addressed to the king (Dan 6:7, 12)[256]—all indicative of supreme royal authority that would have been reserved only for Cyrus. Finally, we should note that Dan 6:28 most probably identifies Darius the Mede as Cyrus by use of an epexegetical *waw*.[257]

וְדָנִיֵּאל דְּנָה הַצְלַח בְּמַלְכוּת דָּרְיָוֶשׁ וּבְמַלְכוּת כּוֹרֶשׁ פָּרְסָאָה

So this Daniel prospered in the reign of Darius, *that is*, in the reign of Cyrus the Persian.

By tying the names *Darius* (the Mede) and *Cyrus* (the Persian) together, Daniel makes the point that Babylon fell to "the Medes and the Persians" (Dan 5:28) in fulfillment of the prophecies that Babylon would fall to the Medes (Isa 13:17; Jer 51:11, 28) in conjunction with the Persians (Isa 21:2).[258]

Although Babylon fell to Persian troops in 539 BC, Cyrus' first regnal year over Babylon did not commence until 1 Nisan (March 24)

---

[255] Herodotus, *Histories*, 1.113–114.

[256] Arrian traced the practice of praying to kings to Cyrus. Arrian, *Anabasis Alexandri*, 4.11.

[257] The conjunction *waw* is often used epexegetically in Daniel. It also is used to identify the Assyrian king Pul as Tiglath-pileser at 1 Chr 5:26.

[258] At Isa 21:2 the prominent Persian city of Elam is used as a reference to the Persians.

538 BC. During this time before 1 Nisan 538 BC (i.e., during the accession year of Cyrus), the events narrated in Dan 6 took place. We can reconstruct the chronology of those events by combining information from Dan 6 and the Nabonidus Chronicle.[259]

The city of Babylon was entered by the Persian commander Gubaru on 16 Tishri (October 12) 539 BC. Cyrus arrived in the city on 3 Marcheshvan (October 29), 539 BC. Cyrus then appointed Gubaru governor of Babylon. Gubaru, in turn, began appointing lesser officials. Gubaru died unexpectedly on 11 Marcheshvan (November 6). Babylonian records do not indicate who was governor of Babylon between 11 Marcheshvan 539 BC and 1 Nisan 538 BC. However, beginning in 1 Nisan 538 BC Cyrus' son Cambyses was placed on the throne of Babylon as coregent with his father. This coregency lasted only nine months before Cambyses was removed, probably due to difficulty he had working with Babylonian officials. Starting from this time a different Gubaru was appointed governor of Babylon. From the beginning of the tenth month of his first year and lasting to the end of his reign, Cyrus alone was called "king of Babylon, king of lands."[260]

Dan 6:2 indicates that Daniel was Cyrus' presumptive choice to be the person appointed over the province of Babylon. However, Dan 6 never reports that Daniel was appointed to that position. Given the trouble caused by jealousy among Babylonian officials (as evidenced by Dan 6), it appears that Cyrus instead chose to appoint his son as Babylonian coregent, implying that the plot against Daniel took place late in 539n. The sequence of events around Dan 6 would then be:

---

[259] *ANET*, 306. For a more complete discussion of this reconstruction see Steinmann, *Daniel*, 301–304.

[260] *King of Babylon* was the traditional Babylonian title of the monarch; *King of Lands* was the traditional Persian title.

Table 44
Chronology of Daniel 6

3 Marcheshvan 539 (Oct 29)	Cyrus arrived in Babylon; Gubaru appointed governor
4–10 Marcheshvan 539 (Oct 30–Nov 5)	Gubaru appointed officials
11 Marcheshvan 539 (Nov 6)	Gubaru died
12–29 Marcheshvan 539 (Nov 7–24)	Cyrus completed appointing officials along with three overseers (Dan 6:1–2)
Kislev 539–Shebat 538 (Nov 25–Feb 21)	Daniel distinguished himself; Cyrus planned to appoint him governor (Dan 6:3)
Late Shebat–Adar 538 (Feb–Mar)	Plot against Daniel hatched (Dan 6:4–27);[261] Daniel rescued from lions' den
1 Nisan 538 (Mar 24)	Cambyses made coregent

Three other important events reported in the Old Testament take place during Cyrus' early years. In his first year, 538n, Cyrus issued a proclamation allowing Judeans to return to Jerusalem to rebuild the temple (2 Chr 36:22–23; Ezra 1:1–4). That same year Daniel received a revelation about a restored Jerusalem (Dan 9). In Cyrus' third year,

---

[261] After Cyrus captured Babylon, the Babylonian Chronicle relates that he ordered the gods that Nabonidus had taken from various cities to Babylon be restored to their original cities. This repatriation of the gods took place from Kislev 539 to Adar 538 (November 25, 539 to March 23, 538). This would have been an opportune time for Darius' counselors to suggest that until the gods could be found again in their accustomed places, prayers could only be made to Darius. The dates here assume that this 30-day period of prayer to Darius was at the end of this time. See Steinmann, *Daniel*, 303.

536n, on 24 Nisan (April 23) Daniel received his final vision (Dan 10–12).

SOME JUDEANS RETURN TO JERUSALEM TO BUILD THE TEMPLE

Despite the fact that the book of Ezra is filled with chronological references,[262] one of the most important events in post-exilic history—the first return of Judeans from captivity in Babylon to Jerusalem—is not accompanied by a chronological notice.[263] Many commentaries on Ezra and works dealing with the chronology of this period simply assume that this return took place during Cyrus' first year, although there is no indication in the text that this was the case.

It must have happened sometime after Cyrus' decree in 538 BC in his first year and sometime before the end of his reign in 530 BC,[264] since Ezra 4:5 indicates that the effort to rebuild the temple in Jerusalem was stalled during the reign of Cyrus. The return probably occurred with at least a few years left in Cyrus' reign, since after the return, the work on the temple began but then was stopped for "all the days of King Cyrus of Persia" (Ezra 4:5), and that phrase seems ill-suited if the return to Jerusalem (and subsequently the start of the work on the temple) had only taken place during the last year or two of his reign.

Moreover, Ezra also indicates that another leader was in charge of the return: Sheshbazzar. This man was entrusted by Cyrus with the vessels that were captured by Nebuchadnezzar from the Jerusalem

---

[262] Ezra 1:1; 3:1, 6, 8; 4:24; 5:13; 6:3, 15, 19; 7:7, 8, 9 (twice); 8:31, 33; 10:9, 16, 17.

[263] For a fuller treatment of this subject see Steinmann, *Ezra and Nehemiah*, 29–39; Steinmann, "A Chronological Note: The Return of the Exiles under Sheshbazzar and Zerubbabel (Ezra 1–2)."

[264] Cyrus was killed in battle toward the end of July 530 BC, and Cambyses probably assumed the throne in August 530 when his father's death was reported in Babylon (Parker and Dubberstein, *Babylonian Chronology 626 B.C.–A.D. 75*, 14; Yamauchi, *Persia and the Bible*, 92).

temple that had been built by Solomon (Ezra 1:7–11), and Sheshbazzar is credited with laying the foundation of the rebuilt temple according to the letter of Tattenai to Darius (Ezra 5:13–16). Tattenai's letter calls Sheshbazzar the "governor" (פֶּחָה)[265] whom Cyrus appointed (Ezra 5:14) and states that the temple had been under construction since Sheshbazzar's day (Ezra 5:16).

SHESHBAZZAR AND ZERUBBABEL

HAGGAI, ZECHARIAH, AND 1 ESDRAS

Some scholars hold that the chronological information in Ezra is suspect and that the books of Haggai and Zechariah are more reliable indicators of the time of Zerubbabel's return.[266] The prophecies in Haggai take place in the second year of Darius I (Hag 1:1, 15; 2:10), that is, 520 BC, which is also the year in which Zechariah begins to prophesy (Zech 1:1, 7). Both prophets mention Zerubbabel (e.g., Hag 1:1; Zech 4:6) and the high priest Joshua (e.g., Hag 1:1; Zech 3:1).[267] These scholars interpret those prophetic passages to mean that in 520 BC Zerubbabel had only recently led exiles to Jerusalem. Neither prophet mentions earlier work on the temple while Haggai notes that the temple still lies in ruins (Hag 1:4, 9) and Zechariah speaks of it as not yet rebuilt (Zech 1:16; 4:9). Some scholars, therefore, assume that Ezra's reference to earlier work on the temple is an error. Zechariah also seems to contradict Ezra (5:16) in that the prophet credits Zerubbabel with laying the foundation of the temple (Zech 4:9; cf.

---

[265] This is the word consistently used for the governors of Yehud in the Aramaic portions of Ezra. In the Hebrew portions of Ezra and in Nehemiah, the noun for governor is the Persian loanword תִּרְשָׁתָא (Ezra 2:63; Neh 7:65, 69; 8:9; 10:2 [10:1 in English Bibles]).
[266] Cross, "A Reconstruction of the Judean Restoration," 15; Halpern, "A Historiographic Commentary on Ezra 1–6."
[267] Joshua is called Jeshua, the Aramaic version of his name, in Ezra and Nehemiah.

Hag 2:18; Zech 8:9). Moreover, 1 Esd 5:1–6 places Zerubbabel's
return under Darius I, early in the second year of his reign (520 BC).
The returnees built houses after they arrived (Hag 1:4, 9), but
according to this interpretation, they did not begin to build the temple
until the prophecies of Haggai and Zechariah later in 520 BC (see Ezra
5:1; 6:14).

However, it is not necessary to extrapolate from Hag 1:4, 9 that no
work on rebuilding the temple had begun. Instead the temple could
still be said to be "desolate" because only the foundation had been
laid and then the work was interrupted. That Haggai does not mention
the foundations laid in Sheshbazzar's day (Ezra 5:16) is no proof that
they were not in place during the ministry of the prophet. His concern
is not with what had been done a decade or more before, but with
what was not being done as he spoke: labor on God's house had been
halted, though the people had by now built themselves "paneled
houses" (Hag 1:4). That description in itself indicates that the prophet
was not speaking to newly arrived residents, but to those who had
lived in the land long enough to furnish their own homes with a
measure of luxury.

In addition, the reference to the laying of the temple's foundation
in Haggai's prophecy which was delivered on 24 Kislev (December
18), 520 BC (Hag 2:10–19), does not contradict the assertion in Ezra
5:16 that Sheshbazzar laid the foundations of the temple. It is
particularly important to understand the statement in Hag 2:18
correctly: "Consider from this day forward, from the twenty-fourth
day of the ninth month. Since the day that the foundation of
Yahweh's temple was laid [לְמִן־הַיּוֹם אֲשֶׁר־יֻסַּד הֵיכַל־יְהוָה], consider
. . . " When used temporally in Biblical Hebrew, the compound
preposition לְמִן, "since," always refers to an event from the past,[268] so

---

[268] Exod 9:18; Deut 4:32; 9:7; Judg 19:30; 2 Sam 7:6; 2 Sam 7:11 ‖ 1 Chr
17:10; 2 Sam 7:19 ‖ 1 Chr 17:17; 2 Sam 19:24; 2 Kgs 19:25 ‖ Isa 37:26
(twice); Isa 7:17; Jer 7:7, 25; 25:5; 32:31; Dan 1:18; Mal 3:7.

Haggai regards "the day that the foundation of Yahweh's temple was laid" as a past event. Haggai is not referring to the recent activity begun three months earlier on 24 Elul (September 21), 520 BC (Hag 1:14–15). That recent activity is described in Hag 2:15 as laying one stone upon another, which is the process of building the temple itself. Neither Hag 1:14 nor Hag 2:15 uses any form of the verb יסד ("lay a foundation") or any cognate noun ("a foundation"), so these verses do not refer to laying the foundation. Instead Haggai describes the recent commencement of construction on 24 Elul in more general terms: "and they did work on the house of Yahweh of hosts, their God" (Hag 1:14).

Other than Ezra 5:16, the Ezra texts that refer to laying the foundation of the temple are all in Ezra 3 and refer to the activity led by Zerubbabel under the governorship of Sheshbazzar (Ezra 3:6, 10–12; see the discussion beginning on page 186). Thus Haggai does not offer more reliable information than Ezra, but instead simply offers complementary information. As I will argue below beginning on page 186, Zech 4:9 does not contradict Ezra 5:16 either, since Zerubbabel was in charge of the construction of the foundation under Sheshbazzar and later was governor when the temple was completed. As for 1 Esd 5:1–6, it should be noted that it is set after a very fanciful tale about a wisdom contest held in Darius' presence and involving royal bodyguards (1 Esd 3–4). This particular story about Zerubbabel is inserted into 1 Esd 2–7, which is otherwise a close retelling of Ezra 1–6 (though with some rearranging of the order of the material in Ezra; see Table 45). Zerubbabel, who is presented as one of Darius' bodyguards, wins the contest, and for his prize he requests that Darius keep the promise made by Cyrus to allow the temple in Jerusalem to be rebuilt. Zerubbabel is then commissioned to rebuild the temple. Given this setting, it is difficult to understand 1 Esd 3:1–5:6 as an accurate portrayal of historical events. The inaccuracy of 1 Esd 2–7 is confirmed when its material is compared to its parallels in Ezra 1–6, as shown in Table 45.

Table 45
Parallels between 1 Esdras 2–7 and Ezra 1:1–6:22

1 Esd 2:1–14	Ezra 1:1–11	Cyrus' decree and preparations to return to Jerusalem
1 Esd 2:15–26	Ezra 4:7–24	Letter to Artaxerxes and the reply
1 Esd 3:1–5:6		Zerubbabel wins a wisdom contest and claims his prize
1 Esd 5:7–70	Ezra 2:1–4:5	The return to Jerusalem; laying of the temple's foundation; opposition to the building project
1 Esd 6:1–7:15	Ezra 5:1–6:22	Resumption of building; letter of Tattenai and the reply; completion of the temple; dedication of the temple; Passover

Clearly, the author of 1 Esdras has rearranged the material in Ezra to accommodate the story about the wisdom contest and its consequences. He moved the letter to Artaxerxes to follow Sheshbazzar's return to Jerusalem in order to explain why the temple restoration was not started in his day, but this creates a glaring anachronism and destroys the integrity of the Aramaic document of Ezra 4:8–6:18.[269] Then he inserted the account of the wisdom contest in order to create a second return of exiles under Zerubbabel. He placed next the remaining material in Ezra 2–7 that spans the laying of the foundation to the eventual completion of the temple. In the

---

[269] I would argue in agreement with Steiner that Ezra 4:8–6:18 is a composite document made up of letters as well as some narrative so as to produce a report to Artaxerxes about the situation in Jerusalem in his day and under previous kings. See Steiner, "Bishlam's Archival Search Report in Nehemiah's Archive."

process of this reorganization, the author of 1 Esdras had no place in his scheme for the opposition under Xerxes, so he simply omitted Ezra 4:6. The entire account in 1 Esd 2–7 is a rearrangement of Ezra 1–6 in order to accommodate the implausible account of the wisdom contest and its aftermath.

In addition, 1 Esd 6:17 makes Zerubbabel and Sheshbazzar contemporaries in coming to Jerusalem instead of leading separate groups at different times, contradicting the portrayal in 1 Esd 2:9–14 and 3:1–5:6. Another contradiction is that the vessels of Jerusalem's temple are returned from Babylon by Sheshbazzar in 1 Esd 2:9–14, but according to 1 Esd 4:57 they are to be returned by Zerubbabel. However, these contradictions disappear without the account concerning Zerubbabel and his wisdom in 1 Esd 3:1–5:6. This is further demonstration that 1 Esd 2–7 is not historically reliable, but instead is a purposeful rearrangement of Ezra 1–6 in order to accommodate a fictional story.

SHESHBAZZAR VERSUS ZERUBBABEL

Some have attempted to reconcile these two seemingly contradictory views of the return. Medieval rabbis simply equated Sheshbazzar and Zerubbabel, claiming that these were two names for the same person, but this view has only a few more recent advocates. A more common explanation is to posit that there are two returns implied by the first chapters of Ezra: one led by Sheshbazzar in the reign of Cyrus (Ezra 1:1–11; 5:13–16) and a later one led by Zerubbabel in the reign of Darius (Ezra 2:1–70).[270] This seems to solve the problem until one turns to Neh 7:4 –73. Here we find a list, similar to the one in Ezra 2:1–70, of those who returned to Judah and Jerusalem. Moreover, this list is said to contain the names of "those who first came up [from Babylon] . . . who came with Zerubbabel, Jeshua, [and others]" (Neh 7:5, 7). Thus Zerubbabel's return was the first return according to Nehemiah 7. Either one has to discount Ezra's statement about a

---

[270] Halpern, "A Historiographic Commentary on Ezra 1–6," 89.

return under Sheshbazzar as inaccurate, or another explanation is needed.

ZERUBBABEL AS LEADER; SHESHBAZZAR AS GOVERNOR

A more likely scenario is that Zerubbabel was one of the prominent men in the return under Sheshbazzar and that Zerubbabel succeeded Sheshbazzar as governor. Note that Zerubbabel is at the head of a list of several leaders among the returning exiles in Ezra 2:2 (‖Neh 7:7). This would explain why in Darius' day Sheshbazzar is spoken of in distant historical terms: "King Cyrus . . . gave them to a certain Sheshbazzar" (Ezra 5:14), and "that Sheshbazzar came and laid the foundations of the house of God" (Ezra 5:16). This would also explain why Sheshbazzar is called governor when the foundation is laid (Ezra 5:14–16). Under Sheshbazzar's authority, Zerubbabel was placed in charge of the actual construction (Ezra 3:8). Thus Zerubbabel, as chief of construction, also could be said to have laid the temple's foundation. A decade or more later, an angel of Yahweh promised that Zerubbabel (now governor) would also see to its completion (Zech 4:9).[271] It is noteworthy that in Ezra, Zerubbabel by name is never called "governor,"[272] and that phenomenon is easily

---

[271] Thus it is not necessary to try to distinguish between the Akkadian loanword אֻשַּׁיָּא in Ezra 5:16, "foundation," and the Hebrew verb יסד, "to found, lay a foundation," used elsewhere in Ezra (3:6, 10–12) and in Haggai (2:18) and Zechariah (4:9; 8:9). Some interpreters have distinguished these two words in order to claim that the Akkadian noun signifies the "subfoundation" and the Hebrew verb is a more general word, so that Sheshbazzar worked only on the subfoundation, but Zerubbabel laid the rest of the foundation. See VanderKam, *From Joshua to Caiaphas*, 8–9, who presents this argument. Instead it is more likely that the Akkadian word is used in Ezra 5:16 because it is in an official document of the empire written in Aramaic, whereas the Hebrew verb is used in the Hebrew texts of Ezra, Haggai, and Zechariah.
[272] However, Ezra 6:7, part of an Aramaic source document, refers to "the governor of the Judeans," apparently meaning Zerubbabel.

explained, because all but one of the references to him in Ezra concern his work when he was under the governor Sheshbazzar (Ezra 2:2; 3:2, 8; 4:2–3). The lone exception is Ezra 5:2 when Zerubbabel resumes the work on the temple after it had been interrupted. In this case the writer may avoid calling him governor because of the influence of the previous passages. The author simply continues his established pattern of not referring to any officials of Yehud[273] by their name and official title simultaneously. However, Haggai does tell us that Zerubbabel was governor in the second year of Darius (Hag 1:1, 14; 2:2, 21).[274]

This understanding of Zerubbabel and Sheshbazzar as contemporaries is also stated in 1 Esdras. 1 Esd 2:9–14 (cf. the parallel in Ezra 1:7–11) relates that the vessels from the temple in Jerusalem captured by Nebuchadnezzar were turned over to Sheshbazzar and that he returned them to Jerusalem. However, 1 Esd 6:17 says that they were turned over to Zerubbabel and Sheshbazzar, making the two men contemporaries when the foundation of the temple was laid (1 Esd 6:19). It should be noted that 1 Esd 6:8–21 is parallel to Ezra 5:7–17, since both contain the letter of Tattenai to Darius. That 1 Esd 6:17 mentions both Zerubbabel and Sheshbazzar, whereas Ezra 5:14, the parallel verse in Ezra, mentions only Sheshbazzar, testifies that even in antiquity the narrative in Ezra 1:1–4:4 was understood as occurring under the governorship of Sheshbazzar when Zerubbabel, a scion of the house of David, was one of the prominent leaders of the Judeans.

Therefore, the most plausible understanding of Ezra 1–6 is that Zerubbabel, as one of the leaders of the exiles, returned with Sheshbazzar. There is no need to posit that Zerubbabel returned to

---

[273] Yehud was the name of the Persian name for the administrative district around Jerusalem where the Judeans settled after returning from Babylon.
[274] Both Haggai and Zechariah refer to Joshua as high priest (Hag 1:1, 12, 14; 2:2, 4; Zech 3:1, 8; 6:11), though Ezra (who calls him *Jeshua*) never explicitly connects him with that office.

Jerusalem at a later date than did Sheshbazzar. Some time after the return, Zerubbabel replaced Sheshbazzar as governor.

WHEN DID ZERUBBABEL COME TO JERUSALEM?

Having concluded that Zerubbabel came to Jerusalem with Sheshbazzar, we now need only to establish when the exiles first returned to Jerusalem. Since the biblical text gives no unambiguous statement about the date of this first return to Jerusalem, external evidence must be sought.

Such external evidence exists in the form of the postexilic cycle of Sabbatical Years. The law concerning Sabbatical Years is treated in the Torah of Moses briefly in Exod 23:10–11, but more thoroughly in Lev 25:1–7. The counting of years up to the seventh year, which was to be the first Sabbatical Year, was to begin "when you come into the land that I am giving you" (Lev 25:2). The Israelites would have begun to count the years for the Sabbatical cycles when they first began to conquer the land under Joshua in 1406 BC. They would have started a new cycle of counting when they returned to the land after their exile in Babylon during the reign of Cyrus.

Therefore, if we can determine the Sabbatical Years in the postexilic era, we can determine when the Judeans returned. The first Sabbatical Year in the postexilic era should mark the seventh year after the return, so we can count back from the first Sabbatical Year to arrive at the year of the return from exile. Cyrus' reign over Babylon and its empire lasted only nine years (538–530 BC), and it is unlikely that the return took place in his first year or in the last year or two of his reign.

In 1857 Benedict Zuckermann published a schedule of Sabbatical cycles based on *Seder 'Olam*, 30, and statements of Moses Maimonides.[275] This became the accepted theory, especially after it was adopted by Emil Schürer in his magisterial *A History of the Jewish People in the Time of Jesus Christ*. However, in 1973, Ben

---

[275] Zuckermann, *A Treatise on the Sabbatical Cycle and the Jubilee.*

Zion Wacholder demonstrated that Zuckermann's schedule was incorrect by one year; each Sabbatical Year should be one year later than in Zuckermann's schedule.[276] More recently Young has demonstrated that Zuckermann did not correctly understand *Seder 'Olam*, 30, but that a correct understanding of it agrees with Wacholder's schedule of Sabbatical Years.[277] Key to Wacholder's schedule of Sabbatical Years is nine literary references to specific Sabbatical Years:

1. The remission of taxes under Alexander the Great for the Sabbatical Year 331t.

2. The second Battle of Beth-zur in the summer of the Sabbatical Year 163t.

3. The murder of the Hasmonean Simon in the Sabbatical Year 135t.

4. The conquest of Jerusalem by Herod on 10 Tishri after the previous Sabbatical Year 37t.[278]

5. The recital of Deut 7:15 by Agrippa I in a post-Sabbatical Year, making the Sabbatical Year AD 41t.

6. A note of indebtedness from Wadi Murabba'at: indicating AD 55t as a Sabbatical Year.

7. The destruction of the temple in Jerusalem at the end of the Sabbatical Year AD 69t.

8. Rental contracts of Simon bar Kosiba ("bar Kochba") indicating AD 132t as a Sabbatical Year.

---

[276] Wacholder, "The Calendar of Sabbatical Cycles during the Second Temple and the Early Rabbinic Period." See also Wacholder, "Chronomessianism" and "The Calendar of Sabbath Years during the Second Temple Era."

[277] Young, "*Seder Olam* and the Sabbaticals Associated with the Two Destructions of Jerusalem: Part 1."

[278] See also Steinmann, "When Did Herod the Great Reign?"

9. Three fourth- and fifth-century tombstones in Sodom indicating AD 433t and 440t as Sabbatical Years.

All of these Sabbatical Years occur as multiples of seven years in relation to each other, indicating that there was a consistent reckoning of Sabbatical Years for over 750 years from the days of Alexander the Great to the fifth century AD. More importantly, as Wacholder has noted, Neh 10:31 demonstrates an awareness of the established nature of this cycle already in the time of Ezra and Nehemiah.[279] Apparently, some had been neglecting the Sabbatical Years, but the returnees in Neh 10 pledged to keep them by foregoing the crops each seventh year.

Counting backward from the known postexilic Sabbatical Years indicates that during the reign of Cambyses 527t would have been a Sabbatical Year. Since this would have been the seventh year after the exiles returned to the land, the first year—the year of the return—would have been 533 BC, some five years after Cyrus' decree in 538 BC permitting the return.

While five years may seem like a long time between Cyrus' decree and the return to Jerusalem, the details in Ezra 1–2 would indicate that an immediate return would have been unlikely. First of all, a time of preparation was required before they could return. Ezra 1:6 indicates a concerted effort by those who remained in Babylon to help equip and finance those who were determined to return. This was probably not a quick process given all that was donated. Second, it is unlikely that the returnees simply dropped everything in order to return. There was property to sell, accounts to settle, travel arrangements to be made. Third, Ezra 2:64–65 (||Neh 7:66–67) indicates that almost 50,000 people made the trip to Jerusalem. Organizing such a large group would take time. Finally, it would have been unlikely that Cyrus' treasurer Mithredath would have turned

---

[279] Wacholder, "The Calendar of Sabbatical Cycles during the Second Temple and the Early Rabbinic Period," 157–58.

over the temple vessels to just any Judean who presented himself as leader of the returning Judeans, no matter how prominent he may have been (Ezra 1:8). Instead it is more reasonable to assume that the exiles first organized themselves and then their leaders requested that one of them be named governor of Yehud and be entrusted with the vessels.

For these reasons, a five-year period of planning and organization is not at all unreasonable. Furthermore, this five-year delay may help explain why the Judeans, after making only a beginning by laying the temple foundation, were forced to stop. Had they returned immediately with the decree of Cyrus still new, it is unlikely that their building program could have been successfully opposed in the court of Cyrus as indicated by Ezra 4:5. It simply would have been unlikely for the king or his officials to reverse policy so abruptly and quickly. If, however, the Judeans returned five years later in 533 BC and began to build in 532 during their second year in Jerusalem (Ezra 3:8), the decree would have been some six years old—far enough in the past that it was capable of being opposed by current leaders in Samaria, allowing for the opposition to persuade Persian authorities to halt the work. Thus from the text of Ezra and the evidence of the Sabbatical cycles of the postexilic era, we can be reasonably certain that Sheshbazzar and Zerubbabel and the Judeans who accompanied them returned to Yehud and Jerusalem in 533 BC.

This enables us to construct a chronology for the events of Ezra 1–4 during the reign of Cyrus.

Table 46
Events in Ezra during the Reign of Cyrus

538	Cyrus' decree	Ezra 1
Summer (?) 533	Arrival in Jerusalem	Ezra 2:68
Elul (?) 533	Altar in built	Ezra 3:2
1 Tishri (20 Sep) 533	First sacrifices on new altar	Ezra 3:6
Iyyar 532	Second temple begun	Ezra 3:8
531 (?)	Work on temple halted	Ezra 4:4–5

DARIUS I (521–486)

During the early years of the long reign of Darius I several important events in the life of the Judeans living in and around Jerusalem took place. In Darius' second year, 520n, on 24 Elul (September 21) the work on the temple resumed. This work was spurred by the preaching of Haggai and Zechariah, who date several of their prophecies to this year:

Table 47
Prophecies of Haggai and Zechariah in 520 BC

Hag 1:1–13	1 Elul	Tuesday, August 29
Hag 1:14–16	24 Elul	Thursday, September 21
Hag 2:1–9	21 Tishri	Tuesday, October 17
Zech 1:1–6	Marcheshvan	October/November
Hag 2:10–19	24 Kislev	Monday, December 18
Hag 2:20–23	24 Kislev	Monday, December 18

Although Haggai's prophetic ministry lasted less than five months, Zechariah would continue to prophesy, and two of his prophecies date to the next two years. On 24 Shebat (Thursday, February 15) 519 BC he would receive his night visions (Zech 1:7–6:15). On 4 Kislev (Saturday, December 7) 518 BC he preached repentance (Zech 7–8).

On 3 Adar (Saturday, March 12) 515 BC the new temple in Jerusalem was dedicated (Ezra 6:15). The Passover celebration followed on 14 Nisan (Thursday, April 21). It was an especially joyous celebration (Ezra 6:19–22).

XERXES (485–465)

The reign of Xerxes is barely mentioned in Ezra, but, of course, takes center stage in Esther.[280] The story of Esther can be coordinated with the known events of Xerxes' reign from classical sources.[281]

---

[280] Xerxes (from the Greek pronunciation of the name) is called אֲחַשְׁוֵרוֹשׁ in Hebrew, which in many English Bibles is transliterated as *Ahasuerus*. Both

Darius I died in late 486 BC, probably in November.[282] At that time Egypt was in open rebellion against Persian rule. Thus, Xerxes ruled during the last months of 486 BC and the early months of 485 BC before his first official regnal year began in Nisan 485 BC. It is during this accession period that the accusatory letter against the Judeans in Jerusalem mentioned in Ezra 4:6 was written. The letter most likely accused the Judeans of complicity in the Egyptian rebellion. It is significant that Ezra 4:6 states that the letter was written "at the beginning of his reign" (בִּתְחִלַּת מַלְכוּתוֹ), not in Xerxes' first year. This phrase most likely was chosen to signify Xerxes' accession period.

Since the first Egyptian inscriptions dating to Xerxes' reign are from 484 BC, he must have successfully suppressed the Egyptian revolt during his first regnal year, 485n. With Egypt pacified, Xerxes was free to turn his attention to the conquest of Greece, which had aided the Egyptians in their rebellion. This would have been the setting for the 180-day banquet in Xerxes' third year mentioned at Esth 1:3. This banquet would have been part of Xerxes' planning his westward campaign and raising support for it among his nobles and commanders. Since Susa was not usually the royal residence during the hot summer months, it is likely that this banquet took place in late winter. This appears to be confirmed by Esth 1:5 which notes that Xerxes provided a seven-day feast for everyone in Susa. This most likely coincided with the new year commencing Xerxes' fourth regnal year on 1 Nisan (Saturday, April 3) 482 BC. That would mean that the 180-day banquet spanned 4 Tishri (Sunday, October 4) 483 BC–30

---

the Hebrew and Greek pronunciations are reflections of the Old Persian name *Xšayāršā*. See Shea, "Esther and History," 246, note 4.

[281] Much of this section is based on the discussion in Shea, "Esther and History."

[282] Xerxes' accession most probably took place in Marcheshvan 486 BC. See Parker and Dubberstein, *Babylonian Chronology 626 B.C. – A.D. 75*, 17.

Adar (Friday, April 2), 482 BC, and the seven-day feast ran from 1 Nisan (Saturday, April 3) to 7 Nisan (Friday, April 9) 482 BC.

Xerxes apparently suppressed a Babylonian revolt in his fourth year, since for his fifth year Xerxes, most likely in irritation with the Babylonians, dropped the title "King of Babylon," and Persian kings would never again use that appellation.[283] This would explain why the Greek invasion was delayed until Xerxes' fifth year.

In May 480 BC Xerxes set out to invade Greece from Sardis in Lydia. After failing to complete his conquest of Greece in light of the defeat of his fleet at the Battle of Salamis, he returned to Sardis in December 480 BC. Xerxes turned his attention from Greece to his court, and it is likely that he arranged the search for a new queen at this time (Esth 2:1–4). This matches well with Esth 2:12 which states that the young girls who were candidates underwent 12 months of preparation. Since Esther was presented to Xerxes in Tebeth 479/478 BC (Esth 2:16),[284] she entered into the preparations no later than Shebat (February) 479 BC. From this point forward we can easily construct the rest of the chronology of Esther as shown in Table 48.

Table 48
Biblical Events during the Reign of Xerxes

Late 486/early 485		Letter to Xerxes	Ezra 4:6
25 Elul 483– 30 Adar 482	Sat, Oct 3, 483– Fri, Apr 2, 482	180-day banquet	Esth 1:3
1–7 Nisan 482	Sat, Apr 3– Fri, Apr 9, 482	Seven-day feast	Esth 1:5

---

[283] Ctesias places the Babylonian revolt before the Greek campaign, whereas Arrian places it afterwards. The dropping of the title "King of Babylon" supports Ctesias. See Shea, "Esther and History," 236; Cameron, "Darius and Xerxes in Babylonia," 324–325.

[284] Tebeth spanned December 22, 479–January 20, 478 BC during Xerxes' seventh year.

Shebat–Tebeth 479	Feb–Dec 479	12-month preparation	Esth 2:12
Tebeth 479/478	Dec 479/Jan 478	Esther presented to Xerxes	Esth 2:16
1 Nisan 474	Fri, Apr 5, 474	Haman casts the Pur	Esth 3:7
13 Nisan 474	Wed, Apr 17, 474	Haman issues edict	Esth 3:12
23 Sivan 474	Mon, Jun 25, 474	Mordecai issues edict	Esth 8:9
13 Adar II 473	Thu, Apr 5, 473	Judeans defend themselves	Esth 3:13; 8:12; 9:1
14 Adar II 473	Fri, Apr 6, 473	Purim celebrated	Esth 9:15; 9:17

ARTAXERXES I (464–424)

The activities of both Ezra and Nehemiah were set during the reign of Artaxerxes. However, there were three Achaemenid kings by that name, and two of them reigned more than 32 years (cf. Neh 5:14; 13:6). Moreover, Ezra appears in the book of Ezra during the seventh year of Artaxerxes (Ezra 7:7) and later in the book of Nehemiah in what is apparently Artaxerxes' twentieth year (Neh 2:1; cf. Neh 8). Dating the work of Ezra and Nehemiah—especially Ezra—is complicated and has drawn much attention by scholars. The following lengthy discussion reviews the evidence and various theories proposed in the past to argue that Ezra began his work in 458 BC under Artaxerxes I and was still active in Jerusalem when Nehemiah arrived in 445 BC.[285]

THE DATE OF EZRA'S MISSION TO JERUSALEM

THE TRADITIONAL VIEW

Ezra 7:7 states that Ezra and those with him returned to Jerusalem in the seventh year of Artaxerxes. There were three Persian kings with this name, and they all reigned more than seven years. However, the book of Nehemiah also tells us that Ezra was in Jerusalem (Neh 8:1–2, 4–6, 9, 13; 12:26, 36) when Nehemiah came to Jerusalem in the

---

[285] For more details see Steinmann, *Ezra and Nehemiah*, especially 40–51.

twentieth year of Artaxerxes (Neh 2:1–8). Since evidence external to the Bible indicates that Nehemiah must have returned in the twentieth year of Artaxerxes I (see discussion below beginning on page 209), Ezra must have returned in the seventh year of Artaxerxes I, 458n. This may be called the traditional view, since it was the most commonly held view before the rise of critical theories that placed Ezra's mission at a later time. Most recent scholarship has also supported this view.

However, three other theories have been put forth, and it is important to understand their arguments, since they can be found in the literature about Ezra.

THE VAN HOONACKER THEORY

First proposed by Maurice Vernes in a footnote in his book *Précis d'histoire juive*,[286] this idea was developed into a full theory by Albin van Hoonacker in a series of works between 1890 and 1924.[287] This theory holds that Ezra came to Jerusalem in the seventh year of Artaxerxes II, 398n. This theory was most popular from the early- to mid-twentieth century, and it continues to have adherents.

Pivotal to this theory is the contention that the material in Neh 8 that mentions Ezra and his reading of the Law was displaced from its original position in Ezra.[288] This contention allows the further claim that Ezra and Nehemiah were not contemporaries, since the original Nehemiah material never mentioned Ezra, and Neh 12:26 and 12:36 allegedly are later glosses. Instead this theory proposes that Ezra came to Jerusalem about thirty years after Nehemiah's final work there. To support this contention scholars observe that 1 Esdras moves immediately from the account of the banishing of foreign wives (1 Esd 8:88–9:36; cf. Ezra 10:1–44) to Ezra's reading of the

---

[286] Vernes, *Précis d'histoire juive*, 582.

[287] A bibliography of van Hoonacker's publications on this subject can be found in Rowley, *The Servant of the Lord*, 133, note 1.

[288] Snaith, "The Date of Ezra's Arrival in Jerusalem," 64.

Law (1 Esd 9:37–55; cf. Neh 7:73–8:12). According to this view 1 Esdras ends abruptly, cutting off in the middle of the account of Ezra reading the Law and its aftermath. For instance, the NRSV ends 1 Esdras with this translation:

> Then they all went their way, to eat and drink and enjoy themselves, and to give portions to those who had none, and to make great rejoicing; because they were inspired by the words which they had been taught. And they came together. (1 Esd 9:54–55)

> καὶ ᾤχοντο πάντες φαγεῖν καὶ πιεῖν καὶ εὐφραίνεσθαι καὶ δοῦναι ἀποστολὰς τοῖς μὴ ἔχουσιν καὶ εὐφρανθῆναι μεγάλως ὅτι καὶ ἐνεφυσιώθησαν ἐν τοῖς ῥήμασιν οἷς ἐδιδάχθησαν καὶ ἐπισυνήχθησαν[289]

Some scholars who espouse this view speculate that perhaps 1 Esdras originally contained all of the material about Ezra as found in Ezra 8 but that the end of the book was lost.

Van der Kooij has demonstrated that the ending of 1 Esdras is not abrupt when properly understood. He argues that the ὅτι clause that ends 1 Esdras should be understood as a compound clause with καὶ linking two verbs within the clause instead of signaling a new sentence.[290] Thus the end of 1 Esdras should be translated like this:[291]

> Then they all went their way, to eat and drink and enjoy themselves and to give portions to those who had none and to make great rejoicing because they were inspired by the words that they had been taught and [because] they had gathered together. (1 Esdras 9:54–55)

Van der Kooij concludes: "There is no compelling reason to suppose that the present ending of 1 Esdr does not constitute the original

---

[289] Note that the NRSV agrees with the Göttingen LXX, which places a period after ἐπισυνήχθησαν followed by a dash before καὶ (Hanhart, *Esdrae Liber I*, 148).

[290] Van der Kooij, "On the Ending of the Book of 1 Esdras," 44–46.

[291] See the similar translation in *NETS*.

one."[292] Since 1 Esdras shows all the signs of being a compilation of material from Ezra and Nehemiah (and Chronicles) and not an earlier edition of those books, the central thesis of the van Hoonacker theory is untenable, making the entire theory unlikely. Moreover, eliminating Neh 8 and its references to Ezra also requires claiming that Ezra's name is a gloss in Neh 12:26, 36. Yamauchi has noted that Ezra cannot be simply stricken from Neh 12:36 because then the second procession along the wall of Jerusalem would have had no leader.[293]

However, other objections to the traditional view have been raised by van Hoonacker and others. These also will be briefly examined.

1. *It has been claimed that Ezra and Nehemiah "ignored" each other, with little or no interaction between the men.* Emerton writes: "No meeting between them is recorded, and they never both play active parts in the same action; one is active and, at most, the other's name is mentioned in passing."[294] However, this argument is unconvincing, since as Tuland observes about two other men in the same era: "The prophets Haggai and Zechariah provide a parallel example. They were concerned with the *same* problems, lived in the *same* place and were contemporaries, but Haggai does not mention Zechariah, nor does Zechariah mention Haggai."[295]

2. *Nehemiah, it is claimed, is silent about those who returned with Ezra (Ezra 8:1–14).* However, the list in Nehemiah 7 (cf. Ezra 2) of returnees who had returned with Zerubbabel includes at least a dozen names of ancestors of those who

---

[292] Van der Kooij, "On the Ending of the Book of 1 Esdras," 47.

[293] Yamauchi, "The Reverse Order of Ezra/Nehemiah Reconsidered," 9.

[294] Emerton, "Did Ezra Go to Jerusalem in 428 B.C.?" 16; see also Snaith, "The Date of Ezra's Arrival in Jerusalem," 59–63.

[295] Tuland, "Ezra-Nehemiah or Nehemiah-Ezra?" 49. We should also note that Ezra 5:1 and 6:14 confirm that Haggai and Zechariah were contemporaries.

returned with Ezra.[296] Since the list in Ezra 8:1–14 includes twelve of the seventeen names in Nehemiah's list (Neh 7:8–24), it would appear that the Ezra's contingent is made up largely of those who had ties to the first returnees. This is more likely to be the case the closer the return of Ezra is to the first return, since over time these family ties would be forgotten or weakened. The traditional view separates the two returns by 75 years—distant, but still close enough to preserve these ties. The van Hoonacker theory separates the two returns by 135 years, making the large overlap of names in the two lists less likely.

3. *Nehemiah supposedly came to a Jerusalem that was sparsely inhabited (Neh 7:4; 11:1–2), whereas Ezra came to a bustling city (Ezra 9:4; 10:1). In a similar vein, Ezra supposedly found the priests, Levites, and family heads living in Jerusalem (Ezra 8:29; 10:1, 5), while Nehemiah had to recruit these groups to live in the city (Neh 11:1–19).* Allegedly, these two observations indicate that Ezra came after Nehemiah. However, the first part of the first supposition is not true; note that when Nehemiah built the wall of the city there were many inhabitants who lived in the city who repaired sections of the wall near their houses (Nehemiah 3). Moreover, regarding the second part of the first supposition, the large crowd in Ezra 10:1 may have come not only from Jerusalem, but also from the surrounding area. A similar argument could be made about the priests, Levites,

---

[296] Tuland, "Ezra-Nehemiah or Nehemiah-Ezra?" 53, lists them: Parosh (Ezra 8:3; Neh 7:8); Pahath-moab (Ezra 8:4; Neh 7:11); Zattu (Ezra 8:5; Neh 7:13); Adin (Ezra 8:6; Neh 7:20); Elam (Ezra 8:7; Neh 7:12); Shephatiah (Ezra 8:8; Neh 7:9); Joab (Ezra 8:9; Neh 7:11); Bani/Binnui (Ezra 8:10; Neh 7:15; cf. Ezra 2:10); Bebai (Ezra 8:11; Neh 7:16); Azgad (Ezra 8:12; Neh 7:17); Adonikam (Ezra 8:13; Neh 7:18); Bigvai (Ezra 8:14; Neh 7:19).

and family leaders who are mentioned in Ezra 8:29. The weighing of the temple vessels in the presence of these groups took place on the fourth day after Ezra's arrival (Ezra 8:33–34), perhaps because it took that long to notify and gather members of these groups who were living in Yehud outside of Jerusalem.

4. *Nehemiah found the wall of Jerusalem broken down, but Ezra thanked God for acting "to give us a protective wall in Judah and in Jerusalem" (Ezra 9:9), which supposedly refers to the city wall and therefore indicates that Ezra came after the city wall had been rebuilt under Nehemiah.* However, in Ezra 9:9, the noun translated as "protective wall" is גָּדֵר, which usually refers to an enclosure made of loose stone that protected a vineyard or marked off one's property (Num 22:24; Pss 62:3; 80:12; Prov 24:31; Eccl 10:8; Isa 5:5; Ezek 13:5; 22:30; 42:7, 10; Hos 2:6; Micah 7:11). It is different than the usual noun for a "city wall," חוֹמָה. Tuland furthermore notes that the repeated preposition בְּ in Ezra 9:9 ("*in* Judah and *in* Jerusalem") is not the preposition associated with a city wall: "Wherever the Hebrew text refers to a wall *around* a city, it does not use the particle *bᵉ*, 'in,' but the word *sābîb*, 'around.' "[297] Finally, when Ezra refers to this "wall in Judah," he is clearly employing a metaphor for God's protection, since it is obvious that there was no literal wall encompassing the whole territory of Judah. This metaphorical "wall" follows a similar metaphor in Ezra 9:8, where God is said to have given his people a "peg" or "stake" (יָתֵר) in God's sanctuary.[298] Van Hoonacker's literalistic construal of

---

[297] Tuland, "Ezra-Nehemiah or Nehemiah-Ezra?" 55, citing 1 Ki 3:1; 2 Chr 14:6 (14:7 in English Bibles); cf. Ezek 40:5.

[298] Snaith, "The Date of Ezra's Arrival in Jerusalem," 59.

Ezra 9:9 is so tendentious that even followers of the van Hoonacker theory have disavowed it.[299]

5. *Nehemiah was a contemporary of the high priest Eliashib (Neh 3:1, 20–21; 13:4, 7), but Ezra was a contemporary of the high priest Jehohanan/Johanan, who was Eliashib's grandson (Ezra 10:6; cf. Neh 12:10–11, 22–23). From two Aramaic papyri from Egypt written in 407 BC, we know that at that time Johanan was high priest.[300] This means that Ezra could not have been in Jerusalem in 445 BC, but must have come to Jerusalem in the seventh year of Artaxerxes II, at least a generation after Nehemiah.* There are several problems with this argument. One is that it equates the priest Eliashib who "had been put in charge of the storerooms of the house of God" (Neh 13:4, 7) with the high priest Eliashib (Neh 3:1, 20; cf. Neh 3:21; 12:10, 22–23). However, the Eliashib in Neh 13:4 is simply called "the priest," which in biblical texts normally indicates he was not the high priest (note the distinction in Neh 3:1). Therefore, there were at least two priests with this name. The same could be observed concerning "Jehohanan son of Eliashib" in Ezra 10:6. In this verse neither this Jehohanan nor this Eliashib is called "high priest." Thus it is likely that there were two priests named Eliashib and two named Jehohanan/Johanan. One Eliashib and one Jehohanan/ Johanan were from the high priestly family, and this Eliashib was the grandfather of Jehohanan/Johanan (see Neh 3:1, 20; 12:10–11[301] and 12:22). The other Eliashib and Jehohanan/Johanan consisted of ordinary priests who were probably father and son (Ezra

---

[299] Snaith, "The Date of Ezra's Arrival in Jerusalem," 58–59.

[300] *TAD* 1:68–75 (A4.7; A4.8), where his name is spelled "Jehohanan."

[301] In Neh 12:11, "Jonathan" is probably another name, or a scribal mistake, for "Johanan" (Neh 12:22–23).

10:6). In fact, Eliashib appears to be a common name at this time, since at least three other men had this name (Ezra 10:24, 27, 36). The name Jehohanan/Johanan also was common, since it was borne by at least five other men (Ezra 8:12; 10:28; Neh 6:18; 12:13; 12:42). Nehemiah was indeed a contemporary of the high priest Eliashib (Neh 3:1, 20–21). But since Ezra 10:6 is talking about a different Jehohanan/Johanan, there is no evidence that Ezra was a contemporary of the high priest Jehohanan/Johanan, Eliashib's grandson (Neh 12:22).

6. *No members of the families who returned with Ezra (Ezra 8:1–20) are among the lists of those who helped build the wall in Nehemiah's day, indicating that these families returned with Ezra after the wall had already been built.* However, Tuland has identified at least two prominent Levites, Sherebiah and Hashabiah, who returned with Ezra and who are also mentioned in connection with Nehemiah's activity. These two are specifically connected with both Nehemiah and Ezra in Neh 12:24–26: Sherebiah (e.g., Ezra 8:18, 24; Neh 12:24), and Hashabiah (e.g., Ezra 8:19, 24; Neh 3:17; 12:24).[302] This makes both Ezra and Nehemiah contemporaries of these men. Neither of these Levites could have journeyed with Ezra if he came to Jerusalem in 398 BC, since in 445 BC they were already old enough to be leaders. In 398 BC they would have been too old to make such a journey. Another Levite associated with both Ezra and Nehemiah was Jozabad (Ezra 8:33; 10:23; Neh 8:7; 11:16). In addition, the priest Meremoth son of Uriah (Ezra 8:33) might be among those associated with the activity of both Ezra and Nehemiah, since there is also a Meremoth son of Uriah

---

[302] Tuland, "Ezra-Nehemiah or Nehemiah-Ezra?" 59–60. See also Yamauchi, "The Reverse Order of Ezra/Nehemiah Reconsidered," 10.

named in Neh 3:4, 21. However, the man in Neh 3:4, 21 is not designated as a priest, so these texts may be speaking about two different people with the same name, one a priest and one a layman.[303] In addition, Malchijah son of Harim was a contemporary of both Ezra and Nehemiah (Ezra 10:31; Neh 3:11). However, the most important observation is that Neh 3 lists only the chief builders of the wall, not all who participated. Therefore, it would at most be an argument from silence (the weakest form of argument) if none of those in the group that returned with Ezra were named as part of the group that helped Nehemiah build the wall of Jerusalem. However, the Levites Sherebiah and Hashabiah, who returned with Ezra, are also associated with Nehemiah, and Hashabiah is named as one of those who helped build the wall.

7. *If Ezra returned to Jerusalem in the seventh year of Artaxerxes I (458 BC), why did he wait for thirteen years until 445 BC to read the Law of Moses publicly (Neh 8:1–12)?* This argument has often been cited by the proponents of the van Hoonacker theory as strong support for their view. However, it reads too much into the text. Nehemiah 8 does not indicate that this was Ezra's first public reading of the Law. He may have read it publicly several times before this. In fact, there were two Sabbatical Years (457t and 450t) between 458 and 445 BC. He may have read the Law on both the occasions, as required by Moses' command (Deut 31:10–13). It would be an argument from silence to contend that just because we are not told that Ezra read the Law in the seven months between the time he arrived in Jerusalem on 1 Ab 458 BC (August 4, 458; Ezra 7:9) and the end of the book of Ezra on 1 Nisan 457 BC (March 27, 457; Ezra 10:17) he must never have read

---

[303] Yamauchi, "The Reverse Order of Ezra/Nehemiah Reconsidered," 9.

it at any time after those events but before the convocation in 445 BC.

8. *Finally, some argue that if Ezra preceded Nehemiah, Ezra's effort to reform marriage practices failed (Ezra 9–10), since Nehemiah had to correct the problem again at a later time (Neh 13:23–28). Moreover, they suggest that Ezra's reform had to be later since his actions were more severe (requiring divorce) than Nehemiah's actions (simply requiring an oath that the people would not allow their children to engage in the practice).* This argument is hardly convincing. First, many men of God are only temporarily successful at reform. Note, for example, how the Judean kings Hezekiah and Josiah, despite their faithfulness and zeal, were unable to effect lasting reforms within unfaithful Israel as a whole. Cross agrees:

> I am not impressed by such an argument. One may say that all the prophets and reformers failed in biblical history. A fairly close analogy is found in the reforms of Hezekiah and Josiah, both of which failed.[304]

Second, Nehemiah's actions of cursing, beating, pulling out hair, and forcing the people to take oaths (Neh 13:25) are more verbally and physically severe than Ezra's actions, considering that Ezra did not resort to either cursing or violence to enforce his reforms.

9. Another piece of evidence makes the van Hoonacker theory unlikely is this: Hattush, a descendant of David, accompanied Ezra to Jerusalem (Ezra 8:2). Hattush was the great-grandson of Zerubbabel (1 Chr 3:17–22). This means that he would

---

[304] Cross, "A Reconstruction of the Judean Restoration," *Int* 29 (1975): 198, n. 60. (This quotation does not appear in the version of this article published in *JBL*.)

have been about seventy years old in 398 BC.[305] It is unlikely that a man of that age (were he still living) would make the arduous trip from Babylon to Jerusalem. However, Hattush would have been about ten years old in 458 BC when he made the journey with Ezra.

Thus upon close inspection there is little to recommend the van Hoonacker theory. None of its assumptions and arguments are convincing, and some are plainly wrong. For this reason it has largely fallen out of favor among scholars.

THE MEDIATING THEORY

Because the book of Nehemiah indicates that Ezra and Nehemiah were contemporaries, some critical scholars have sought to place Ezra after Nehemiah—but close in time—thereby attempting to mediate between the traditional view and the van Hoonacker theory. Key to this theory is the text of Ezra 7:7–8:

וַיַּעֲלוּ מִבְּנֵי־יִשְׂרָאֵל וּמִן־הַכֹּהֲנִים וְהַלְוִיִּם וְהַמְשֹׁרְרִים וְהַשֹּׁעֲרִים
וְהַנְּתִינִים אֶל־יְרוּשָׁלָ͏ִם בִּשְׁנַת־שֶׁבַע לְאַרְתַּחְשַׁסְתְּא הַמֶּלֶךְ: וַיָּבֹא
יְרוּשָׁלַ͏ִם בַּחֹדֶשׁ הַחֲמִישִׁי הִיא שְׁנַת הַשְּׁבִיעִית לַמֶּלֶךְ:

Some of the Israelites, some of the priests, the Levites, the singers, the gatekeepers, and the temple servants went up to Jerusalem in the seventh year of King Artaxerxes. He came to Jerusalem in the fifth month (it was the king's seventh year).

Scholars have proposed that a word has dropped out of the dating of the regnal years in one or both of these verses. In 1895 Julius Wellhausen proposed that "twenty" (עֶשְׂרִים) had dropped out.[306] The

---

[305] Demsky, "Who Came First, Ezra or Nehemiah? The Synchronic Approach," 7–8.

[306] Julius Wellhausen, "Die Ruckkehr der Juden aus dem babylonischen Exil," *Nachrichten von der königliche Gesellschaft der Wissenschaften zu Göttingen, Philologisch-Historische Klasse* (Göttingen: 1895), 186, cited by Demsky, "Who Came First, Ezra or Nehemiah: The Synchronic Approach,"

number in Ezra 7:7–8 would then be twenty-seven. This would place Ezra's arrival in Jerusalem seven years after Nehemiah arrived, but during Nehemiah's twelve-year term as governor (Neh 5:14). In 1896 Josef Markwart proposed that the number "thirty" (שְׁלֹשִׁים) had dropped out.[307] This would place Ezra's arrival in 428 BC, seventeen years after Nehemiah, probably during Nehemiah's second governorship of Yehud. Wellhausen's view attracted few supporters, but Markwart's view has had quite a few advocates. Some argue that homoioarchton ("same beginning") led to the omission of "thirty." In Hebrew both "thirty" and "year" begin with שׁ, and after a scribe had written שְׁנַת, "year," he could have skipped over שְׁלֹשִׁים, "thirty," thinking that he had already written that (different) word that starts with the same consonant, שׁ.

The most obvious problem with this view is that there is neither Hebrew manuscript evidence nor any evidence from the LXX or from any of the other ancient versions to support it. It is simply conjecture.

There are also further problems with this view. The way to refer to the "thirty-seventh" year would be to use two cardinal numbers, שְׁלֹשִׁים וְשֶׁבַע, literally, "thirty and seven," as in 2 Kgs 13:10; 25:27; Jer 52:31. Hebrew has no separate forms for cardinal and ordinal numbers above ten. Ezra 7:7 employs the cardinal number "seven" (שֶׁבַע), but Ezra 7:8 has the ordinal number "seventh" (הַשְּׁבִיעִית). Even if, hypothetically, the text of Ezra 7:7 were corrupted by the omission of the cardinal number שְׁלֹשִׁים, "thirty," that same process of corruption would not account for the text of Ezra 7:8, with its ordinal "seventh" (שְׁבִיעִית). The ordinal "seventh" (שְׁבִיעִית) must be the original text of Ezra 7:8, since the alleged restoration of שְׁלֹשִׁים, "thirty," would produce the reading שְׁנַת שְׁלֹשִׁים הַשְּׁבִיעִית, which

---

8, n. 29 (cf. Yamauchi, "The Reverse Order of Ezra/Nehemiah Reconsidered," 12).

[307] According to Yamauchi, "The Reverse Order of Ezra/Nehemiah Reconsidered," 12.

would not be the correct syntax for saying "the thirty-seventh year."[308] It is difficult to accept that both verses originally had שְׁלֹשִׁים וְשֶׁבַע, that "thirty" (שְׁלֹשִׁים) dropped out of both verses simultaneously, and that subsequently a scribe changed שֶׁבַע ("seven") to שְׁבִיעִית ("seventh") in Ezra 7:8 but did not change שֶׁבַע ("seven") in Ezra 7:7.

There is another, less obvious objection to the mediating theory, which is, nevertheless, a fatal objection: Ezra participated in the dedication of the wall of Jerusalem (Neh 12:27–47; see especially Neh 12:36). Why would Nehemiah delay the dedication seven or seventeen years after completing the project?[309]

Thus either of the forms of the mediating theory has little to recommend it. Furthermore, it relies on many of the arguments that are part of the van Hoonacker theory that Ezra must have come to Jerusalem after Nehemiah—arguments that are unconvincing.

THE SABBATICAL YEAR THEORY

A more recent theory has been proposed by Aaron Demsky.[310] He theorizes that the Ezra source that he perceives behind the narratives about Ezra in both Ezra 7–10 and in portions of Nehemiah follows a different calendrical system than Nehemiah's memoirs. The Ezra source supposedly used reckoning according to Sabbatical Years, whereas Nehemiah's memoirs used the regnal years of the Persian monarch. He proposes that Ezra 7:7–8 has been corrupted by a scribe who did not understand the presence of these two different systems in

---

[308] Emerton, "Did Ezra Go to Jerusalem in 428 B.C.?"18–19; Demsky, "Who Came First, Ezra or Nehemiah: The Synchronic Approach," 8.

[309] Cf. Demsky, "Who Came First, Ezra or Nehemiah? The Synchronic Approach," 9. If a scholar wishes to omit Ezra's name in Neh 12:36 as a later gloss in order to support the mediating theory, the second procession along the wall would be left without a leader (Yamauchi, "The Reverse Order of Ezra/Nehemiah Reconsidered," 9).

[310] Demsky, "Who Came First, Ezra or Nehemiah? The Synchronic Approach."

the text. According to Demsky, Ezra 7:7–8 originally did not contain the phrases "of King Artaxerxes" or "of the king." By Demsky's reckoning these were added by a scribe who did not understand that the references to "the seventh year" meant the Sabbatical Year. The scribe instead took them to be the regnal years of Artaxerxes and added the appropriate phrases to make them read that way. Thus for Demsky, Ezra returned in 444t during a Sabbatical Year. This is why Ezra could follow Nehemiah and yet be at the dedication of the wall, which apparently was delayed about a year after its completion.[311]

There are several problems with Demsky's theory. The most serious is the speculative nature of his assumptions. A dating system that is based on the Sabbatical Year is completely hypothetical: there is no place in the OT or even in Hellenistic Jewish literature where historical narratives employ a Sabbatical Year dating system.[312] Indeed, such a system would be highly impractical, since it would simply repeat a seven-year-long cycle. It would quickly become confusing since a "first year" and every year up to the "seventh year" would be repeated once every seven years. Without some other system to which to tie such dating, it would not be possible to tell which ordinal year ("first," "second," etc.) was intended. The proposal that "of King Artaxerxes" and "of the king" are later glosses is also hypothetical, since all of the textual evidence supports their inclusion.

In addition, Demsky's reckoning of Sabbatical Years follows the erroneous tables of Zuckermann instead of the correct tables of Wacholder.[313] The Sabbatical Year would have been one year later than Demsky assumes, meaning that Ezra would not have arrived in

---

[311] Neh 6:15 states that the wall was completed on 25 Elul. Demsky agrees that this is in Artaxerxes' twentieth year, 445 BC.

[312] The only indisputably explicit mention of an actual Sabbatical Year in the Bible or the Apocrypha is in 1 Macc 6:53, where the mention of the Sabbatical Year is not a dating device, but is used to explain why stores of foodstuffs were running low in the late summer of that year.

[313] See the discussion above beginning on page 188.

Jerusalem until 442 BC, which would leave more than two years between the completion of the wall in 445 BC and its dedication. However, it is irrelevant whether there were one or two years between the completion and the dedication of the wall. The flow of the narrative in Nehemiah from Neh 6:15 to Neh 9:1 leaves the impression that the wall was dedicated in the same year as it was completed and that this was the same year that Nehemiah first arrived in Jerusalem.

There is no compelling reason to adopt the highly speculative Sabbatical Year theory. Instead the traditional view that Ezra came to Jerusalem in 458 BC in the seventh year of Artaxerxes I provides the correct chronological setting for the events of Ezra 7–10.

Since all the alternatives to the traditional theory have serious drawbacks, the best position is that of the traditional theory: Ezra returned to Jerusalem in the seventh year of Artaxerxes I, 458n.

THE DATE OF NEHEMIAH'S GOVERNORSHIP OF YEHUD

In Neh 5:14 Nehemiah states that he was governor of Yehud from the twentieth to the thirty-second year of Artaxerxes, having been appointed in the first month (Nisan) of Artaxerxes' twentieth year (Neh 2:1). However, these biblical references could be either to Artaxerxes I (464–424 BC) or to Artaxerxes II (404–359 BC). Artaxerxes I and Artaxerxes II each ruled for more than thirty-two years.

Two Aramaic papyri from Egypt, which are drafts of a letter dated to 407 BC, suggest that Nehemiah was active during the reign of Artaxerxes I (464–424 BC).[314] There are two indications of this in the Aramaic letter. First, it names Johanan/Jehohanan as the high priest in Jerusalem at that time.[315] Johanan was the grandson of Eliashib and the son of Joiada, the high priests in Nehemiah's day (Neh 3:1, 20; 13:28). This means that Nehemiah was governor sometime before

---

[314] *TAD* 1:68–75 (A4.7; A4.8).

[315] *TAD* 1:68–75 (A4.7.18; A4.8.17), where his name is spelled "Jehohanan."

407 BC, placing him in the reign of Artaxerxes I. Confirming this, the end of the Aramaic letter mentions Delaiah and Shelemiah, sons of Sanballat, governor of Samaria.[316] From the context it appears that Sanballat is now an aged man and his sons are looking after his affairs. Sanballat apparently had been governor since Nehemiah's day (Neh 2:10, 19; 4:1, 7; 6:1–2, 5, 12, 14; 13:28).

Additional evidence that Nehemiah was active during the reign of Artaxerxes I (464–424 BC) is found in the inscription on a silver bowl discovered at Tell el-Maskhuta in Lower Egypt in 1947. The inscription reads, "That which Qaynu son of Gashmu, king of Qedar, brought in offering to Han-'ilat," and can be dated paleographically to about 400 BC.[317] The Gashmu of the inscription is called Geshem in Nehemiah (Neh 2:19; 6:1–2; but Gashmu at Neh 6:6). Geshem was leader of the Arabian kingdom of Qedar, and he opposed Nehemiah when Nehemiah was governor. Since his son was king of Qedar about 400 BC, Geshem (and therefore Nehemiah) had to be active before that time.

Finally, as Heltzer has noted, in the late first century or early second century AD, the Greek historian Plutarch wrote that at some point during the reign of Artaxerxes I, he outlawed punishing nobles by flogging them and plucking their beards. Therefore Nehemiah must have meted out this punishment to the nobles of Jerusalem (Neh 13:25) at an earlier time in the reign of Artaxerxes I, before Artaxerxes published this decree.[318]

All of the evidence, therefore, converges to confirm that Nehemiah was governor of Yehud from the twentieth to the thirty-second year of Artaxerxes I (445–433 BC). Because of this

---

[316] *TAD* 1:68–75 (A4.7.29; A4.8.28).

[317] Dumbrell, "The Tell el-Maskhuta Bowls and the 'Kingdom' of Qedar in the Persian Period," 33–38; see also Cross, "Geshem the Arabian."

[318] Heltzer, "The Flogging and Plucking of Beards in the Achaemenid Empire and the Chronology of *Nehemiah*," 306–7, citing Plutarch, *Moralia*, 173D.1, 3.

overwhelming evidence there is near-universal agreement on the dates of Nehemiah's tenure in Jerusalem.[319]

---

[319] See, for example, Green, "The Date of Nehemiah," who argues for the fifth-century date after reexamining the evidence and attempting to harmonize it with Josephus' account in *Antiquities*, 11. However, Josephus' chronology for this period is extremely unreliable, making it difficult to harmonize his accounts of Jewish history under the Persians with biblical or other extrabiblical evidence. Like Green, Saley attempts to harmonize the data from Josephus with the books of Ezra and Nehemiah ("The Date of Nehemiah Reconsidered"). He comes to the conclusion that there is insufficient information to determine whether Nehemiah served during the reign of Artaxerxes I or Artaxerxes II. However, his conclusion is dependent upon the conjectural reconstruction of the succession of high priests proposed by Cross, "A Reconstruction of the Judean Restoration." That reconstruction is doubtful, calling into question Saley's conclusion as regards the viability of dating Nehemiah to the reign of Artaxerxes II.

In one of the few studies in the last quarter century that challenges the consensus on the date of Nehemiah's activities, McFall attempts to rearrange the materials in Nehemiah, making his first term as governor run from 465 to 454 BC (thus bringing him to Jerusalem before Ezra came in 458 BC) and dating his second trip to Jerusalem to 445 BC ("Was Nehemiah Contemporary with Ezra in 458 BC?"). According to McFall, Nehemiah's second stay in Jerusalem was brief and mainly occupied with repairing the wall of the city. Ezra, according to McFall, did not stay long after completing his work in 458 BC, but returned to Babylon. Later he returned with Nehemiah in 445 BC. McFall accepts the chronological information in Nehemiah as accurate, but believes there are three different ways of reckoning years employed by the author(s) of Ezra and Nehemiah. One of these ways of reckoning is dynastic, that is, in Neh 5:14 and 13:6, the twentieth and thirty-second years of Artaxerxes are actually reckoned from the beginning of the reign of Xerxes, since in this system of reckoning, the reigns of Xerxes and Artaxerxes are counted as one reign. Dynastic reckoning, though uncommon, was used at times in the ancient Near East (e.g., 2 Chr 16:1; see Thiele, *Mysterious Number*, 84–87, 198). However,

Nehemiah's return to Jerusalem after his governorship (Neh 13:6–7), therefore, must have taken place sometime after 433 BC. Nehemiah's return took place after a public reading of the Teaching of Moses (Neh 13:1), and such public readings were to be held at the Feast of Tabernacles in Tishri during Sabbatical Years (Deut 31:10–13). The only Sabbatical Year that occurred after 433 BC but still in the reign of Artaxerxes I began in 429 BC. Therefore, Nehemiah returned to Jerusalem to find Tobiah's property in a temple storeroom (Neh 13:7–8) sometime after Tishri 429 BC but before the end of Artaxerxes' reign in 424 BC. Since Nehemiah's actions to cleanse the temple of the Ammonite Tobiah (Neh 13:9) is connected with this reading of Moses' Teaching, a date of late 429 BC or early 428 BC is the most reasonable for Nehemiah's return. This would still leave about four more years for the last part of the reign of Artaxerxes I, during which he promulgated his decree outlawing the plucking of beards (see the discussion on page 210).

CHRONOLOGY OF THE WORK OF EZRA AND NEHEMIAH

Having established the time when Ezra came to Jerusalem and when Nehemiah served as governor we can proceed to compile a list of dates for various occurrences during the work of these two men.

"THE TWENTIETH YEAR" IN NEH 1:1

The only vexing question left to answer is the meaning of "the twentieth year" in Neh 1:1.[320] In this verse Nehemiah relates the time and the place that he received news about Jerusalem. He mentions "the twentieth year," which scholars usually assume is a reference to Artaxerxes' twentieth year as king. The problem with this reckoning

dynastic reckoning in the ancient Near East is only documented in cases where a dynasty begins with a ruler from a new family line or a collateral family line (as in the case of Darius I). Dynastic reckoning is not documented in a case like the one proposed by McFall, where a son had succeeded his father as king. This and other problems with McFall's theory make it doubtful.

[320] This discussion is based on Steinmann, *Ezra and Nehemiah*, 385–387.

is that Nehemiah later approached Artaxerxes in the month of Nisan in the twentieth year of his reign (Neh 2:1–8). Since the Persians normally counted regnal years as beginning in Nisan and Neh 1 takes place the previous Kislev, Neh 1:1 cannot refer to Artaxerxes' twentieth regnal year.

Several other theories have been put forward that pose solutions to this issue.[321] One popular solution proposes that Nehemiah reckoned the new year as beginning with the month of Tishri in the early autumn instead of Nisan in the early spring.[322] Yet Williamson notes: "Without any explanation, this would be a confusing procedure, however, for it runs counter to all known Jewish practice of the period."[323] A similar suggestion by Bickerman is that Nehemiah was reckoning years from Artaxerxes' month of accession to the throne, which he dates to Ab 465 BC.[324] This theory also runs counter to all known practice—Jewish and Persian—and once again would be a confusing procedure without further explanation. Another proposal is that "twentieth year" is a mistake and that "nineteenth year" is the actual date. This, however, is simply conjecture without any textual support.

The best solution to the problem is that Nehemiah was reckoning from some other event important to him. This likelihood is supported by the fact that Nehemiah does not label this year as one of the years of Artaxerxes, but everywhere else he does count years in terms of the reign of Artaxerxes (Neh 2:1; 5:14; 13:6). Most likely this "twentieth year" was Nehemiah's twentieth year of service to the Persian court, beginning shortly before Artaxerxes' first official year. Perhaps Nehemiah was part of Artaxerxes' new administration when he assumed the throne sometime in 465 BC.

The enigmatic dating in Neh 1:1 probably also indicates that this extract from Nehemiah's memoirs (Neh 1:1–8:1a) was taken from

---

[321] A good summary can be found in Williamson, *Ezra, Nehemiah*, 169–170.

[322] Thiele, *Mysterious Numbers*, 53, 180.

[323] Williamson, *Ezra, Nehemiah*, 169.

[324] Bickerman, "En marge de l'Écriture," 19–23.

somewhere in the middle, although the superscription (Neh 1:1a) may have come from the beginning. An earlier part of the memoirs probably made clear what starting point Nehemiah used for this other method of chronological reckoning, and so here Nehemiah did not need to specify the reference point for "the twentieth year." However, that point of reference was lost when the author/compiler of the book of Nehemiah extracted this portion of Nehemiah's work.

DATES FOR THE WORK OF EZRA AND NEHEMIAH

Table 49
Chronology of the Work of Ezra and Nehemiah

1 Nisan 458	Sat Apr 8	Ezra leaves Babylon	Ezra 7:7–9
12 Nisan 458	Wed Apr 19	Ezra leaves Ahava Canal	Ezra 8:31
1 Av 458	Fri Aug 4	Ezra arrives in Jerusalem	Ezra 7:7–9
4 Av 458	Mon Aug 7	Vessels weighed	Ezra 8:33
17 Kislev 458	Sat Dec 16	Proclamation to assemble	Ezra 10:7–8
20 Kislev 458	Tue Dec 19	Convocation re: intermarriage	Ezra 10:9
1 Tebeth 458	Fri Dec 29	Examination of intermarriage	Ezra 10:16
1 Nisan 457	Wed Mar 27	Examination ends	Ezra 10:17
Kislev 446	Nov/Dec	Hanani reports to Nehemiah	Neh 1:1
Nisan 445	Apr/May	Nehemiah before Artaxerxes	Neh 2:1
445–433		Nehemiah governor of Yehud	Neh 6:15; 13:6
3 Ab 445	Mon Aug 11	Walls of Jerusalem started	Neh 6:15
25 Elul 445	Thu Oct 2	Walls of Jerusalem completed	Neh 6:15
1 Tishri 445	Wed Oct 8	Nehemiah holds convocation	Neh 7:73; 8:2
2 Tishri 445	Thu Oct 9	Ezra leads Torah study	Neh 8:13
15–21 Tishri 445	Oct 22–28	Feast of Tabernacles	Neh 8:14, 18
22 Tishri 445	Wed Oct 29	Assembly	Neh 8:18
24 Tishri 445	Fri Oct 31	Fast	Neh 9:1
Late 429/early 428		Nehemiah returns to Jerusalem	Neh 13:6–7

10

BETWEEN THE TESTAMENTS

BIBLICAL SOURCES: 1 AND 2 MACCABEES

While not considered inspired Scripture by Jews or Protestants, the books of the Apocrypha have traditionally been included in Bibles in some Protestant traditions. Luther included the Apocrypha in his German translation of the Scriptures, placing it between the Old and New Testaments, a tradition followed by later Bible translations, most notably in 1611 with the publication of the King James Version of the Bible. The placement of these books between the Old and New Testaments was fitting, since most of the books of the Apocrypha originated in the years between the composition of the last books of the Old Testament and the birth of Jesus.

Among the Apocrypha are two historical books that relate events in Jewish history during the Hellenistic era which followed the fall of Persia to the forces of Alexander the Great (1 Macc 1:1). These books, 1 and 2 Maccabees, chronicle the turbulent times of the second century BC that saw faithful Jews resisting the forced Hellenization of Judea by Antiochus IV Epiphanes (175–163 BC) and the rise of the Jewish priestly Hasmonean dynasty starting with Mattathias (d. 166 BC) and his sons Judas Maccabeus (d. 160 BC), Jonathan (d. 142 BC), and Simon (d. 134 BC).

1 MACCABEES

Probably composed sometime in the first half of the first century BC, 1 Maccabees covers events in Palestine from the beginning of the reign of Antiochus IV Epiphanes in 175 BC (1 Macc 1:10) to the accession of John Hyrcanus to the Hasmonean throne in 134 BC (1 Macc 16:11–24). Although it has a tendency to glorify the Hasmonean dynasty, 1 Maccabees is generally regarded as an accurate historical source, and its narrative of events can often be corroborated by reference to Polybius or other Greek historians.

2 MACCABEES

The author of 2 Maccabees claims that his work is a condensation of a five-volume work by Jason of Cyrene (2 Macc 2:23). The author or a later editor has added two letters to Jews in Egypt at the beginning of the book (2 Macc 1:1–2:18). 2 Maccabees parallels 1 Macc 1–8, but is generally considered somewhat less historically accurate. It covers events from 176–161 BC.

PTOLEMAIC AND SELEUCID KINGDOMS

After the unexpected death of Alexander the Great in 323 BC, a struggle to rule his kingdom ensued among his generals and successors. Eventually Alexander's empire was split into several parts, the two most important being the Ptolemaic kingdom in Egypt and the Seleucid Empire that ruled Syria, Babylonia, Persia and parts of Asia Minor. Initially the Ptolemaic Kingdom ruled Palestine, but in the early second century BC the Seleucids wrested control of the Jewish homeland from them.

Since both 1 and 2 Maccabees are set during the Seleucid domination of Palestine, it is not surprising that they generally use the Seleucid method of numbering years. The Seleucid Era began in 311 BC with the return of Seleucus I Nicator to Babylon from exile in Egypt. The Seleucids considered this date to be the founding of their empire, so that the years of the Seleucid era begin with 311 BC as year 1.[325] Since the Babylonian calendar was used by the empire, these years began in Nisan.

---

[325] The Seleucids (and Josephus and 1 Maccabees) reckoned this from 311n, following the Babylonian custom. The Macedonians and Egyptians

CHRONOLOGY OF EVENTS IN 1 AND 2 MACCABEES

Both 1 and 2 Maccabees date a number of events. These events along with their dates are given in Table 50.

Table 50
Dated Events in 1 and 2 Maccabees

Seleucid Date	Julian Date	Event	Reference
137	175n	Antiochus IV begins to reign	1 Macc 1:10
143	169n	Temple in Jerusalem sacked	1 Macc 1:20
15 Kislev 145	Dec 6, 167	Altar in temple desecrated	1 Macc 1:54
146	166n	Mattathias dies	1 Macc 2:70
25 Kislev 148	Dec 14, 164	Temple in Jerusalem cleansed	1 Macc 4:52
148	164n	Letter of Lysias to the Jews[326]	2 Macc 11:21
15 Xanthicus 148	Mar 163	Letter of Antiochus V[327]	2 Macc 11:33
15 Xanthicus 148	Mar 163	Letter from Rome	2 Macc 11:38
149	163n	Antiochus V attacks Judas	2 Mac 13:1
150	162n	Spring: Citadel in Jerusalem attacked; Summer: 2nd battle of Beth-Zur[328]	1 Macc 6:20
151	161n	Alcimus seeks high priesthood	2 Macc 14:4
Nisan 152	Apr 160	Demetrius attacks Jerusalem	1 Macc 9:3
Iyyar 153	May 159	Inner courtyard wall torn down	1 Macc 9:54
Tishri 160	Oct 152	Jonathan made high priest	1 Macc 10:21

(Ptolemies) reckoned this from the fall equivalent of Tishri (i.e., 312t). See Finegan, *Handbook of Biblical Chronology*, 102, §193.

[326] The date is given as 24 Dioscorinthius in year 148 (of the Seleucid Era). The month and day cannot be determined, however, since this is the only ancient reference to the otherwise unknown month of Dioscorinthius.

[327] Xanthicus was equated with Adar. According to Parker and Duberstein, *Babylonian Chronology 626 B.C–A.D. 75*, 41, there was both an Adar and a second (intercalated) Adar in 163 BC. If this was the first Adar, 15 Xanthicus would have occurred on March 2. If it was the second Adar, 15 Xanthicus would have occurred on March 31.

[328] The Second Battle of Beth-Zur took place in the summer of this year near the end of sabbatical year, when food stores in Palestine were running low (1 Macc 6:53). Therefore the attack on the citadel took place earlier in the year, probably in the spring.

169	143n	Letter to Egyptian Jews	2 Macc 1:7
170	142n	Demetrius II frees Judah from taxation	1 Macc 13:41
23 Iyyar 171	Jun 4, 141	Simon conquers Jerusalem's citadel	1 Macc 13:51
18 Elul 172	Sep 13, 140	Monument to Simon erected	1 Macc 14:27
Shebat 177	Feb 134	Simon assassinated	1 Macc 16:14
Bef. Kislev 188	Bef. Dec 124	Letter to Jews in Egypt	2 Macc 1:10

From these dates the other events related in 1 and 2 Maccabees can be approximately dated. For instance the First Battle of Beth-Zur (1 Macc 4:28–35) took place in 164 BC before the cleansing of the temple later that year in Kislev. In a similar way, Demetrius deposed Antiochus V as Seleucid king sometime in 161 BC (2 Macc 14:1–2) before Alcimus sought to ingratiate himself with Demetrius in an attempt to be reappointed high priest (2 Macc 14:3–5).

Figure 1
Hasmoneans in 1 and 2 Maccabees

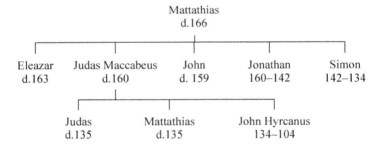

11

JESUS' BIRTH

The New Testament contains a number of chronological indications of the time of Jesus' birth. He was born during the reigns of Augustus (Luke 2:1) and Herod (Matt 2:1). Quirinius was "governing Syria" (ἡγεμονεύοντος τῆς Συρίας) at the time, and there was a census (Luke 2:2). In addition, Jesus was "about thirty years old" (ὡσεὶ ἐτῶν τριάκοντα) when he was baptized (Luke 3:23), and this was during the fifteenth year of Tiberius' reign (Luke 3:1).

One way to estimate the date of Jesus' birth would be to count backward from the fifteenth year of Tiberius. Following the death of Augustus on August 19, AD 14, Tiberius was named head of the Roman state by the Senate on September 17. Tiberius' fifteenth year would have been September 17, AD 28–September 16, AD 29, or if official Roman regnal years were intended, January 1–December 31, AD 29.[329] Since it was most likely summer when John began to preach

---

[329] Some, following a suggestion first made by Theodor Mommsen in 1887, would argue that Tiberius' reign should be reckoned as the beginning of his joint rule of the provinces with Augustus sometime between AD 11 and AD 13. (See the discussion in Finegan, *Handbook of Biblical Chronology,* 330–337, esp. §578; Hoehner, *Chronological Aspects of the Life of Christ*, 31–37; Messner, "'In the Fifteenth Year' Reconsidered," especially 202–205 and note 3.) However, as far as is known, ancient sources always counted Tiberius' reign as commencing after the death of Augustus. Martin, "The Nativity and Herod's Death," 89, notes that surviving coins and inscriptions also reckon Tiberius' reign from either January 1 or August 19, AD 14.

in the wilderness and Jesus came to be baptized, the summer of AD 29 is the likely date of Jesus' baptism.[330] Jesus, therefore, would have been born sometime from the summer of 3 BC to the summer of 1 BC if he were "about 30"—between 29 and 31 years old at his baptism.[331] This, in fact, is the date favored by the church fathers for Jesus' birth.[332]

However, the consensus of modern scholarship is that Jesus was born before the spring 4 BC, because the end of the reign of Herod the Great is commonly dated to that time. For this reason we must examine the way Herod's reign is dated before we can make any conclusions about the date of Jesus' birth.

---

[330] This is confirmed by John 2:13, 20, 23. See discussion below beginning on page 262. It would be possible on the basis of Luke 3:1, 23 alone to place Jesus' baptism in late September AD 28, if one dated Tiberius' reign from the time that the senate declared him emperor. However, John 2:20 makes this impossible.

[331] While some might argue that Luke's notice that Jesus was "about 30" at his baptism should be taken very loosely so that he might have been as old as 33 or 34, Luke's only other similar notice contradicts this. At Luke 8:42 he reports that a synagogue ruler had a daughter "about twelve." Since Luke did not use a more general description to indicate merely that the girl was a young adolescent, he must have been indicating her age as accurately as was known—within a year or so of twelve. Certainly he did not mean that she could have been as old as fifteen or sixteen or as young as eight or nine. See the more detailed discussion in Steinmann, "When Did Herod the Great Reign?" 18–19.

[332] Finegan, *Handbook of Biblical Chronology*, 291, Table 139.

THE REIGN OF HEROD THE GREAT

THE CONSENSUS VIEW

The general consensus is that Herod was named king of Judea by the Romans in 40 BC, began his reign in Jerusalem after conquering the city in 37 BC, and died in 4 BC.[333] The logic for this is as follows:[334]

1. Herod was named king by Antony and Octavian "in the one hundred eighty-fourth Olympiad, the consuls being Gnaeus Domitius Calvinus for the second time and Gaius Asinius Pollio."[335] The one hundred eighty-fourth Olympiad ran from July 1, 44 BC to June 30, 40 BC. Calvinus and Pollio were named consuls in 40 BC. This dates Herod's appointment to 40 BC.

2. Herod took Jerusalem "during the consulship at Rome of Marcus Agrippa and Caninius Gallus, in the one hundred eighty-fifth Olympiad."[336] The one hundred eighty-fifth Olympiad ran from July 1, 40 BC to June 30, 36 BC, and Agrippa and Gallus were named consuls in 37 BC. This dates the beginning of Herod's reign in Jerusalem to 37 BC.

3. Herod died shortly after a lunar eclipse, but before the Passover.[337] The eclipse is usually taken to be the partial lunar eclipse on March 13/14, 4 BC, twenty-nine days before the Passover on April 11.

4. Herod's sons and successors also appear to indicate that he died in 4 BC. Herod Archelaus was banished in AD 6 after a

---

[333] The discussion of the dates of Herod's reign is based on Steinmann, "When Did Herod the Great Reign?"

[334] This is based on Schürer, *A History of the Jewish People in the Time of Jesus Christ*, 1.281 n.3; 1.2. 84n. 11; 1.327, n.1.

[335] Josephus, *Ant.* 14.389 [14.14.5].

[336] Josephus, *Ant.* 14.487–488 [14.16.4]; *J.W.* 1.343 [1.17.8].

[337] Josephus, *Ant.* 17.167, 213 [17.6.4; 17.9.3]; *J.W.* 2.10 [2.1.3].

reign of 10 years over Judea, Samaria and Idumea.[338] Herod Antipas lost the tetrarchy of Galilee and Perea in the second year of Gaius (AD 38 or 39) after a reign of 43 years according to numismatic evidence.[339] Herod Philip died in the twentieth year of Tiberius (AD 33) after a reign of 37 years over Gaulanitis.[340] All of these point to the beginning of their reigns as 4 BC.

This consensus is heavily reliant on a particular interpretation of the relevant portions of Josephus' *Antiquities* and *The Jewish War*. However, when using Josephus we must exercise caution, since it is well documented that he was not always accurate in his portrayal of events. Like historians of all ages, Josephus was dependent upon sources which themselves had to be understood and interpreted, and his understanding of his sources may have been deficient or his interpretation of them may at times have been mistaken. Like many other ancient historians, he at times modified events to suit his rhetorical and ideological purposes. Josephus' accounts especially need to be examined when he reports speeches, which are not verbatim transcripts of what was said, but often contain the historian's account of what should have been said, could have been said, or what the historian wanted to have been said given his ideological biases. In addition, when Josephus reports on people's motives or is attempting to convince his audience of the reasons for a person's actions, he may well be embellishing the truth in order to accomplish his rhetorical goal of persuading his readers to adopt his view of events and their causes.

Nevertheless, there is one area in which everyone who attempts to reconstruct the chronology of Herod's reign agrees: Josephus' chronological notices are more-or-less reliable.

---

[338] Josephus, *Ant.* 17.342 [17.13.2].

[339] Josephus, *Ant.* 18.252 [18.7.2], Finegan, *Handbook of Biblical Chronology*, 300, §516.

[340] Josephus, *Ant.* 18.106 [18.4.6].

PROBLEMS WITH THE CONSENSUS VIEW

There are numerous problems with the Consensus View that make it highly suspect. For instance, to make Herod begin his reign in 40 BC and 37 BC in Jerusalem and end at 4 BC, the Consensus View allows only 36 years for his reign and 33 in Jerusalem, although Josephus reports 37 and 34 years respectively. To justify this the Consensus View must hold that Herod's reign was reckoned inclusively (i.e., by non-accession year reckoning, counting both the beginning and ending years and all years between), although there is no evidence for this—and every other reign in this period, including those of the Jewish high priests, are reckoned non-inclusively by Josephus.

THE STARTING DATE FOR HEROD'S REIGN

There are at least three reasons to doubt Josephus' chronology at this point, casting doubt on the dating of Herod's appointment to 40 BC.

1. The one hundred eighty-fourth Olympiad ended on June 30, 40 BC. However, Calvinus and Pollio were not appointed consuls until after the Treaty of Brundisium on October 2. Josephus must be in error here.

2. Appian contradicts Josephus. He mentions Herod's appointment by Antony, along with a number of other kings. From the context, it is clear that Appian places Herod's appointment in 39 BC.[341]

3. There is a discrepancy in Josephus' writings in that he implies that Herod did not journey to Rome until winter,[342] making the earliest date for his appointment late 40 BC, during the one hundred eighty-fifth Olympiad.

---

[341] Appian, *Civil War* 5.8.75. Sections 69–76 cover the year 39 BC, which can be determined by comparison to Dio's *Roman History*. This was first noted by Filmer, "Reign of Herod," 285.

[342] Josephus, *Ant.* 14.376 [14.14.2].

Josephus' notice of Herod's appointment is somehow in error. Either Herod was appointed late in 40 BC or sometime in 39 BC, but not in the first half of 40 BC as Josephus' Olympian synchronism would imply.

Moreover, a date of 40 BC does not fit with the known movements of Marc Antony nor with Josephus' own relating of the events connected with him.[343] In 44 BC Julius Caesar was murdered and his assassins were defeated by Octavian and Antony at the Battle of Philippi at the end of 42 BC. Antony then went to Asia where he met and fell in love with Cleopatra. This must have been in 41 BC. Josephus relates that Antony appointed Herod and his brother Phasaelius tetrarchs at this time. Two years later, Josephus tells us, the Parthians conquered Syria and deposed Hyrcanus as Jewish high priest, installing Antigonus as both Judean king and high priest. This must have been in 39 BC. Only after this event did Herod travel to Rome where he was appointed king to replace Antigonus. Thus, Josephus' own narrative contradicts his dating of Herod's appointment to 40 BC during the one hundred eighty-fourth Olympiad. Instead, the narrative, like the narrative in Appian, implies that Herod was appointed in 39 BC.

If Herod was appointed in the winter of 39 BC, then his first official year would have been 38 BC. After a reign of 37 years, he would have died shortly before Passover in 1 BC. This, in turn, places Jesus' birth sometime from late 3 BC to late 2 BC, and he would have been 30 or 31 years of age at his baptism, in agreement with Luke 3:1, 23.

THE DATE FOR HEROD'S CONQUEST OF JERUSALEM

Although Herod had been named king by the Romans, the Parthians had made the Hasmonean Antigonus king and high priest in

---

[343] Filmer, "Reign of Herod," 287; Josephus, *Ant.* 14.301, 324, 330 [14.12.2; 14.3.1, 3].

Jerusalem. Therefore, Herod was forced to raise an army and, with the help of the Roman general Sossius, he conquered Jerusalem and deposed Antigonus three years after having been named king.

Josephus' description of Herod's conquest of Jerusalem is found in *Ant.* 14.487–491 [14.16.4]. He claims that Herod conquered Jerusalem during the consulship of Marcus Agrippa and Caninius Gallus in the one hundred eighty-fifth Olympiad, in the third month of the Greek calendar (September) on the Day of Atonement (10 Tishri). He also states that it was 27 years to the day after the Roman general Pompey conquered Jerusalem. Furthermore, he says "thus did the government of the Hasmoneans cease, one hundred twenty-six years after it was first set up."

The consular year and Olympiad given by Josephus indicate that Herod took Jerusalem in 37 BC. However, the other two pieces of information given by Josephus contradict this:

1. Jerusalem fell to Herod exactly 27 years after it fell to Pompey. Pompey took Jerusalem on the Day of Atonement in 63 BC. This indicates that Herod took Jerusalem in 36 BC.

2. Shortly after Jerusalem fell to Herod, Antigonus was taken to Antony, who had him executed. This ended 126 years of Hasmonean government. If Herod took Jerusalem in 37 BC as Josephus' consular year suggests (and as the Consensus View holds), then the government set up by the Hasmoneans should have started in 163 BC. However, no such government is mentioned in any of the sources for this period. On the other hand, if Herod took Jerusalem in 36 BC, the Hasmonean government should have been founded in 162 BC. In fact this is exactly what is reported in both Josephus and 1 Maccabees. In 162 BC Antiochus V made peace with Judas Maccabeus: "the king sent to Judas, and to those that were besieged with them, and promised to give them peace, and to permit them to

make use of, and live according to the laws of their fathers."[344] Subsequently, Judas behaved as if he had authority over a sovereign state and made a treaty of "the Jewish nation" with Rome.[345]

There are several other indications that Josephus gave the wrong consular year for Herod's conquest of Jerusalem. The first is in Josephus' own writings. He states that Pompey reinstated Hyrcanus II as high priest after he conquered Jerusalem in Tishri 63 BC and that Hyrcanus reigned twenty-four more years (i.e., to Tishri 39 BC). This was followed by Antigonus' reign of three years and three months (or six months).[346] This puts Antigonus' execution in December 36 BC (or March 35 BC). This fits well if Herod conquered Jerusalem in September 36 BC. The three (or six) additional months would have been the time needed to take Antigonus to Antony, for Antony to receive Herod's bribe and request that Antigonus be killed, and to arrange for Antigonus' execution. Thus, Josephus own chronology of the high priests of this period date Herod's conquest to 36 BC, not 37 BC.

Second, Dio's *Roman History* casts doubt on Josephus' consular year. Dio reports that during 37 BC Sossius engaged in no military activity, and Dio specified that Sossius did this because he did not want to be seen as doing anything to advance Antony's interests.[347] Thus, Dio's statement implies that Sossius would not have helped Herod that year, since Herod was favored by Antony.

Finally, Josephus states that Herod besieged Jerusalem at the end of a Sabbatical year when food supplies were running low.[348] However, the summer of 37 BC when Herod supposedly besieged Jerusalem according to Josephus' consular year notice was not the

---

[344] Josephus, *Ant.* 12.382 [12.9.7]; cf. 1 Macc 6:59.
[345] Josephus, *Ant.* 12.414–419 [12.10.6]; 1 Macc 8.
[346] Josephus, *Ant.* 20.244–245 [20.10.4] reports three years and three months. *Ant.* 14.97 [14.6.1] reports three years and six months.
[347] Dio, *Roman History,* 49.23.1–2.
[348] Josephus, *Ant.* 14.475 [14.16.2].

end of a sabbatical year. In contrast, the summer of 36 BC was the end of a sabbatical year that had begun in Tishri of 37 BC.[349]

Once again, despite a consular year notice to the contrary, most of Josephus' information and information from Dio point to a different year. In this case the evidence indicates that Jerusalem fell to Herod in Tishri 36 BC. If Herod conquered Jerusalem in 36 BC, then after a reign of 34 years in Jerusalem (beginning in Tishri 36 BC), he would have died shortly before Passover in 2t, that is, in late Adar or early Nisan 1 BC. This, in turn, once again places Jesus' birth sometime from late 3 BC to late 2 BC, and he would have been 30 or 31 years of age at his baptism, in agreement with Luke 3:1, 23.

THE NUMBER OF HIGH PRIESTS

Josephus reports that the number of high priests from "the times of Herod" (τῶν Ἡρώδου χρόνων) to Titus' burning of the Temple in AD 70 was 28 and that the total of their reigns was 107 years.[350] The Consensus View has generally held that the "times of Herod" began with his conquest of Jerusalem. Since Titus conquered Jerusalem during Ab in AD 70,[351] and the Consensus View holds that Herod conquered Jerusalem on 10 Tishri 37 BC, the Consensus View allows only about 106 years.[352] The Consensus View consistently holds that in *Antiquities* Josephus reckoned all of Herod's regnal years from Herod's conquest of Jerusalem. There are four additional references to Herod's regnal years in *Antiquities* and one in *The Jewish War*:

---

[349] See the discussion of post-exilic Sabbatical years beginning on page 188.

[350] Josephus, *Ant.* 20.250 [20.10.5]. See the discussion in Steinmann, "When Did Herod the Great Reign?" 25–28.

[351] Josephus, an eyewitness to the destruction of the temple, dates the conflagration to 10 Ab (*J.W.* 6.250 [6.4.5]).

[352] The Consensus View holds that Josephus was counting beginning and ending partial years and that he was reckoning inclusively. Thus, the spring of 31 BC is said to be Herod's sixth year according to the consensus view. However, Josephus explicitly called it Herod's seventh year (*Ant.* 15.121 [15.5.2]), calling into doubt that Josephus was reckoning years inclusively.

Table 51
Josephus' References to Herod's Regnal Years

Reference	Regnal Year	Event
Antiquities 15.121 [15.5.2]	Seventh	Battle of Actium (Sept 2, 31 BC)
Antiquities 15.354 [15.10.3]	Eighteenth[353]	Caesar in Syria (Spring 20 BC)
Antiquities 15.380 [15.11.1] *J.W.* 1.401 [1.21.1]	Eighteenth Fifteenth	Work on temple begun
Antiquities 16.136 [16.5.1]	Twenty-eighth	Work on Caesarea Sebaste[354] finished

Since in *Antiquities* Herod's seventh year must correlate to the year of the Battle of Actium, and Herod's eighteenth year must correlate to Caesar's presence in Syria, the Consensus View holds that this numbering is from Herod's conquest of Jerusalem. It must also maintain that Josephus' reference to Herod's fifteenth year in *The Jewish War* 1.401 [1.21.1] is a mistake.

However, in *Antiquities* Josephus was not reckoning from Herod's conquest of Jerusalem, but from his appointment by the Romans. This is demonstrated by his noting that there were 28 high priests from "the times of Herod" to Titus's destruction of the temple. When Herod conquered Jerusalem he appointed Ananel high priest.[355] Counting high priests from Ananel to Pannias, the last high priest before the temple was burned, yields only 27 high priests. Clearly, Josephus was including Antigonus in the total of 28. However, Antigonus was high priest when Herod was appointed by the Romans.

---

[353] Literally "Herod already had reigned seventeen years" (Ἤδη δ᾿ αὐτοῦ τῆς βασιλείας ἑπτακαιδεκάτου).

[354] The city was named Caesarea Sebaste by Herod in honor of Augustus. It is also known as Caesarea Palaestina or Caesarea Maritima to distinguish it from Caesarea Philippi.

[355] Josephus, *Ant.* 15.22 [15.2.4].

Therefore, in *Antiquities* Josephus was reckoning the "times of Herod" from his appointment by the Romans. This, in turn, means that the "fifteenth year" in *The Jewish War* 1.401 [1.21.1] was not a mistake, but was reckoned from Herod's conquest of Jerusalem and corresponds to the "eighteenth year" in *Antiquities* 15.380 [15.11.1], which was reckoned from Herod's appointment by the Romans three years earlier.

Contrary to the Consensus View, Herod was appointed in late 39 BC. He began to count his regnal years from 38 BC, probably beginning in Tishri.[356] This would mean that when Titus burned the temple in Ab of AD 70, it would have been the eleventh month of Herod's one hundred seventh year, precisely as Josephus reports. This also justifies the rest of Josephus' references to Herod's regnal years:

Table 52
Herod's Regnal Years Coordinated to Julian Dates

Reference	Regnal Year	Event
Antiquities 15.121 [15.5.2]	Seventh (32t)	Battle of Actium (Sept 2, 31 BC)
Antiquities 15.354 [15.10.3]	Eighteenth (21t)	Caesar in Syria (Spring 20 BC)
Antiquities 15.380 *J.W.* 1.401 [1.21.1]	Eighteenth (21t)/ Fifteenth (21t)	Work on temple begun (Spring or Summer 20 BC)
Antiquities 16.136 [16.5.1]	Twenty-eighth (11t)	Caesarea Sebaste finished (10 BC)

Thus, there is no need to declare Josephus' statement about Herod's fifteenth year in *The Jewish War* 1.401 [1.21.1] to be a mistake. Instead, most of Josephus' discussion of Herod's reign is accurate, and the only inaccuracies in Josephus' work are his dating Herod's reign to consular years. Once again we are led to conclude that Herod's 37 year reign ended in 1 BC.

---

[356] See the discussion in Steinmann, "When Did Herod the Great Reign?" 26–27.

HEROD'S DEATH

Unlike the dates for the beginning of Herod's reign, Josephus simply relates that Herod died after a lunar eclipse but before Passover. According to Josephus, the eclipse occurred the night following the execution of Matthias, son of Margalothus, who was condemned to death by Herod for inciting some young men to pull down a golden eagle Herod had erected at the temple's east gate. Between 7 BC and 1 BC there were three total and one partial lunar eclipses viewable in Palestine:[357]

Table 53
Lunar Eclipses 7 BC to 1 BC

Date	*Type of Eclipse*	*Eclipse to Passover*
March 23, 5 BC	Total	29 days
September 15, 5 BC	Total	7 months
March 13, 4 BC	Partial	29 days
January 10, 1 BC	Total	89 days

The eclipse of March 5 BC would require Herod's death to have been in April of 5 BC, too early even for the Consensus View. The September 5 BC eclipse would imply that Herod died in late 5 BC. While some have defended this eclipse as possibly the one to which Josephus refers, it is unlikely. Josephus reports that Herod was nearly 70 years old shortly before his death and that he was 25 years old when his father Antipater many him governor of Galilee in 47 BC.[358] Herod, therefore, was born about 72 BC. In late 5 BC he would have been only 66 or 67.

---

[357] Finegan, *Handbook of Biblical Chronology*, 295, Table 142.

[358] At death: Josephus, *Ant.* 17.148 [17.6.1]; *J.W.* 1.647 [1.33.1]; when made governor: Josephus, *Ant.* 14.158 [14.9.2]. The Greek text reads "fifteen years old," but this must reflect a scribal mistake for "twenty-five years old," as generally acknowledged by all.

The Consensus View holds that the eclipse is the partial eclipse of March 13, 4 BC. This also presents a problem concerning Herod's age, since he would have been only 67 or 68 in early 4 BC. However, there is another problem with this date. There were only 29 days between the eclipse and the Passover that year, and all of the events that happened between these two would have taken a minimum of 41 days had each one of them taken place as quickly as possible.[359] A more reasonable estimate is between 60 and 90 days.

Moreover, one of the events Josephus reports is that Herod had Matthias, son of Margalothus, and his co-conspirator Judas, son of the Sepphorean,[360] executed for inciting some young men to pull down a golden eagle Herod had erected at the temple's east gate. If the Consensus view is correct, then Herod had these rabbis executed on March 13, 4 BC. That was 15 Adar in the Jewish calendar, the second day of Purim. As upset as Herod was about the two rabbis' actions, he certainly would not have been so politically insensitive as to have two popular leaders executed during Purim when he could have waited a day and avoided any number of political repercussions that would have been created by such timing.

For these reasons, the 4 BC eclipse is unlikely to be the one to which Josephus refers. Moreover, in Josephus' narrative the eclipse is

---

[359] There are twelve items for which to account, some of them requiring several days minimum to several weeks maximum. See Steinmann, "When Did Herod the Great Reign?," 13–17.

[360] At *J.W.* 1.648 [1.33.2] Judas is called "son of the Sepphorean" (υἱὸς Σεπφεραίου). *Ant.* 17.149 [17.6.2] calls him "son of Saripheus" (ὁ Σαριφαίου), some manuscripts of *Antiquities* call him "the son of the Sepphorean" (ὁ Σεπφεραίου). Clearly, the reading "son of Saripheus" is a scribal corruption and the correct reading is "son of the Sepphorean." Lodder noted that late Jewish literature mentions both a house of Seripha and sons of Seripha. Thus the cause of the scribal corruption was likely the unconscious shift from the geographic name Sepphoris to the more common family name Saripheus. (Lodder, *Die Schätzung des Quirinius bei Flavius Josephus*, 41.)

obviously used as an ominous portent of Herod's death, and the 4 BC eclipse was a partial eclipse—hardly a candidate for an ominous precursor of death.

Schwartz has argued that the eclipse is not connected by Josephus to the execution of the rebel Matthias, but to an incident during the high priesthood of a different man named Matthias.[361] Josephus injects the account of the high priest Matthias' dream as a digression in the account of the golden eagle incident. The relevant passage is *Ant.* 17:164–167 [17.6.4]:[362]

> But the people, on account of Herod's barbarous temper, and for fear he should be so cruel and to inflict punishment on them, said, what was done, was done without their approbation, and that it seemed to them that the actors might well be punished for what they had done. But as for Herod, he dealt more mildly with others [of the assembly]; but he deprived Matthias of the high priesthood, as in part an occasion of this action, and made Joazar, who was Matthias' wife's brother, high priest in his stead. Now it happened, that during the time of the high priesthood of this Matthias, there was another person made high priest for a single day, that very day which the Jews observed as a fast. The occasion was this:—This Matthias the high priest, on the night before that day when the fast was to be celebrated, seemed, in a dream, to have intercourse with his wife; and because he could not officiate himself on that account, Joseph, the son of Ellemus, his kinsman, assisted him in that sacred office. But Herod deprived this Matthias of the high priesthood, and burnt the other Matthias, who had raised the sedition, with his companions, alive. *And that very night* there was an eclipse of the moon.

---

[361] Schwartz, "Joseph ben Illem and the Date of Herod's Death." Schwartz, 158–159, concedes that the events narrated by Josephus cannot fit between the 4 BC eclipse and the Passover, noting "Anyone who reads Josephus' account of the interval [between the eclipse and Herod's death] should be very surprised if he were told that it covers only a month. . . ."

[362] Whiston's translation.

The most natural reading of this passage is that the eclipse took place the night following the execution of the rebel Matthias. This is why nearly all scholars understand the eclipse as taking place the night of Matthias' execution. However, reviving an argument first put forward in 1873 by Marcus Brann, Schwartz argues that the reference of "that very night" (τῇ αὐτῇ νυκτὶ) is not the night following the rebel Matthias' execution, but the "the night before that day when the fast was to be celebrated" when the high priest Matthias had his dream. This, according to Schwartz, is the only night in the immediate context of the phrase "that very night."

There are several problems with Schwartz' argument, however. First, it should be noted that the account of the high priest Matthias is a long digression into the main narrative—it is not part of the context of the main narrative, which is set contextually at the time of the rebel Matthias' execution. This digression has its own historical and literary context and is set some years earlier. It is not part of the account of Matthias' execution.

Second, it should also be noted that the digression is set off by an inclusio—it is marked by similar phrases at its beginning and end: " . . . he [Herod] deprived Matthias of the high priesthood . . . Herod deprived this Matthias of the high priesthood."[363] The second mention of Matthias being deposed from the high priest's office signals that the digression has ended and that the main narrative has resumed. Thus, the comment about the eclipse that follows the notice of the rebel Matthias' execution is in the context of the main narrative, not the digression. While the mention of the night of the high priest's dream is in close proximity to the phrase "that same night," *it is not close in context*. What is close in context to the phrase "that same night" is the execution of the rebel Matthias, and the eclipse is clearly tied to time of his execution. In fact, the reason for the digression

---

[363] " . . . Ματθίαν δὲ τὸν ἀρχιερέα παύσας ἱερᾶσθαι . . . Ἡρώδης δὲ τόν τε Ματθίαν ἐπεπαύκει τῆς ἀρχιερωσύνης . . ."; Josephus, *Ant.* 17.164, 167 [17.6.4]. I am indebted to my colleague John Rhoads for this insight.

about the high priest in the middle of the account of the rebel may be a double connection between the high priest and the rebel: they shared the same name and both were connected with nights that had ominous portents.

There is yet another problem with Schwartz's theory: he must posit that the night of the high priest's dream to which he claims Josephus' eclipse refers corresponded to the September 5 BC eclipse.[364] The problem with this is that Josephus reports that at the time of Herod's funeral those who mourned the execution of the rabbis Judas and Matthias took Herod's death as vindication for their rabbis' actions.[365] They demanded that Archelaus remove the high priest Joazar from office, a demand to which Archelaus acceded.[366] If almost seven months had passed between the execution of Judas and Matthias (September 5 BC to March 4 BC), it is hard to see how their followers made any connection between their rabbis' execution and Herod's death. However, if the January 1 BC eclipse was the occasion of the rabbis' execution, then only about three months had passed between the eclipse and Herod's death, and it would have been entirely possible that his followers would have made the connection between the two.

Having ruled out the 4 BC eclipse, we can note that the 1 BC eclipse fits well with everything Josephus reports. The 89 days between the eclipse and the Passover comfortably fits Josephus' narration of events. In addition, Herod would have been 70 years old in 1 BC. Moreover, the eclipse was a total eclipse, a fitting prelude to Herod's death. Thus, once again we are led to the conclusion that the Consensus View that Herod died in 4 BC is incorrect. Instead, the evidence indicates that Herod died in 1 BC.

---

[364] Schwartz, "Joseph ben Illem and the Date of Herod's Death," 163–166.

[365] *Ant.* 17.206, 213 [17.9.1; 17.9.3].

[366] *Ant.* 17.207–208 [17.9.1].

THE REIGNS OF HEROD'S SUCCESSORS

The only remaining evidence that supports the Consensus View that Herod died in 4 BC are the reigns of Herod's sons Archelaus, Antipas and Philip. Each of these reckoned their reigns from about 4 BC, which appears to indicate that Herod must have died in that year. To understand how Herod's sons might have reckoned their reigns from 4 BC although Herod died in 1 BC, it is necessary to understand what Josephus tells us about Herod's heirs during his last years.

Originally Herod had named his son Antipater to be his heir and had groomed Antipater to take over upon his death. However, a little over two years before Herod's death Antipater had his uncle, Herod's younger brother Pheroras, murdered. Pheroras had been tetrarch of Galilee under Herod. Antipater's plot was discovered, and Archelaus was named Herod's successor in place of Antipater. Seven months passed before Antipater, who was in Rome, was informed that he had been charged with murder. Late in the next year he would be placed on trial before Varus, governor of Syria. Eventually Herod received permission from Rome to execute Antipater. During his last year Herod wrote a will disinheriting Archelaus and granting the kingdom to Antipas. In a later will, however, he once again left the kingdom to Archelaus. Following his death his kingdom would eventually be split into three parts among Archelaus, Antipas, and Philip.

Josephus is careful to note that during his last year Herod was forbidden by Augustus from naming his sons as his successors.[367] However, in several passages Josephus also notes that Herod bestowed royalty and its honors on his sons. At Antipater's trial Josephus quotes Herod as testifying that he had yielded up royal authority to Antipater.[368] He also quotes Antipater claiming that he was already a king because Herod had made him a king.[369]

---

[367] Josephus, *Ant.* 16.129 [16.4.5]; *J.W.* 1.461 [1.23.5].
[368] Josephus, *J.W.* 1.625 [1.32.2].
[369] Josephus, *J.W.* 1.631–632 [1.32.3].

When Archelaus replaced Antipater as Herod's heir apparent some two years before Herod's death, Antipater may have been given the same prerogatives as Archelaus had previously enjoyed. After Herod's death Archelaus went to Rome to have his authority confirmed by Augustus. His enemies charged him with seemingly contradictory indictments: that Archelaus had already exercised royal authority for some time and that Herod did not appoint Archelaus as his heir until he was demented and dying.[370] These are not as contradictory as they seem, however. Herod initially named Archelaus his heir, and at this point Archelaus may have assumed royal authority under his father. Then Herod revoked his will, naming Antipas his heir. Ultimately, when he was ill and dying, Herod once again named Archelaus his heir. Thus, Archelaus may not have legally been king until after Herod's death in early 1 BC, but may have chosen to reckon his reign from a little over two years earlier in late 4 BC when he first replaced Antipater as Herod's heir.

Since Antipas would eventually rule Galilee, it is entirely possible that under Herod he already had been given jurisdiction over Galilee in the wake of Pheroras' death. This may explain why Herod briefly named Antipas as his heir in the year before his death. Since Antipas may have assumed the jurisdiction over Galilee upon Pheroras' death sometime in 4 BC, like Archelaus, he also may have reckoned his reign from that time, even though he was not officially named tetrarch of Galilee by the Romans until after Herod's death.

Philip also appears to have exercised a measure of royal authority before Herod's death in 1 BC. Philip refounded the cities of Julias and Caesarea Philippi (Paneas). Julias was apparently named after Augustus' daughter, who was arrested for adultery and treason in 2 BC. Apparently Julias was refounded before that date. As for Caesarea Philippi, the date of its refounding was used to date an era, and the first year of the era was 3 BC. Apparently Philip chose to antedate his

---

[370] Josephus, *J.W.* 2.31 [2.2.5]; *Ant.* 17.238 [17.9.5]; *J.W.* 2.26 [2.2.5].

reign to 4 BC, which apparently was the time when Herod first entrusted him with supervision of Gaulanitis.

Additional support for Philip having been officially appointed tetrarch after the death of his father in 1 BC may be found in numismatics. A number of coins issued by Philip during his reign are known.[371] The earliest bear the date "year 5," which would correspond to AD 1. This fits well with Philip serving as administrator under his father from 4–1 BC. He counted those as the first four years of his reign, but since he was not officially recognized by Rome as an independent client ruler, he had no authority to issue coins during those years. However, he was in position to issue coinage soon after being named tetrarch sometime in 1 BC, and the first coins appear the next year, AD 1, antedating his reign to 4 BC. While the numismatic evidence is not conclusive proof of Herod's death in 1 BC, it is highly suggestive.

Given the explicit statements of Josephus about the authority and honor Herod had granted his sons during the last years of his life, we

---

[371] Coins bearing the dates of years 5, 12, 16, 19, 30, 33, 34, 37 of Philip's reign are known (Meshorer, *Ancient Jewish Coinage*, volume 2, 244–246). Unfortunately, we do not have similar evidence from the reigns of his brothers Archelaus and Antipas. All known coins issued by Archelaus bear no date, while the earliest known dated coins issued by Antipas are from the twenty-fourth year of his reign (Meshorer, *Ancient Jewish Coinage*, 2.240–243). Most likely Archelaus and Antipas, who ruled regions with large Jewish populations avoided dated coins. Dated coins may have been viewed by their subjects as unacceptably adopting pagan customs, and, therefore, to be avoided. Only later in the century would dated coins by Jewish rulers become common. Note that Herod the Great issued only one dated coin, a "year 3" coin that probably was issued for the year he conquered Jerusalem. Perhaps adverse reaction among the populace led Herod to decree that all subsequent coins remain undated. Philip, however, ruled Ituraea and Trachonitis, regions with much smaller Jewish populations. Therefore, he was able to issue dated coins much earlier than his brothers.

can understand why all three of his successors decided to antedate their reigns to the time when they were granted a measure of royal authority while their father was still alive. Although they were not officially recognized by Rome as ethnarch or tetrarchs until after Herod's death, they nevertheless appear to have reckoned their reigns from about 4 BC.

HEROD'S REIGN AND JESUS' BIRTH

Since we now have established that Herod died in early 1 BC after January 10 but before Passover (April 8), we can now confirm that Jesus was born no earlier than midyear 3 BC and no later than the end of 2 BC. Given the events surrounding Jesus' birth we can surmise that at least a few months passed between Jesus' birth and Herod's death. The arrival of the magi in Jerusalem was after Jesus' birth, but before Herod's death (Matt 2:1). Herod waited some time for the Magi to return before ordering execution of the boys in Bethlehem (Matt 2:16). Since he ordered the execution of boys up to two years old, matching the time when the magi indicated they had first seen the star (Matt 2:7, 16), the magi first observed the star no earlier than about 4 BC. Joseph and Mary's flight to Egypt with the infant Jesus shortly after the visit of the Magi (Matt 2:13–15) should probably be dated after mid-2 BC and no later than early 1 BC.

QUIRINIUS AND THE CENSUS

Another chronological marker in the NT for the birth of Jesus is found in Luke 2:1–4:

> Ἐγένετο δὲ ἐν ταῖς ἡμέραις ἐκείναις ἐξῆλθεν δόγμα παρὰ Καίσαρος Αὐγούστου ἀπογράφεσθαι πᾶσαν τὴν οἰκουμένην. αὕτη ἀπογραφὴ πρώτη ἐγένετο ἡγεμονεύοντος τῆς Συρίας Κυρηνίου. καὶ ἐπορεύοντο πάντες ἀπογράφεσθαι, ἕκαστος εἰς τὴν ἑαυτοῦ πόλιν. Ἀνέβη δὲ καὶ Ἰωσὴφ ἀπὸ τῆς Γαλιλαίας ἐκ πόλεως Ναζαρὲθ εἰς τὴν Ἰουδαίαν εἰς πόλιν Δαυὶδ ἥτις καλεῖται Βηθλέεμ, διὰ τὸ εἶναι αὐτὸν ἐξ οἴκου καὶ πατριᾶς Δαυὶδ . . .

In those days a decree went out from Caesar Augustus that all the world should be registered in a census. This was the first census registration when Quirinius was governing Syria, and everyone went to be registered, each to his own city. So Joseph also went up from Galilee, from the city of Nazareth, to Judea, to the city of David, which is called Bethlehem, because he was of the house and lineage of David. . . .

We should be careful to note what this passage says. It indicates that Augustus in his capacity as censor ordered a tax census for his entire realm. It indicates that Quirinius had some type of governing function in Syria. However, unlike most English versions of Luke 2:2, *it does not state that Quirinius was governor*. The verb ἡγεμονεύω denotes exercising of authority in a governing capacity, but does not necessarily denote holding the office of governor.[372] Finally, this passage notes that the census registration took place in each person's "own city." This is what brought Joseph and Mary to Bethlehem.

Some scholars have questioned whether the Romans would have taken a census in Judea during Herod's reign, since he was ruling a client state, not a Roman province. However, recent studies have demonstrated that an imperial census could have occurred during Herod's reign.[373]

THE MODERN DATING OF THE CENSUS

The current consensus holds that the census administered in Palestine by Quirinius took place in AD 6 or 7. This is based on Josephus' dating of the census to the year that Archelaus was deposed as ethnarch over Judea, Samaria and Idumea. Josephus explicitly states

---

[372] It should also be noted that Josephus never calls Quirinius governor. Instead, he depicts him as coming to take account of Jewish property in the province of Syria, which included Judea (*Ant.* 17.354 [17.13.5]; 18.1, 2, 26, 29 [18.1.1; 18.2.1; 18.2.2]; 20.102 [20.5.2]). Josephus depicts Quirinius as *legatus juridicus* (δικαιοδότης τοῦ ἔθνους). Governors of provinces were *legati pro praetore*. See the discussion in Finegan, *Handbook of Biblical Chronology*, 304–305, §522; Lawrence, "Publius Sulpicius Quirinius and the Syrian Census," 199.

[373] Pearson, "The Lukan Censuses Revisited."

that the census (ἀποτιμήσεων) was completed in "the thirty-seventh year of Caesar's victory over Antony at Actium."[374]

Since all other evidence, including Luke 1:5, requires Jesus' birth to have taken place during the reign of Herod the Great who had died—as we have seen—seven years earlier in 1 BC, there has been much discussion of how Luke 2:1–4 can be reconciled to the rest of the evidence for the date of Jesus' birth.[375] A number of scholars have simply declared Luke to be in error concerning the census.[376] It has been suggested—without any manuscript evidence—that Quirinius in Luke 2:2 is a scribal mistake for Quintilius, the second name of P. Quintilius Varus who was governor of Syria during Herod's last years. One scholar has proposed the Herod of the Luke's account is Herod Archelaus instead of Herod the Great![377] The latter theory contracts the clear statement of Matt 2:22 that after Herod had died and Joseph returned from Egypt with Mary and Jesus, he settled in Galilee to avoid living under the rule of Archelaus. Thus, Matthew unequivocally identifies Herod the Great as the Judean monarch when Jesus was born.

---

[374] Josephus, *Ant.* 18.26 [18.2.1]. Since the Battle of Actium took place on September 2, 31 BC, the thirty-seventh year of Actium ran from September 2, AD 6 to September 1, AD 7.

[375] Brindle, "The Census and Quirinius: Luke 2:2"; Finegan, *Handbook of Biblical Chronology*, 302–306; Hoehner, *Chronological Aspects of the Life of Christ*, 13–23; Jones, "Luke's Unique Interest in Historical Chronology," 379–380; Lawrence, "Publius Sulpicius Quirinius and the Syrian Census"; Ogg, "The Quirinius Question To-day"; Porter, "The Reasons for the Lukan Census"; Rist, "Luke 2:2: Making Sense of the Date of Jesus' Birth"; Schwartz, "On Quirinius, John the Baptist, the Benedictus, Melchizedek, Qumran and Ephesus"; Smith, "Of Jesus and Quirinius."

[376] See Schwartz, "On Quirinius, John the Baptist, the Benedictus, Melchizedek, Qumran and Ephesus," 635.

[377] Smith, "Of Jesus and Quirinius."

A popular way to reconcile Luke 2:1–4 with a birth of Jesus during Herod the Great's reign is to hold that Luke's sentence αὕτη ἀπογραφὴ πρώτη ἐγένετο ἡγεμονεύοντος τῆς Συρίας Κυρηνίου should be translated "This was the census registration *before* Quirinius was governor of Syria."[378] This suggestion, which notes that πρῶτος, "first" was at times used as the equivalent of πρότερος, "former, earlier," was first proposed by Herwartus in 1612, and has enjoyed a certain popularity since it was revived by Lagrange in 1911.[379] The chief problem with this theory is that it is a very unnatural reading of the Greek text, since there is no other passage in Luke or elsewhere in the NT where πρῶτος with the meaning *before* is followed by genitive absolute as at Luke 2:2.

JOSEPHUS MISDATED THE CENSUS

However, there is another approach that is more likely—that Josephus misdated Quirinius and the census. This argument was made a century ago by Zahn, Spitta, Weber, and Lodder and has most recently been revived by Rhoads.[380]

Before delving into that argument, we should note that some evidence external to Josephus that may indicate that Quirinius' census may have occurred under Herod the Great comes from Eusebius who dates the census to Augustus' forty-second year (March 17, 3 BC– March 16, 2 BC) and the twenty-eighth year from Actium (September

---

[378] Brindle, "The Census and Quirinius: Luke 2:2"; Hoehner, *Chronological Aspects of the Life of Christ*, 20–22.

[379] Ogg, "The Quirinius Question To-day," 232–233.

[380] Lodder, *Die Schätzung des Quirinius*; Spitta, "Die Chronologische Notizen und die Hymnen in Lc 1 U. 2"; Weber, "Der Census des Quirinius nach Josephus"; Zahn, "Die Syrische Statthalterschaft und die Schatzung des Quirinius"; Rhoads, "Josephus Misdated the Census of Quirinius," *JETS* 54 (2011): 65–88. The discussion here follows that of Rhoads.

2, 4 BC–September 1, 3 BC).[381] This would imply that the census took place in the spring or summer of 3 BC.

Finegan notes that Augustus' own account of his acts, known as the *Res gestae divi Augusti*, notes that Augustus was declared Father of his Country (*Pater Patriae*) on Feb 5, 2 BC by "the whole people of Rome."[382] He theorizes that there was an empire-wide registration taken in preparation for this honor and that it likely was the time reported by Josephus during Herod's reign that the entire Jewish nation with the exception of 6000 Pharisees took an oath of loyalty to Caesar.[383] This would place an empire-wide census in 3 BC, and Finegan notes that this is exactly what the fourth-century Christian historian Orosius describes in commenting on Luke 2:1–4 as the "first and greatest census" in which all great nations took an oath of loyalty to Caesar "and were made part of one society."

THREE ACCOUNTS OF REBELLION

In close proximity with Quirinius' presence in Judea, Josephus also noted a rebellion led by a man named Judas. In fact, in *Antiquities* Josephus recounts three rebellions led by an insurgent or insurgents named Judas.

1. Judas, son of the Sepphorean, (Ἰούδας ὁ Σεπφεραίου)[384] gathered disciples around himself and a rabbi named

---

[381] Eusebius, *Hist. eccl.* 1.5.

[382] Finegan, *Handbook of Biblical Chronology*, 305–306, §525.

[383] Josephus, *Ant.* 17.41–45 [17.2.4–17.3.1].

[384] At *J.W.* 1.648 [1.33.2] Judas is called "son of the Sepphorean" (υἱὸς Σεπφεραίου). *Ant.* 17.149 [17.6.2] calls him "son of Saripheus" (ὁ Σαριφαίου), some manuscripts of *Antiquities* call him "the son of the Sepphorean" (ὁ Σεπφεραίου). Clearly, the reading "son of Saripheus" is a scribal corruption and the correct reading is "son of the Sepphorean." Lodder noted that late Jewish literature mentions both a house of Seripha and sons of Seripha. Thus the cause of the scribal corruption was likely the unconscious shift from the geographic name *Sepphoris* to the more common family name *Saripheus*. (Lodder, *Die Schätzung des Quirinius bei Flavius Josephus*, 41.)

Matthias, son of Margalothus. They urged zeal for the Law of Moses and looked for a lasting reward in death. Judas incited some of the young men who were his followers to pull down a golden eagle Herod had erected at the temple's east gate. Herod the Great had those directly involved in this incident executed. (*Ant.* 17.148–167 [17.6.1–4]; *J.W.* 1.648–655 [1.33.2–3]; See the discussion of this incident beginning on page 231.)

2. While Archelaus was in Rome seeking confirmation of his father's will naming him king, there were a number of uprisings in Palestine. Among these were one led by Judas the Galilean, son of Hezekiah. He was active around Sepphoris in Galilee (περὶ Σέπφωριν τῆς Γαλιλαίας) and attempted to raid Herod's armory. (*Ant.* 17.269–285 [17.10.4–8])

3. A rabbi named Judas the Galilean gathered a group of disciples around himself and a Pharisee named Sadduc. They were zealous for the Law of Moses and were willing to die for it in expectation of a greater, lasting reward. Judas led a revolt against taxation tied to the census of Quirinius. (*Ant.* 18:4–23 [18.1.1–6]; *J.W.* 2.117–118 [2.8.1]).[385]

The first and second accounts are parallel in that Judas has a very similar description in each: son of the Sepphorean versus active around Sepphoris. The second and third accounts are parallel in that Judas is called a Galilean. The first and third accounts are parallel in that zeal for the Law of Moses and expectation of a lasting reward after death are characteristic of the teachings of Judas in partnership with a second teacher.

---

[385] Judas is called a Gaulonite (Γαυλανίτης) in *Antiquities*, but a Galilean (Γαλιλαῖος) in *J.W.* The label *Galilean* is confirmed in Gamaliel's speech at Acts 5:37.

Another tie between the first and third accounts is that Josephus connects both with the high priesthood of Joazar, son of Boethus, making an easy reconstruction of his high priesthood problematic. In the first account Herod deposed Matthias from the high priesthood. In his place he honored Joazar, Matthias' brother-in-law, with the high priesthood in reward for his opposition to Judas.[386] In the third account Joazar helped persuade the people to cooperate with the census that Judas was opposing.[387] Yet between these two accounts Josephus reports that Archelaus twice deposed a high priest—Joazar was deposed and replaced with his brother Eleazar, and Eleazar was replaced with Jesus, son of Sie.[388] How, then, was Joazar once again high priest under Archelaus—especially since Josephus does not mention his being restored to the high priesthood? Moreover, Josephus strangely also reports that before the census was completed Quirinius deposed Joazar, who had been so helpful in gaining cooperation of the people.[389] It appears as if Josephus has confused the entire account of the census and the rebellions associated with it as well as the succession of high priests during this era. We should, therefore, be cautious about accepting his explicit dating of the census.

FIRST ACCOUNT:
THE GOLDEN EAGLE INCIDENT IN THE TEMPLE

As was noted above, the golden eagle incident is associated with the final days of Herod the Great, just about three months before his death (see the discussion beginning on page 231). Herod executed Judas and Matthias by having them burned. What is noteworthy here is that this incident led to the promotion of Joazar to the high priesthood, but was also the ultimate reason for his removal about

---

[386] Josephus, *Ant.* 17.164 [17.6.4].

[387] Josephus, *Ant.* 18.3 [18.1.1].

[388] Josephus, *Ant.* 17.339, 341 [17.13.1].

[389] Josephus, *Ant.* 18.26 [18.2.1].

four months later by Archelaus, when Judas' followers demanded his removal because they saw Herod's death as vindication of their slain leader.

SECOND ACCOUNT:
DISTURBANCES WHILE ARCHELAUS WAS IN ROME

The account of the insurrection of Judas the Galilean while Archelaus was in Rome is part of a large account by Josephus of disturbances in Palestine following the death of Herod the Great. The account includes the movements of Varus, the Roman governor of Syria and Sabinus, Caesar's procurator of Syrian affairs. Sabinus went to Jerusalem, and seized Herod's effects to secure them. Reconstruction of the movements of Varus and Sabinus and the insurrections to which they were responding is complicated, partly because Josephus reports them twice.[390]

While the various ways one might reconstruct the events need not concern us here, we should note three things: First, that Josephus may well have presented the movements of Varus and Sabinus twice when they actually are simply two accounts of the same movements from two different sources. Josephus simply did not understand that his two sources were describing the same events from different perspectives.

Second, we should note that there is at least one indication that the disturbances began *before* Herod the Great's death—Josephus reports that the unrest was "foreseen by Varus" and "it was manifest that the nation would not be at rest."[391] Thus, it is possible that Josephus mistakenly included the raid by Judas the Galilean as part of the disturbances following Herod's death when it actually occurred during the last days of Herod's reign.

Third, we should note that Sabinus appears to be of consular rank. He acted contrary to the wishes of the Syrian governor Varus by

---

[390] Josephus, *Ant.* 17.219–223 [17.9.3]; *J.W.* 2.14–19 [2.2.1–2]; then *Ant.* 17.250–255 [17.10.1–2]; *J.W.* 2.39–42 [2.3.1].
[391] Josephus, *J.W.* 2.40 [2.3.1].

going to Jerusalem to secure Herod's effects following Herod's death. Moreover, he took command of the legion that Varus left in Judea. Only a man of high rank could dare defy a governor's wishes in these ways.

THIRD ACCOUNT:
TAX REVOLT AT THE TIME OF THE CENSUS

There are significant differences in the way that Josephus reports the tax revolt in *The Jewish War* and in *Antiquities*. In *The Jewish War* there is no mention of Quirinius. The revolt is simply reported as occurring under the administration of Coponius, the first prefect of Judea after Archelaus was exiled. In contrast, *Antiquities* contains much more detail, including the role played by the high priest Joazar who persuaded the people to cooperate with Quirinius during the census. Josephus does not mention the prefecture of Coponius at this juncture, but delays it until after recounting the acts of Herod Philip and Herod Antipas during their terms as tetrarchs.

The difference is significant. In his earlier work, *The Jewish War*, Josephus links the arrival of Coponius as part of Quirinius' command at the beginning of Coponius' term as prefect (i.e., AD 6).[392] In this way the tax revolt of the zealots under the leadership of Judas is linked to Coponius' prefecture. However, in *Antiquities* Judas' tax revolt is not linked at all to Coponius' prefecture. This may indicate that Josephus had reconsidered the timing of the tax revolt and now disconnected it from Coponius, implying that it may have taken place before Coponius' prefecture. However, he still appears to place it near the time of Coponius' prefecture, probably in the interim between Archelaus' exile and Coponius assuming the office of prefect. The parallel between the rebellion of a Judas at the end of the reign of Herod Archelaus and the acts of a Judas at the end of the reign of

---

[392] Josephus, *J.W.* 2.117–118 [2.8.1].

Herod the Great may suggest that Josephus somehow has displaced the census account, thereby connecting it with the wrong Herod.

JUDAS AND THE CENSUS UNDER QUIRINIUS

It would appear that the three accounts of insurrections by Judas may be three accounts of the same rebel's various activities. The first two clearly connect Judas to the city of Sepphoris in Galilee. Moreover, Judas in the second account is called the son of Hezekiah, a Galilean bandit killed by Herod some 44 years prior to Judas' uprising, strengthening the identification of Judas as the same man in both accounts.

This would imply that the tearing down of the golden eagle in the temple precincts and the raid on Herod's armory were part of the same series of rebellious acts that took place in the last months of Herod the Great's reign. Since Josephus describes the Judas of the first account and the Judas of the third account as having nearly identical theological teachings, we should also suspect that this is the same Judas in all three accounts.

The role of Joazar also appears to indicate this. He is elevated to the high priesthood because of his cooperation with the authorities— he opposed Judas, and he persuaded the people to cooperate with the census. However, after Herod's death he was removed from the high priesthood. According *Ant.* 17.207–208 [17.9.1] *Archelaus* removed Joazar because of the will of the people following Herod's death. The people saw Herod's death as a vindication of Judas. However, according to *Ant.* 18.26 [18.2.1] *Quirinius* removed Joazar because of popular discontent.

Whether it was Archelaus or Quirinius, these two very similar accounts of the removal of Joazar suggest that Josephus displaced the arrival of Quirinius in Judea from its original historical setting. He has put it at the end of the reign of Herod Archelaus instead of the reign of Herod the Great. Perhaps his source simply called the ruler "Herod," and he mistakenly thought the ruler was Herod Archelaus. Why would he have done that? Because of Coponius, who arrived with Quirinius, as Josephus himself relates.[393] Thus, it appears that Coponius, a man of equestrian rank, originally came to Judea under Quirinius, a man of consular rank. Over a decade later Coponius would be named prefect. It most likely was the presence of Coponius, who was better known for his service as prefect, that led Josephus to misplace the census of Quirinius to a time at the end of the reign of the wrong Herod and to associate it with Coponius' prefecture.

However, there is still another item to deal with, if this is the case: the identity of Sabinus, who appears to be a powerful man and who is active in Judea at the time of Herod's death. According to Josephus, Sabinus was a procurator of Syria (ὁ τῆς Συρίας ἐπίτροπος) or Caesar's procurator of affairs in Syria (Καίσαρος ἐπίτροπος τῶν ἐν Συρίᾳ πραγμάτων).[394] This description is similar to Josephus' description of Quirinius, whom Josephus depicts as being sent by Caesar to Syria as *legatus juridicus* (δικαιοδότης τοῦ ἔθνους).[395]

In addition, there are other striking similarities between the two men. We have already noted that Sabinus was of consular rank, and there is no doubt that Quirinius held consular rank. Both Quirinius and Sabinus were concerned about taxation in Judea. Sabinus wrote letters to Augustus about revenues from Judea.[396] Quirinius was censor (τιμητὴς τῶν οὐσιῶν) of Syria.[397] Moreover, Josephus depicts both men as seeking to secure the property of Herod. In the case of Sabinus, it is the property of Herod the Great.[398] In the case of Quirinius, Josephus claims it was Herod Archelaus, though we have argued above that this was a mistake on Josephus' part.[399]

---

[393] Josephus, *Ant.* 18.2, 29 [18.1.1; 18.2.2].

[394] Josephus, *J.W.* 2.16 [2.2.2]; *Ant.* 17.221 [17.9.3].

[395] Josephus, *Ant.* 18.1 [18.1.1].

[396] Josephus, *J.W.* 2.25 [2.2.4].

[397] Josephus, *Ant.* 18.1 [18.1.1].

[398] Josephus, *Ant.* 17.221 [17.9.3]; *J.W.* 2.16 [2.2.2].

[399] Josephus, *Ant.* 18.2 [18.1.1].

Weber argued that Josephus had misread his sources and had mistakenly written "Sabinus" for "Quirinius."[400] More probable is the suggestion of Rhoads—that Sabinus is not a family name but an ethnic designation—he was "the Sabine."[401] This fits well with Quirinius, who was born in Lavinium, and most likely was a Sabine. This would explain the many striking parallels between Josephus' descriptions of Quirinius and Sabinus, and would also argue that Josephus had two sources for his information, one that used the name Quirinius and another that used the name Sabinus. However, Josephus did not realize that these were the same person.

In summary, it is likely that Josephus misplaced the arrival of Quirinius in Judea and, therefore, misdated the census. The initiation of the census in Judea should be dated to the spring or summer of 3 BC. That census prompted Judas' rebellion. Once again the date of Jesus' birth must have been sometime in late 3 BC or early 2 BC.

THE MAGI AND THE STAR

The account of the visit of the Magi to the Christ child in Matt 2:1–18 has often been a cause for speculation about the astronomical phenomenon described by Matthew and whether it can be used as a chronological marker for the birth of Jesus.[402] As a result, a number of studies have attempted to identify a particular astronomically observable event that could be the star to which the magi refer in Matt 2:2 and which Matthew describes in Matt 2:9–10. Perhaps most well-known is the suggestion by Johannes Kepler of a conjunction of Jupiter and Saturn on May 27, October 6 and December 1, 7 BC.[403] However, on those occasions Jupiter and Saturn did not come close

---

[400] Weber, "Der Census des Quirinius nach Josephus," 313–314.

[401] Rhoads, "Josephus Misdated the Census of Quirinius." *JETS* 54 (2011): 82–84.

[402] See the extensive bibliography in Finegan, *Handbook of Biblical Chronology*, 306–307.

[403] Finegan, *Handbook of Biblical Chronology*, 313–314, §538.

enough to each other to appear as a single star. Others have proposed different conjunctions of planets with each other or planets with stars, comets or supernovas as candidates for the Magi's star.[404]

Despite all of these attempts to identify the star, there is no way to identify the astronomical phenomenon which Matthew describes. First of all, this should be obvious from the many different astronomical events which are proposed. Can one prove that any one of them fits Matthew's description better than each of the other competing candidates?

Secondly, it is often assumed that the Magi saw the star in the east and that it moved across the sky to guide them to Jerusalem where they met with Herod. However, Matthew says no such thing. The Magi simply report that they had seen the star "in the east" (or "when it rose"; ἐν τῇ ἀνατολῇ) and were prompted to find the newborn king of the Jews (Matt 2:2). They may have simply observed some astronomical phenomenon, connected it with a prophecy of a coming Jewish king (such as Num 24:17), and decided to go to Jerusalem to find him. None of this requires navigation using the star itself.

Third, the only implication that the Magi followed the star is in the last, very short leg of their journey from Bethlehem to Jerusalem. For this Matt 2:9 says,

> . . . ὁ ἀστήρ, ὃν εἶδον ἐν τῇ ἀνατολῇ, προῆγεν αὐτούς, ἕως ἐλθὼν ἐστάθη ἐπάνω οὗ ἦν τὸ παιδίον.

> . . . the star, which they had seen in the east, went before them until it came to stand over the place where the child was.

If we assume that they travelled at night, then this happened in one night, since the trip southward from Jerusalem to Bethlehem takes only a few hours. Thus, the Magi's star could have been any astral object that would have appeared to have been in the southern sky

---

[404] See the extensive discussion in Finegan, *Handbook of Biblical Chronology,* 306–320 as well as Humphreys, "The Star of Bethlehem"; "The Star of Bethlehem, A Comet in 5 BC and the Date of Christ's Birth."

when the Magi were in Jerusalem but was approximately directly overhead in Bethlehem during some portion of the night.[405]

Given that there is no way to determine what astronomical event Matt 2:1–19 describes, this passage offers no help in dating Jesus' birth. At most we can say that the star could have appeared as early as 4 BC, no more than two years before Jesus' birth.[406]

THE BIRTHS OF JOHN THE BAPTIST AND JESUS

Luke gives a fair amount of detail about the events surrounding the births of John and Jesus (Luke 1:5–38). Following Gabriel's announcement of a son to Zechariah (Luke 1:5–23), Zechariah's wife Elizabeth became pregnant and confined herself to home for five months (Luke 1:24–25). During the sixth month was the Annunciation (Luke 1:26–38, esp. vv. 26, 36). Thus, John was about 5½ months older than Jesus.

---

[405] Due to the rotation of the earth, any star except one directly over the North or South Pole (e.g., Polaris) will appear to slowly move across the night sky from east to west. What Matthew intended to mean by "until it stood over the place where the child was" cannot be determined. Does it mean that it appeared to stop moving across the night sky? Does it mean that it was overhead when the Magi got to Bethlehem and appeared to quit moving because dawn was near, and it was last visible directly over Bethlehem before dawn? Matthew's description simply is not worded specifically enough to determine what—in modern astronomical terms—the observed phenomenon was.

[406] Matt 2:16 states that Herod had all the boys two years old and younger killed in Bethlehem, and that he determined this age by what the Magi told him about the first appearance of the star. However, this does not mean that the star appeared two years earlier. For instance, the Magi may have told Herod that they saw the star one year earlier, but Herod decided that he would give himself a margin of error by killing all boys who were not yet ambulatory or talking, that is, about two years of age.

Shortly after the Annunciation, Mary spent three months in Judea with Elizabeth (Luke 1:39–56, esp. vv. 39, 56). John was born after Mary returned to Bethlehem (Luke 1:57–80).[407] Sometime after this Joseph took Mary with him to Bethlehem for the census (Luke 2:1–4).[408] If the census commenced sometime in the spring or summer of 3 BC, then Joseph may have arrived in Bethlehem in late summer or early autumn. This would place Jesus' birth no earlier than late summer of 3 BC and no later than the first months of 2 BC (Luke 2:5–21).[409] In turn, John's birth took place between late spring and late autumn of 3 BC.

Forty days after Jesus' birth came the time for Mary's purification, and Jesus was presented in the temple (Luke 2:22–38). The visit of the Magi seems to have occurred at this time, because Joseph and Mary would likely still have been lodging in Bethlehem when they came to Jerusalem for Mary's purification rites 40 days after Jesus' birth (Lev 12:1–4).[410] They would have stayed with relatives in

---

[407] The human gestation period is approximately 280 days or about 9½ lunar months. Mary must have returned to Nazareth shortly before John's birth.

[408] It is impossible to determine how many months Mary had been pregnant before the trip to Bethlehem. It was at least 3, but less than 9½ lunar months.

[409] Beckwith attempts to place the Nativity either between mid-January and mid-February or between late June and early August based on the fact that Zechariah, a priest of the course of Abijah (Luke 1:5) would have been on duty in the temple twice each year at specific times of the year. However, the enterprise founders on the fact that Beckwith assumes that John was conceived immediately after Zechariah returned home. (Beckwith, "St. Luke, The Date of Christmas and the Priestly Courses at Qumran.") Luke's language, however, is much more indeterminate. He simply says, "After these days his wife Elizabeth conceived." (Μετὰ δὲ ταύτας τὰς ἡμέρας συνέλαβεν Ἐλισάβετ ἡ γυνὴ αὐτοῦ, Luke 1:24). The period between Zechariah's return and Elizabeth's conception could have been as little as one day or as much as six months (i.e., up to the next time the course of Abijah reported for duty in the temple again).

[410] The chronology of the Magi's visit offered here employs some

Bethlehem until the 40 days were completed.[411] At the time of Mary's purification Joseph and Mary were poor, as shown by the type of offering that they presented (Luke 2:24; Lev 12:8). Had the Magi seen the child and his mother earlier than the time of the purification ceremony, Joseph and Mary, who were careful to observe the Law of Moses, could not have honestly given only two doves or pigeons for the offering. The visit of the Magi most likely dates immediately after Mary's purification rites, because after the Magi had departed from Bethlehem, Mary and Joseph, now no longer poor, fled to Egypt (Matt 2:13–14). The gifts were such as could be exchanged at a high price in Egypt to provide for their sustenance while there and for their living expenses afterward. The gifts were also the kind that could easily be carried furtively by refugees. The family stayed in Egypt until the death of Herod, after which they returned to their home town of Nazareth. The visit of the Magi, therefore, most likely occurred sometime in 2 BC, 40 to 50 days after the birth of Jesus. The flight to Egypt occurred immediately after the Magi left. The return to Nazareth was after Herod's death in the first quarter of 1 BC.

Table 54
Chronology of Herod's Reign and the Birth of Jesus

Date	Event
Late 39	Herod appointed king
Tishri 38	Beginning of Herod's first regnal year
10 Tishri 36	Herod conquers Jerusalem
Dec 36 or Mar 35	Antigonus executed
Tishri 35	Beginning of Herod's first regnal year in Jerusalem

suggestions offered by Rodger C. Young (private correspondence, June 2010).

[411] While they could have made a trip back to Nazareth during these 40 days, it is unlikely that they would have made a trip to Nazareth and back in such a short period of time, especially with a newborn baby.

31	Battle of Actium (September 2)
20	Caesar in Syria (spring)
20	Herod begins work on the temple[412]
Late 19 or early 18	Work on temple completed[413]
12	Work on the temple precincts completed[414]
11 or 10	Work on Caesarea Sebaste completed
5	Magi observe the star
4	Murder of Pheroras
4	Antipater deposed as Herod's heir
4	Archelaus named Herod's heir
3 or 2	Tax revolt of Judas
Mid 3	John the Baptist born
Late 3 or early 2	Jesus born
40-50 days after birth	Flight to Egypt
First quarter 1	Herod dies
Later in 1	Return to Nazareth

---

[412] Josephus, *Ant.* 15.380 [15.11.1].

[413] Josephus, *Ant.* 15.421 [15.11.5].

[414] Josephus, *Ant.* 15.420 [15.11.5].

Figure 2
Herodians in the New Testament

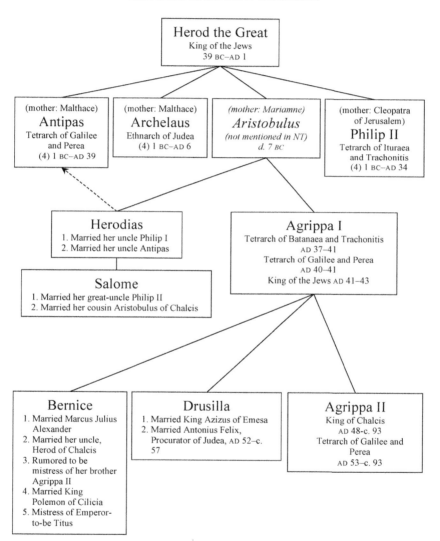

Herod the Great
King of the Jews
39 BC–AD 1

(mother: Malthace)
Antipas
Tetrarch of Galilee
and Perea
(4) 1 BC–AD 39

(mother: Malthace)
Archelaus
Ethnarch of Judea
(4) 1 BC–AD 6

(mother: Mariamne)
Aristobulus
(not mentioned in NT)
d. 7 BC

(mother: Cleopatra
of Jerusalem)
Philip II
Tetrarch of Ituraea
and Trachonitis
(4) 1 BC–AD 34

Herodias
1. Married her uncle Philip I
2. Married her uncle Antipas

Salome
1. Married her great-uncle Philip II
2. Married her cousin Aristobulus of Chalcis

Agrippa I
Tetrarch of Batanaea and Trachonitis
AD 37–41
Tetrarch of Galilee and Perea
AD 40–41
King of the Jews AD 41–43

Bernice
1. Married Marcus Julius
Alexander
2. Married her uncle,
Herod of Chalcis
3. Rumored to be
mistress of her brother
Agrippa II
4. Married King
Polemon of Cilicia
5. Mistress of Emperor-
to-be Titus

Drusilla
1. Married King Azizus of Emesa
2. Married Antonius Felix,
Procurator of Judea, AD 52–c.
57

Agrippa II
King of Chalcis
AD 48–c. 93
Tetrarch of Galilee and
Perea
AD 53–c. 93

12

JESUS' MINISTRY

Apart from a notice about the return from Egypt to Nazareth (late 1 BC or early AD 1; Matt 2:19–23; cf. Luke 2:39) and the account of Jesus in the Temple when he was 12 years old (Nisan, AD 10; Luke 2:41–52), the Gospels tell us nothing of Jesus' childhood or early adult years. Instead, all four Gospel concentrate mainly on Jesus' ministry from his baptism to his crucifixion and resurrection.

THE LENGTH OF JESUS' MINISTRY

Various proposals have been put forward about the length of Jesus' ministry. Perhaps the most extreme and least likely was the theory of Irenaeus that Jesus' ministry must have lasted over a decade.[415] He reasoned that since Jesus was about 30 years old when he began his ministry, and since some of Jesus' opponents stated that he was not yet 50 years old near the end of his ministry (John 8:57), he must have been in his forties. However, Jesus' opponents were pointing out that he could not have possibly seen Abraham (cf. John 8:56). They appear to have been using 50 years old as the threshold of being elderly. Thus, they are stating that Jesus was too young to be considered elderly, much less old enough to have seen Abraham. They are not making a statement that he was nearly 50 years old. For this reason, Irenaeus' theory has found almost no support in the nineteen centuries since he proposed it.

---

[415] Irenaeus, *Haer.* 22.5–6.

Two theories have dominated the discussion of the length of Jesus ministry: that it lasted about one and one-half years or that it lasted about three and one-half years.[416]

A ONE AND ONE-HALF YEAR MINISTRY

The Synoptic Gospels explicitly mention only one Passover during Jesus' ministry, the one during which he was crucified (Matt 26:2; Mark 14:1; Luke 22:1). Jesus' Galilean ministry included at least one spring when the disciples plucked grain in a field (Matt 12:1; Mark 2:23; Luke 6:1), and this spring appears to come after Jesus' baptism and during the early part of his Galilean ministry but before the spring with the Passover at Jesus' crucifixion. Therefore, at least one year and a few months are required for Jesus' ministry. This, apparently, was the position of the Gnostic teacher Valentinus in the second century.[417] Valentinus seems to have based his reasoning on Luke 4:19 where Jesus read Isaiah 61:2 concerning the "acceptable year of the Lord" and claimed it was fulfilled. Thus, Jesus' ministry was to have lasted one year. The one-year ministry was also accepted by Clement of Alexandria and Origen in the late second and early third centuries.[418]

While the Synoptic Gospels mention only one Passover, they appear to mention at least *two* other spring times. One is the springtime when the disciples plucked grain. All of the Synoptic Gospels place this early in Jesus' Galilean ministry (Matt 12:1; Mark 2:23; Luke 6:1). The second is connected with the Feeding of the 5000, a miracle recorded in all of the Gospels near the end of Jesus' Galilean ministry (Matt 14:13–21; Mark 6:32–41; Luke 9:10–17; John 6:1–15). Mark 6:39 notes that the grass was green, indicating

---

[416] Some have proposed a two-year or four-year ministry, but those schemes require either a radical rearrangement of the text of the Gospel of John or positing additional Passovers not implied in any Gospel. See Hoehner, *Chronological Aspects of the Life of Christ*, 48–55.

[417] Irenaeus, *Haer.* 22.5–6.

[418] Clement, *Strom.* 1.21.146; Origen, *Princ.* iv.1.5.

another spring, and John 6:4 explicitly states that the Passover was near.[419] There are far too many events between the beginning of the Galilean ministry and the Feeding of the 5000—that is, between Matt 4:12 and Matt 14, Mark 2 and Mark 6 and Luke 6 and Luke 9—to compress into a single year.[420] It is more likely that several months more than one year are required, given that there is a good amount of material in the Synoptics before the disciples plucked grain. Moreover, it is impossible to hold that all of the events from the Feeding of the 5000 to the Passover of Jesus' crucifixion—including the ministry in Judea and Perea—took place in just two or three weeks as would have to be the case if the Passover that was near the Feeding of the 5000 was the same as the Passover of Jesus' crucifixion. Therefore, there is another year between the Feeding of the 5000 and Jesus' crucifixion. Thus, the Synoptic Gospels require at least a two and one-half year ministry.

In addition, one would have to propose a radical rearrangement of the Gospel of John to coordinate a one-year Galilean ministry of the Synoptic Gospels with it. On the other hand, the Synoptics fit quite well with John's chronological notices. Like the Synoptics, John records the beginning of the Galilean ministry (Matt 4:12–17; Mark 1:14–15; Luke 4:14–15; John 4:1–3, 43–46).

Between the beginning of the Galilean ministry and the Feeding of the 5000 John records Jesus going to Jerusalem for a Feast (John 5:1). This cannot be the Passover, since in all other passages in John the

---

[419] Note that John 6:10 is similar to Mark 6:39 in that it states that there was a lot of grass (χόρτος πολύς).

[420] It might be possible if one were to hold that none of the Synoptic Gospels arranged the events of the Galilean ministry primarily in chronological order. However, given the general agreement among the Synoptics on the sequence of many of Jesus' acts during this period, it is highly unlikely that the Galilean ministry in any of the Synoptics radically strays from a chronological arrangement of Jesus' teachings and miracles.

Passover is always explicitly called *Passover* when it is first mentioned (John 2:13, 23, 6:4; 11:55 [twice]; 12:1; 13:1; 18:39; 19:14).[421] Since Jesus made a special trip to Jerusalem for this event, it was most likely one of the other two pilgrim feasts—Pentecost or Tabernacles. While either of these is possible, the Feast of Tabernacles appears more likely to be the one mentioned here. In both the OT and the NT this pilgrim festival is the more often mentioned of the two.

Now it ought to be noted that after the Passover mentioned at John 2:13, 23 but before beginning his Galilean ministry, Jesus spent a fair amount of time in Judea making and baptizing more disciples than John (John 3:22–23; 4:1). This, in turn, implies that the Galilean ministry began only a few months before the spring when the disciples plucked grain. Therefore, the feast of John 5:1, be it Pentecost or Tabernacles, had to have come *after* the spring when the disciples were plucking grain but before the Passover associated with the Feeding of the 5000. Thus, John confirms that the Galilean ministry lasted over a year and adds what must have been several months in a Judean ministry that preceded it.

Given this evidence, it is extremely unlikely that Jesus' ministry lasted only about one and one-half years. The other major alternative is that Jesus' ministry lasted three and one-half years.

A THREE AND ONE-HALF YEAR MINISTRY

Because of the difficulty of fitting the entire ministry of Jesus into a one and one-half year period, from ancient times the most favored view is that Jesus had a three and one-half year ministry. The Gospel of John explicitly mentions a number of feasts, including three Passovers (first: John 2:13, 23; second: 6:4; third: 11:55 [twice]; 12:1;

---

[421] Note that the Passover appears to be called "the feast" twice at John 4:45, but that feast had been previously identified as the Passover (John 2:13, 20). The same holds for "the feast" at John 11:56; 12:12, 20; 13:29, which is first identified as the Passover at John 11:55 and again at John 12:1; 13:1.

13:1; 18:39; 19:14), Tabernacles (John 7:2), Dedication (John 10:22), and an unnamed feast, which must be either Tabernacles or Pentecost (John 5:1; see discussion above beginning on page 259). In addition, the Synoptic Gospels report the disciples plucking grain near the beginning of Jesus' Galilean ministry when John is silent about a Passover. This implies a fourth Passover during Jesus' ministry (Matt 12:1; Mark 2:23; Luke 6:1; see the discussion above on page 258).[422] Since Jesus' baptism took place before the first Passover mentioned in John (John 1:32), Jesus' ministry began some months before. Therefore, the Gospel of John implies the following three and one-half year ministry:

Table 55
Jesus' Ministry According to the Gospel of John

Before First Year	Jesus' Baptism	John 1:32
First Year:		
Nisan	First Passover	John 2:13, 23
Second Year:		
Nisan	Second Passover	Unmentioned[423]
Tishri (?)	Tabernacles (?)	John 5:1
Third Year:		
Nisan	Third Passover	John 6:4
Tishri	Tabernacles	John 7:2
Kislev	Dedication	John 10:22
Nisan	Fourth Passover	John 11:55

---

[422] This cannot be identified as the Passover that John mentions at John 6:4, since that Passover is associated with the Feeding of the 5000. All four Gospels place the feeding of the 5000 near the end of Jesus' Galilean Ministry (Matt 14:13–21; Mark 6:32–44; Luke 9:10–17; John 6:1–15).
[423] Required by Matt 12:1; Mark 2:23; Luke 6:1.

DATING JESUS' MINISTRY

As has already been noted, Jesus' baptism took place during Tiberius' fifteenth year, AD 29, probably in the late summer (see the discussion above on page 219). Confirmation for this can be found in a statement made by some of Jesus' opponents during the first Passover mentioned in John. They say:

τεσσεράκοντα καὶ ἓξ ἔτεσιν οἰκοδομήθη ὁ ναὸς οὗτος

This temple has been built for 46 years. (John 2:20)

Josephus notes that Herod began to build the temple sometime after the spring of the year that Caesar came to Syria (20 BC), that is, during the second half of 20 BC or in 19 BC.[424] The temple building proper (ναὸς) was completed in one year and six months—in late 19 BC at the earliest but, more likely, in mid-to-late 18 BC.[425] The rest of the temple precincts were completed after eight years in 12 BC.[426] Thus, the forty-sixth anniversary of the temple's completion occurred sometime in mid-to-late AD 29. If Jesus was in Jerusalem at the Passover forty-six years after the completion of the temple building (ναός), then the Passover would have been the one in AD 30. Therefore, his baptism occurred in AD 29. The fourth Passover during which Jesus was crucified would have occurred in AD 33.

---

[424] Josephus, *Ant.* 15.354 [15.10.3]; *J.W.* 1.398–399 [1.20.4].

[425] Josephus, *Ant.* 15.421 [15.11.6]. Ναός refers to the building itself (Matt 23:17; John 2:20; 1 Cor 3:16, 17; 6:19; 2 Cor 6:16; Rev 11:19; 15:5, 8; 21:22). The building and the surrounding precincts are τὸ ἱερόν (e.g., John 2:14–15; 5:14; 7:14, 28; 8:2, 20, 59; 10:23; 11:56; 18:20). Some have attempted to read the aorist οἰκοδομήθη as if it means "has been under construction" (cf. Ezra 5:16 LXX). This would describe the temple precincts (τὸ ἱερόν) well, since they continued to be worked long after Herod's construction, but it does not describe the temple itself (ὁ ναός). See Hoehner, *Chronological Aspects of the Life of Christ*, 40–43; Finegan, *Handbook of Biblical Chronology*, 346 (§590), 348–349 (§595), 366 (§627).

[426] Josephus, *Ant.* 15.420 [15.11.5].

AN OUTLINE OF JESUS' MINISTRY

Now that we have established the dates for Jesus' ministry, we can outline the events in the Gospels relating to it. In Table 56 dates in *italics* are estimated from the flow of the events in the Gospels. A discussion of some dates follows Table 56.

Table 56
Outline of Jesus' Ministry

29	*Spring*	1. John the Baptist begins his ministry (in Judea or Perea; Matt 3:1–12; Mark 1:1–8; Luke 3:1–18)
	Summer	2. Jesus' baptism (in Judea or Perea; Matt 3:13–17; Mark 1:9–11; Luke 3:21–22)
	Summer or early Autumn	3. The Temptation (40 days; Matt 4:1–11; Mark 1:12–13; Luke 4:1–13)
	Autumn	4. Testimony of John the Baptist; Calling of John (?), Andrew, Peter, Philip, Nathaniel; Wedding at Cana (John 1:19–2:12)
30	Nisan	5. Jesus in Jerusalem at the Passover (John 2:13–3:21)
	Nisan–Bul	6. Jesus and John the Baptist in Judea (John 3:22–36)
	Kislev	7. John the Baptist Arrested (Matt 4:12; Mark 1:14a; [Luke 3:19–20])
		8. Jesus travels through Samaria (John 4:1–42)
31	*Tebeth 31– Adar 32*	9. Ministry in Galilee (Matt 4:12–14:12; Mark 1:14–6:31; Luke 4:14–9:9; John 4:43–54)
	Tishri	10. Jesus in Jerusalem for the Feast of Tabernacles (John 5)
32	*Tebeth*	11. John the Baptist Executed (Matt 14:3–12; Mark 6:17–29; [Luke 3:19–20]; cf. Josephus, *Ant.* 18.116–119 [18.5.2])

263

	Nisan	12. Further ministry in Galilee: Feeding 5000; Walking on Water; Healing at Gennesaret (Matt 14:13–36; Mark 6:32–56; Luke 9:10–17; John 6:1–24)
	Iyyar–Ab	13. Ministry in Galilee ends, Tyre and Sidon, Decapolis, Caesarea Philippi (Matt 15–18; Mark 7–9; Luke 9:18–17:10; John 6:25–7:1)
	Elul	14. Ministry on the border of Samaria (Luke 17:11–18:14)
32	Tishri	15. Jesus in Jerusalem for the Feast of Tabernacles (John 7:2–8:59)
	Tishri 32– 8 Nisan 33	16. Ministry in Judea and Perea (Matt 19–20; Mark 10; Luke 18:15–19:27; John 9:1–10:21; 11:1–12:11)
	Kislev	17. Jesus in Jerusalem at the Feast of Dedication (John 10:22–42)
33	9–16 Nisan	18. Triumphal entry (9 Nisan); Crucifixion (14 Nisan); Resurrection (16 Nisan) (Matt 21:1–28:15; Mark 11–16; Luke 19:28–24:49 ; John 12:12–20:31; Acts 1:3–5)
	17 Nisan–24/25 Iyyar[427]	19. Great Commission in Galilee; By the Sea of Tiberias; Ascension (40 days; Matt 28:16–20; Luke 24:49–53; John 21; Acts 1:6–11)

DATING OF SPECIFIC EVENTS IN JESUS' MINISTRY

4. JESUS' EARLY MINISTRY IN JOHN 1 AND 2

The first part of Jesus ministry as record in the Gospel of John is a series of days that occurred sometime following the Temptation. Note that Jesus' baptism was past (John 1:32–34). Since the Temptation immediately followed Jesus' baptism (Matt 4:1; Mark 1:12; Luke

---

[427] The lunar months alternated 29-day months with 30-day months. If Nisan was a 30-day month that year, then Jesus' ascension took place on 25 Iyyar. If Nisan had 29 days, then the Ascension took place on 26 Iyyar.

4:1), the first days of Jesus' ministry in John must follow the Temptation. There are a series of days that John carefully records:

First day: John's testimony at Bethany in Perea (John 1:19–28)

Second day: John identifies Jesus as the Lamb of God (John 1:29–34)

Third day: Jesus calls Peter, Andrew and another disciple (probably John; John 1:35–42)

Fourth day: Jesus decides to go to Galilee and calls Philip and Nathaniel (John 1:43–51)

Sixth day: Jesus, back in Galilee, attends the wedding at Cana (John 2:1–11). This happens on "the third day," that is, Jesus had a three-day journey to the wedding—the fourth, fifth and sixth days.

Several more days: Jesus, his mother, brothers and disciples stay in Capernaum (John 2:12)

7 & 8. JOHN ARRESTED; JESUS TRAVELS THROUGH SAMARIA

Apparently, after Jesus attended the Passover in the spring of AD 30, he remained in Judea and began his ministry (John 3:22). He continued this ministry for some time until the Pharisees learned that he was making more disciples than John the Baptist (John 4:1), which prompted his return to Galilee. John does not explain why Jesus left Judea, but it was probably because of John's arrest, which both Matthew and Mark connect with Jesus' return to Galilee (Matt 4:12; Mark 1:14). Jesus probably stopped baptizing in the same region as John to avoid being arrested as John had, especially since it was now known that his ministry was more prominent than John's.

It is not possible to know how long Jesus' initial Judean ministry lasted, but it must have been several months for it to become apparent that Jesus' ministry was reaching more Judeans than was John's. Perhaps a hint of the end of the Judean ministry can be found at John 4:35. Here the disciples engaged Jesus in a conversation following his conversation with the Samaritan woman at the well. Jesus quoted an aphorism:

ἔτι τετράμηνός ἐστιν καὶ ὁ θερισμὸς ἔρχεται

"There are still four months and [then] the harvest comes."

This saying probably means that even though one has been awaiting some event, it cannot be rushed. It will come in its own time.

Some have argued that this is not an aphorism that Jesus quoted, but a statement of fact—the disciples had been discussing that the harvest was still four months away.[428] One argument against this saying being an aphorism is that it is unattested elsewhere. But, of course, that is an argument from silence, which does not prove that it was not a known saying.

Another argument is that "still" (ἔτι) is inappropriate for an aphorism—that the proverb should instead mention sowing seed and say something like "there are four months between seedtime and harvest."[429] However, this misses the point. The aphorism assumes that seed has been sown. It is not a saying about how long there is between seedtime and harvest. One must still wait four more months for the harvest. Therefore, "still" is quite appropriate in this aphorism.

A third argument is that there were six months between seedtime and harvest (autumn to spring) in Palestine, not four months. This also misses the point of the aphorism which is that even though one has been waiting a while (i.e., two months), there is still even more time to wait (i.e., four months).

Finally, we should note that the way that Jesus introduces this aphorism with a present tense verb (λέγετε) points to it being proverbial and not simply a statement made by the disciples. He says, "Don't you say that . . . " (οὐχ ὑμεῖς λέγετε ὅτι . . .). If he had been

---

[428] Hoehner, *Chronological Aspects of the Life of Christ*, 56–57.
[429] Hoehner, *Chronological Aspects of the Life of Christ*, 57, note 53, quoting Hendrickson.

simply quoting the disciples' conversation, it is more likely that John would have used an aorist verb to say, "Didn't you say that . . . " (οὐχ ὑμεῖς εἴπατε ὅτι . . .).

Although John 4:35 is not a statement of fact by the disciples, one must still ask why Jesus quoted this particular aphorism at this time. Until Jesus quoted this aphorism, the conversation had been about eating food (John 4:31–34). Jesus uses this aphorism to switch the subject to harvesting. Why did Jesus choose this particular aphorism, and why did he switch metaphors from eating to harvesting? Not only did Jesus use this metaphor to introduce the reason for his Galilean ministry, but he may have chosen this particular aphorism because it was especially timely.[430] It may have fit the season when he spoke it. That is, it may have been in winter, perhaps the month of Kislev in AD 30 when one had over a quarter year to wait for the harvest.

While we cannot be certain of this, it fits quite well with the circumstances. Jesus would have been making disciples in Judea for about eight months (Nisan to Kislev), a long enough time for it to become evident that he was baptizing more disciples than John. It would allow about four or five months (Tebeth to Nisan or Iyyar; Matt 12:1–8; Mark 2:23–28; Luke 6:1–5). Therefore, we can tentatively date John's arrest to Marcheshvan or Kislev in late AD 30 and Jesus' return to Galilee to Kislev AD 30 or Tebeth AD 31.

11. JOHN THE BAPTIST BEHEADED

In both Matthew and Mark the death of John the Baptist is related just before the Feeding of the 5000 in Nisan of AD 32 (Matt 14:3–12;

---

[430] Although Jesus' use of harvest as a metaphor in Matt 9:37–38||Luke 10:2 is well-known, the Gospels do not portray this metaphor as a particularly common one in Jesus' teachings. It occurs nowhere else, and is not employed as the controlling metaphor in any parable. Harvest imagery is employed in two parables in support of other controlling metaphors: the Parable of the Sower (Mark 4:8) and the Parable of the Tares in the Wheat (Matt 13: 30, 39).

Mark 6:17–29).[431] In both cases the setting is Jesus' growing fame and Herod Antipas' consternation about Jesus being John raised from the dead. Therefore, by Nisan AD 32 John was dead. However, late in Jesus' Galilean ministry John was still alive (Matt 11:2–19; Luke 7:18–35). We can estimate that John was executed in early AD 32, perhaps in the month of Tebeth. This would allow two or three months for Jesus' fame to grow in John's absence and eventually reach Antipas.

12, 13 & 14. *EVENTS OF NISAN–ELUL 32*

All four Gospels report the Feeding of the 5000 in Nisan AD 32 (Matt 14:13–21; Mark 6:32–44; Luke 9:10–17; John 6:1–15). In addition, Matthew, Mark and John report Jesus' walking on the Sea of Galilee immediately afterward (Matt 14:22–33; Mark 6:45–52; John 6:16–21). Both Matthew and Mark report Jesus and his disciples landing at Gennesaret the next day. There Jesus healed many (Matt 14:34–36; Mark 6:53–56; cf. John 6:22–25).

Shortly thereafter Jesus completed his ministry in Galilee, probably in Capernaum (John 6:59), and traveled to the region of Tyre and Sidon, through the Decapolis and near Caesarea Philippi. He returned to Galilee, briefly reviving his ministry there before leaving (Matt 17:22; 19:1; Mark 9:30, 33; Luke 10:38–42; 13:22; 17:11; John 7:1–9). He then traveled along the border of Samaria (Luke 17:11–18:14) towards Perea and Judea.

16. *MINISTRY IN JUDEA AND PEREA*

John reports Jesus traveling to Jerusalem for the Feast of Tabernacles in Tishri 32 (John 7:10–8:59) and also recounts Jesus' visit to Jerusalem two months later for the Feast of Dedication (John 10:22–39). The Feast of Tabernacles probably marked the beginning of Jesus' ministry in Judea and Perea. This would explain his visit to

---

[431] Luke includes the account of John's death with the report of John's arrest (Luke 3:19–20).

Jerusalem during the Feast of Dedication (Hanukkah)—he was not far away and went to Jerusalem for Hanukkah, even though it was not a pilgrimage festival. Thus, Jesus' ministry in Judea and Perea occupied the last six months of his ministry before his triumphal entry into Jerusalem.

13

HOLY WEEK, CRUCIFIXION, AND RESURRECTION

The four canonical Gospels contain much detail about Jesus' final week in Jerusalem before his resurrection. However, the many details are not always easily integrated into a coherent chronology of the events of this week, especially of the period beginning with Jesus' Passover meal with his disciples through the crucifixion. Therefore, we will have to carefully examine their witness to the time of Jesus' crucifixion to determine when it occurred.

THE DAY OF THE CRUCIFIXION

THE DAY OF THE WEEK

All four Gospels clearly indicate that the day of the crucifixion was a Friday, since they describe the following day as a Sabbath (Matt 28:1a; Mark 15:42; Luke 23:56; John 19:31), and place the resurrection on a Sunday, "the first day of the week" (Matt 28:1b; Mark 16:2; Luke 24:1; John 20:1). This is confirmed by the frequent mention of Jesus' resurrection "on the third day" (τῇ τρίτῃ ἡμέρᾳ or τῇ ἡμέρᾳ τῇ τρίτῃ), that is, with the Friday crucifixion being the first day (Matt 16:21; 17:23; 20:19; Luke 9:22; 18:33; 24:7,46; Acts 10:40; 1 Cor 15:4). This way of counting days inclusively is confirmed at Luke 13:32 where Jesus speaks of doing his work "today, tomorrow, and the third day" (σήμερον καὶ αὔριον καὶ τῇ τρίτῃ).

Despite this strong evidence, some have sought to place the crucifixion on Thursday or even Wednesday.[432] Several passages in particular have prompted such theories. The most important one is Matt 12:40 where Jesus says that the Son of Man will be in the heart of the earth three days and three nights. It is reasoned that if Jesus was buried late in the day on Friday and rose on Sunday morning, the most one could count would be three days (late in the day Friday, Saturday during the day, and Sunday just after dawn) and two nights (Friday night and Saturday night). Therefore, the crucifixion must have taken place on a Thursday (if one is allowed to count partial days) or Wednesday (if one must count full days and nights). In support of this, it is noted that several passages quote Jesus as saying that he will rise *"after* three days" (μετὰ τρεῖς ἡμέρας; Matt 27:63; Mark 8:31; 9:31; 10:34).

Matt 12:40 appears to be the strongest evidence against a Friday crucifixion. However, an examination of OT passages demonstrates that the interpretation given to "three days and three nights" by those who would insist on a very literal reading fails to understand this idiom. Consider Esth 4:16; 5:1. Esther asked Mordecai to have the Judeans in Susa fast for "three days, night and day" (שְׁלֹשֶׁת יָמִים לַיְלָה וָיוֹם) before she approached Xerxes (Esth 4:16). Then she went in to see Xerxes "on the third day" (בַּיּוֹם הַשְּׁלִישִׁי). Clearly, three days and three nights did not transpire. Similarly, at Gen 42:17 Joseph imprisoned his brothers for "three days" (שְׁלֹשֶׁת יָמִים). However, he released them "on the third day" (בַּיּוֹם הַשְּׁלִישִׁי), even though three entire days had not transpired.

When examining the phrase "after three days," we should note that, although this is the only way Mark refers to the time of Jesus' resurrection, Matthew had no trouble using the phrase interchangeably with his more usual "on the third day." Moreover, at Matt 27:63 the Pharisees quoted Jesus as using the phrase "after three

---

[432] See the discussion in Hoehner, *Chronological Aspects of the Life of Christ*, 65–71; Storey, "The Chronology of Holy Week," 72.

days" so that they could have the tomb sealed. However, they interpreted Jesus' meaning as "until the third day" (ἕως τῆς τρίτης ἡμέρας), not "until after three days would pass." The guards were at the tomb on the first day of the week when Jesus arose (Matt 28:1, 4), and Matthew is clearly depicting this as the third day.

Therefore, the Gospels are consistent in depicting Jesus' crucifixion as taking place on a Friday. His resurrection came, as he had predicted, on the third day beginning with his being rejected, delivered to Gentiles, flogged, mocked, spat upon, and crucified (Matt 16:21; 17:23; 20:19; Luke 9:22; 18:33; 24:7).

THE LUNAR DATE

All three Synoptic Gospels are clear that Jesus had his disciples prepare at Passover meal on "the first day of Unleavened Bread" (Matt 26:17; Mark 14:12; Luke 22:7–8). This indicates that evening was the beginning of Passover on 14 Nisan, placing Jesus' crucifixion on the following day which was also 14 Nisan.[433] This agrees with Paul's statement that "Christ our Passover [lamb] has been sacrificed" (1 Cor 5:7).

However, many have seen a conflict between the Synoptics and John on the time of Jesus' crucifixion. It has been noted that John 19:14 states that Jesus' trial took place on "the day of Preparation of the Passover" (παρασκευὴ τοῦ πάσχα), and this is understood to mean that it was the day before the Passover when the Passover was prepared and when the Passover lambs were slaughtered in the late afternoon.[434] Moreover, John states that on the early morning when Jesus' accusers brought him to Pilate

αὐτοὶ οὐκ εἰσῆλθον εἰς τὸ πραιτώριον, ἵνα μὴ μιανθῶσιν ἀλλὰ φάγωσιν τὸ πάσχα

---

[433] That is, 14 Nisan ran from sundown Thursday to sundown Friday.
[434] Finegan, *Handbook of Biblical Chronology*, 355, §607. This understanding is reflected in some English versions which translate the phrase as "the day of Preparation *for* the Passover" (e.g., NRSV).

They did not enter the Praetorium so that they would not be defiled, but might eat the Passover. (John 18:28)

Thus, it is argued that according to John, it was 13 Nisan—the day before the Passover—and the next day would be the Passover. Jesus' accusers did not wish to become ceremonially defiled by entering Pilate's residence, thereby disqualifying them from eating the Passover meal during the following evening.

There have been many attempts to reconcile the Synoptics and John on this point.[435] Perhaps the most radical was the suggestion that Jesus and his disciples followed the calendar of *Jubilees*, which always placed the Passover on Tuesday.[436] Jesus' accusers, however, followed the traditional calendar according to this theory.

Another theory proposes that Jesus and his disciples reckoned days from sunup instead of sundown. However Jesus' accusers reckoned days from sundown.[437] This would make for a half-day difference in the Passover and could be used to explain why Jesus and his disciples ate the Passover meal an evening earlier than Jesus' accusers.

Still another theory proposes that when Jesus' accusers did not enter the Praetorium in order to be able to "eat the Passover" what was meant was that they wished to be able to eat the sacrifices offered during the Passover or the sacrifices for the first day of the Feast of Unleavened Bread on 15 Nisan (Num 28:18–23).[438] One problem with this theory is that Jesus' accusers included not only priests, but also lay members of the Sanhedrin, and those laymen would not have been eligible to eat the sacrifices under any circumstances.[439]

---

[435] Finegan, *Handbook of Biblical Chronology*, 355–358; Hoehner, *A Chronology of the Life of Christ*, 76–90.

[436] Jaubert, *La date de la Cène*.

[437] This is favored by Hoehner, *A Chronology of the Life of Christ*, 85–90. See also Finegan, *Handbook of Biblical Chronology*, 356–357, §611.

[438] Smith, "The Chronology of the Last Supper," 32–39.

[439] Note that John calls the accusers "the Jews" not "the chief priests." This

Other theories suppose that the Jesus' and his disciples ate a Passover meal, and John must be mistaken about the Passover or that Jesus' meal was not a Passover meal, despite the clear statements in the Synoptic Gospels.[440]

None of these solutions are satisfying, and most of them involve either denying the clear statements of one or more of the Gospels or relying on unproven speculation about alternate ways that the Passover may have been celebrated.

The solution to the seeming conflict between the Synoptic Gospels and John is a careful examination of their language. First, we should note that nowhere does John deny that the Last Supper was a Passover meal. In fact, there are several indications in John that it was a Passover meal:[441] It was held in Jerusalem, although Jesus was staying in Bethany for the festival (John 12:1). Jesus and his disciples did not return to Bethany that evening—it was required that the Passover night be spent within the ritual limits of the city. Jesus' statement that those who have washed need only their feet cleaned implies that the disciples had washed before the meal (John 13:10). This would have been a ceremonial cleansing to prepare for the Passover meal. The disciples thought that Judas left the meal to buy (additional?) provisions for the feast or to donate money to the poor. It was customary to donate to the poor on Passover night. Thus, there are good reasons to believe that John was depicting a Passover meal, and there is no compelling reason to believe that he was depicting any other type of supper.

With regards to John 19:14, it should be noted that "the day of Preparation" was customarily a way of referring to a Friday, a day before a Sabbath. Mark specifically defines the day of Preparation as

---

agrees with the Synoptics that the chief priests, elders and Sanhedrin brought Jesus to Pilate (Matt 27:1; Mark 15:1; Luke 22:66; 23:1).

[440] See the discussion in Hoehner, *A Chronology of the Life of Christ*, 76–85; That Jesus' meal was not a Passover meal is favored by Finegan, *Handbook of Biblical Chronology*, 357–358, §613.

[441] Smith, "The Chronology of the Last Supper," 31–32.

the day before the Sabbath (Mark 15:42).[442] Luke 23:54 appears to confirm this.[443] John 19:31 also confirms that the Preparation meant that it was a Friday.[444] John 19:42 also implies that the day of Preparation was a term for Friday.[445] Outside of the NT, Josephus also confirms that the phrase "day of Preparation" was a term for Friday.[446]

As for the phrase, "the day of Preparation *of the Passover,*" the ambiguity of the word *Passover* (πάσχα) during this era should also be noted. Since the Feast of Unleavened Bread was a week immediately following Passover, at times "Passover" indicated the entire eight-day period. Luke states this explicitly:

Ἤγγιζεν δὲ ἡ ἑορτὴ τῶν ἀζύμων ἡ λεγομένη πάσχα.

The Feast of Unleavened Bread, which is called "Passover" was near. (Luke 22:1; cp. Acts 12:3–4)

It appears likely that Luke had the entire eight-day period in mind also at Luke 2:41:

---

[442] ἦν παρασκευὴ ὅ ἐστιν προσάββατον; "it was the day of Preparation, that is, the day before the Sabbath."

[443] ἡμέρα ἦν παρασκευῆς καὶ σάββατον ἐπέφωσκεν; "it was the day of Preparation, and the Sabbath was beginning."

[444] παρασκευὴ ἦν, ἵνα μὴ μείνῃ ἐπὶ τοῦ σταυροῦ τὰ σώματα ἐν τῷ σαββάτῳ, ἦν γὰρ μεγάλη ἡ ἡμέρα ἐκείνου τοῦ σαββάτου; " . . . it was the day of Preparation, so that the bodies would not remain on the cross on the Sabbath. For that Sabbath was a great Sabbath."

[445] διὰ τὴν παρασκευὴν τῶν Ἰουδαίων, ὅτι ἐγγὺς ἦν τὸ μνημεῖον, ἔθηκαν τὸν Ἰησοῦν; "because it was the Jews' day of Preparation, that the grave was nearby, they placed Jesus' body there." Note also the mention of the day of Preparation in the parallels at Matt 27:62; Mark 15:42; Luke 23:54, 56.

[446] Josephus, *Ant.* 16.163 [16.6.2]; ἐν σάββασιν ἢ τῇ πρὸ αὐτῆς παρασκευῇ; "on the Sabbath or the day of Preparation before it."

Καὶ ἐπορεύοντο οἱ γονεῖς αὐτοῦ κατ' ἔτος εἰς Ἰερουσαλὴμ τῇ ἑορτῇ τοῦ πάσχα.

Now his parents would go every year to Jerusalem for the Feast of the Passover.

It is unlikely that Jesus' parents made the trip to Jerusalem for only a day.

In a similar way, the phrase *Feast of Unleavened Bread* could be used to refer to the Passover plus the seven-day feast that followed.

Καὶ τῇ πρώτῃ ἡμέρᾳ τῶν ἀζύμων, ὅτε τὸ πάσχα ἔθυον

Now on the first day of Unleavened Bread when the Passover was sacrificed . . . (Mark 14:12; cp. Matt 26:17; Luke 22:7)

It is likely that Acts 12:3; 20:6 also refer to the entire eight-day period as "the days of Unleavened Bread."

This same merging of the Passover and the Feast of Unleavened Bread can be found in Josephus:

τῆς τῶν ἀζύμων ἐνστάσης ἑορτῆς ἣ πάσχα παρὰ Ἰουδαίοις καλεῖται

. . . the coming of the Feast of Unleavened Bread, which is called Passover by Jews (*J.W.* 2.10 [2.1.3])

κατὰ τὸν καιρὸν τῆς τῶν ἀζύμων ἑορτῆς ἣν πάσχα λέγομεν

. . . at the time of the Feast of Unleavened Bread, which we call Passover (*Ant.* 14:21 [14.2.1])

τὸν καιρὸν ἑορτῆς ἐν ᾗ Ἰουδαίοις ἄζυμα προτίθεσθαι πάτριον φάσκα δ' ἡ ἑορτὴ καλεῖται

. . . the time of the feast in which unleavened bread was appointed ancestrally, which is called Passover (*Ant.* 17.213 [17.9.3])

τῶν ἀζύμων τῆς ἑορτῆς ἀγομένης ἣν πάσχα καλοῦμεν

. . . the Feast of Unleavened Bread, which is called Passover was being celebrated (*Ant.* 18.29 [18.2.2])[447]

In addition, Philo notes the fusing of Passover and Unleavened Bread:

συνάπτει δὲ τοῖς διαβατηρίοις ἑορτὴν διάφορον ἔχουσαν καὶ οὐ συνήθη τροφῆς χρῆσιν, ἄζυμα, ἀφ᾿ οὗ καὶ ὠνόμασται.

And there is another festival combined with the feast of the Passover, using food different from the usual, and not customary—namely, Unleavened Bread, from which it derives its name. (*Spec. Laws* 2.150)

Given this evidence, the phrase "the day of Preparation of the Passover" does *not* denote the day when the Passover was prepared (13 Nisan), but a Friday during the Feast of Unleavened Bread broadly understood.[448] That is, it was a Friday during the eight-day period encompassing Passover and the Feast of Unleavened Bread. This also explains why John would say of the day following Jesus' crucifixion "that Sabbath was a great Sabbath" (John 19:31). That is, it was not only a Sabbath, but it was the first day of the Feast of Unleavened Bread, on which special sacrifices were to be offered (Num 28:18–23). Therefore, John 19:14 does not contradict the Synoptic Gospels.

As for the notice at John 18:28, it does not mean that the following day was the Passover. Note that two of the three Synoptic Gospels as well as John state that Jesus was brought to Pilate early in the morning at the end fourth watch of the night (πρωΐ), that is, after about 4:30 am. Jesus' accusers had been busy all night long. They had gathered a crowd to arrest Jesus, had put him on trial during the night, and confined him while they contemplated their next move—taking him to Pilate. Unlike Jesus and his disciples, they had not yet had

---

[447] See also Josephus, *Ant.* 18.90 [18.4.3]; 20.106 [20.5.3].

[448] This sense is conveyed by the NIV translation of John 9:14a: "It was the day of Preparation of Passover Week." In other words, it was Friday of Passover Week.

time to eat the Passover meal, which had to be eaten before dawn (Exod 12:10; 34:25; Deut 16:4 cp. Exod 23:18; 29:34; Lev 7:15). They were hoping to remain undefiled so that they could eat it *after* Pilate gave them permission to crucify Jesus.

Jesus' accusers apparently expected a quick ruling from Pilate. However, their refusal to enter the Praetorium may have actually delayed Pilate's ruling, as a close reading of John's portrayal of the events suggests. At first, Pilate did not see a capital offense in their accusations, but told Jesus' captors to judge him by their laws (John 18:29–31). They insisted, however, that Jesus had committed a capital crime, so Pilate took Jesus into the Praetorium and interviewed him. Although Jesus claimed a kingship, Jesus' responses denied that he was an insurrectionist (John 18:33–36). Moreover, Pilate appears to be convinced that Jesus was some type of philosopher whose concern was for truth, hardly making him a threat to Roman interests (John 18:37–38). Hoping that flogging Jesus would mollify the crowd, Pilate presented him as innocent (John 19:1–5). They were not mollified, but demanded Jesus be executed (John 19:6). When the chief priests and Sanhedrin accused Jesus of making himself the Son of God, Pilate again interviewed Jesus in the Praetorium (John 19:7–11). Jesus' ultimate answer that acknowledged Pilate's authority convinced the Roman prefect of Jesus' innocence, and he tried to find a way to release him (John 19:12a). Only when the crowd played their trump card—that if Pilate released Jesus, the prefect would not be a friend of Caesar's—did Pilate hand Jesus over to be crucified.

Thus, Jesus' accusers did not enter the Praetorium, hoping for a quick decision from Pilate so that they could eat the Passover meal before sunrise. However, they would end up missing the Passover meal, since the cautious and thorough Pilate did not give them permission until sometime around dawn (John 19:14). John is subtle—but very effective—in showing that Jesus' captors were not in charge of the flow of events. By a comparison of John 18:28 and

John 19:14 the reader is led to conclude that Jesus' life is not being taken from him, but he is laying it down willingly (John 10:17–18).[449]

Moreover, John is also using irony to demonstrate that by rejecting Jesus, his accusers were placing themselves in a position of bearing the guilt of their own sin instead of having Jesus bear it for them. Had they entered the Praetorium and become defiled, they could have eaten the Passover meal one month later than usual (Num 9:6–12). However, if a person was clean, but did not eat the Passover meal, that person was to be excluded from God's people and would bear his own sin (Num 9:13).

A careful reading of John's Gospel demonstrates that it agrees with the Synoptic Gospels in depicting the crucifixion as taking place on Passover. Moreover, all four Gospels state that 14 Nisan that year was a Friday, a "Day of Preparation" (Matt 27:62; Mark 15:42; Luke 23:54; John 19:14, 31, 42).

THE YEAR OF THE CRUCIFIXION

We have already demonstrated that Jesus' ministry began in mid-to-late AD 29 and that it lasted somewhat over three years. That would necessitate that his crucifixion took place on Passover of AD 33. However, since dates from AD 21 to AD 36 have been proposed, with

---

[449] Matthew and Mark make a similar point when they note that the chief priests and elders plotted to take Jesus' life " . . . but not during the feast, lest there be an uproar among the people" (Matt 26:5; Mark 14:2). Despite their plan, they ended up doing just what they said they would not do. The delay during the late evening and morning before Jesus' crucifixion is even more striking when all four Gospels are compared, since there were at least two other unexpected delays that contributed to Jesus' accusers missing the Passover meal: the failure to sustain the charges against Jesus at his trial before the Sanhedrin (Matt 26:59–60‖Mark 14:55–56) and Pilate sending Jesus to Herod Antipas (Luke 23:6–12).

AD 30 being the most popular alternative,[450] further discussion of the year of the crucifixion is warranted here.

The mention of several officials during Jesus' trial determines a possible range of dates for the crucifixion. Caiaphas (Joseph bar Kayafa; Matt 26:3, 57; Luke 3:2; John 11:49; 18:13, 14, 24, 28) was high priest from AD 18 to AD 37. Pontius Pilate was procurator of Judea from approximately AD 26 to AD 36. Herod Antipas (Luke 23:7–12, 15) was tetrarch of Galilee and Perea from 1 (4) BC to AD 38. Thus, judging from these officials, the crucifixion can roughly be placed from AD 26 to AD 36.

A YEAR WITH A FRIDAY PASSOVER

As we have already seen, the Passover at Jesus' crucifixion commenced on Thursday evening at sundown and lasted throughout the daytime hours of the following Friday. Thus, Jesus' crucifixion occurred in a year when, in our terms, the Passover fell on a Friday. Only two years between AD 26 and AD 36 had Friday Passovers: Friday, April 7, AD 30 was a Passover, and Friday, April 3, AD 33 was a Passover.[451] Since the Passover of AD 30 was the first Passover of Jesus' ministry (see discussion beginning on page 262), the date for Jesus' crucifixion is most likely April 3, AD 33.

---

[450] E.g., Kokkinos, "Crucifixion in A.D. 30."

[451] Fotheringham, "The Evidence of Astronomy and Technical Chronology for the Date of the Crucifixion," 158–160. Fotheringham favors April 3, AD 33 (p. 161). See also, Goldstine, *New and Full Moons 1001 B.C. to A.D. 1651*, 80, 87. The tables in Parker and Dubberstein, *Babylonian Chronology 626 B.C.–A.D. 75*, 44 assume an intercalated second Adar in the early spring of AD 33. If no such month is assumed, the date for 14 Nisan would agree with Fotheringham. While in earlier years Judea was ruled from the east and would have been under the sway of Babylonian reckoning, those political ties had been severed when Judea came under Roman domination in 63 BC with Pompey's conquest of Jerusalem. Thus, from 63 BC onward, Parker and Dubberstein can only be used as a rough guide, especially in years with an intercalated second Adar.

ROMAN POLITICS AND THE CRUCIFIXION

Political developments in the Roman Empire during the third and fourth decades of the first century also favor AD 33 as the year of the crucifixion.[452] As we will see, two incidents from Jesus' trial before Pilate are illuminated by these political developments.

In AD 26 Pontius Pilate was nominated to be procurator of Judea by Lucius Aelius Seianus, commonly known as Sejanus. Sejanus was a friend and confidant of Tiberius and prefect of the Praetorian Guard.

In AD 26 Tiberius left for an extended stay on Capri. He would remain there until his death on March 16, AD 37. Control of the empire was left in the hands of Sejanus. Sejanus controlled all of the information that passed between Capri and Rome, allowing Sejanus to continue to consolidate power in his hands.

Sejanus was virulently anti-Jewish.[453] His attitude seems to have influenced Tiberius, who expelled the Jews from Rome in AD 19. When Pilate assumed office in Judea, his policies reflected Sejanus' attitude toward Jews, and several incidents are recorded by Josephus. Early in his administration Pilate's troops marched into Jerusalem with medallions bearing the imperial image among their regimental standards. This sparked a five-day Jewish demonstration in Caesarea Maritima seeking the removal of the images as a violation of Jewish law against graven images. Pilate was forced to order the offended images removed.[454] Later Pilate built an aqueduct for Jerusalem, paying for it by confiscating the fund from the Corban in the temple treasury. Another riot ensued, which Pilate suppressed with much

---

[452] This discussion is based upon Maier, "Sejanus, Pilate, and the Date of the Crucifixion," 8–13; see also Doyle, "Pilate's Career and the Date of the Crucifixion"; Maier, "The Episode of the Golden Shields at Jerusalem"; Finegan, *Handbook of Biblical Chronology*, 362; Hoehner, *Chronological Aspects of the Life of Christ*, 105–111.

[453] Philo, *Flaccus*, 1.1; *Embassy*, 1.159–161

[454] Josephus, *J.W.* 2.169–174 [2.9.2–3]; *Ant.* 18.55–59 [18.3.1].

bloodshed.[455] Luke also reports one of Pilate's atrocities, noting that he had mingled the blood of some Galileans with their sacrifices (Luke 13:1). In addition, in AD 30–31 Pilate minted bronze *quadrans* coins in Judea. These displayed a crosier, a symbol of the pagan Roman augurs—priests whose main function was to read omens from the gods. This also would have offended Jewish sensibilities.

Sejanus reached the height of his power in AD 30. The Roman Senate declared that his birthday should be publicly celebrated. Prayers and sacrifices were offered on behalf of Tiberius and Sejanus jointly. Oaths were sworn by Tiberius and Sejanus jointly. Statues were erected in his honor. Sejanus was named consul with Tiberius for AD 31.

However, Sejanus' fall from power was swift. His political intrigues against the imperial family were exposed, and Sejanus was condemned. On October 18, AD 31 he was executed, and his body was unceremoniously thrown down the Gemonian Stairs where a crowd tore it asunder. It was revealed that Sejanus had poisoned Tiberius' son Drusus, leading Tiberius to purge Rome of Sejanus' family and supporters.

In this political climate, Pilate, who was appointed by Sejanus, now had to navigate the political waters carefully. He needed to be careful to demonstrate his loyalty to Tiberius and to distance himself from any hint of treason. One way he apparently sought to demonstrate his loyalty to the emperor was by placing some gold shields inscribed with a dedication to Tiberius in Herod's palace in Jerusalem.[456] These shields had no images on them and were not displayed in public. Despite the aniconic nature of the shields, the Jews in Jerusalem, led by four of Herod's sons, protested to Pilate. However, Pilate refused to remove the shields. They then appealed to Tiberius, who ordered the shields removed. This incident clearly took

---

[455] Josephus, *J.W.* 2.175–177 [2.9.4]; *Ant.* 18.60–62 [18.3.2].

[456] Philo, *Embassy*, 1.299–308; see Maier, "The Episode of the Golden Roman Shields at Jerusalem."

place after Sejanus' downfall, most likely in AD 32.[457] Not only did Tiberius rule in favor of the Jews, but he was able to receive the appeal from Jerusalem, something that would not have been permitted by Sejanus when he was in control of correspondence between Rome and Capri.

The affair of the golden shields serves to illuminate the interplay between Pilate and Herod Antipas during Jesus' trial (Luke 23:6–12). Luke reports that before this time Pilate and Antipas were hostile toward each other (Luke 23:12). This probably stemmed from the role played by Antipas, one of Herod's sons, who appealed to Tiberius against Pilate. However, Pilate's gesture of sending Jesus to Antipas mended their relationship. Antipas had been wary of Jesus for some time (Matt 14:1–2; Mark 6:15–16). Thus, Luke 23:6–12 indicates that Jesus was crucified *after* AD 32. Since only AD 33 qualifies both as a year after the golden shields affair and as a year with a Passover falling on a Friday, it is the year of the crucifixion.

Another indication that AD 33 was the year of the crucifixion is the claim by Jesus' accusers that finally moved Pilate to turn Jesus over to them, although he was inclined to release him instead. They said:

ἐὰν τοῦτον ἀπολύσῃς, οὐκ εἶ φίλος τοῦ Καίσαρος· πᾶς ὁ βασιλέα ἑαυτὸν ποιῶν ἀντιλέγει τῷ Καίσαρι.

If you release this man, you are no friend of Caesar's. Everyone who makes himself a king defies Caesar. (John 19:12)

This comment caused Pilate to immediately accede to the Jewish leaders' demand that Jesus be turned over to them for crucifixion (John 19:13–16). Pilate even made a public display of washing his hands of the entire affair, declaring himself innocent of Jesus' blood (Matt 27:24).

---

[457] Doyle, "Pilate's Career and the Date of the Crucifixion."

Had the crucifixion taken place before Sejanus' downfall in late AD 31, the veiled threat of Jesus' accusers that they would appeal to Tiberius, claiming that Pilate was protecting an insurrectionist, would have rung hollow. Before AD 31 Sejanus controlled the information that Tiberius received, and Sejanus certainly would not have looked favorably upon an appeal from Jewish authorities. The only setting in which the threat of the Jewish authorities would have been able to move Pilate to change his mind so suddenly was in the aftermath of Sejanus' downfall.

Moreover, Pilate was careful to distance himself publicly from the execution of a Jew whom he considered to be innocent of the charges brought against him. Since Tiberius had reversed Sejanus' anti-Jewish policy, it would have been risky for Pilate to have appeared to continue practices encouraged under Sejanus. He needed to appear to be neutral and impartial.

Therefore, both John 19:12 and Matt 27:24 indicate that Jesus was crucified after October AD 31. Pilate was caught on the horns of a dilemma because of the political climate during the final years of Tiberius' reign. He could not appear to be disloyal to Tiberius by harboring an insurrectionist, but he could not appear to be persecuting Jews by shedding their blood without cause. All he could do was release Jesus to the Jewish authorities, but maneuver them into declaring that Jesus' blood was on them (Matt 27:25). Once again the evidence supports April 3, AD 33 as the date of the crucifixion.

ASTRONOMY AND THE DATE OF THE CRUCIFIXION

Several phenomena in nature are reported in the Gospels in connection with the crucifixion. Darkness was over the land from noon until about 3:00 pm (Matt 27:45; Mark 15:33; Luke 23:44). At Jesus' death there was an earthquake (Matt 27:51). Neither of these phenomena can be verified from extra-biblical sources. However, there is a third phenomenon that can be verified.

On April 3, AD 33 at about 6:30 pm the moon rose over the horizon at Jerusalem.[458] It was in the midst of a lunar eclipse with about 20 percent of its disc in the umbra of the earth's shadow and the rest of its disc in the penumbra. The true umbral eclipse lasted until 6:45 pm, and the perceived eclipse ended ten minutes later at 6:55 pm. Although only 20 percent of the moon was within the umbra, this section was positioned close to the leading edge of the rising moon.

The umbral shadow is normally blood red in color. For partial eclipses with the moon high in the sky against a starry backdrop there is a large contrast between the obscured and unobscured parts of the moon so that the obscured part appears missing from the disc with the rest of the disc appearing white. However, in Jerusalem on April 3, AD 33 the eclipsed moon was just above the horizon against the relatively bright early evening sky. The most probable color of the rising moon would have been red for the portion in the umbral shadow—most of the visible portion of the moon as it arose that evening. The rest of the moon would have appeared to be yellow-orange. If a dense dust storm had been responsible for the darkening of sun earlier in the day, any remaining dust in the atmosphere would have tended to modify and even deepen these colors. The Passover would have been ending at sunset as the moon arose. The Jews in Jerusalem would have been observing these phenomena closely. They would have witnessed a dramatic blood red moon rising over Jerusalem with a significant portion of it appearing to "turn to blood."

On the day of Pentecost the first prophet quoted by Peter was Joel:

> "'And in the last days it shall be,' God declares, 'that I will pour out my Spirit on all flesh, and your sons and your daughters will prophesy, and your young men will see visions, and your old men will dream dreams. Even on my male and female servants in those days I will pour out my Spirit, and they will prophesy. *I will show wonders in the heavens above*

---

[458] This discussion is based on Humphreys and Waddington, "Astronomy and the Date of the Crucifixion," 176–179.

and signs on the earth below, blood, and fire, and clouds of smoke. The sun will be turned to darkness and the moon to blood before the day of the Lord comes, the great and magnificent day. (Acts 2:16–20, quoting Joel 2:28–31 [Hebrew text 3:1–4])

This quotation took advantage of the phenomena observed in nature at the crucifixion as well as the pouring out of the Spirit at Pentecost. Joel had prophesied these things, and the dramatic events in nature at Jesus' crucifixion coupled with the signs of the Spirit at Pentecost verified Peter's claim that God had ushered in the messianic "last days" precisely as prophesied by Joel. The coupling of the sun being turned dark with the moon being turned to blood and with the additional reference to "clouds of smoke" which may be the way that the sun appeared to be darkened (i.e., by a smoky-looking dust cloud) made Peter's sermon very powerful and led to his listeners being "pierced in the heart" (κατενύγησαν τὴν καρδίαν; Acts 2:37).

The lunar eclipse of April 3, AD 33 is an additional verification that this is the likely date of Jesus' crucifixion. It is the only viable date for the crucifixion that provides the background for Peter's choice of Joel 2:28–31 as the opening for his Pentecost sermon.[459]

In Table 57 lunar days are from sundown (separated by dashed lines). Julian days are from midnight (separated by solid lines). References in brackets denote where one Gospel has an item or related topic out of chronological order or in a different order or context from the other Gospels.

---

[459] This also is a dramatic demonstration of the benefit of an accurate understanding of biblical chronology and the way it illuminates the events and theological claims of the Scriptures.

THE CHRONOLOGY OF HOLY WEEK AND EASTER

Table 57
Holy Week and Easter

Lunar Date	Julian Date	Event	Matthew	Mark	Luke	John
9 Nisan	March 29 Sunday	1. Triumphal Entry	21:1–11	11:1–10	19:28–40	12:12–19
		2. Weeping over Jerusalem			19:41–44	
		3. Some Greeks Seek Jesus				12:20–36a
		4. Visit to Temple: Return to Bethany	21:14–17	11:11		12:36b–43 (?)
10 Nisan	March 30 Monday	5. Cursing the Fig Tree	21:18–19	11:12–14		
		6. Cleansing the Temple	[21:12–13]	11:15–17	19:45–46	
		7. Priests and Scribes Seek to Destroy Jesus		11:18	19:47–48	
		8. Return to Bethany		11:19		
11 Nisan	March 31 Tuesday	9. Lesson of the Fig Tree	21:20–22	11:20–26		
		10. Teaching in the Temple	21:23–23:39	11:27–12:44	20:1–21:4	
		11. Jesus Foretells Destruction of Temple	24:1–2	13:1–2	21:5–6	
		12. The Olivet Discourse	24:3–25:46	13:3–37	21:7–36	
		13. Teaching in the Temple			21:37–38	
12 Nisan	April 1 Wednesday	14. Jesus Predicts His Crucifixion	26:1–2			
		15. Priest and Scribes Plot to Kill Jesus	26:3–5	14:1–2	22:1–2	[11:45–53]
		16. Jesus Anointed at Bethany [8 Nisan ?]	[26:6–13]	[14:3–9]		12:1–8
		17. Judas Agrees to Betray Jesus	26:14–16	14:10–11	22:3–6	
13 Nisan	April 2 Thursday	18. The Disciples Prepare the Passover Meal	26:17–19	14:12–16	22:7–13	
14 Nisan		19. The Passover Meal	26:20–29	14:17–25	22:14–38	13:1–17:26
		20. Jesus Foretells Peter's Denial	26:30–35	14:26–31	[22:32–34]	[13:36–38]
		21. Praying at Gethsemane	26:36–46	14:32–42	22:39–46	

Lunar Date	Julian Date	Event	Matthew	Mark	Luke	John
14 Nisan	April 2					
	Thursday	22. Jesus Arrested	26:47–56	14:43–52	22:47–53	18:1–12
	April 3	23. Jesus before Caiaphas	26:57–68	14:53–65	22:54	18:13–14; 19–24
	Friday	24. Peter Denies Jesus	26:69–75	14:66–72	22:55–62	18:15–18; 25–27
		25. Jesus Is Mocked			22:63–65	
		26. Jesus Delivered to Pilate	27:1–2	15:1	23:1	18:28
		27. Judas Hangs Himself	27:3–10		Acts 1:16-19	
		28. Jesus before Pilate	27:11–14	15:2–5	23:2–5	18:29–38
		29. Jesus before Herod			23:6–17	
		30. Barabbas Freed	27:15–23	15:6–15	23:18–25a	18:39–40
		31. Pilate Has Jesus Scourged	[27:26b]	15:15a		19:1–3
		32. Pilate Seeks to Release Jesus	27:24–25			19:4–15
		33. Pilate Hands Jesus over to be Crucified	27:26	15:15b	23:25b	19:16
		34. Soldiers mock Jesus	27:27–31	15:16–20		[19:21]
		35. Jesus Is Crucified	27:32–56	15:21–41	23:26–49	19:17–37
		36. Jesus Buried	27:57–61	15:42–47	23:50–56a	19:38–42
15 Nisan		37. Guard at the Tomb	27:62–66			
	April 4					
	Saturday	38. Rest on the Sabbath			23:56b	
16 Nisan	April 5					
	Sunday	39. The Resurrection	28:1–10	16:1–9	24:1–12	20:1–18
		40. Report of the Guard	28:11–15			
		41. Jesus Appears on the Road to Emmaus		16:12–13	24:13-35	
17 Nisan		42. Jesus Appears to the Disciples			24:36–49	20:19–23

289

SPECIFIC EVENTS DURING HOLY WEEK

1. TRIUMPHAL ENTRY

John 12:1 places Mary's anointing of Jesus six days before the Passover. The date was, therefore, 8 Nisan or Saturday, March 28 according to the Julian calendar. John 12:12 places the triumphal entry on the next day. Therefore Jesus entered Jerusalem on 9 Nisan, or Sunday, March 29.[460]

5. CLEANSING OF THE TEMPLE

As is evident from comparing Matthew with the other Synoptic Gospels, Matthew tends to follow the chronological order of events during Holy Week. However, he occasionally places items out of chronological order to treat them topically.[461] One of these items is the cleansing of the temple, which Mark and Luke clearly place on Monday, but which Matthew places with the visit to the temple on Sunday after Jesus' entry into Jerusalem.

---

[460] The contention of Hoehner that the Triumphal entry took place on a Monday is without basis. Hoehner posits a day between Mary's anointing of Jesus and the Triumphal entry. He places the narrative of the plot to kill Lazarus (John 12:9–11) on this intervening day. The reasoning is specious, however. John is careful to note the day of the anointing and the day of the entry into Jerusalem. It strains credulity to suppose that he would leave no explicit notice of the intervening day. Hoehner places the triumphal entry on Monday in order to avoid a "silent Wednesday" during which there is no account in the Gospels for Jesus' activity. However, Luke 21:37–38 accounts for Jesus' activity on Wednesday (cp. Matt 26:55; Mark 14:49; Luke 19:47), and Matt 26:5 and Mark 14:2 place some events on Wednesday, two days before Passover. See Hoehner, *Chronological Aspects of the Life of Christ,* 68, 90–91.

[461] This is also the case with Matthew's account of the withering of the fig tree (Matt 21:20–22) and Pilate having Jesus scourged (Matt 27:26b).

9. WITHERING OF THE FIG TREE

Matthew treats the cursing and withering of the fig tree together (Matt 21:18–22), without noting that the cursing took place on Monday morning as Mark does (Mark 11:12–14), but the disciples do not note that the fig tree has withered until Tuesday morning (Mark 11:20–26). Once again, Matthew has obscured the chronology in order to group events topically.

However, it is evident that Matt 21:18–22 spans two days. The event immediately preceding the cursing of the fig tree is the return to Bethany on Sunday evening (Matt 21:17). The cursing of the fig tree took place the next morning (Matt 21:18). The incident following the fig tree reported by Matthew is the challenge to Jesus' authority (Matt 21:23–27). By comparison to Mark 11:27–33 and Luke 20:1–8, this happened on Tuesday. Therefore, Matt 21:18–22 combines events from two mornings.

Matthew's notice that ἐξηράνθη παραχρῆμα ἡ συκῆ should be translated "immediately the fig tree *began to wither* (Matt 21:19). This reading takes the aorist verb ἐξηράνθη as ingressive (or inchoative) and thus describes the beginning of the withering which became evident the next morning.[462]

10 & 13. TEACHING IN THE TEMPLE

All three Synoptic Gospels record Jesus' teachings in the temple and set it on Tuesday. However, Luke appears also to place some teachings of Jesus in the temple on Wednesday and, perhaps, Thursday (Luke 21:37–38). It would appear that when Jesus was arrested he confirmed that this teaching in the temple was not confined to a single day, but occurred "day after day" (καθ᾽ ἡμέραν; Matt 26:55; Mark 14:49; cp. Luke 19:47). Thus, the teachings reported in the Synoptics in connection with Tuesday may be a summary of several days' teachings.

---

[462] On the ingressive or inchoative aorist see *BDF* §331; Wallace, *Greek Grammar Beyond the Basics*, 558–559.

14, 15 & 17. EVENTS OF WEDNESDAY, APRIL 1

Matt 26:2 and Mark 14:1 state that it was now two days before the Passover. This places Jesus' prediction of his crucifixion, the plot of the priests and scribes to arrest and kill Jesus and Judas' agreement to betray Jesus on that day. Since the plot to kill Jesus was originally planned not to occur on the Passover (Matt 26:5; Mark 14:2), the original plan must have been to arrest Jesus on Wednesday night or Thursday morning. However, for reasons not revealed in the Gospels, that plan was delayed until late Thursday night.

16. JESUS' BODY ANOINTED

Matt 26:6–13 and Mark 14:3–8 record Jesus being anointed in Bethany at the home of Simon the Leper, and they place it with the narrative for Wednesday. This anointing has many points in common with Mary's anointing of Jesus in Bethany on the previous Saturday (John 12:1–8). In Matthew and Mark the reaction of some at dinner and Jesus' reply is very similar to Judas' reaction and Jesus' reply in John. The estimate of the price of the ointment is the same in Matthew and John. The one major difference is that John records Mary as anointing Jesus' feet and wiping them with her hair (John 12:3). In contrast, Matthew and Mark record the anointing of Jesus' head (Matt 26:7; Mark 14:3).

It is difficult to decide whether these are two separate incidents or the same one. The probability, however, is that Matthew and Mark have placed the anointing out of chronological order to connect the anointing and the reaction of Judas without explicitly naming him. Note that in both Matthew and Mark the following narrative is the account of Judas agreeing to betray Jesus (Matt 26:14–16; Mark 13:10–11).

THE CHRONOLOGY OF THE PASSOVER

Beginning with the Passover meal, there are several chronological notices that help to orient the reader to the passage of time during events of the Passover—14 Nisan—which ran from sundown on Thursday, April 2 to sundown on Friday, April 3.

The Passover meal took place in the evening, after sundown (Matt 26:20; Mark 14:17; cf. Exod 12:8). The meal would have begun no earlier than 6:00 pm and may have lasted a couple of hours. Following the meal, Jesus and his disciples left the upper room and crossed the Kidron Valley to the Mount of Olives. There at Gethsemane Jesus prayed. From his comment to the disciples that they could not stay awake with him even one hour, we can assume that roughly an hour passed before Jesus' arrest (Mark 14:37).

Upon his arrest Jesus was taken to the high priest Caiaphas where a late night trial was held. As Jesus was being tried, Peter, who was in the courtyard, denied Jesus. The trial must have lasted most of the night, since by morning Jesus' captors had not had time to eat the Passover (John 18:28).

Early in the day, before sunrise, Jesus was taken to Pilate. The time was at the end of the fourth watch of the night (πρωΐας/πρωΐ), before about 6:00 am, possibly as early as 4:30 am (Matt 27:1; Mark 15:1; Luke 23:1; John 18:28). During this time Jesus was interviewed by Pilate, sent to Herod Antipas who interviewed him and mocked him, and sent back to Pilate. Pilate sought to release Jesus. First he offered Barabbas and Jesus as options for a prisoner to be released at the Feast. The crowd chose Barabbas. Then Pilate had him scourged, and the soldiers mocked him.

At "about the sixth hour" (ὥρα ἦν ὡς ἕκτη; John 19:14) Pilate presented Jesus to the crowd as their king. They demanded his crucifixion. Pilate washed his hands of the affair and released Jesus to be crucified.

John's mention of the sixth hour has led to discussion of whether John is at odds with the Synoptic Gospels which state that Jesus was on the cross at the sixth hour (Matt 27:45; Mark 15:33; Luke 23:44).[463] Moreover, Mark states that the crucifixion began at "the

---

[463] Finegan, *Handbook of Biblical Chronology*, 358–359; §614. Finegan

third hour" (ἦν δὲ ὥρα τρίτη; Mark 15:25). Since time was normally reckoned from dawn (i.e., the first hour being about 6:00 am to 7:00 am), it appears that John depicts Jesus having been released at noon. The Synoptics have Jesus on the cross with darkness descending on the land at noon. However, Mark has Jesus on the cross as early as 9:00 am.

---

rejects the time notices at John 19:14 and Mark 15:25 as "interpolations." Finegan's understanding of John 19:14 as referring to the sixth hour as measured from sunrise, however, is not consistent with the passages everywhere else in his book in which he demonstrates that John measured the hours from midnight, in keeping with the Roman or Graeco-Roman audience for which John's Gospel was intended. To demonstrate that John measured the hours from midnight, Finegan notes (p. 8, §13) that when John says (20:1) that Mary Magalene came to the tomb very early on Sunday before sunrise, it could be explained by assuming that John was measuring the day from midnight, "in terms of the official Roman day which, as Pliny told us (§11), began at midnight." On page 10, §19, Finegan writes, "When various hourly notations are considered in the Gospel according to John, it is found that they do in fact work out well in terms of the Roman reckoning. For example, in John 1:39 a reckoning from the morning would make the 'tenth hour' four o'clock in the afternoon, but a reckoning from midnight would make it ten o'clock in the morning, the lat[t]er being more appropriate to the fact that the two disciples then stayed with Jesus 'that day.' In John 4:6, the 'sixth hour' would be midday in one case [Jewish reckoning], but six o'clock in the evening in the other [Roman reckoning], and the latter would be a very likely time for the gathering at the well. In John 4:52 the 'seventh hour' would be one p.m. or seven p.m., and the latter may be more likely for the arrival at Cana from Capernaum, a journey of twenty miles." Despite these persuasive arguments, when treating John 19:14, Finegan assumes that John has switched to the Hebrew mode of reckoning, and thus he sees an "interpolation" or mistake. Finegan is not consistent in his counting of the hours—but John is. Texts demonstrating that John was writing for a non-Jewish audience are John 1:38; 2:13; 3:1; 5:1; 6:4; 7:2, 15; 10:22; 11:55; 19:40, 42 and 21:1 (note Sea of *Tiberius* instead of Sea of *Galilee*).

The key to understanding the Gospels' time indications surrounding the crucifixion is to understand notations of time in the ancient world.[464] John used Roman reckoning, starting at midnight, whereas the Synoptic Gospels used Jewish reckoning, staring at dawn (about 6:00 am). Often time references were approximations. Thus, John explicitly approximates the time when Jesus was handed over to be as "*about* the sixth hour." It was most likely about 6:00 am—not noon—since John was using Roman hours.[465] Between then and noon (the "sixth hour" of the Synoptic Gospels) Jesus was led away, nailed to the cross (Mark's "third hour"; i.e., 9:00 am) and crucified. This makes good sense, since it appears that Jesus was brought to Pilate very early, certainly before sunrise. In order to accomplish all the events narrated in the Gospels between then and the crucifixion, most of the morning would have been required. Thus, John's note that it was "about the sixth hour" when Pilate declared "Behold, your king!" means that it was going on 6:00 am. After the crowd demanded Jesus' crucifixion, Pilate released him (John 19:15–16).

---

[464] See Cadbury, "Some Lukan Expressions of Time," 277–278," and especially Miller, "The Time of the Crucifixion." Miller discusses the various schemes previously proposed to make sense of the Gospel accounts. These include assuming one or more of the Gospels is incorrect about the time (Miller, "The Time of the Crucifixion," 157–158), or positing that John used Roman civil time, reckoned from midnight (Miller, "The Time of the Crucifixion," 158–163). Miller rules out the latter, claiming that it does not comport well with other time notices in John and that surviving evidence indicates nighttime was not commonly divided into hours. However, the other time notices in John work well assuming Roman reckoning (see footnote 463), and Miller offers no convincing evidence that nighttime was not commonly divided into hours. In fact, Acts 23:23 appears to contradict Miller's assertion about nighttime hours.

[465] Consistent with John's use of Roman timekeeping, the Holman Christian Standard Bible translation of John 19:14b reads, "It was about six in the morning."

The other time indications also should be understood as approximations. Note that the Synoptic Gospels appear to divide the day into quarters parallel to the night watches (see the discussion on page 10). The crucifixion began at the third hour (Mark 15:25) and darkness was over the land from the sixth hour to the ninth hour (Matt 27:45; Mark 15:33; Luke 23:44). Thus, these are indications of the twelve daylight hours being divided into quarter days of about three hours each with each quarter called by the ending hour of the previous quarter day. Mark's notice that when Jesus was crucified "it was the third hour" probably means nothing more than that it was between about 9:00 am and noon. Thus, Mark does not conflict with John. Nor does Mark conflict with the other Synoptic Gospels. All of the Gospels indicate that before darkness struck the land in the afternoon Jesus was on the cross, and a number of things happened during that time (Matt 27:32–44; Mark 15:21–32; Luke 23:32–43).

Then there was darkness over the land during the third quarter of the daylight hours from "the sixth . . . until the ninth hour" (Ἀπὸ δὲ ἕκτης ὥρας . . . ἕως ὥρας ἐνάτης—Matt 27:45; ὥρας ἕκτης . . . ἕως ὥρας ἐνάτης—Mark 15:33; ὡσεὶ ὥρα ἕκτη . . . ἕως ὥρας ἐνάτης—Luke 23:44). This was from about noon until Jesus' death at 3:00 pm.

Following Jesus' death, Joseph of Arimathea got permission from Pilate to bury Jesus' body. Just before sunset when the Sabbath was to begin, Joseph completed the burial (Luke 23:54). The burial was apparently accomplished quickly and before sunset so that those who handled the body would be ritually clean and able to celebrate the Sabbath and the first day of Unleavened Bread (John 19:42; cf. Lev 11:31).

Table 58
The Passion—14 Nisan, AD 33

Time	Event	Matthew	Mark	Luke	John
6:00–8:00 pm	A. The Last Supper	26:26–29	14:17–25	22:14–38	13:1–17:26
8:00–11:00 pm	B. Jesus Foretells Peter's Denial; Praying at Gethsemane	26:30–46	14:26–31	22:39–46	

11:00 pm– 4:30 am	C. Jesus arrested; Jesus before Caiaphas; Peter denies Jesus	26:47–76	14:43–73	22:47–63	18:1–27
4:30– 6:00 am	D. Jesus delivered to Pilate; Judas hangs himself; Jesus before Pilate; Jesus before Herod	27:1–14	15:1–5	23:1–12	18:28–38
	E. Barabbas freed; Jesus scourged and handed over to be crucified; soldiers mock Jesus	27:15–32	15:6–21	23:13–25	18:39–19:17
6:00 am– 9:00 am	F. Simon forced to carry Jesus' cross; Jesus addresses the crowd; criminals led away with Jesus; Jesus offered wine	27:33–34	15:22–24	23:25–32	
9:00 am	G. Jesus crucified		15:25	23:33	19:18
9:00 am– Noon	H. Garments divided; charge placed on cross; mocked by crowds, priests, soldiers; priests protest to Pilate; Jesus addresses his mother	27:35–44	15:26–32	23:34–43	19:19–27
Noon– 3:00 pm	I. Sun darkened	27:45	15:33	23:44–45a	
3:00 pm	J. Jesus dies; thieves' legs broken; Jesus' side pierced; curtain in temple torn; earthquake; saints rise	27:46–56	15:34–41	23:45b–49	19:28–37
3:00– 6:00 pm	K. Joseph gets permission from Pilate and buries Jesus' body	27:57–61	15:42–47	23:50–56a	19:38–42
6:30– 6:55 pm	L. Lunar eclipse—moon appears blood red in the evening sky at the beginning of 15 Nisan			Cf. Acts 2:16–20	

THE CHRONOLOGY OF EASTER

All four Gospels indicate that Jesus' resurrection and the immediately ensuing events took place on early Sunday morning shortly after dawn (Matt 28:1–10; Mark 16:1–9; Luke 24:1–12; John 20:1–18). The Gospels mention several women from Galilee going to the tomb. The resurrected Jesus instructed them to tell the disciples to go to Galilee (Matt 28:16; Mark 16:7). Peter and another disciple, presumably John, also went to the tomb after the women reported the resurrection to the disciples.

That same morning the men who guarded the tomb reported the resurrection to the chief priests. They accepted a bribe to publicly report that the disciples had stolen Jesus' body (Matt 28:11–15).

That afternoon Jesus first appeared to two disciples on the Emmaus road (Luke 24:13–35; Mark 16:12–13). Later that evening he appeared to the disciples (except Thomas) in a locked room somewhere in Jerusalem (Luke 24:36–49; Mark 16:14; John 20:19–23).

FROM EASTER TO THE ASCENSION

The Gospels also record several post-Easter appearances of Jesus before his ascension. He appeared to his disciples a week after his resurrection. Thomas was present at the time, but no location—be it Jerusalem or Galilee—is given (John 20:24–29). The date was 23 Nisan or Sunday, April 12 on the Julian calendar.

In Galilee Jesus gave his disciples the commission to make disciples of all nations (Matt 28:16–20). Jesus also appeared to Simon Peter, Thomas, Nathanael, James, John and two other disciples by the Sea of Tiberias (John 21).

Forty days after his resurrection (Acts 1:3), Jesus ascended to heaven (Luke 24:50–52; Acts 1:6–11). The date was 25 or 26 Iyyar, depending on whether Nisan had 30 or 29 days that year. The Julian date was Thursday, May 14.

14

THE CHURCH: FROM PENTECOST TO THE END OF PAUL'S MINISTRY

The remaining events of the NT books are chronicled mainly by Luke in the book of Acts. However, a few statements from Paul's letters are also relevant to the chronology of this period. Any biblical chronology that accepts the authenticity of all of Paul's letters contained in the NT canon as well as the historical accuracy of the book of Acts must account for these statements.[466]

BENCHMARKS FROM EXTRA-BIBLICAL SOURCES

A number of references in Acts and Paul's letters to persons or events during this period provide absolute chronological benchmarks when compared to extra-biblical sources. These can be used as a framework

---

[466] A number of influential studies attempt to reconstruct a chronology of Paul's life based primarily on the letters of Paul that critical scholars accept as actually written by him and discounting the other canonical Pauline letters as well as many of the chronological notices in Acts. E.g., Knox, *Chapters in the Life of Paul*: Jewett, *A Chronology of Paul's Life*; Luedemann, *Paul, Apostle to the Gentiles*. Finegan, who rejects this approach, affirms that Acts is a reliable source to reconstruct Paul's life, stating, "If the relevant materials in the book of Acts are taken as they stand, certain problems are raised, particularly in the earlier part, but a relatively detailed chronology, particulary in the later part, can be worked out." (Finegan, *Handbook of Biblical Chronology*, 390; §673.

on which to reconstruct the chronology of the earliest history of the church.

PETER AND JOHN BEFORE THE SANHEDRIN

In Acts 3 Luke recounts Peter and John in the temple one day at the time of prayer during the evening sacrifice at "the ninth hour," that is after 3:00 pm (Acts 3:1). There Peter healed a lame beggar at the Beautiful Gate and proclaimed the Gospel. Because Peter and John were teaching Jesus' resurrection of the dead, the priests, the captain of the temple guard, and the Sadducees had them arrested and placed in custody until the next day (Acts 4:1–3).

The next day Peter and John were brought before the Sanhedrin. Annas, the former high priest, and Caiaphas, the present high priest, were there. In addition, their relative John—most likely the man who would succeed Caiaphas as the high priest—was also present. Since Caiaphas was high priest during Jesus' crucifixion and continued to serve as high priest until AD 37, this incident took place between AD 33 and AD 37, most likely around AD 34.[467] The reason for this dating is that the next chronological benchmark in this era—the martyrdom of Stephen after the outbreak of persecution of Jesus' followers in Jerusalem—most likely is to be dated to late AD 35 or early AD 36. However, at this earlier time the Jewish authorities only threatened the apostles and declined to persecute them (Acts 4:18–22), also indicating that this happened early in this period between AD 33 and AD 36.

---

[467] See Josephus, *Ant.* 18.90–95 [18.4.3]. John or Jonathan was appointed by Vitellius, the Roman governor of Syria. After Vitellius had sent Pilate back to Rome to answer for his actions against the Samaritans, Vitellius appointed Marcellus to be procurator of Judea. This happened in late AD 35 or early AD 36. Then, on the following Passover in AD 37 Vitellius came to Jerusalem, deposed Caiaphas and appointed his brother Jonathan to the high priesthood.

THE MARTYRDOM OF STEPHEN

Stephen was stoned after having appeared before the Sanhedrin and the high priest (Acts 6:12–7:60, esp. 6:12; 7:1, 58). That the high priest and the Sanhedrin could assume the authority to condemn someone to death and carry out the sentence indicates that Roman governance of Judea was in flux at the time (cp. John 18:31). Most scholars agree that Stephen's execution took place in the interregnum between Pilate's dismissal by Vitellius, the Roman governor of Syria and the arrival of his replacement Marcellus. Because of a complaint by the Jews, Pilate was ordered to appear before Tiberius when he reached Rome. However, Tiberius died before Pilate arrived in Rome.[468]

Tiberius died on March 16, AD 37. Since travel on the Mediterranean was often not undertaken in winter and early spring to avoid losing ships in storms, Pilate must have been dismissed during the winter of AD 36. Immediately before this Josephus indicates Pilate was involved with the Samaritans, having attacked and killed a number of them.[469] Thus, during the last year of Pilate's time in Judea he was distracted with the Samaritans and then dismissed from office. This was the ideal time for the high priest and the Sanhedrin to assert themselves and escalate their previous opposition to the Christians in Jerusalem to violent persecution (cf. Acts 8:1–3).

The most likely date for Stephen's martyrdom, then, is sometime in AD 36, with Paul's conversion shortly thereafter.

PAUL'S ESCAPE FROM DAMASCUS

Paul's life was threatened in Damascus, and he had to escape from the city by being lowered in a basket from an opening in the wall, since his enemies were watching for him at the gates. This incident is recorded in Acts 9:23–25. Paul also mentions it in 2 Cor 11:32–33 (cp. Gal 1:17–18). Paul noted that it was the "ethnarch of King

---

[468] Josephus, *Ant.* 18.89 [18.4.2].

[469] Josephus, *Ant.* 18.85–88 [18.4.1–2].

Aretas" (ὁ ἐθνάρχης Ἀρέτα τοῦ βασιλέως) that sealed the city gates in order to apprehend Paul. This provides a date for Paul's escape from the city.

The Nabataean king Aretas IV Philopatris (4 BC–AD 40) was the father-in-law of Herod Antipas. Antipas married Aretas' daughter Phasaelis. Later he divorced her in order to marry his brother Philip's wife Herodias (cf. Matt 14:3–4; Mark 6:17–18; Luke 3:19–20). In AD 36 Phasaelis fled to her father. As a result, Aretas IV invaded Antipas' territory. He defeated Antipas' army and captured some regions controlled by Antipas, including Bantanaea, south of Damascus. Apparently Aretas projected his power and influence as far north as Damascus and appointed an ethnarch over the city.[470] Antipas then appealed to Tiberius, who ordered the governor of Syria to attack Aretas. But because of the Tiberius' death in AD 37, this action was never carried out.[471]

After Tiberius' death, Antipas' nephew Agrippa I was appointed by Gaius (Caligula) as governor over Bantanaea and Trachonitis. While Agrippa may have ended Aretas' control over Bantanaea and his influence in Damascus as early as AD 37,[472] it is just as likely that Aretas' control did not cease until sometime in AD 38. This is confirmed by the fact that in the autumn of AD 39 Agrippa returned to Rome and engineered the banishment of Antipas, getting himself appointed ruler of Antipas' territories of Galilee and Perea.[473] Thus, it was not until autumn AD 39 that Agrippa felt secure enough in his control of Bantanaea to return to Rome, indicating that he needed until AD 38 or later to end Aretas' influence over the territories north of Nabataea.

---

[470] This theory is supported by Campbell, "An Anchor for Pauline Chronology." He notes that this theory is also supported by Bowersock, *Roman Arabia*, 65–69.

[471] Josephus, *Ant.* 18.109–125 [18.5.1–3].

[472] As held by Campbell, "An Anchor for Pauline Chronology," 297.

[473] Schwartz, *Agrippa I*, 57–58.

Therefore, we can date Paul's escape from Damascus sometime between AD 36 and AD 38. Since Paul indicated that he went to Jerusalem three years after his conversion (Gal 1:18), and that immediately followed his escape from Damascus (Acts 9:26), AD 38 is the likely year of Paul's escape.[474]

THE DEATH OF AGRIPPA I

The death of Agrippa I can be dated by information from Josephus and Eusebius.[475] Josephus says that Agrippa reigned four years under Gaius (Caligula) and three years under Claudius for a total of seven years.[476] For the first three years of his reign Agrippa ruled Bantanaea and Trachonitis. In the fourth year Gaius added the territories of Antipas (Galilee and Perea). When Gaius was assassinated, Agrippa gave Claudius advice that helped him become emperor, and Claudius rewarded Agrippa by adding Judea and Samaria to his realm. Schwartz has found reason in Josephus to hold that Agrippa reckoned his reign from Tishri each year, starting with his first year as AD 36t as his accession year.[477] This would make AD 43t his last year. Agrippa died at Caesarea Maritima in AD 43t during the fourteenth celebrations of the games held there. The celebrations were begun by Herod the Great when he finished building Caesarea in the twenty-eighth year of his reign (10t BC).[478] The festival took place once every four years, making the fourteenth celebrations AD 43t.[479] Schwartz

---

[474] This is required by Paul's conversion shortly after Stephen's martyrdom in AD 35 or 36 (Acts 8:1–3; 9:1–19). Paul is apparently reckoning inclusively—AD 36–38.

[475] See the discussion in Finegan, *Handbook of Biblical Chronology*, 370–373; §§635–637.

[476] Josephus, *Ant.* 19.350–351 [19.8.2].

[477] Schwartz, *Agrippa I*, 2–5.

[478] Josephus, *Ant.* 16.136–141 [16.5.1].

[479] Josephus, *Ant.* 16.138 [16.5.1] says the games were held in a five-year cycle (κατὰ πενταετηρίδα). This counts the year of one games, the three years between the games, and the year of the next games. In our way of

concludes that Agrippa died between Tishri AD 43 and Shebat AD 44, most likely in September or October of AD 43.[480]

Acts 12:1–23 relates the persecution of Christians in Jerusalem by Agrippa, whom Luke simply calls "Herod." Since Agrippa assumed authority over Judea in early AD 41 and died in late AD 43, the events related in Acts 12 under Agrippa must have taken place during those years.

THE PROCONSULSHIP OF GALLIO

Acts 18:12 states:

Γαλλίωνος δὲ ἀνθυπάτου ὄντος τῆς Ἀχαΐας κατεπέστησαν ὁμοθυμαδὸν οἱ Ἰουδαῖοι τῷ Παύλῳ καὶ ἤγαγον αὐτὸν ἐπὶ τὸ βῆμα

But when Gallio was proconsul of Achaia, the Jews made a unified attack on Paul and brought him before the tribunal.

This incident took place in Corinth. Paul had been in Corinth at least 18 months by this time (Acts 18:11), and it appears from the wording of Acts 18:12 that Gallio had only recently arrived in Corinth.

Junius Annaeus Gallio was son of the rhetorician Seneca the Elder and elder brother of Nero's advisor Seneca the Younger. Normally the term of office of a proconsul of a senatorial province such as Achaia was one year, though in exceptional cases a proconsul may have served a second year. At Delphi an inscription was found that mentions Gallio in his office as proconsul. The inscription dates to the twenty-sixth acclamation of Claudius as *imperator*, which took place sometime between January 25 and August 1, AD 52.[481] The beginning date of the period is established by the inscription, which states that it

---

reckoning this is every four years.

[480] The outer limits would be between September AD 43 and February AD 44. Schwartz, *Agrippa I*, 109–111, 203–207.

[481] Finegan, *Handbook of Biblical Chronology*, 392; §677; Ogg, *Chronology of the Life of Paul*, 107–108. Slingerland, "Acts 18:1–18, The Gallio Inscription, and Absolute Pauline Chronology," 444, has the beginning date as January 25, 51 which is clearly a mistake.

was also the twelfth tribunican power of Claudius. Tribunican power began on January 25 of every year. The ending date is established by the dedicatory inscription on the Aqua Claudia at Rome which names Claudius as having tribunican power for the twelfth time and as *imperator* for the twenty-seventh time in AD 52. Thus, the twenty-seventh and twenty-sixth acclamations must have come sometime before August 1. If we allow some time before August 1 for the twenty-seventh acclamation, most likely Gallio was serving as proconsul during the first half of AD 52 when the twenty-sixth acclamation was made. Since proconsuls normally were appointed to office on May 1, it appears that Gallio was proconsul from the second half of AD 51 to the first half of AD 52.

From this information it appears as if Paul was brought before Gallio in mid-year AD 51. Paul's arrival in Corinth, then, was at least 18 months earlier, or in late AD 49. This is confirmed by Acts 18:2:

καὶ εὑρών τινα Ἰουδαῖον ὀνόματι Ἀκύλαν, Ποντικὸν τῷ γένει προσφάτως ἐληλυθότα ἀπὸ τῆς Ἰταλίας καὶ Πρίσκιλλαν γυναῖκα αὐτοῦ, διὰ τὸ διατεταχέναι Κλαύδιον χωρίζεσθαι πάντας τοὺς Ἰουδαίους ἀπὸ τῆς Ῥώμης

And he found a certain Jew named Aquila, a native of Pontus, recently come from Italy and his wife Priscilla, because Claudius had commanded all the Jews to leave Rome.

Orosius, citing Josephus and Suetonius, says that Claudius expelled the Jews from Rome in the ninth year of his reign, AD 49.[482] Paul's arrival in late AD 49 agrees well with the presence of Aquila and Priscilla in Corinth at that time.

Thus, the Gallio inscription offers a benchmark for most of Paul's ministry. One can reckon backward to at least the end of the first missionary journey as well as forward to the end of the book of Acts.

---

[482] PL 31.1075.

PAUL'S VISITS TO JERUSALEM

Resolving the number and occasions of Paul's visits to Jerusalem after his conversion is pivotal to reconstructing the chronology of this period. Acts mentions Paul's visits at:

9:26–30—Barnabas introduces Paul to the apostles

11:29–30 (cf. 12:25)—Barnabas and Paul deliver aid in response to a prophecy by Agabus.

15:1–29—Council at Jerusalem on whether Gentile Christian must be circumcised and observe the Law of Moses.

18:22—After Paul's second missionary journey, he greets the church.[483]

21:15–17—After Paul's third missionary journey he visits Jerusalem.

Paul's letters mention three visits:

Gal 1:18–19—Paul met with Peter and James privately three years after his conversion.

Gal 2:1–10—Fourteen years after his conversion,[484] Paul went to Jerusalem with Barnabas, taking Titus with him. The visit was prompted by a revelation (κατὰ ἀποκάλυψιν). Paul set his case before "those who seemed influential" (τοῖς δοκοῦσιν) in a private meeting (κατ᾽ ἰδίαν). Titus was not forced to be circumcised, and Paul defended freedom in Christ not to

---

[483] Acts 18:22 does not mention Jerusalem explicitly but states ". . . and when he arrived at Caesarea, he went up to greet the church. He [then] went down to Antioch" (καὶ κατελθὼν εἰς Καισάρειαν, ἀναβὰς καὶ ἀσπασάμενος τὴν ἐκκλησίαν κατέβη εἰς Ἀντιόχειαν).

[484] Opinion is split as to whether Paul went to Jerusalem fourteen years after his conversion or fourteen years after the previously-mentioned visit. The majority opinion, with which the present author agrees, is that Paul is counting from his conversion.

circumcise before "false brothers" (ψευδαδέλφους). Peter (Cephas), James and John were entrusted with ministry to the circumcised. Paul and Barnabas were sent to the Gentiles. Paul was asked to remember the poor.

1 Cor 16:2–4 and Rom 15:25—Paul planned a future visit to bring contributions to the poor to Jerusalem.

In Galatians the mention of these visits is embedded within a larger pericope in which Paul discusses the Gospel that he preached and how he received it. He presents an autobiographical sketch of his life and interaction with the Gospel (Gal 1:11–2:14). It includes the following:

1. Paul's former life in Judaism—he persecuted the church (Gal 1:11–14).

2. God revealed his Son to Paul so that Paul might preach the Gospel among the Gentiles (Gal 1:15–16a).

3. Paul did not consult with anyone. Instead he went to Arabia and returned to Damascus (Gal 1:16b–17).

4. After three years Paul went to Jerusalem for fifteen days, where he met with Peter and James (Gal 1:18–19).

5. Paul went to Syria and Cilicia. He was unknown to the churches in Judea at this time, although they had heard about his conversion and preaching (Gal 1:21–24).

6. After fourteen years Paul went to Jerusalem *again with Barnabas* taking Titus with him (Gal 2:1–10).

    a. Paul went up because of a revelation.

    b. Paul set before those who seemed influential the Gospel he proclaimed among the Gentiles.

    c. Even Titus was not forced to be circumcised, although he was a Greek.

d. Because of false brothers who slipped in, "we" (Paul and Barnabas?) did not yield so that the truth of the Gospel could be preserved among the Galatians.

e. Those who were influential added nothing; they saw that Paul was entrusted with the Gospel to the uncircumcised, just as Peter was entrusted with the Gospel to the circumcised.

f. James, Cephas, and John gave the right hand of fellowship to Barnabas and Paul.

g. The apostles asked Barnabas and Paul to remember the poor.

7. When Cephas came to Antioch, Paul opposed his hypocrisy (Gal 2:11–14)

a. Before some men came from James, Cephas ate with the Gentiles.

b. After men came from James, Peter separated himself, because he feared the circumcision party.

c. The rest of the Jews—even Barnabas—acted hypocritically in this way.

d. Paul challenged Peter in front of them all.

Clearly the first visit at Gal 1:18 where Paul met with Peter and James corresponds to the visit in Acts 9:26–29, which Paul states took place three years after his conversion. The planned visit mentioned at 1 Cor 16:2–4 and Rom 15:25 just as clearly corresponds to Acts 21:15, since it is certain that Romans and 1 Corinthians were written during Paul's third missionary journey.

Several possibilities exist for the second visit mentioned in Galatians, but it clearly is not the visit in Acts 18:22 which Luke mentions in passing and where Paul was said to "greet the church" (ἀσπασάμενος τὴν ἐκκλησίαν).[485] Nor is it the visit after his third

---

[485] It has been argued by Knox, Jewett and Lüdemann that Gal 2:1–10 is the

missionary journey (Acts 21:15–17). This leaves the visits at Acts 11:29–30 (relief ministry) and Acts 15:1–29 (Jerusalem council).

Three major theories have been advanced to address which of these two visits to which Paul refers in Gal 2:1–10.[486] It has been suggested that the famine relief visit best matches Gal 2:1–10. Others have suggested that the Jerusalem council best matches Gal 2:10. A third suggestion is that the famine relief visit in Acts 11:29–30 and the Jerusalem council visit at Acts 15:1–29 are the same visit told from two perspectives.

THE FAMINE MINISTRY = THE JERUSALEM COUNCIL VISIT

The most recent major theory, developed by critical scholars in the late nineteenth century, attempts to reconcile the two visits Paul describes in Gal 1–2 with the three visits in Acts 9, 11, and 15 by equating the famine ministry with the Jerusalem Council visit and with the second visit in Galatians.[487] These, then, are one visit described from different points of view which Luke derived from different sources.

One major assumption of all the variations of this theory is that Luke mistakenly made two visits out of one because he

---

Jerusalem Council of Acts 15:1–30, but that it actually took place during the visit of Acts 18:22, and Luke was mistaken about its placement. This requires that Luke invented the famine relief ministry of Acts 11:29–30. Since this theory denies the historical accuracy of Acts, it has not been widely accepted by evangelicals or others who hold that Acts is historically accurate (see the discussion in Trebilco, "Itineraries, Travel Plans, Journeys, Apostolic Parousia," 452–452; §6.1).

[486] There are other theories, all of which involve calling Luke's historical accuracy into question. See the discussion in Trebilco, "Itineraries, Travel Plans, Journeys, Apostolic Parousia," 451–452.

[487] Dockx, "The First Missionary Voyage of Paul," 211–213; Lake, "The Apostolic Council of Jerusalem," 201–204. (Lake notes that this theory was developed by Karl Heinrich Weizsäcker, Arthur C. McGiffert and A. Schwartz); Daniel Schwartz, "The End of the Line," 6–7.

misunderstood that his sources for Paul's second visit were parallel to one another and were not, as he assumed, describing different visits. Dockx assumes that in addition to all of these inaccuracies, Luke simply fabricated the account of Paul's first missionary journey (Acts 13–14) to fill out the material between the two visits he had made out of one.[488] Schwartz, on the other hand, assumes that the first missionary journey was misplaced by Luke and that it actually followed the Jerusalem Council.[489]

None of these approaches are acceptable to those who believe Luke to be an accurate reporter of events. Moreover, they make it virtually impossible to argue for a particular chronology for this period in Paul's life, since any resulting chronology is dependent on what a particular scholar believes is accurately recorded in Paul and on what that scholar also chooses to discard as fabricated or mistaken.

One need not necessarily believe that Luke was confused to hold this theory. Instead, one could hold that Luke was accurately recording events but that he simply chose to digress frequently. That is, he related the situation in the church at Antioch culminating in Agabus' prophecy (Acts 11:19–28a). Then he skipped forward in time to the reign of Claudius when the famine struck and the relief ministry of Barnabas and Paul was undertaken (Acts 11:28b–30). He then related Agrippa's persecution of the Jerusalem church which took place "about that time" (Κατ' ἐκεῖνον δὲ τὸν καιρὸν; Acts 12:1–24). Next he reported the return of Barnabas and Paul to Antioch (Acts 12:25). Then Luke skipped backward in time again to the church in Antioch, when Barnabas and Paul were sent out on their missionary journey (Acts 13:1–4). Finally, Luke related the missionary journey (Acts 13:5–14:28). He now had caught up to the time of the famine relief ministry, which corresponds to the trip of Barnabas and Paul to the Jerusalem Council (Acts 15).

---

[488] Dockx, "The First Missionary Voyage of Paul," 213–216.

[489] Schwartz, "The End of the Line," 7–9.

Such a scenario is not only very complicated, it can be certain of only one drastic jump in time by Paul—the jump forward from Agabus' prophecy to the notice of when the famine actually occurred (Acts 11:28b). Moreover, the required digression between Paul and Barnabas' return to Antioch at Acts 12:25 and the new scene in the church at Antioch beginning at Acts 13:1 is far from obvious since there is no explicit indication of a digression in the text of Acts 13:1. Added to this is the notice that when Barnabas and Paul returned from Jerusalem they brought John, who was called Mark, with them (Acts 12:25). This seems to be chronologically prior to John accompanying Barnabas and Paul on the first part of their missionary journey (Acts 13:5, 13).

Thus, there is little to recommend equating the two visits of Paul and Barnabas to Jerusalem in Acts 11 and 15 with each other. This theory has more drawbacks than benefits.

THE FAMINE MINISTRY = GALATIANS 2:1–10

While historically the equation of Gal 2:1–10 with the famine ministry of Acts 11:29–30 has found few supporters, during the last century many scholars, especially evangelicals, have sought to make this identification.[490] According to this view, Paul came to Jerusalem with Barnabas to distribute the famine relief and while there met privately with some leaders of the Jerusalem church.

Those who hold this view have offered several arguments in its favor. For instance, it has been argued that since Barnabas was sent to Antioch because of the conversion of Gentiles there (Acts 11:19–26), it would make sense to have a discussion about Gentiles when

---

[490] McGough, "A Chronology of Acts," 75–77; Morgado, "Paul in Jerusalem." Morgado, 65 note 33, notes that this view was held as early as John Calvin.; Treblico, "Itineraries, Travel Plans, Journeys, Apostolic Parousia," 453–455; §§6.3; Toussaint, "The Chronological Problem of Galatians 2:1–10."

Barnabas came back to Jerusalem.[491] The problem with this view is that Acts 11 never mentions Gentiles. The conversion is among Hellenists, who in Acts 6:1 are clearly Jews who have adopted Greek language and cultural traits or circumcised Gentile converts to Judaism who are no longer considered Gentiles. The same seems to be true of the Hellenists who opposed Paul at Acts 9:29. Acts 6 takes place before the first conversion of Gentiles—the household of Cornelius (Acts 10). Therefore, the Hellenists are *not* uncircumcised Gentiles. Some of them may have been Gentiles who converted to Judaism and were circumcised, becoming observant Jews. Others may have been Jews whose primary language and culture was Greek. However, unlike the Gentiles who converted to Christianity, their presence in the church was *not* considered anything novel or un-Jewish. Yet Paul's discussion in Galatians is not about the freedom of circumcised Gentiles in the Gospel, but about the freedom of uncircumcised Gentile Christians.

Another argument often used is that Paul states that he went to Jerusalem "as a result of a revelation" (κατὰ ἀποκάλυψιν; Gal 2:2).[492] This revelation is taken to be the famine prophecy of Agabus (Acts 11:28). However, this is mere speculation. Paul does not specify which revelation led him to go to Jerusalem. It is equally possible that the revelation he mentions in Gal 2:2 is Peter's vision in Acts 10:9–16. On the basis of that vision, he may have gone to Jerusalem to argue that the Gentiles need not be circumcised. Peter's vision may have even been part of the discussion that Barnabas and Paul had with the circumcision advocates in Antioch before going to the Jerusalem Council (Acts 15:2).

Another argument often advanced in defense of identifying the famine ministry with Gal 2:1–10 is that Paul states that he was asked to continue to remember the poor (Gal 2:10).[493] This, it is said, fits

---

[491] Treblico, "Itineraries, Travel Plans, Journeys, Apostolic Parousia," 453.

[492] Morgado, "Paul in Jerusalem," 66.

[493] Morgado, "Paul in Jerusalem," 66.

well with the famine ministry, where continuing aid was needed.[494] However, Paul made collections for the poor Christians well beyond the famine in the days of Claudius. He was still collecting for Jerusalem's poor at the end of his third missionary journey during Nero's reign, and he brought contributions to Jerusalem on his final trip there (Acts 24:17). Thus, remembering the poor cannot be facilely taken as referring to the famine.

Still another argument is that following the meeting mentioned in Gal 2:1–10 Peter came to Antioch, and both Peter and Barnabas succumbed to pressure from the circumcision advocates (Gal 2:11–14). This, it is contended, would not have happened after the Jerusalem Council and the issuing of its decree, especially since Peter publically opposed imposing the Law on Gentiles (Acts 15:7–11).[495] However, it is too simplistic to think that the issue of circumcision immediately died with the decision of the apostles and elders in Jerusalem, or that the circumcision party would not have continued to have a large following in Judea and would not have continued to exert pressure even on leaders like Paul and Barnabas. That Peter would give in to peer pressure even after having supported Paul at the Jerusalem Council is not at all out of character for him given his actions as portrayed at Matt 26:31–35‖Mark 14:27–31‖Luke 22:31–34 contrasted with Matt 26:69–75‖Mark 14:66–72‖Luke 22:55–62.

Paul calls on God as a witness that he is telling the truth (Gal 1:20). This is understood to be Paul attesting that he only went to Jerusalem twice.[496] However, it should be noted that Paul's oath does not apply to the second visit. It follows his statement that during his first visit he met with only Peter (Cephas) and James, and applies only to that (Gal 1:19). The oath is meant to emphasize that Paul did

---

[494] Certainly the force of the subjunctive clause ἵνα μνημονεύωμεν is "that we continue to remember."

[495] Morgado, "Paul in Jerusalem," 65; Treblico, "Itineraries, Travel Plans, Journeys, Apostolic Parousia," 453–454.

[496] McGough, "A Chronology of Acts," 81, note 20.

not receive the Gospel from the apostles, but from Jesus himself (Gal 1:11–12). Paul is not taking an oath that he only visited Jerusalem twice after his conversion before writing Galatians.

Finally, it is argued that if Paul had the decision of the Jerusalem Council on his side of the argument with the Judaizers, he surely would have mentioned it in Galatians.[497] Therefore, Gal 2:1–10 cannot be referring to the Jerusalem Council visit, but to the famine relief visit. We ought to note, however, that the issue at stake in Galatians is Christian freedom in the Gospel (Gal 1:6–9, 11; 2:2, 4, 5, 7, 14; 3:8; 4:13; 5:1, 13). This freedom is represented first and foremost in Galatians by the issue of circumcision (Gal 2:3, 12; 5:2, 3, 6, 11; 6:12, 13, 15). The council's letter, however, mentions neither the Christian's freedom from the requirements of the Law of Moses nor the issue of circumcision (Acts 15:23–29). However, this certainly was the substance of the council's deliberations (Acts 15:19). Thus, Paul's argument against the Judaizers would not have been helped by mentioning the council's letter or the decision behind it (Acts 15:19–21). Indeed, the council's letter advises Gentile Christians to avoid certain practices forbidden in the Law of Moses (Acts 15:28–29). This could have been misused by Paul's opponents in Galatia if not properly understood as being a request (not a command) to avoid offending Jews who as a result of being offended might reject the Gospel (Acts 15:21). Therefore, Paul had good reason not to mention the council's decision directly in Gal 2:1–10.

More importantly, Paul makes the claim that the Gospel he preached was not confirmed by men, but was given to him by Christ. It needed no confirmation by the Jerusalem Council, so any appeal to the Council's decision would have run counter to Paul's argument.

There are also a number of other considerations that weigh against identifying the famine ministry in Acts with Gal 2:1–10. First is the discussion of Titus in Gal 2:3–5. Paul states that during his visit Titus

---

[497] Morgado, "Paul in Jerusalem," 63–65.

was not compelled to be circumcised even though false brothers tried to impinge on Christian freedom. This mirrors Acts 15:5 quite well, but finds no parallel in the famine relief ministry. This is congruent with the discussions at the Council, and can be understood as Paul's appeal to the Council's practical and theological import for the Galatians. Thus, Paul may well be appealing to the Council through his discussion of Titus.

This leads to a second objection to identifying Gal 2:1–10 with the famine relief visit—there is no evidence anywhere in Acts 11 that any doctrinal issues were raised with Paul and Barnabas during their time in Judea ministering to the poor. The supposition that Gal 2:1–10 fits into the famine relief visit necessarily involves taking the silence of Acts 11 as regards doctrinal issues as license to inject a doctrinal discussion into that narrative.

A third objection is that Acts 11 nowhere pictures Paul and Barnabas meeting with any apostles. The aid was sent "to the elders" (πρὸς τοὺς πρεσβυτέρους; Acts 11:30). While at times the NT can treat the apostles as elders, it should be noted that in Acts 15 the apostles are distinct from the elders (τε οἱ ἀπόστολοι καὶ οἱ πρεσβύτεροι; Acts 15:2; cf. 15:4, 6, 22, 23). Thus, there is no evidence that Paul and Barnabas met with Peter or the other apostles during the famine relief ministry.

Another objection was expressed by Lake, who noted, " . . . if the whole question [of circumcision] had really been settled beforehand by the Apostles at the Second Visit to Jerusalem, why did they pretend to argue it all *de novo* at the meeting described in Acts 15, as though they had never discussed, much less settled, the problem?"[498]

A final objection has to do with chronology. The advocates of equating Gal 2:1–10 with the famine relief visit usually date this visit to AD 46.[499] This means that Paul's conversion came fourteen years

[498] Lake, "The Apostolic Council of Jerusalem," 201.

[499] Tousasaint, "The Chronological Problem of Galatians 2:1–10," 238–239. McGough, "A Chronology of Acts," 75 is less specific, giving the range AD 44–48.

earlier in AD 32 or, perhaps, AD 33, if Paul was reckoning the span of years inclusively (Gal 2:1). However, we have already seen that the most likely date for the crucifixion is AD 33, which of necessity places Paul's conversion several years later. (See the discussion of the dates of Jesus' ministry and crucifixion in chapters 12 and 13 and especially the discussion of the year of the crucifixion beginning on page 280.)

THE JERUSALEM COUNCIL VISIT = GALATIANS 2:1–10

Historically most authorities, as early as the church father Irenaeus, have identified the Jerusalem Council visit of Acts 15 with the visit described by Paul in Gal 2:1–10.[500] This remains the majority view among scholars.[501]

There are obvious reasons why this identification has been made. In both texts Paul and Barnabas met with Peter and other influential leaders in the Jerusalem church (Acts 15:6–7, 13; Gal 2:2, 6–7). In both the issue of circumcision is prominent (Acts 15:1, 5; Gal 2:3). The ministries of both Peter and Paul are mentioned in both texts (Acts 15:3–4, 7–8; Gal 2:7–9). Both Peter during the Jerusalem meeting in Acts 15:9–11 and Paul in his application of the Jerusalem meeting at Gal 2:16 speak of sinners receiving God's grace through faith and not by human effort.

The most obvious objection to identifying the Jerusalem Council visit with Gal 2:1–10 is that Acts clearly portrays the Jerusalem Council visit as Paul's third since his conversion, whereas at Gal 2:1–10 Paul is speaking about a second visit. It is often argued that if Paul had purposely omitted a visit to Jerusalem between Gal 1:18–19 and Gal 2:1–10, he would have given his opponents in Galatia an opportunity to call into question his veracity, thereby casting doubt on

---

[500] Morgado, "Paul in Jerusalem," 60.

[501] Finegan, *Handbook of Biblical Chronology*, 395; §684; Moody, "A New Chronology for the Life and Letters of Paul," 258–259.

his arguments.[502] However, we need to ask whether Paul is attempting to document for the Galatians every trip he made to Jerusalem. A close examination of Gal 1:11–12, Paul's preface to the autobiographical section of Galatians (Gal 1:13–2:14), would appear to argue that Paul was not relating every trip. In these verses Paul makes the claim that the Gospel he proclaimed was not a mere human message and that he did not receive the Gospel from anyone except Jesus himself. Given that preface, it is clear that Paul is relating those visits to Jerusalem where the Gospel was a matter of discussion or debate. This is certainly the case during Paul's first visit where Barnabas testified to the Gospel that Paul had received directly from Jesus and which Paul subsequently preached (Acts 9:27). It is also the case with the Jerusalem Council (Acts 15:12; note the parallel with Gal 1:16 in the preacing of the Gospel to the Gentiles). However, there is no indication that the Gospel was under discussion during the famine relief ministry. Therefore, Paul may have omitted it as irrelevant to the discussion at hand. *The Jerusalem Council visit was Paul's second visit to Jerusalem when the Gospel that Paul had received from Jesus and which he preached was the topic of discussion.*

In fact, Paul may hint at the famine visit at Gal 2:1 without mentioning it.[503] He says:

---

[502] Morgado, "Paul in Jerusalem," 61.

[503] This argument is based on the observation of Morgado, who does not understand it properly. He uses it to attempt to prove that Gal 2:1–10 is the famine visit, since "Barnabas 'again' being with him [Paul], just as in the first visit of [Gal] 1:18." (Morgado, "Paul in Jerusalem," 60.) However, if Morgado's analysis of the syntax is correct, μετὰ Βαρναβᾶ modifies ἀνέβην. This would mean that it was the second time that Paul went up *with Barnabas*. However, in Paul's first visit to Jerusalem, he did not go up with Barnabas. Instead, Barnabas found Paul in Jerusalem and took him to the apostles (Acts 9:27).

Ἔπειτα διὰ δεκατεσσάρων ἐτῶν πάλιν ἀνέβην εἰς Ἱεροσόλυμα μετὰ Βαρναβᾶ συμπαραλαβὼν καὶ Τίτον·

Then after fourteen years, I again went up to Jerusalem with Barnabas, taking Titus also with me.

In this sentence, "again" (πάλιν) modifies "I went up" (ἀνέβην). The prepositional phrases "to Jerusalem" (εἰς Ἱεροσόλυμα) and "with Barnabas" (μετὰ Βαρναβᾶ) also modify "I went up." It is possible that Paul means that this is another time that he went to Jerusalem with Barnabas. The first time he went to Jerusalem with Barnabas was the famine ministry visit (Acts 11:30).[504] Then he went *again with Barnabas* to the Jerusalem council (Acts 15:2). This, however, is not a conclusive argument, since it relies on the Galatians having prior knowledge of all of Paul's trips to Jerusalem to have been able to understand Paul in this way. We do not know, however, if Paul's movements during the fourteen years after his conversion were known to the Galatians.

Another objection to identifying Gal 2:1–10 with the Jerusalem Council visit is that Paul states that he placed the Gospel he proclaimed to the Gentiles before the influential members of the Jerusalem church in private (Gal 2:2), whereas the Jerusalem Council was a public meeting before the church as a whole. The problem with this objection is the assumption that the Jerusalem Council was a public meeting before the entire church. This is without warrant in the text. Certainly, the dispute over circumcision which precipitated the Council occurred before the entire church (Acts 15:4–5). The Council itself, however, involved only the apostles and the elders (Acts 15:6), and it was there that Paul and Barnabas presented their work among the Gentiles (Act 15:12). The presence of only the apostles and elders corresponds quite nicely with what Paul characterizes as a private meeting with "those who were influential' (τοῖς δοκοῦσιν).

---

[504] Barnabas first appears in the narrative of Paul's first trip to Jerusalem *after* Paul arrived in the city (Acts 9:26–27).

Still another objection is that Paul mentions going to Syria and Cilicia between his two visits to Jerusalem (Gal 1:21). If the second visit is equated with the Jerusalem Council visit, then Paul also went on his first missionary journey to Cyprus, Pamphylia, Pisidia and Galatia (Acts 13–14). It is claimed that "This goes against the natural reading of the verse. . . ."[505] However, the "natural reading" of the verse is not that Paul went *only* to Syria and Cilicia between his two visits. In fact, Paul may have felt no need to chronicle his first missionary journey, since the Galatians were well aware that he had visited them during that time.

In favor of identifying Gal 2:1–10 with the Jerusalem Council visit is that at the Council Paul was recognized as the "Apostle to the Gentiles" (Gal 2:7–8).[506] Since the Jerusalem Council occurred after Paul's first missionary journey, and during the Council Paul reported about his activities among the Gentiles on that missionary journey (Acts 15:12), it fits well Paul's being recognized as Apostle to the Gentiles. In contrast, there is no evidence that Paul preached the Gospel specifically to Gentiles before the famine ministry visit.[507]

---

[505] Treblico, "Itineraries, Travel Plans, Journeys, Apostolic Parousia," 454.

[506] Stein, "The Relationship of Galatians 2:1–10 and Acts 15:1–35," 242.

[507] The argument of Morgado, "Paul in Jerusalem," 67, that Paul must have preached to Gentiles during his time in Arabia, Tarsus and Antioch is an attempt to fill Acts' silence about Paul's activities with a supposed Gentile mission during those years. Morgado posits this supposed Gentile mission, although there is not even a scintilla of textual evidence in Acts or Paul's letters that he engaged in Gentile missions in Arabia, Tarsus or Antioch prior to the famine relief ministry in Acts 11:30. Although Paul is mentioned as preaching during some of those periods, Luke does not portray Paul as specifically targeting Gentiles with the Gospel until his first missionary journey (Acts 13:46–48; 14:2). The success of Gentile missions first came as (welcome) news at Antioch after Paul's first missionary journey (Acts 14:27) and then was reported to Phoenicia, Samaria, and Jerusalem (Acts 15:3, 12).

Another factor in favor of identifying Gal 2:1–10 with the Jerusalem Council is chronology. As we have already established, Stephen's martyrdom is most probably to be dated to AD 36 (see the discussion beginning on page 301). Since Paul's conversion followed Stephen's martyrdom and probably came later in that same year, the setting for Paul's trip to Jerusalem described at Gal 2:1 would be fourteen years after his conversion—AD 50 or AD 49, if Paul is counting inclusively. Since Paul had been in Corinth 18 months before Gallio arrived, he arrived in the city in late AD 49 or early AD 50 on his second missionary journey (Acts 18:1; see the discussion beginning on page 304). This means that the Jerusalem Council must have met very early in AD 49. Thus, the chronological information given by Paul at Gal 2:1 also argues that the second visit in Galatians is the Jerusalem Council visit.

CHRONOLOGY OF THE EARLY CHURCH

FROM THE ASCENSION UNTIL THE STONING OF STEPHEN

Sometime during the ten days between Jesus' ascension (Acts 1:6–11) and Pentecost (Acts 2:1–41), Matthias was chosen to be Judas Iscariot's replacement as an apostle (Acts 1:12–26). This would place Matthias' apostleship between 25 or 26 Iyyar (May 14, AD 33) and 6 Sivan (May 24, AD 33).

Luke devotes Acts 2:1–41 to a description of the sending of the Holy Spirit at Pentecost and Peter's sermon. Acts 2:45–47 is the first of several summary statements about the church's growth or a general description of activity that signals the end of sections in much of Acts. These summary statements, while not strict chronological markers, most likely signal some passage of time between the major events that Luke narrates.

The next major narrative in Acts relates an afternoon some time later when Peter and John were in the temple at "the hour of prayer, the ninth hour" (ἐπὶ τὴν ὥραν τῆς προσευχῆς τὴν ἐνάτην; Acts 3:1). They healed a lame beggar, and Peter preached about Jesus (Acts

3:1–26). They were arrested by the temple authorities and the next day were taken before the Sanhedrin which eventually told them not to speak about Jesus and then released them (Acts 4:1–22). Upon their release they prayed with other believers (Acts 4:23–31).

These events cannot be dated precisely, but there are indications that they probably took place late in AD 33 (see the discussion beginning on page 300). Peter and John hold the crowd in the temple and the Sanhedrin responsible for Jesus' death (Acts 3:13–17; 4:10–11), an indication that the crucifixion was not yet long passed. Moreover, the Sanhedrin recognized Peter and John as companions of Jesus (Acts 4:13), perhaps indicating that not much time had passed since the events of Nisan of AD 33.

Following another of Luke's summary statements (Acts 4:32–37), the incident of Ananias and Sapphira is related (Acts 5:1–11). A reasonable chronological setting for this incident is the first half of AD 34. This account is followed by another summary section (Acts 5:12–16).

The account of the apostles' arrest, imprisonment, release from prison by an angel of the Lord, and appearance before the Sanhedrin (Acts 5:17–41) appears to have happened sometime later, perhaps in mid-to-late AD 34. It is followed by another short summary statement (Acts 5:42).

The complaint by the Hellenists must have occurred in late AD 34 or early AD 35. It led to the appointment of Stephen and six others who would minister at tables (Acts 6:1–6). This would allow time for Stephen's work of "great wonders and signs among the people" (τέρατα καὶ σημεῖα μεγάλα ἐν τῷ λαῷ) to bring him to the attention of the men of the Synagogue of the Freedman (Acts 6:9). The choosing of the seven is followed by another summary section (Acts 6:7).

As already discussed, Stephen's martyrdom took place in AD 36 (Acts 6:8–8:3; see discussion beginning on page 301). At this point Luke introduces Saul for the first time (Acts 7:58; 8:1). Saul is clearly linked with the persecution of the church in Jerusalem that happened even as Stephen was being buried. Saul's persecution of the church led to the scattering of disciples as far as Caesarea Maritima (Acts 8:40).

PHILIP'S MINISTRY (ACTS 8:4–40)

The ministry of Philip, one of the seven,[508] that followed Stephen's death must have taken place from AD 36 to about AD 37. His activity covered an unnamed "city of Samaria" (Acts 8:5),[509] a place somewhere between Gaza and Jerusalem (Acts 8:26), and from Azotus to Caesarea Maritima (Acts 8:40), perhaps including Lydda and Joppa.[510] Depending on how long Philip spent in each place, he could have spent a year or more on this missionary journey.

Philip baptized an Ethiopian eunuch who was in the service of "Queen Candace of the Ethiopians" (Κανδάκης βασιλίσσης Αἰθιόπων; Acts 8:27). Kandake was a title held by queens who reigned in Nubia at Meroë.[511] This particular Kandake was Amantitere, who ruled AD 25–41.

PAUL'S CONVERSION AND FIRST YEARS AS A CHRISTIAN

After relating Philip's missionary work along the Mediterranean, Luke turns his attention to Paul's activity during the same period.

---

[508] This must be Philip who is mentioned as one of the seven at Acts 6:5—not the apostle Philip—since Luke specifically states that the apostles remained in Jerusalem during the persecution (Acts 8:1).

[509] The text reads [τὴν] πόλιν τῆς Σαμαρείας. The evidence for including the article is strong, but there are also good reasons for viewing it as a secondary reading (since Samaria is usually a region, not a city, in the NT). There are several cities that may be the one Luke had in mind, including Sebaste (known in the OT as Samaria), Sychar, or Shechem.

[510] There were disciples in Lydda and Joppa later when Peter arrived at these cities (Acts 9:32, 36). This may have been a result of Philip's missionary activity.

[511] Fluehr-Labban, "Nubian Queens in the Nile Valley and Afro-Asiatic Cultural History."

Paul's trip to Damascus and conversion (Acts 9:1–19) most likely took place before the middle of AD 36 by which time Marcellus would have been firmly in charge of Judea as the new proconsul. Paul must have received his authorization from the high priest before Marcellus established his authority. After Paul's conversion Luke says that Paul stayed "some days" (ἡμέρας τινὰς) where his preaching "confounded the Jews by proving that Jesus is the Christ" (Acts 9:22).

Luke does not mention Paul's time in Arabia where his preaching and the controversy that resulted from it undoubtedly came to the attention of the Nabataean King Aretas (Gal 1:17; 2 Cor 11:32). The "Arabia" to which Paul refers probably included Nabataea. Given the flow of events, it is likely that Paul was in Arabia for much of AD 37 but returned to Damascus late in the year.

Luke places Paul's escape from Damascus (Acts 9:21–25; cf. 2 Cor 11:32–33) after "many days had passed" (ἐπληροῦντο ἡμέραι ἱκαναί; Acts 9:23), and this fits well with a date of AD 38 for Paul's arrival in Jerusalem shortly thereafter—three years after Paul's conversion (counting inclusively, Gal 1:18; see the discussion beginning on page 301).

Paul then traveled to Jerusalem, where the disciples were afraid of him until Barnabas intervened and introduced him to them (Acts 9:26–27). There Paul met Peter and James, the brother of Jesus, and stayed fifteen days (Gal 1:18–19). However, during those fifteen days Paul's preaching brought him into conflict with the Hellenists, and they sought to kill him (Acts 9:29). The disciples, however, conducted Paul from Jerusalem to Caesarea Maritima where he was put on a boat to Tarsus, his hometown. Apparently he would stay there for about two years.

PETER'S MINISTRY IN JUDEA AND SAMARIA

Luke next turns his attention to Peter's ministry in Judea (Acts 9:32–10:48). This ministry cannot have taken place until after Paul's trip to Jerusalem. This is indicated by the presence of disciples in Lydda and Joppa (Acts 9:32, 36) which were most likely a result of Philip's prior missionary activity (Acts 8:4–40). Moreover, Peter was in Jerusalem when Paul arrived (Gal 1:18). Thus, we can date Peter's Judean ministry to about AD 39.

Peter first travelled to Lydda where he healed Aeneas (Acts 9:32–34). This gave him opportunity to evangelize in Lydda and the surrounding Plain of Sharon (Acts 9:35). While at Lydda the disciples at Joppa begged Peter to come to them after the death of Tabitha (also called Dorcas; Acts 9:36–43). After Tabitha was restored to life, Peter stayed at the home of the tanner Simon for "a number of days" (ἡμέρας ἱκανὰς; Acts 9:43), and Luke appears to indicate that he continued to evangelize the city.

From Joppa Peter was instructed to go to Cornelius' house in Caesarea Maritima (Acts 10:19–20). As a result of his visit to Cornelius the first Gentile converts to the Christian faith were added to the church (Acts 10:1–48). Peter was asked to remain there "some days" (ἡμέρας τινάς; Acts 10:48).

All of these activities must have taken the better part of AD 39 before Peter returned to Jerusalem to report on his activities. By the time he arrived, news that "also the Gentiles had received the Word of God" (καὶ τὰ ἔθνη ἐδέξαντο τὸν λόγον τοῦ θεοῦ; Acts 11:1) had preceded him. Thus, Peter's report is most likely to be dated to late AD 39.

THE CHURCH IN ANTIOCH

The next topic in Acts is the church at Antioch (Acts 11:19–30). Luke briefly digresses to note that those who were scattered in the persecution following Stephen's death in AD 35 or 36 travelled as far as Phoenicia, Cyprus and Antioch and that they evangelized only Jews (Acts 11:19). When they came to Antioch, however, they also evangelized the Hellenists (τοὺς Ἑλληνιστὰς; Acts 11:20). While this is often taken to be a reference to Gentile missions, it ought to be noted that the only other references to Hellenists in the NT are at Acts 6:1; 9:29. The reference in those passages to Hellenists may have included Gentiles who converted to Judaism and were circumcised, becoming observant Jews. Others may have been ethnically Jewish, but their primary language and culture was Greek. However, unlike the Gentiles who converted to Christianity, their presence in the church was *not* considered anything novel or un-Jewish. Therefore, we should not be quick to think Luke here is talking about missions to Gentiles who are in no way connected with Judaism. Instead, if the Hellenists at Antioch were Gentiles, they were most likely circumcised Gentiles who had converted to Judaism in contrast to the Jews (Ἰουδαίοις) of the previous verse who were likely ethnically Jewish and had not adopted Greek as their primary language.

In response to news that a great number of Hellenists joined the church at Antioch, the church at Jerusalem sent Barnabas to Antioch. He not only encouraged them, but also went to Tarsus to fetch Paul. For an entire year (ἐνιαυτὸν ὅλον; Acts 11:26) Paul and Barnabas taught at Antioch, where the disciples adopted the name *Christians*. Barnabas most likely arrived in Antioch in late AD 39. With the influx of many Hellenists who had adopted Gentile culture and language, the church in Jerusalem most likely was responding to Antioch in light of Peter's experience at Cornelius' house in Caesarea. This would place Paul's year in Antioch in about AD 40.

Luke next reports the arrival in Antioch of prophets from Jerusalem (Acts 11:27). This leads to the account of the prophecy of Agabus concerning a future famine throughout the Roman Empire and the response of the church of Antioch to the prophecy (Acts 11:28–30). Luke parenthetically adds that the famine took place in the days of Claudius (Acts 11:28). This strongly implies that the prophecy was received *before* Claudius became emperor in late January AD 41. Most likely Agabus' prophecy came in late AD 40 or very early in January of AD 41.

The timing of the sending of Barnabas and Paul to Jerusalem on the relief ministry with the funds raised as a result of Agabus' prophecy is difficult to determine. Many have sought to place it about

AD 46.[512] Often this is based on Josephus' placing the famine in the proconsulship of Tiberius Alexander from AD 46–48.[513] However, there is no evidence that the great famine took place in Alexander's first year. This theory is sometimes supplemented by the conjecture of Jeremias that AD 47t was a Sabbatical year in which the land would have remained fallow.[514] Thus, the next harvest would have been in the autumn of AD 49, making the famine severe, since it lasted from AD 46 to AD 49. The chief problem with this conjecture is that Jeremias relied on the erroneous tables of Sabbatical years by Zuckermann rather than the accurate tables of Wacholder (see the discussion beginning on page 188). The Sabbatical year actually occurred one year later in AD 48t.

Compounding the problem of this theory is that while localized famines sporadically occurred during much of Claudius' reign, Dockx has demonstrated that the great famine that struck the entire empire as prophesied by Agabus actually followed the Sabbatical year of AD 48t. It began with a drought in the east in AD 49. The famine reached the western part of the empire in AD 50.[515] This would accord well with Paul being asked during the Jerusalem Council to continue to remember the poor in Jerusalem (Gal 2:10).

More likely, the relief ministry of Barnabas and Paul should be dated to AD 43, since Luke seems to indicate that Barnabas and Paul returned to Antioch shortly after the death of Agrippa (Acts 12:23–25). How, then, should we understand the chronology of the Agabus'

---

[512] E.g., Moody, "A New Chronology for the Life and Letters of Paul," 258; Morgado, "Paul in Jerusalem," 67; Toussaint, "The Chronological Problem of Galatians 2:1–10," 339.

[513] Josephus, *Ant.* 20.100–101 [20.5.2]. ἐπὶ τούτου δὲ καὶ τὸν μέγαν λιμὸν κατὰ τὴν Ἰουδαίαν συνέβη γενέσθαι "under this one [Alexander] the great famine throughout Judea occurred. . . ."

[514] E.g., Moody, "A New Chronology for the Life and Letters of Paul," 258.

[515] Dockx, "The First Missionary Voyage of Paul," 210; *Chronologies néotestamentaires et vie de l'Eglise primitive*, 62–63.

prophecy and the relief ministry (Acts 11:28–30)? Agabus prophesied in late AD 40, and the church at Antioch began to collect money for the relief of the Judean Christians. By AD 43 they had gathered enough to send aid, and they sent Barnabas and Paul to deliver it to the elders in the churches in Judea. All this happened about the time that Agrippa was persecuting the church in Judea (Acts 12:1–23).[516] The persecution ended with Agrippa's death in late AD 43 (see the discussion beginning on page 303), and shortly thereafter Paul and Barnabas returned to Antioch, bringing John Mark with them (Acts 12:25).

Several items ought to be noted in connection with Luke's account of the relief effort. First of all, Luke nowhere states that the relief was sent during the famine, as so many have assumed. In fact, the point of the prophecy was that God had given the church in Antioch foreknowledge of the famine so that they could anticipate the needs of the Christians in Jerusalem. Secondly, the relief ministry of Barnabas and Paul may have been preemptive in anticipation of the coming famine. In fact, for all we know it may have been the first of several relief efforts during those years. Third, Luke's summary statement at the end of the account of Agrippa's persecution of the Judean church includes the return of Barnabas and Paul to Antioch (Acts 12:24–25), placing the return in close proximity to Agrippa's death and implying that the two events occurred relatively close together in time.[517]

In summary, then, the events in the church at Antioch in Acts 11:19–30 began with Barnabas' arrival in late AD 39, followed by

---

[516] Note especially the link between the relief effort in Antioch and the persecution by Agrippa, who was appointed king of Judea in AD 41: Κατ' ἐκεῖνον δὲ τὸν καιρὸν . . . "now about that time. . . ."

[517] Note a similar summary statement at 4:32–37 which also ends with a notice about Barnabas and is designed to connect it to the following narrative of Ananias and Sapphira, just as the summary statement here with the presence of John Mark connects to the next narrative concerning the beginning of Paul's first missionary journey.

Barnabas bringing Paul to Antioch for an entire year, AD 40. Late in AD 40 Agabus prophesied the famine, and a collection was gathered starting in AD 41 and lasting until the latter part of AD 43 when Barnabas and Paul were sent to Judea to deliver the aid to the elders.

AGRIPPA'S PERSECUTION OF THE CHURCH IN JERUSALEM

The second great persecution of the church in Jerusalem occurred after Agrippa had been named king of Judea in AD 41 (Acts 12:1–23). During this persecution Agrippa, whom Luke simply calls "Herod," killed the apostle James, the brother of John, and imprisoned Peter, intending to kill him. However, Peter was freed from prison by an angel and escaped Jerusalem. Luke then recounts Agrippa's death.

When exactly was James martyred and Peter imprisoned? The text of Acts gives the impression that Peter was imprisoned during the Feast of Unleavened Bread (Acts 12:3) that preceded Agrippa's death (Acts 12:20–23), which occurred in September or October of AD 43 (see the discussion beginning on page 303). Finegan, however, has argued that Peter was imprisoned in AD 41 and that Luke has juxtaposed the accounts of Peter's imprisonment and Agrippa's death to make Agrippa's death appear to be divine retribution for the persecution of the church.[518] Finegan's proposal, however, is impossible, since Agrippa was crowned king of Judea by Claudius in Rome during the early months of AD 41. Agrippa did not return to the east until after May of that year, too late to be in Jerusalem for the Feast of Unleavened Bread.[519] However, it is nearly certain that Agrippa was in Judea not later than the beginning of AD 42.

A more likely scenario for the events of Acts 12 is this: Agrippa arrived in Judea in the summer of AD 41. After consolidating his administration over his realm, sometime in AD 42 Agrippa came to Jerusalem and began to "lay hands on some members of the church to harm them" (ἐπέβαλεν Ἡρῴδης ὁ βασιλεὺς τὰς χεῖρας κακῶσαί τινας

---

[518] Finegan, *Handbook of Biblical Chronology*, 373–374; §640.

[519] Schwartz, *Agrippa I*, 107.

τῶν ἀπὸ τῆς ἐκκλησίας; Acts 12:1). Late in AD 42 or early in AD 43 he had James executed (Acts 12:2). After he saw that James' execution pleased his Jewish subjects, he moved against Peter in April of AD 43 during the Feast of Unleavened Bread, intending to execute him on the day after the Feast (Acts 12:3). Peter, however, escaped on the last evening of the Feast with the angel's help (Acts 12:6). According to Luke, Peter "went to another place" (ἐπορεύθη εἰς ἕτερον τόπον), and this may have been Rome where he worked among Jews to found the church there, as tradition holds.[520] However, by early AD 49 Peter had returned to Jerusalem, since he was there for the Jerusalem Council.

Agrippa spent some time the next day searching for Peter (i.e., the day after the angel had freed him from prison), but he could not find Peter (Acts 12:19). Then Agrippa left for Caesarea Maritima, which most likely served as the administrative capital for his realm. Later in September or October, Agrippa died in Caesarea during the fourteenth games held there (Acts 12:20–23; Josephus, *Ant.* 19.343–350 [19.8.2]).

PAUL'S FIRST MISSIONARY JOURNEY

The scene in Acts next shifts back to Antioch after Barnabas and Paul had returned from Jerusalem (Acts 12:25). Luke introduces the church in Antioch by noting that there were several "prophets and teachers" (προφῆται καὶ διδάσκαλοι) there. Among them was a certain Manaen, who was "a close friend of Herod the tetrarch" (Ἡρῴδου τοῦ τετραάρχου σύντροφος; Acts 13:1). The reference to Herod, that is Herod Antipas, ties this account to the previous one, which was about a different Herod—Agrippa, nephew of Antipas. While Luke's summary statement at Acts 12:24–25 probably serves to indicate some time had passed since Agrippa's death, the characterization of Manaen probably indicates not many years had elapsed. This would place the beginning of this account no earlier than AD 45 and no later than AD 47.

---

[520] E.g., Irenaeus, *Haer.* 3.1.5.

Paul's first missionary journey must have ended with his return to Antioch sometime in AD 48. This is required by Luke's notice that Paul and Barnabas stayed in Antioch "no little time" (χρόνον οὐκ ὀλίγον; Acts 14:28) before going to Jerusalem where the Jerusalem Council was held in early AD 49 (see the discussion beginning on page 320).

Thus, Paul and Barnabas must have been absent from Antioch for at least two years and possibly as many as four. Many chronologies date the first missionary journey to AD 47–48 or AD 46–48. The shorter timeframe, which can be at most 20 months, is usually required because Barnabas' and Paul's trip to Jerusalem for the relief ministry is often dated to AD 46,[521] which, as we have seen is probably about three years too late (see the discussion beginning on page 320). The longer timeframe, which is at most 32 months, is more reasonable, given the chronological clues in Acts 13–14. However, even this makes for a rather hurried itinerary for Paul and Barnabas.

During the missionary journey Paul and Barnabas must have spent at least some months on Cyprus (Acts 13:4–12), "remained a long time" (ἱκανὸν μὲν οὖν χρόνον διέτριψαν) at Iconium (Acts 14:3), not to mention their time at Pisidian Antioch (Acts 13:13–52), Derbe (Acts 14:20), and Perga (Acts 14:25). While Paul was in Pisidian Antioch for at least two Sabbaths (Acts 13:14, 42, 44), his stay there cannot have terminated after only two weeks. After being rejected in the synagogue, he and Barnabas turned to Gentile mission work in Pisidia (Acts 13:46–47). As a result "the word of the Lord was spreading throughout the whole region" (Acts 13:49). Only with this success did persecution arise which eventually drove Paul and Barnabas from that area (Acts 13:50). This would seem to require a number of months— perhaps approaching the better part of a year—to have been spent in and around Pisidia.

---

[521] E.g., Moody, "A New Chronology for the Life and Letters of Paul," 258–259. See also Finegan, *Handbook of Biblical Chronology*, 402, table 194.

Given all these chronological clues, it is entirely possible to reconstruct a more reasonable pace for the first missionary journey (Acts 13:4–14:28): Paul and Barnabas were sent from Antioch to Cyprus sometime in mid-to-late AD 45 (Acts 13:4–12), came to Pisidia in the spring of AD 46 (Acts 13:13–52) and to Iconium in the latter part of that year (Acts 14:1–5). They could have left Iconium in the first part of AD 47 and spent the rest of AD 47 evangelizing in Galatia at Lystra and Derbe, where they made many disciples (Acts 14:6–21a). Then, in AD 48 they returned to Lystra, Iconium, and Antioch where they appointed elders for the churches before going to Pamphylia where they spoke the word of God in Perga (Acts 14:21b–25a). Then they went to Attalia to board a ship back to Antioch where they spent the last months of the year (Acts 14:25b–28).

THE JERUSALEM COUNCIL AND THE CHURCH IN ANTIOCH

As discussed above, the Jerusalem Council most likely took place in very early AD 49, probably in January (Acts 15:4–29; Gal 2:1–10; see the discussion beginning on page 320). This would place the arrival of men from Jerusalem who were teaching the necessity of circumcision (Acts 15:1–2) to the last months of AD 48, and the journey of Paul, Barnabas and others through Phoenicia and Samaria (Acts 15:3) to December of that year.

Paul and Barnabas must have returned from Jerusalem to Antioch in late January AD 49 (Acts 15:30–35). Peter probably arrived in Antioch about February of the following year, and Paul confronted him in March or April (Gal 2:11–14). This would allow the departure of Barnabas to Cyprus by ship in April or May when travel on the Mediterranean was safe (Acts 15:39). At the same time Paul and Silas would have left to travel overland to Cilicia (Acts 15:41).

PAUL'S SECOND MISSIONARY JOURNEY

Paul initiated the second missionary journey with a suggestion to Barnabas that they again visit the cities they had evangelized on the first missionary journey (Acts 15:36). The dispute that arose between

Barnabas and Paul over John Mark (Acts 15:37–38; cf. Acts 13:13) caused them to split the cities between them.[522] Barnabas may have felt a need to defend his cousin Mark (Col 4:10), and it is gratifying to note that Paul's rift with Barnabas was not permanent (1 Cor 9:6). When Barnabas took Mark and sailed for Cyprus, Paul took Silas to travel through Syria to the cities in Cilicia, Pamphylia and Galatia (Acts 15:39–40).

Paul's trip through Asia Minor was relatively quick, since by late AD 49 he arrived in Corinth (see the discussion of the Proconsulship of Gallio beginning on page 304). Luke indicates that Paul strengthened the churches by delivering to them the decisions of the Jerusalem Council (Acts 15:41; 16:4–5). This would not have involved a long time in any city. Thus, in a matter of three or four months, Paul could have traveled through Syria, Cilicia, and Galatia, stopping at Derbe and Lystra where he had Timothy circumcised before taking him along on the rest of the journey (Acts 15:40–16:5).

By late July AD 49 Paul must have been in Troas where he had a vision calling him to go to Macedonia (Acts 16:6–10). This would place his ministry in Philippi during August of that year (Acts 16:11–40). There he baptized Lydia, was harassed by a slave girl with a spirit of divination for "many days" (πολλὰς ἡμέρας; Acts 16:18), and was imprisoned.

Leaving Philippi, Paul, Silas, and Timothy traveled through Amphipolis and Apollonia before arriving in Thessalonica, where they stayed at least three weeks before being forced to leave the city (Acts 17:1–8, esp. 17:2). By now it was probably the end of September.

Paul's time in Berea was more brief than that of Silas and Timothy, and he was forced to move on to Athens (Acts 17:10–15).

---

[522] There may have been underlying tension between Paul and Barnabas because of the circumcision party that came from Jerusalem earlier that year. Much to Paul's chagrin, Barnabas had joined Peter in separating himself from the Gentile believers (Gal 2:13).

In Athens he was able to make a few disciples before leaving (Acts 17:16–34). We can estimate that Paul spent October and November of AD 49 in Berea and Athens.

By December of AD 49, Paul had arrived in Corinth, where he first became acquainted with Aquila and Priscilla, who had come from Rome and apparently were Christians—perhaps converted to the faith through the work of Peter in Rome (Acts 18:1–3). Paul's work in Corinth lasted another eighteen months until he was brought before Gallio's tribunal, probably in June of AD 51 (Acts 18:4–17). After "remaining a number of days" (ἔτι προσμείνας ἡμέρας ἱκανὰς; Acts 18:18), Paul set sail for Syria accompanied by Priscilla and Aquila, probably in early August.

Paul's stay in Corinth is probably when he wrote 1 Thessalonians, which would date from AD 50 or 51. Paul mentions that God's wrath had come upon the Jews (1 Thess 2:16), which may be a reference to Claudius' edict banning Jews from Rome.[523] Though this is not certain, it would also suggest a date of about AD 50 for this letter.

After what appears to be a short stop at Cenchreae, Paul arrived in Ephesus where he briefly taught in the synagogue (Acts 18:19–21). Leaving Priscilla and Aquila in Ephesus, Paul sailed for Caesarea Maritima. After landing in Caesarea, he went to Jerusalem and then back to Antioch, where he spent some time (Acts 18:22–23a). A reasonable chronology for these events brings Paul to Caesarea in mid-September and to Antioch in November, where he may have stayed a month or so.

PAUL'S THIRD MISSIONARY JOURNEY

Probably in the early months of AD 52 Paul left Antioch and went through Galatia and Phrygia "strengthening all the disciples" (ἐπιστηρίζων πάντας τοὺς μαθητάς; Acts 18:23b). It is likely that this part of his trip lasted until late spring when he arrived in Ephesus. From Luke's account, it appears that during this time Apollos arrived

---

[523] Moody, "A New Chronology for the Life and Letters of Paul," 263.

at Ephesus, was instructed by Priscilla and Aquila, and left for Corinth (Acts 18:24–28).

After Apollos arrived in Corinth, Paul travelled to Ephesus, probably arriving in April of AD 52. There he found some disciples who had known only the baptism of John, probably from Apollos' early teaching in Ephesus (Acts 19:1–7; cp. Acts 18:25). Paul's first three months in Ephesus (probably April through June) were spent teaching in the synagogue (Acts 19:8). After some of the members of the synagogue became stubborn, Paul moved to the hall of Tyrannus where he taught for two more years (probably July AD 52–June AD 54; Acts 19:9–10). During this time Paul performed miracles which the seven sons of Sceva attempted also to produce by invoking the name of Jesus (Acts 19:11–20).

By the time his two years of teaching in the hall of Tyrannus were drawing to a close in June of AD 54, Paul had decided to travel through Macedonia and Achaia and then to Jerusalem. He also decided that after Jerusalem he would go to Rome (Acts 19:21). Paul sent Timothy and Erastus ahead to Macedonia, but he remained in Asia (Acts 19:22). However, the furor caused by the silversmith Demetrius led to Paul's departure from Ephesus, probably in August (Acts 19:23–20:1).

During his stay in Ephesus, Paul likely wrote more of his letters. 2 Thessalonians most likely dates to AD 52, during the early days of Paul's time in Ephesus.

Galatians may also have been written during Paul's time in Ephesus, perhaps in AD 53. It appears from the tone of Paul's letter that some men from the circumcision party had made their way to Galatia. Since Paul had visited the Galatians in AD 49 and again in AD 52 without any hint of controversy over circumcision recorded in Acts, it is likely that the circumcision party arrived after Paul's third visit to Galatia. They began to contradict the Gospel that Paul preached, and when word reached Paul, he responded with the Galatian letter. It is also interesting to note that Paul mentions that he was asked to remember the poor in Jerusalem (Gal 2:10), but he does not ask the Galatians to participate in the collection as he does when he writes to the Corinthians. This may indicate that he was not anticipating returning to Galatia, providing further support to the dating of Galatians to Paul's time in Ephesus.

It is likely that 1 Corinthians was written during April or May of AD 54. In it Paul mentions the collection for the saints which he will take to Jerusalem (1 Cor 16:1–4). He states that he will pass through Macedonia before coming to them to spend the winter (1 Cor 16:5–7). However, he also says that he would remain in Ephesus until Pentecost (1 Cor 16:8).[524] 2 Corinthians probably was sent from Ephesus in July. Paul had changed his travel plans, perhaps in response to the problems in the Corinthian congregation that occupied his several letters to Corinth during this period. Paul had revised his travel plans in order travel to Corinth, then to Macedonia, and finally back to Corinth before departing for Judea (2 Cor 1:15–16). Now, however, due to the delay, he would follow his original plans to travel through Macedonia before arriving in Corinth.

After Paul travelled through Macedonia, "encouraging them with many words" (παρακαλέσας αὐτοὺς λόγῳ πολλῷ; Acts 20:2), he arrived in Greece, where he spent three months before planning to sail to Syria (Acts 20:3a). This would place Paul's time in Macedonia during September, October, and November, and his three months in Greece to December of AD 54 and January and February of AD 55— he had said he intended to stay in Corinth for the winter (1 Cor 16:6).

It is likely that Paul wrote Romans during his stay in Greece just before his intended departure. He states that it was his desire to come to Rome to preach the Gospel (Rom 1:8–15). In addition, he sends greetings to Prisca and Aquila (Rom 16:3). They apparently had returned to Rome after Claudius died in October of AD 54. Claudius

---

[524] If the churches were following the same soli-lunar calendar as was followed in Mesopotamia, Pentecost that year would have fallen in June. (Parker and Dubberstein, *Babylonian Chronology 626 B.C.–A.D. 75*, 47.)

had banned Jews from Rome, but with Claudius' death, Jews may have been free to return to the imperial city. Since Prisca and Aquila had been in Ephesus in April or May of AD 54 when Paul wrote 1 Corinthians (1 Cor 16:19), they must have returned to Rome sometime in early AD 55.[525]

Paul's plans changed when some Jews plotted against him, so he travelled back through Macedonia to Philippi. After the Feast of Unleavened Bread in early May AD 55 he sailed to Troas, arriving five days later (Acts 20:3b–6).[526] Paul stayed in Troas seven days before traveling to Miletus (Acts 20:7–15). His goal was to be in Jerusalem by Pentecost in the latter part of June (Acts 20:16). By late May Paul was in Miletus and met with the Ephesian elders before continuing his trip to Jerusalem (Acts 20:17–38).

---

[525] Because Paul had at this point never visited Rome, and yet was well acquainted with the numerous individuals listed in Rom 16, many scholars have held that Rom 16 is really a letter from Paul to the Ephesian church. Additional evidence in support of this thesis is: 1. Chapter 15 has a proper ending for the epistle; 2. Chapter 16 starts with the kind of salutation that would be used at the beginning of a letter of recommendation (cp. 2 Cor 3:1) for the bearer of the epistle, assumed to be Phoebe; 3. There is no evidence, except that inferred from this chapter, that Priscilla and Aquila (Rom 16:3) ever returned from Ephesus to Rome, and they were in Ephesus when 1 Corinthians was written (1 Cor 16:19) and some years later when 2 Timothy was written (2 Tim 4:19); 4. In Rom 16:5 Epaenetus was the first convert "in Asia," and Ephesus was in the province of Asia; 5. Paul had such close, and apparently long-term, contacts with Rufus and his mother (Rom 16:13), that he said that Rufus' mother was his mother also.

However, the majority of scholars believe that Rom 16 was intended for the church at Rome.

[526] If the churches were following the same soli-lunar calendar as was followed in Mesopotamia, the Feast of Unleavened that year would have fallen in early May. (Parker and Dubberstein, *Babylonian Chronology 626 B.C.–A.D. 75*, 47.)

Paul traveled to Jerusalem by way of Cos, Rhodes and Patara (Acts 21:1). From there he caught a ship to Phoenicia that sailed south of Cyprus on a direct line to Tyre, where Paul stayed one week before the ship left for Ptolemais (Acts 21:2–7). After a day in Ptolemais, Paul went to Caesarea Maritima. There he stayed with Philip for many days (ἡμέρας πλείους; Acts 21:10), and Agabus arrived and prophesied his arrest (Acts 21:8–14).

Finally, Paul went to Jerusalem to stay at Mnason's home (Acts 21:15–16). Luke does not say whether Paul met his goal of arriving in Jerusalem by Pentecost, but a date near that time—about mid-to-late June—is a reasonable estimation for Paul's arrival. Paul's stay in Jerusalem was a brief nine days (Acts 21:17–23:30). The day after his arrival he visited James and was counseled to undergo the rite of purification. When the seven days of the purification were nearly completed, Paul was arrested in the temple (Acts 21:27). The next day he was arraigned before the Sanhedrin (Acts 22:30), and in the third hour of the night on the next day (Acts 23:12, 23), Paul was sent under armed guard to Caesarea Maritima via Antipatris, because some Jews had plotted to kill him (Acts 23:12–15, 31–35).

An interesting chronological confirmation of Paul's time in Jerusalem is the mention of an Egyptian who had recently stirred up a rebellion in Judea (Acts 21:38). The tribune Claudius Lysias who arrested Paul (cf. Acts 23:26) had mistaken him for this Egyptian. Josephus reports on the activity of this Egyptian. From Josephus' account it appears that the Egyptian's activities took place during the mid-part of the Roman procurator Felix's tenure in Judea (AD 52–c. AD 57), or about AD 54 or early AD 55.[527] This corresponds nicely with Paul's presence in Jerusalem after Pentecost of AD 55.

PAUL IN CAESAREA AND JOURNEY TO ROME

Five days after arriving in Caesarea Paul was examined before the procurator Felix when the high priest Ananias came from Jerusalem

---

[527] Josephus, *J.W.* 2.261–263 [2.13.5].

(Acts 24:1–21). It was most likely early July of AD 55. At this point Felix put off the any decision on Paul's case until the tribune Lysias, who had arrested Paul, could come to Caesarea (Acts 24:22–23).

Some days later Felix and his wife Drusilla summoned Paul in order to hear his message about Christ, but dismissed him summarily when Paul's message challenged Felix's morality (Acts 24:24–25). Marcus Antonius Felix had divorced his first wife Drusilla of Mauretania, second cousin of the emperor Claudius, to marry Drusilla, daughter of Agrippa I. This Drusilla had previously been married to King Azizus of Emesa. The marriage of Felix to his second wife Drusilla could not have taken place before AD 54,[528] coinciding nicely with Paul's appearance before the couple sometime in the late summer of AD 55.

Paul's imprisonment during Felix's term lasted two years until he was replaced by Marcus Porcius Festus in AD 57 (Acts 24:27).[529] Although there is no firm extra-biblical evidence as to when Felix was recalled and replaced by Festus, the chronology of Acts implies that Felix assumed office in early July of that year.[530] Numismatic evidence also points to AD 57 as the start of Festus' term as procurator of Judea.[531] A new series of coins for Judea was minted in Nero's fifth year—which began in October AD 58. Felix had

---

[528] Bruce, "Chronological Questions in the Acts of the Apostles," 284.

[529] For a detailed argument that Luke's reference to two years is from the beginning of Paul's imprisonment see Moody, "A New Chronology for the Life and Letters of Paul," 252.

[530] Josephus is no help here. He notes that Festus succeeded Felix, but gives no clue as the exact date. Josephus, *J.W.* 2.271 [2.14.1]; *Ant.* 20.185 [20.8.10].

[531] Smallwood, *The Jews under Roman Rule*, 269, note 40; Moody, "A New Chronology for the Life and Letters of Paul," 253 argues that Festus was appointed in AD 56 and arrived in Judea in AD 57. Finegan also argues that Festus assumed his post in Judea in AD 57. Finegan, *Handbook of Biblical Chronology*, 398–399; §691 and §692.

previously minted a large number of coins, and was not likely to have changed to a new series. However, the change makes sense if Festus replaced Felix in AD 57 and ordered a new series of coins that would have been minted the following year.

Three days after arriving in Judea, Festus went to Jerusalem to hear the charges that had been brought against Paul (Acts 25:1–5). Some eight or ten days later he returned to Caesarea, and the next day he heard Paul's case. At that time Paul appealed his case to Caesar (25:6–12).

Some days later Agrippa II and his sister Bernice came to Caesarea for an extended stay (Acts 25:13–14). During this visit Festus discussed Paul's case with Agrippa (Acts 25:15–22), and the next day Paul was brought before Agrippa and Bernice and given an opportunity to defend himself (Acts 25:23–26:32). Agrippa and Festus agreed that Paul did not deserve to be punished, and Agrippa noted that he could have been set free if he had not appealed to Caesar. It was probably August of AD 57 when it was decided that Paul must be sent to Rome.

Key to dating Paul's departure from Caesarea for Rome is Acts 27:9, which states that Paul arrived in Fair Havens on Crete after "the Fast," that is after the Day of Atonement on 10 Tishri. Thus, it was early October.[532] Working backward and considering that the winds were against the direction of travel (Acts 27:4, 7) and that Paul changed ships in Myra (Acts 27:5–6), Paul must have left for Rome in early September.

Since sailing the Mediterranean was considered risky after the middle of September, why was Paul sent to Rome at that time and not held in Caesarea until spring of AD 58? Political factors may have played a large part in Festus' decision to send Paul to Rome in the

---

[532] If the churches were following the same soli-lunar calendar as was followed in Mesopotamia, the Day of Atonement in AD 57 would have fallen on September 29. (Parker and Dubberstein, *Babylonian Chronology 626 B.C.–A.D. 75*, 47.)

autumn. Josephus reports that Felix's term as procurator was marked by Jewish rebellions that were harshly repressed,[533] and Festus may have wanted to be rid of Paul in order to remove another reason for Jewish restlessness as he tried to calm Judea. Another reason to send Paul to Rome was to remove him from the threat of assassination, since on at least two occasions there had been plots against his life (Acts 23:12–22; 25:3).

Thus, in September Paul left Caesarea for Rome in the custody of the centurion Julius (Acts 27:1–2). A day later the ship put in at Sidon, where Paul was allowed shore leave (Acts 27:3). Sailing north of Cyprus, the ship put in at Myra, where Julius found a ship sailing for Italy (Acts 27:4–6). With difficulty the ship came to Cnidus off the southwest coast of Asia Minor and then sailed across open sea to Crete, coming to Fair Havens. There Paul advised them to stay the winter (Acts 27:7–10). By now it was early October or later.

The ship's captain and owner wished to make port at Phoenix on Crete and so put out to sea when the winds turned favorable (Acts 27:11–13). The weather changed, however, before the ship could reach Phoenix. Getting swept along by a storm, the ship was carried westward across the Mediterranean for two weeks (Acts 27:27, 33). The ship's crew and passengers were eventually shipwrecked on Malta (Acts 28:1). It was now late October or early November.

For three days Paul and his companions were hosted by Publius (Acts 28:7). Paul healed Publius' father and other people on Malta (Acts 28:8–10).

Three months later Paul and others left on a ship that had wintered on Malta (Acts 28:11). It would have been late January or early February. In quick succession Paul came to Syracuse, where he stayed three days, then to Rhegium and to Puteoli on the second day. Paul stayed there a week (Acts 28:14). Next Paul traveled overland to the Forum of Appius and Three Taverns before arriving in Rome (Acts 28:15–16). Thus, Paul arrived in Rome about March of AD 58.

---

[533] Josephus, *J.W.* 2.252–270 [2.13.2–7]; *Ant.* 20.160–178 [20.8.5–7].

After three days in Rome, Paul met with the Jewish leaders there (Acts 28:17). When they subsequently rejected the Gospel, Paul notified them that he would work among the Gentiles instead (Acts 28:23–29). Luke tells us that Paul lived "two complete years" (διετίαν ὅλην) in Rome, implying that he was released from custody in the spring of AD 60.

Paul's time in Rome is the most likely setting for his Prison Letters of Ephesians, Philippians, Colossians, and Philemon (Eph 6:20; Col 4:18; Phlm 1). Some would posit that these letters were written when Paul was confined in Caesarea, and others would even posit an otherwise unattested imprisonment in Ephesus.[534] However, Phil 4:22 mentions Christians in Caesar's household and, therefore, almost certainly places the composition of Philippians in Rome.

BEYOND PAUL'S CONFINEMENT IN ROME

Strong tradition places the deaths of Peter and Paul in Rome during the last year of Nero's reign, which ran from October 13, AD 67 to his suicide on June 9, AD 68.[535] Considering the additional information about Paul's movements in the Pastoral Letters, we can estimate Paul's movements from his release from custody in Rome in AD 60 to his martyrdom with Peter in AD 67 or 68.[536]

Paul had expressed his desire to evangelize Spain after visiting Rome (Rom 15:24, 28). A reasonable estimate of his time in Spain is from his release from custody in Rome in the spring of AD 60 to the spring of AD 64. During the time Paul was in Spain, James, the brother of Jesus, was martyred in Jerusalem. Josephus reports that

---

[534] Moody, "A New Chronology for the Life and Letters of Paul," 265–266. His explanation that Paul's reference to Caesar's household might apply to Cornelius or others in Nero's service is strained.

[535] Finegan, *Handbook of Biblical Chronology*, 387–388; §669–671; Moody, "A New Chronology for the Life and Letters of Paul," 268–270.

[536] Based on Moody, "A New Chronology for the Life and Letters of Paul," 269–270. Moody's chronology for this period was developed by Dockx.

after Festus had died but before Albinus arrived in Judea to succeed him, the high priest Ananus had James executed.[537] This would have been during the first part of AD 62.

In the spring of AD 64 Paul travelled east to Crete, where he left Titus in the spring of AD 65 (Tit 1:5). In the spring and summer of AD 65 Paul was in Ephesus, where he left Timothy (1 Tim 1:3). Then Paul traveled through Macedonia on his way to Nicopolis where he spent the winter (1 Tim 1:3; Tit 3:12). During that time Demas deserted Paul and went to Thessalonica. Crescens went to Galatia and Titus to Dalmatia (2 Tim 4:9–10). Paul returned to Ephesus in spring AD 66 and stayed until autumn (1 Tim 1:3, cf. 2 Tim 1:18). Then Paul spent the winter at Troas during AD 66 to 67 (2 Tim 4:13). Nero came to Greece in AD 67 to participate in the Olympic Games. He may have had Paul arrested at that time and sent back to Rome for trial (2 Tim 4:16). In late AD 67 or early AD 68 both Peter and Paul were martyred in Rome. Although Peter's movements are not recorded in Acts or mentioned in his letters, it is likely that Peter came to Rome sometime after Claudius' death in October AD 54.

Table 59
From Pentecost to the Deaths of Peter and Paul

May 33	Matthias chosen to replace Judas
Late May 33	Pentecost
Late 33	Peter heals a lame beggar/Peter and John before the Sanhedrin
Early–mid 34	Deaths of Ananias and Sapphira
Mid–late 34	The apostles before the Sanhedrin
Late 34/early 35	The seven appointed
Early 36	Stephen martyred
Early 36	Paul persecutes the church
Mid-36	Paul's conversion

---

[537] Josephus, *Ant.* 20.200 [20.9.1].

36–37	Philip's mission in Samaria and Judea
37	Paul in Arabia
Late 37	Paul returns to Damascus
38	Paul escapes Damascus; goes to Jerusalem; arrives in Tarsus
39	Peter's Judean ministry; conversion of Cornelius; Barnabas sent to Antioch
Late 39	In Jerusalem Peter reports on Gentile conversions
40	Barnabas brings Paul to Antioch
Late 40	Agabus' prophecy of the great famine
43	Peter travels to Rome?
43	Barnabas and Paul's relief ministry to Judea
Late 42/early 43	James executed by Agrippa I
April 43	Peter imprisoned by Agrippa I
September/October 43	Death of Agrippa I
October/November 43	Barnabas and Paul return to Antioch, bringing John Mark with them
45–48	*Paul's First Missionary Journey*
Mid-late 45	Barnabas and Paul arrive in Cyprus
Spring 46	Paul and Barnabas arrive in Pisidian Antioch
Mid-late 46	Paul and Barnabas arrive in Iconium
Early 47	Paul and Barnabas leave Iconium
47	Paul and Barnabas in Lystra and Derbe
Mid-48	Elders appointed in Lystra, Iconium and Antioch; preaching at Perga
Late 48	Paul and Barnabas arrive in Antioch
October/November 48	Arrival of circumcision party in Antioch
December 48	Paul, Barnabas and others travel through Phoenicia and Samaria to Jerusalem
January 49	The Jerusalem Council
February 49	Peter arrives in Antioch
March/April 49	Paul confronts Peter in Antioch

49–51	*Paul's Second Missionary Journey*
April/May 49	Barnabas and Mark leave for Cyprus; Paul and Silas leave for Cilicia
May-July 49	Paul travels through Syria, Cilicia, and Galatia to Troas
August 49	Paul in Philippi
September 49	Paul in Thessalonica
October/November 49	Paul in Berea and Athens
December 49	Paul arrives in Corinth
50 or 51	1 Thessalonians written
June 51	Paul before Gallio's tribunal in Corinth
Early August 51	Paul leaves Corinth for Syria
Mid-September 51	Paul arrives in Caesarea
November 51	Paul arrives in Antioch
52–55	*Paul's Third Missionary Journey*
January-March 52	Paul in Galatia and Phrygia
Early 52	Apollos in Ephesus
March 52	Apollos arrives in Corinth
April 52	Paul arrives in Ephesus
April–June 52	Paul teaches in the synagogue at Ephesus
52	2 Thessalonians written
July 52–June 54	Paul teaches in the hall of Tyrannus
53	Galatians written?
April/May 54	1 Corinthians written
June 54	Paul decides to travel through Macedonia and Achaia and to Jerusalem; resolves to go to Rome; sends Timothy and Erastus to Macedonia
July 54	2 Corinthians written
August 54	Paul leaves Ephesus
September–November 54	Paul in Macedonia
December 54–March 55	Paul in Greece
Early 55	Romans written

55	Peter arrives in Rome?
Early May 55	Paul leaves Philippi
Mid-May 55	Paul in Troas for seven days
Late May 55	Paul meets with Ephesian elders in Miletus
Mid–late June 55	Paul arrives in Jerusalem
Early July 55	Paul imprisoned in Caesarea; Paul defends himself before Felix
Late summer 55	Paul before Felix and Drusilla
Early July 57	Paul's case discussed by Festus and the chief priests in Jerusalem
Mid-July 57	In a hearing before Festus, Paul appeals to Caesar
August 57	Paul makes his defense before Agrippa and Bernice
57–58	*Paul's voyage to Rome*
September 57	Paul leaves Caesarea
Early October 57	Paul arrives at Fair Havens on Crete
Early November 57	Paul shipwrecked on Malta
Early February 58	Paul leaves Malta
March 58	Paul arrives in Rome
Spring 60	Paul released from custody; goes to Spain
62	James, brother of Jesus, martyred
Spring 64–Spring 65	Paul in Crete, where he leaves Titus
Spring–Summer 65	Paul in Ephesus, where he leaves Timothy
Summer–Autumn 65	Paul in Macedonia
Winter 65–66	Paul in Nicopolis; Demas to Thessalonica; Crescens to Galatia; Titus to Dalmatia
Spring–Autumn 66	Paul in Ephesus
Winter 66–67	Paul at Troas
Spring 67	Paul arrested and sent to Rome
Late 67 or early 68	Peter and Paul martyred at Rome

APPENDIX
DATED AND DATABLE PROPHECIES

This is a list of prophecies in the historical and prophetic books of the Old Testament that can reasonably be dated to a specific year, month or day. Beginning with the prophets of the last years of Judah a complete accounting by chapter is given for each except Malachi whose work is clearly post-exilic, but who supplies no chronological notices for his prophecies.

JUDGES

Reference	Prophet	Date
4:4–9	Deborah	1217 BC
6:7–10	Anonymous	1172 BC

SAMUEL AND CHRONICLES

Samuel	Chronicles	Prophet	Date
1 Sam 10:1–8		Samuel	c. 1049 BC
2 Sam 7:1–17	1 Chr 17:1–15	Nathan	c. 975 BC
2 Sam 12:1–15		Nathan	c. Summer 997 BC

KINGS AND CHRONICLES

Kings	Chronicles	Prophet	Date
	2 Chr 12:5–8	Shemaiah	Tishri 927–Elul 926 BC
	2 Chr 15:1–7	Azariah	Late 897 BC
	2 Chr 16:7–10	Hanani	Tishri 896–Elul 895 BC
1 Kgs 22:13–28	2 Chr 18:12–27	Micaiah	Nisan–Tishri 853 BC
	2 Chr 19:1–3	Jehu	Nisan 853–Elul 853 BC
1 Kgs 22:48–49	2 Chr 20:35–37	Eliezer	Late 853–Early 852 BC
2 Kgs 1:2–17		Elijah	Nisan–Tishri 852 BC
2 Kgs 2:1–24		Elijah	Nisan–Tishri 852 BC
	2 Chr 24:20–22	Zechariah	Late 797–Early 796 BC
2 Kgs 20:1–11	2 Chr 32:24	Isaiah	Tishri 702–Elul 701 BC
2 Kgs 20:12–19	2 Chr 32:31	Isaiah	Tishri 702–Elul 701 BC
2 Kgs 22:14–20	2 Chr 34:19–28	Huldah	Tishri 623–Nisan 622 BC

ISAIAH

Reference	Date
6	Tishri 740–Elul 739 BC
14:28–32	Tishri 716–Elul 715 BC
20:1–2	711 BC
20:3–6	709 BC
39	Tishri 702–Elul 701 BC

JEREMIAH

Reference	Date	Note
1:1–3	Composed after Av 587 BC	Superscription
1:4–3:5	Tishri 629–Adar 628 BC	Thirteenth year of Josiah
3:6–6:30	641–610 BC	During Josiah's reign
7–19	Undated (Zedekiah's reign?)	No date given at 7:1
20	597–587 BC	During Zedekiah's reign
21–23	10 Tebeth 589–9 Tammuz 587 BC	During siege of Jerusalem
24	Early 597 BC	After Jeconiah's exile
25	Tishri 606–Elul 605 BC	Fourth year of Jehoiakim
26	Late 609 BC	Beginning of Jehoiakim's reign
27–29	Tishri 595–Elul 594 BC	"Beginning" of Zedekiah's reign
30–31	Undated (Zedekiah's reign?)	No date given at 30:1
32	Nisan–Elul 588 BC	Tenth year of Zedekiah
33–34	Tishri 588–Nisan 587 BC	Jeremiah in court of the guard
35	609–598 BC	During Jehoiakim's reign
36:1–8	Summer/Autumn 605 BC	Fourth year of Jehoiakim
36:9–32	Kislev 605 BC	Fifth year of Jehoiakim
37–38	10 Tebeth 589	Zedekiah begins to reign
39–40	Composed after Av 587 BC	Historical narrative
41–43	Composed after Tishri 587 BC	Historical narrative
44	After Tishri 587 BC	After 41–43 (cf. 44:1)
45–47	Tishri 606–Elul 605 BC	Fourth year of Jehoiakim
48–51	Undated (after 9 Tammuz 587 BC?)	No date given at 48:1
52	Composed after 561 BC	Historical narrative

EZEKIEL

Reference	Date	Note
1:1–3:14	5 Tammuz 593 BC	5th day, 4th month, 5th year
3:16–5:12	11 Tammuz 593 BC	"the end of seven days"
6–7	592 BC	Probable date
8–19	5 Elul 592 BC	5th day, 6th month, 6th year
20–23	10 Av 591 BC	10th day, 5th month, 7th year
24–25	10 Tebeth 589 BC	10th day, 10th month, 9th year
26–28	1 Elul 587 BC	1st day, 11th year

Reference	Date	Note
29:1–16	12 Tebeth 588 BC	1st oracle against Egypt
29:17–30:19	1 Nisan 571 BC	6th oracle against Egypt
30:20–26	7 Nisan 587 BC	2nd oracle against Egypt
31	1 Sivan 587 BC	3rd oracle against Egypt
32:1–16	1 Elul 586 BC	4th oracle against Egypt
32:17–32	15 Elul 586 BC	5th oracle against Egypt
33:1–20	15 Elul 586 BC	Ezekiel a watchman
33:21–39:29	5 Tebeth 586 BC	5th day; 10th month; 12th year
40–48	10 Tishri 574 BC	10th day; 1st month; 25th year

DANIEL

Reference	Date	Note
1:1–2	Summer 605–Shebat 604 BC	Historical narrative
1:3–17	Early 604 BC	Historical narrative
1:18–20	603 BC	Historical narrative
1:21	603–538 BC	Historical narrative
2	Late 603 BC or early 602 BC	Historical narrative
3	Kislev or Tebeth 595/594 BC	Historical narrative
4	Between 573 and 569 BC	Historical narrative
5	15 Tishri 539 BC	Historical narrative
6	12 Marcheshvan 539–Adar 538 BC	Historical narrative
7	Nisan 550–Adar 549 BC	Vision
8	Nisan 548–Adar 547 BC	Vision
9	Nisan 538–Adar 537 BC	Vision
10–12	24 Nisan 536 BC	Vision

HAGGAI

Reference	Date	Note
1:1–13	1 Elul 520 BC	1st day, 6th month
1:14–16	24 Elul 520 BC	Historical narrative
2:1–9	21 Tishri 520 BC	21st day, 7th month
2:10–19	24 Kislev 520 BC	24th day, 9th month
2:20–23	24 Kislev 520 BC	24th day

ZECHARIAH

Reference	Date	Note
1:1–6	Marcheshvan 520 BC	8th month, 2nd year
1:7–6:15	24 Shebat 519 BC	During the night
7–8	4 Kislev 518 BC	4th day, 9th month; 4th year

BIBLIOGRAPHY

"The Chronology of the New Testament." Pages 277–283 in vol. 1 of *The Illustrated Bible Dictionary*. Edited by J. D. Douglas. Leicester: Inter-Varsity. 1980.

Ackroyd, Peter R. "Two Old Testament Historical Problems of the Early Persian Period." *JNES* 17 (1958): 13–27.

Aharoni, Yohanan. "Province-List of Judah." *VT* 9 (1959): 225–246.

Ahituv, Shmuel. *Echoes from the Past: Hebrew and Cognate Inscriptions from the Biblical Period*. Jerusalem: Carta, 2008.

Ahlström, G. W. and D. Edelman, "Merneptah's Israel," *JNES* 44 (1985): 59–61.

Albright, William Foxwell. "The Chaldaean Conquest of Judah: A Rejoinder." *JBL* 51 (1932): 381–382.

Althann, Robert. "The Meaning of *'Rb 'Ym Shnh* in 2 Sam 15:7." *Bib* 73 (1992): 248–252.

Amadon, Grace. "Ancient Jewish Calendation." *JBL* 61 (1942): 227–280.

_____. "The Crucifixion Calendar." *JBL* 63 (1944): 177–190.

Andersen, Knud Tage. "Die Chronologie Der Könige Von Israel Und Juda." *ST* 23 (1969): 69–114.

_____. "Noch Einmal: Die Chronologie Der Könige Von Israel Und Juda." *SJOT* 1 (1989): 1–45.

Archer, Gleason L, Jr. "Old Testament History and Recent Archaeology from Abraham to Moses." *BSac* (1970).

Ault, Lester E. "A New Chronology of Passion Week." *Methodist Review* 111 (1928): 297–301.

Ball, E. "The Co-Regency of David and Solomon (1 Kings 1)." *VT* 21 (1977): 268–279.

Barnes, William H. *Studies in the Chronology of the Divided Monarchy of Israel*. Atlanta: Scholars, 1991.

Barnett, Paul W. Bp. "Galatians and Earliest Christianity." *RTR* 59 (2000): 112–129.

Barr, James. "Why the World Was Created in 4004 BC: Archbishop Ussher and Biblical Chronology." *BJRL* 67 (1985): 575–608.

Beare, Francis Wright. "Note on Paul's First Two Visits to Jerusalem." *JBL* 63 (1944): 407–409.

Beckwith, Roger T. "The Day, Its Divisions and Its Limits, in Biblical Thought." *EvQ* 43 (1971): 218–227.

_____. "St Luke, the Date of Christmas and the Priestly Courses at Qumran." *RevQ* 9 (1977): 73–94.

_____. "Cautionary Notes on the Use of Calendars and Astronomy to Determine the Chronology of the Passion," Pages 183–205 in *Chronos, Kairos, Christos: Nativity and Chronological Studies Presented to Jack Finegan.* Edited by Jerry Vardaman and Edwin M. Yamauchi. Winona Lake, IN: Eisenbrauns, 1989.

Ben-Tor, Amnon and Sharon Zuckerman, "Hazor at the End of the Late Bronze Age: Back to Basics," *BASOR* 350 (May 2008): 1–6.

Bercovitz, J. Peter. "Paul and Antioch: Some Observations." *Proceedings of the Eastern Great Lakes and Midwest Biblical Societies* 19 (1999): 87–101.

Bergsma, John Sietze. "Once Again, the Jubilee, Every 49 or 50 Years?" *VT* 55 (2005): 121–125.

_____., *The Jubilee from Leviticus to Qumran: A History of Interpretation.* Edited by. ed. Vol. Leiden: Brill, 2007.

Beyer, David W. "Josephus Reexamined: Unveiling the Twenty-second Year of Tiberius," Pages 85–96 in *Chronos, Kairos, Christos II: Chronological, Nativity, and Religious Studies in Memory of Ray Summers.* Edited by E. Jerry Vardaman. Macon, GA: Mercer University, 1998.

Bickerman, Elias J. "En marge de l'Écriture." *RB* 88 (1981): 19–41.

Bimson, John J. and David P. Livingston. "Redating the Exodus," *BAR* 13, no. 5 (1987): 40–53.

Blosser, Don. "The Sabbath Year Cycle in Josephus." *HUCA* 52 (1981): 129–139.

Bowersock, Glen W. *Roman Arabia.* Cambridge: Harvard University, 1983.

Braund, D. "Four Notes on the Herods." *CQ* 33 (1983): 239–242.

Brindle, Wayne A. "The Census and Quirinius: Luke 2:2." *JETS* 27 (1984): 43–52.

Brownlee, William H. "'Son of Man Set Your Face': Ezekiel the Refugee Prophet." *HUCA* 54 (1983): 83–110.

Bruce, F. F. "Chronological Questions in the Acts of the Apostles." *BJRL* 68 (1986): 273–295.

Brug, John F. "New Testament Chronology: A Followup." *Wisconsin Lutheran Quarterly* 91 (1994): 217–219.

Bunimovits, Shelomoh and Avraham Faust. "Chronological Separation, Geographical Segregation, or Ethnic Demarcation? Ethnography and the Iron Age Low Chronology." *BASOR* 322 (2001): 1–10.

Cadbury, Henry Joel. "Some Lukan Expressions of Time." *JBL* 82 (1963): 272–278.

Cameron, George G. "Darius and Xerxes in Babylonia." *AJSL* 58 (1941): 314–325.

Campbell, Douglas A. "An Anchor for Pauline Chronology: Paul's Flight from 'the Ethnarch of King Aretas' (2 Corinthians 11:32–33)." *JBL* 121 (2002): 279–302.

_____. "Possible Inscriptional Attestation to Sergius Paul[l]us (Acts 13:6–12), and the Implications for Pauline Chronology." *JTS* ns 56 (2005): 1–29.

Casperson, Lee W. "Sabbatical, Jubilee, and the Temple of Solomon." *VT* 53 (2003): 283–296.

Cerny, Edward A. "Recent Studies on the Date of the Crucifixion." *CBQ* 7 (1945): 222–230.

Chapman, Rupert L. "The Dan Stele and the Chronology of Levantine Iron Age Stratigraphy." *BAIAS* 13 (1993): 23–29.

Chapman, William John B. "Palestinian Chronological Data 750–700 B.C., in Their Relation to the Events Recorded in the Assyrian Canon." *HUCA* 8–9 (1931): 151–168.

_____. "The Problem of Inconsequent Post-Dating in II Kings xv 13, 17 and 23." *HUCA* 2 (1925): 57–61.

Chirichigno, Gregory C. *Debt-slavery in Israel and the Ancient Near East*. JSOTSup 141. Sheffield: JSOT, 1993.

Clarke, A. H. T. "The Historic Accuracy of the Old Testament." *EvQ* 3 (1931): 157–167.

_____. "The Bible in the Light of the Latest Science: (Garstang's Joshua and Judges)." *EvQ* 4 (1932): 39–49.

Clines, D. J. A. "The Evidence for an Autumnal New Year in Pre-exilic Israel Reconsidered." *JBL* 93 (1974): 22–40.

Cody, Aelred. "New Inscription from Tell Al-Rimah and King Jehoash of Israel." *CBQ* 32 (1970): 325–340.

Cogan, Mordechai. "Tyre and Tiglath-Pilesar III: Chronological Notes." *JCS* 25 (1973): 96–99.

_____. "Sennacherib's Seige of Jerusalem (2.119b)," Pages 302–303 in *The Context of Scripture II: Monumental Inscriptions from the Biblical World*. Edited by William W. Hallo. Leiden: Brill, 2000.

Collins, Nina L. "The Start of the Pre-Exilic Calendar Day of David and the Amalekites: A Note on 1 Samuel 30:17." *VT* 41 (1991): 203–210.

Cook, Herbert J. "Pekah." *VT* 14 (1964): 121–135.

Couke, V. "Chronologie des rois de Juda et d'Israël," *RBén* 37 (1925): 325–364.

_____. "Chronique biblique" columns 1245–1279 in Volume 1 of *Supplément au Dictionnaire de la Bible*, edited by Louis Pirot. Paris: Libraire Letouzey et Ané, 1928.

Cross, Frank Moore. "Geshem the Arabian," BA 18 (1955) 46–47.

_____. "An Interpretation of the Nora Stone," BASOR 208 (1972): 13–19.

_____. "A Reconstruction of the Judean Restoration," JBL 94 (1975): 4–18.

Dearman, J. Andrew and J. Maxwell Miller. "The Melqart Stele and the Ben Hadads of Damascus: Two Studies." *PEQ* 115 (1983): 95–101.

Declercq, Georges. "Dionysius Exiguus and the Introduction of the Christian Era." *SacEr* 41 (2002): 165–246.

Demsky, Aaron. "Who Came First, Ezra or Nehemiah?" *HUCA* 65 (1994): 1–19.

Depuydt, Leo. "The Date of Death of Jesus of Nazareth." *JAOS* 122 (2002): 466–480.

Derby, Josiah. "Calendar Notations in the Prophets." *JBQ* 29 (2001): 255–258.

Dieckmann, Hermannus D. "Das Fünfzehnte Jahr Des Caesar Tiberius." *Bib* 6 (1925): 63–67.

Dijkstra, Meindert. "Pithom En Raämses." *NedTT* 43 (1989): 89–105.

Dockx, S. *Chronologies néotestamentaires et vie de l'Eglise primitive.* Gembloux: Duculot, 1976.

_____. "The First Missionary Journey of Paul: Historical Reality or Literary Creation of Luke?" Pages 209–222 in *Chronos, Kairos, Christos: Nativity and Chronological Studies Presented to Jack Finegan.* Edited by Jerry Vardaman and Edwin M. Yamauchi. Winona Lake, IN: Eisenbrauns, 1989.

Doron Ben-Ami, "The Iron Age I at Tel Hazor in Light of the Renewed Excavations," *IEJ* 51 (2001): 148–170.

Doyle, A. D. "Pilate's Career and the Date of the Crucifixion." *JTS* 42 (1941): 190–193.

Dumbrell, William J. "The Tell el-Maskhuta Bowls and the 'Kingdom' of Qedar." *BASOR* 203 (1971): 33–44.

Duncan, George S. "Chronological Table to Illustrate Paul's Ministry in Asia." *NTS* 5 (1958): 43–45.

Edwards, Ormond. "Herodian Chronology." *PEQ* 114 (1982): 29–42.

Emerton, J. A. "Did Ezra Go to Jerusalem in 428 B.C.?" *JTS* 17 (1966): 1–19.

Elliger, Karl. *Leviticus.* HAT 4. Tübingen: J.C.B. Mohr [Paul Siebeck], 1966.

Faiman, David. "Chronology in the Book of Judges." *JBQ* 21 (1993): 31–40.

Faulstich, E. W. "Studies in O.T. and N.T. Chronology," Pages 97–118 in *Chronos, Kairos, Christos II: Chronological, Nativity, and Religious Studies in Memory of Ray Summers.* Edited by E. Jerry Vardaman. Macon, GA: Mercer University, 1998.

Fee, Gordon D. "*Caris* in II Corinthians 1:15: Apostolic Parousia and Paul-Corinth Chronology." *NTS* 24 (1978): 533–538.

Ferrari-D'Occhieppo, Konradin. "The Star of the Magi and Babylonian Astronomy," Pages 41–54 in *Chronos, Kairos, Christos: Nativity and Chronological Studies Presented to Jack Finegan.* Edited by Jerry Vardaman and Edwin M. Yamauchi. Winona Lake, IN: Eisenbrauns, 1989.

Filmer, W. F. "Chronology of the Reign of Herod the Great," *JTS* ns 17 (1966): 283–298.

Finegan, Jack. "The Chronology of Ezekiel." *JBL* 69 (1950): 61–66.

———. "Nebuchadnezzar and Jerusalem." *JBR* 25 (1957): 203–205.

———. *Handbook of Biblical Chronology: Principles of Time Reckoning in the Ancient World and Problems of Chronology in the Bible.* Rev. ed. Peabody, MA: Hendrickson, 1998.

Finkelstein, Israel. "Hazor at the End of the Late Bronze Age: A Reassessment. *UF* 37 (2005): 341–49.

Finkelstein, Israel and Eliazer Piasetzky. "The Iron I-IIa in the Highlands and Beyond: 14c Anchors, Pottery Phases and the Shoshenq I Campaign." *Levant* 38 (2006): 45–61.

Fishbane, Michael. *Biblical Interpretation in Ancient Israel.* Oxford: Clarendon, 1985.

Fluehr-Labban, Carolyn. "Nubian Queens in the Nile Valley and Afro-Asiatic Cultural History." Pages 1–9 in *Nubian Studies: 1998 Proceedings of the Ninth Conference of the International Society of Nubian Studies.* North Eastern University, 1998.

Freedman, David Noel. "Headings in the Books of the Eighth-Century Prophets." *AUSS* 25 (1987): 9–26.

Freedy, K. S. and Donald B. Redford. "The Dates in Ezekiel in Relation to Biblical, Babylonian and Egyptian Sources." *JAOS* 90 (1970): 462–485.

Gaechter, Paul. "The Chronology from Mary's Betrothal to the Birth of Christ." *TS* 2 (1941): 145–170.

_____. "The Chronology from Mary's Betrothal to the Birth of Christ. 2." *TS* 2 (1941): 347–368.

Gal, Zvi. "The Iron Age 'Low Chronology' in Light of the Excavations at Horvat Rosh Zayit." *IEJ* 53 (2003): 147–150.

Galil, Gershon. "The Babylonian Calendar and the Chronology of the Last Kings of Judah." *Bib* 72 (1991): 367–378.

_____. *The Chronology of the Kings of Israel and Judah.* Leiden: Brill, 1996.

Garstang, John and J. B. E. Garstang, *The Story of Jericho.* Second ed. London: Marshal, Morgan and Scott, 1948.

Gielen, Marlis. "Paulus—Gefangener in Ephesus? Teil 1." *BN* 131 (2006): 79–103.

Gilchrist, J. M. "Paul and the Corinthians—The Sequence of Letters and Visits." *JSNT* 34 (1988): 47–69.

Gilmer, Graham. "A Week in the Life of Christ." *BSac* 96 (1939): 42–50.

Goldstine, Herman H. *New and Full Moons 1001 B.C. to A.D. 1651.* Philadelphia: American Philosophical Society, 1973.

Gow, James, *A Companion to School Classics.* Third ed. London: Macmillan, 1893.

Grabbe, Lester L. "Maccabean Chronology: 167–164, 168–165 BCE." *JBL* 110 (1991): 59–74.

Green, Alberto R. W. "The Chronology of the Last Days of Judah: Two Apparent Discrepancies." *JBL* 101 (1982): 57–73.

_____. "The Date of Nehemiah: A Reexamination." *AUSS* 28 (1990), 195–209.

Grimal, Nicholas-Christophe. *A History of Ancient Egypt.* Trans. Ian Shaw. Oxford: Blackwell, 1992.

Gruber, Mayer I. "The Reality Behind the Hebrew Expression *K'T Hyh.*" *ZAW* 103 (1991): 271–274.

Guggenheimer, Heinrich W. *Seder Olam: The Rabbinic View of Biblical Chronology.* Lanham: Rowman and Littlefield, 1998.

Guyot, Gilmore Henry "The Chronology of St. Paul." *CBQ* 6 (1944): 28–36.

Hagens, Graham. "Exodus and Settlement: A Two Sojourn Hypothesis." *SR* 36 (2007): 85–105.

Hallo, William W. "From Qarqar to Carchemish: Assyria and Israel in the Light of New Discoveries." *BA* 23 (1960): 34–61.

Halpern, Baruch. "Radical Exodus Redating Fatally Flawed," *BAR* 13, no. 6 (1987): 56–61.

————. "A Historiographic Commentary on Ezra 1–6: A Chronological Narrative and Dual Chronology in Israelite Historiography," pages 81–142 in *The Hebrew Bible and Its Interpreters*, ed. William L Propp, et. al. Winona Lake: Eisenbrauns, 1990.

Hamilton, John. "The Chronology of the Crucifixion and the Passover." *Chm* 106 (1992): 323–338.

Hanhart, Robert. *Esdrae Liber I.* Septuaginta: Vetus Testamentum Graecum 8/1. Göttingen: Vandenhoeck and Ruprecht, 1974.

Hartley, John E. *Levtiticus.* WBC 3. Dallas: Word, 1992.

Hasel, Gerhard F. "The First and Third Years of Belshazzar (Dan 7:1; 8:1)." *AUSS* 15 (1977): 153–168.

Hasel, Michael G. "Israel in the Merneptah Stela." *BASOR* 296 (1994): 45–61.

Hayes, John H. and Paul K. Hooker. *A New Chronology for the Kings of Israel and Judah and Its Implications for Biblical History and Literature.* Louisville: Westminster/John Knox, 1988. Reprint Eugene: Wipf and Stock, 2007.

Helzer, Michael. "The Flogging and Plucking of Beards in the Achaemenid Empire and the Chronology of Nehemiah," *AMI* 28 (1995–96): 305–307.

Hinz, Walther. "Chronologie Des Lebens Jesu." *ZDMG* 139 (1989): 301–309.

Hoehner, Harold W. "Duration of the Egyptian Bondage." *BSac* (1969): 306–316.

_____. "Chronological Aspects of the Life of Christ. Part I, the Date of Christ's Birth Other Titles: Date of Christ's Birth." *BSac* (1973): 338–351.

_____. "Chronological Aspects of the Life of Christ. Part II, the Commencement of Christ's Ministry Other Titles: Commencement of Christ's Ministry." *BSac* (1974): 41–54.

_____. "Chronological Aspects of the Life of Christ. Part III, the Duration of Christ's Ministry Other Titles: Duration of Christ's Ministry." *BSac* (1974): 147–162.

_____. "Chronological Aspects of the Life of Christ. Part IV, the Day of Christ's Crucifixion Other Titles: Day of Christ's Crucifixion." *BSac* (1974): 241–264.

_____. "Chronological Aspects of the Life of Christ. Part V, the Year of Christ's Crucifixion Other Titles: Year of Christ's Crucifixion." *BSac* (1974): 332–348.

_____. "Chronological Aspects of the Life of Christ. Part VI, Daniel's Seventy Weeks and New Testament Chronology Other Titles: Daniel's Seventy Weeks and New Testament Chronology." *BSac* (1975): 47–65.

_____. "The Date of the Death of Herod the Great," Pages 101–112 in *Chronos, Kairos, Christos: Nativity and Chronological Studies Presented to Jack Finegan.* Edited by Jerry Vardaman and Edwin M. Yamauchi. Winona Lake, IN: Eisenbrauns, 1989.

Hoenig, Sidney B. "Sabbatical Years and the Year of Jubilee." *JQR* ns 59 (1969): 222–236.

Hoffmeier, James K. "What Is the Biblical Date for the Exodus? A Response to Bryant Wood." *JETS* 50 (2007): 225–247.

Holladay, William L. "The Years of Jeremiah's Preaching." *Int* 37 (1983): 146–159.

Horn, Siegfried H. "The Chronology of King Hezekiah's Reign." *AUSS* 2 (1964): 40–52.

_____. "Babylonian Chronicle and the Ancient Calendar of the Kingdom of Judah." *AUSS* 5 (1967): 12–27.

_____. "Who Was Solomon's Egyptian Father-in-Law?" *BR* 12 (1967): 3–17.

_____. "From Bishop Ussher to Edwin R Thiele." *AUSS* 18 (1980): 37–49.

Hornung, Erik, Rolf Krauss & David Warburton, eds., *Ancient Egyptian Chronology*. Handbook of Oriental Studies. Leiden: Brill, 2006.

Horton, Stanley M. "Critical Note: A Suggestion Concerning the Chronology of Solomon's Reign." *Bulletin of the Evangelical Theological Society* 4 (1961): 3–4.

Howard, David M., Jr. "'Three Days' in Joshua 1—3: Resolving a Chronological Conundrum." *JETS* 41 (1998): 539–550.

Humphreys, Colin J. "The Star of Bethlehem, a Comet in 5 BC and the Date of Christ's Birth." *TynBul* 43 (1992): 31–56.

_____. "The Star of Bethlehem." *Science and Christian Belief* 5 (1993): 83–101.

Humphreys, Colin J. and W. G. Waddington, "Astronomy and the Date of the Crucifixion," Pages 165–182 in *Chronos, Kairos, Christos: Nativity and Chronological Studies Presented to Jack Finegan*. Edited by Jerry Vardaman and Edwin M. Yamauchi. Winona Lake, IN: Eisenbrauns, 1989.

Hurd, John C. "Sequence of Paul's Letters." *CJT* 14 (1968): 189–200.

Hyatt, James Philip. "Beginning of Jeremiah's Prophecy." *ZAW* 78 (1966): 204–218.

Instone-Brewer, David. "Jesus's Last Passover: The Synoptics and John." *ExpTim* 112 (2001): 122–123.

Jaubert, Annie. *La date de la Cène: calendrier biblique et liturgie chrétienne*. Etudes biblique. Paris: J. Gabalda,1957.

Jepsen, Alfred. "Noch Einmal Zur Israelitisch-Jüdischen Chronologie." *VT* 18 (1968): 31–46.

_____. "Ein Neuer Fixpunkt Für Die Chronologie Der Israelitischen Könige." *VT* 20 (1970): 359–361.

Jewett, Robert. *A Chronology of Paul's Life*. Philadelphia: Fortress, 1979.

Johnson, Douglas. "'And They Went Eight Stades toward Herodeion'," Pages 93–100 in *Chronos, Kairos, Christos: Nativity and Chronological Studies Presented to Jack Finegan*. Edited by Jerry Vardaman and Edwin M. Yamauchi. Winona Lake, IN: Eisenbrauns, 1989.

Jones, David L. "Luke's Unique Interest in Historical Chronology." *SBLSP* 28 (1989): 378–387.

Katzenstein, H. Jacob. "Who Were the Parents of Athaliah?" *IEJ* 5 (1955): 194–197.

Kaufman, Stephen A. "A Reconstruction of the Social Welfare Systems of Ancient Israel," in *In the Shelter of Elyon*. JSOTSup 31. Edited by W. B. Barrick and J. R. Spencer. Sheffield: JSOT, 1984.

Kawashima, Robert S. "The Jubilee, Every 49 or 50 Years? Other Titles: Jubilee, Every Forty-Nine or Fifty Years?" *VT* 53 (2003): 117–120.

Kenyon, Kathleen. "Some Notes on the History of Jericho in the Second Millennium B.C.," *PEQ* (1951): 101–138.

_____. *Archaeology in the Holy Land*. Fourth ed. London: Ernest Benn, 1979.

Kitchen, Kenneth A. *The Third Intermediate Period in Egypt (1100–650 B.C.)*. Warminster: Aris and Philips, 1986.

_____. "Egypt and East Africa," Pages 106–126 in *The Age of Solomon: Scholarship at the Turn of the Millennium*. Ed. Lowell K. Handy. Leiden: Brill, 1997.

_____. "Ancient Egypt and the Hebrew Monarchies: A Review Article." *Them* 26 (2001): 38–50.

_____. "How We Know When Solomon Ruled," *BAR* 27, no. 5 (September/October 2001): 32–37, 58.

_____. *On the Reliability of the Old Testament.* Grand Rapids: Eerdmans, 2003.

Kitchen, Kenneth A. and T. C. Mitchell. "Chronology of the Old Testament." Pages 268–277 in vol. 1 of *The Illustrated Bible Dictionary.* Edited by J. D. Douglas. Leicester: Inter-Varsity. 1980.

Knauf, Ernst Axel. "The 'Low Chronology' and How Not to Deal with It." *BN* 101 (2000): 56–63.

Kokkinos, Nikos. "Crucifixion in A.D. 30: Keystone for Dating the Birth of Jesus," Pages 133–164.

Kraeling, Carl H. "The Episode of the Roman Standards at Jerusalem." *HTR* 35 (1942): 263–289.

Laato, Antti. "New Viewpoints on the Chronology of the Kings of Judah and Israel." *ZAW* 98 (1986): 210–221.

Lake, Krisopp. "The Apostolic Council of Jerusalem." Pages 195–211 in *The Beginnings of Christianity, Part I: The Acts of the Apostles.* Volume 5 Additional Notes to the Commentary. Edited by F. J. Foakes Jackson and Kirsopp Lake. New York: Macmillian, 1933; Reprint. Grand Rapids: Baker, 1979.

Larsson, Gerhard. "When Did the Babylonian Captivity Begin?" *JTS* ns 18 (1967): 417–423.

_____. "Is Biblical Chronology Systematic or Not." *RevQ* 6 (1969): 499–515.

_____. "The Chronology of the Pentateuch: A Comparison of the MT and LXX." *JBL* 102 (1983): 401–409.

_____. "Ancient Calendars Indicated in the OT." *JSOT* 54 (1992): 61–76.

_____. "Chronology as a Structural Element in the Old Testament." *SJOT* 14 (2000): 207–218.

_____. "The Chronology of the Kings of Israel and Judah as a System." *ZAW* 114 (2002): 224–235.

_____. "Septuagint Versus Massoretic Chronology." *ZAW* 114 (2002): 511–521.

_____. "A System of Biblical Dates." *SJOT* 16 (2002): 184–206.

Lasker, Daniel J. "The Date of the Death of Jesus: Further Reflections." *JAOS* 124 (2004): 95–99.

Lawrence, John M. "Publius Sulpicius Quirinius and the Syrian Census." *ResQ* 34 (1992): 193–205.

Lefebvre, Jean-François, *Le jubilé biblique: Lv 25, exégèse et théologie*. OBO 194. Göttingen: Vandenhoeck & Ruprecht, 2003.

Lemche, Niels Peter. "The Hebrew and the Seven Year Cycle." *BN* 25 (1984): 65–75.

Lipiński, Edward. "Ba 'il-Ma'zer II and the Chronology of Tyre." *RSO* 45 (1970): 59–65.

Liver, J. "The Chronology of Tyre at the Beginning of the First Millennium B.C.," *IEJ* 3 (1953): 113–120.

Livingston, David. "Location of Biblical Bethel and Ai Reconsidered." *WTJ* 33 (1970): 20–44.

————. "Further Considerations on the Location of Bethel at El-Bireh." *PE Q* 126 (1994): 154–59.

Lizbarski, Mark. *Handbuch der nordsemitischen Epigraphik nebst ausgewählten Inschriften* 2 vol. (Weimar: Felber, 1898).

Lodder, Willem, *Die Schätzung des Quirinius bei Flavius Josephus. Eine Untersuchung: Hat sich Flavius Josephus in der Datierung der bekannten Schätzung (Luk. 2,2) geirrt*. Leipzig: Dörffling and Franke, 1930.

Lucas, A. "The Date of the Exodus." *PEQ* 73 (1941): 110–121.

Luedemann, Gerd. *Paul, Apostle to the Gentiles: Studies in Chronology*. Philadelphia: Fortress, 1984.

Maier, Paul. "Sejanus, Pilate, and the Date of the Crucifixion." *CH* 37 (1968): 3–13.

————. "The Episode of the Golden Roman Shields at Jerusalem." *HTR* 62 (1969): 109–121.

————. "The Date of the Nativity and the Chronology of Jesus' Life," Pages 113–130 in *Chronos, Kairos, Christos: Nativity and Chronological Studies Presented to Jack Finegan*. Edited by Jerry Vardaman and Edwin M. Yamauchi. Winona Lake, IN: Eisenbrauns, 1989.

Marshak, Adam Kolman. "The Dated Coins of Herod the Great: Towards a New Chronology." *JSJ* 37 (2006): 212–240.

Martin, Ernest L. "The Nativity and Herod's Death," Pages 85–92 in *Chronos, Kairos, Christos: Nativity and Chronological Studies Presented to Jack Finegan.* Edited by Jerry Vardaman and Edwin M. Yamauchi. Winona Lake, IN: Eisenbrauns, 1989.

Martin, Raymond Albert. "The Date of the Cleansing of the Temple in John 2:13–22." *IJT* 15 (1966): 52–56.

Masterman, N. C. "Date of the Triumphal Entry." *NTS* 16 (1969): 76–82.

Mayes, A. D. H. "The Historical Context of the Battle against Sisera." *VT* 19 (1969): 353–360.

Mazar, Amihai. "Iron Age Chronology: A Reply to I Finkelstein." *Levant* 29 (1997): 157–167.

McCarter, P. Kyle, Jr. "Yaw, Son of 'Omri': A Philological Note on Israelite Chronology." *BASOR* 216 (1974): 5–7.

McFall, Leslie. "Did Thiele Overlook Hezekiah's Coregency." *BSac* 146 (1989): 393–404.

_____. "Has the Chronology of the Hebrew Kings Been Finally Settled?" *Them* ns 17 (1991): 6–11.

_____. "A Translation Guide to the Chronological Data in Kings and Chronicles." *BSac* 148 (1991): 3–45.

_____. "Was Nehemiah Contemporary with Ezra in 458 BC?" *WTJ* 53 (1991): 263–293.

_____. "Some Missing Coregencies in Thiele's Chronology." *AUSS* 30 (1992): 35–58.

_____. "Review of Gershon Galil, *The Chronology of the Kings of Israel and Judah*." *VT* 49 (1999): 572–574.

_____. "Do the Sixty-nine Weeks of Daniel Date the Messianic Mission of Nehemiah or Jesus?" *JETS* 52 (2009): 673–718.

_____. "The Chronology of Saul and David," *JETS* 53 (2010): 475–533.

McGough, Michael. "A Chronology of Acts." *TTE* 42 (1990): 71–82.

McHugh, John. "Date of Hezekiah's Birth." *VT* 14 (1964): 446–453.

Merrill, Eugene H. *An Historical Survey of the Old Testament.* Nutley, NJ: Craig, 1966.

_____. "Fixed Dates in Patriarchal Chronology." *BSac* 137 (1980): 241–251.

_____. "Paul's Use of 'About 450 Years' in Acts 13—20." *BSac* 138 (1981): 246–257.

_____. "Palestinian Archaeology and the Date of the Conquest: Do Tells Tell Tales?" *Grace Theological Journal* 3 (1982): 107–121.

_____. "The 'Accession Year' and Davidic Chronology." *JANESCU* 19 (1989): 101–112.

Meshorer, Ya'akov. *Ancient Jewish Coinage.* Two Volumes. Dix Hills, NY: Amphora, 1982.

Messner, Brian. "'In the Fifteenth Year' Reconsidered: A Study of Luke 3:1." *Stone-Campbell Journal* 1 (1998): 201–211.

Milgrom, Jacob. "Did Isaiah Prophesy During the Reign of Uzziah." *VT* 14 (1964): 164–182.

_____. *Leviticus 23–27: A New Translation with Introduction and Commentary.* AB 3B. New York: Doubleday, 2001.

Miller, James E. "The Thirtieth Year of Ezekiel 1:1." *RB* 99 (1992): 499–503.

Miller, J. Maxwell. "Another Look at the Chronology of the Early Divided Monarchy." *JBL* 86 (1967): 276–288.

Miller, Johnny V. "The Time of the Crucifixion." *JETS* 26 (1986): 157–166.

Mitchell, T. C. "Israel and Judah from the Coming of Assyrian Domination until the Fall of Samaria, and the Struggle for Independence in Judah (C. 750–700 B.C.)," Pages 322–370 in *The Cambridge Ancient History.* Edited by John Boardman. Vol. 3, part 2. Cambridge: Cambridge University, 1991.

_____. "Israel and Judah until the Revolt of Jehu (931–841 B.C.)," Pages 442–487 in *The Cambridge Ancient History.* Edited by John Boardman. Vol. 3, part 1. Cambridge: Cambridge University, 1991.

Moberly, Robert B. "New Testament Chronology: Some Current Ideas." *Theology* 97 (1994): 170–179.

Moody, Dale. "New Chronology for the Life and Letters of Paul." *PRSt* 3 (1976): 249–272 = "A New Chronology for the Life and Letters of Paul," Pages 223–240 in *Chronos, Kairos, Christos: Nativity and Chronological Studies Presented to Jack Finegan.* Edited by Jerry Vardaman and Edwin M. Yamauchi. Winona Lake, IN: Eisenbrauns, 1989.

_____. "A New Chronology for the New Testament." *RevExp* 78 (1981): 211–231.

Morgado, Joe, Jr. "Paul in Jerusalem: A Comparison of His Visits in Acts and Galatians." *JETS* 37 (1994): 55–68.

Morgenstern, Julian. "Additional Notes on 'the Three Calendars of Ancient Israel.'" *Hebrew Union College* 3 (1926): 77–107.

_____. "Supplementary Studies in the Calendars of Ancient Israel." *HUCA* 10 (1935): 1–148.

_____. "Chronological Data of the Dynasty of Omri." *JBL* 59 (1940): 385–396.

Mowery, Robert L. "Paul and Caristanius at Pisidian Antioch." *Bib* 87 (2006): 223–242.

Münnich, Maciej M. "Hezekiah and Archaeology: The Answer for Nadav Na'aman." *UF* 36 (2004): 333–346.

Murtonen, A. "On the Chronology of the Old Testament." *ST* 8 (1954): 133–137.

Na'aman, Nadav. "Historical and Chronological Notes on the Kingdoms of Israel and Judah in the 8th Century BC." *VT* 36 (1986): 71–92.

_____. "Chronology and History in the Late Assyrian Empire (631–619 BC)." *ZA* 81 (1991): 243–267.

Neirynck, Frans. "Note on Mark's Chronology: The Holy Week." *ETL* 67 (1991): 395–397.

Nevins, Arthur J. "When Was Solomon's Temple Burned Down? Reassessing the Evidence." *JSOT* 31 (2006): 3–25.

Nicol, George G. "The Chronology of Genesis: Genesis xxvi 1–33 as 'Flashback'." *VT* 46 (1996): 330–338.

North, Robert G. *The Sociology of the Biblical Jubilee.* AnBib 4. Rome: Pontifical Biblical Institute, 1954.

Northcote, Jeremy. "The Schematic Development of Old Testament Chronography: Towards an Integrated Model." *JSOT* 29 (2004): 3–36.

Noth, Martin. *Levtiticus: A Commentary.* OTL. Philadelphia: Westminster, 1965.

Numbers, Ronald L. "'The Most Important Biblical Discovery of Our Time': William Henry Green and the Demise of Ussher's Chronology." *CH* 69 (2000): 257–276.

Ogg, George. "A New Chronology of Saint Paul's Life." *ExpTim* 64 (1953): 120–123.

_____. "Quirinius Question to-Day." *ExpTim* 79 (1968): 231–236.

_____. *Chronology of the Life of Paul.* London: Epworth, 1968.

O'Herlihy, Donal J. "The Year of the Crucifixion." *CBQ* 8 (1946): 298–305.

Orchard, Bernard. "The Problem of Acts and Galatians." *CBQ* 7 (1945): 377–397.

Orr, Avigdor. "Seventy Years of Babylon." *VT* 6 (1956): 304–306.

Oswalt, John N. *The Bible among the Myths: Unique Revelation or Just Ancient Literature?* Grand Rapids: Zondervan, 2009.

Overholt, Thomas W. "Some Reflections on the Date of Jeremiah's Call." *CBQ* 33 (1971): 165–184.

Parker, Edmund A. "Note on the Chronology of 2 Kings 17:1." *AUSS* 6 (1968): 129–133.

Parker, Richard Anthony. "Ancient Jewish Calendation: A Criticism." *JBL* 63 (1944): 173–176.

_____. *The Calendars of Ancient Egypt.* Studies in Ancient Oriental Civilizations. Chicago: University of Chicago, 1950.

_____. "The Lunar Dates of Thutmose III and Ramesses II." *JNES* 16 (1957): 39–43.

Parker, Richard A. and Waldo H. Dubberstein, *Babylonian Chronology 626 B.C.–A.D. 75.* Reprint of *Wipf and Stock.* Edited by. Third ed. Vol., Studies in Ancient Oriental Civilizations. Providence: Brown University, 1956.

Payne, J. Barton. "The Arrangement of Jeremiah's Prophecies." *Bulletin of the Evangelical Theological Society* 7 (1964): 120–130.

Pearson, Brook W. R. "The Lukan Censuses, Revisited." *CBQ* 61 (1999): 262–282.

Petrovich, Douglas. "Amenhotep II and the Historicity of the Exodus-Pharaoh." *MSJ* 17 (2006): 81–110.

_____. "The Dating of Hazor's Destruction in Joshua 11 by Way of Biblical, Archaeological, and Epigraphical Evidence." *JETS* 51 (2008): 489–512.

Pfann, Stephen J. "Dated Bronze Coinage of the Sabbatical Years of Release and the First Jewish City Coin." *BAIAS* 24 (2006): 101–113.

Phillips, Thomas E. "'The Third Fifth Day?' John 2:1 in Context." *ExpTim* (2004): 328–331.

Porter, Stanley, "The Reasons for the Lukan Census." Pages 165–188 in *Paul, Luke and the Graeco-Roman World: Essays in Honour of Alexander J. M. Wedderburn.* Edited by A. J. M. Wedderburn and Alf Christiphersen. London: Sheffield Academic, 2002.

Powell, Cyril H. "'Faith' in James and Its Bearings on the Problem of the Date of the Epistle." *ExpTim* 62 (1951): 311–314.

Power, Edmond. "John 2, 20 and the Date of the Crucifixion Other Titles: John 2:20 and the Date of the Crucifixion." *Bib* 9 (1928): 257–288.

Ray, Paul J., Jr. "The Duration of the Israelite Sojourn in Egypt." *AUSS* 24 (1986): 231–248.

_____. "Another Look at the Period of the Judges," *Beyond the Jordan: Studies in Honor of W. Harold Mare.* Edited by Edited by Glenn A. Carnagey Sr., Glenn Carnagey Jr., and Keith N. Schoville. Eugene, OR: Wipf and Stock, 2005.

Rea, John. "The Time of the Oppression and the Exodus." *Bulletin of the Evangelical Theological Society* 3 (1960): 58–69.

Reade, Julian. "Mesopotamian Guidelines for Biblical Chronology." *Syro-Mesopotamian Studies* 4 (1981): 1–9.

Reventlow, Hennig Graf. *Das Heiligkeitsgesetz formgeschichtlich untersucht.* WMANT 6. Neukirchen-Vluyn: Neukirchener, 1961.

Redford, Donald B. "The Coregency of Tutmosis III and Amenophis II." *JEA* 51 (1965): 107–122.

_____. "On the Chronology of the Egyptian Eighteenth Dynasty." *JNES* 25 (1966): 113–124.

Rhoads, John, "Josephus Misdated the Census of Quirinius," *JETS* 54 (2011): 65–88.

Rist, John M. "Luke 2:2: Making Sense of the Date of Jesus' Birth." *JTS* ns 56 (2005): 489–491.

Roberts, J. J. M. "The Babylonian Chronicles." *ResQ* 9 (1966): 275–280.

Robertson, A. T. "Points of Chronology in Luke's Writings." *Methodist Review Quarterly* 70 (1921): 144–154.

Robinson, Donald W. B. Abp. "The Date and Significance of the Last Supper." *EvQ* 23 (1951): 126–133.

Rose, Lynn E. "The Astronomical Evidence for Dating the End of the Middle Kingdom of Ancient Egypt to the Early Second Millennium: A Reassessment." *JNES* 53 (1994): 237–261.

Rosenzweig, Michael L. "Life History Data in the Bible, from Abraham to Joshua." *Judaism* 29 (1980): 353–359.

Rowley, Harold Henry. "The Date of the Exodus." *PEQ* 73 (1941): 152–157.

_____. *The Servant of the Lord and Other Essays on the Old Testament.* London: Lutterworth, 1952.

Rowlingson, Donald T. "The Jerusalem Conference and Jesus' Nazareth Visit: A Study in Pauline Chronology." *JBL* 71 (1952): 69–74.

Rowton, Michael B. "The Problem of the Exodus." *PEQ* 85 (1953): 46–60.

Russell, Henry G. "Which Was Written First, Luke or Acts?" *HTR* 48 (1955): 167–174.

Saarnivaara, Uuras. "Date of Crucifixion in the Synoptics and John." *LQ* 6 (1954): 157–160.

Saley, Richard J. "The Date of Nehemiah Reconsidered." Pages 151–165 in *Biblical and Near Eastern Studies: Essays in Honor of William Sanford LaSor.* Ed. Gary A. Tuttle. Grand Rapids: Eerdmans, 1978.

Sanchez Bosch, Jorge. "La Chronologie De La Premiere Aux Thessaloniciens Et Les Relations De Paul Avec D'autres Eglises." *NTS* 37 (1991): 336–347.

Sarna, Nahum M. "Zedekiah's Emancipation of Slaves and the Sabbatical Year," in *Orient and Occident: Essays Presented to Cyrus H. Gordon on the Occasion of His Sixty-Fifth Birthday.* Edited by Harry Hoffner, Jr. Neukirchen: Butzon and Bercker Kevelaer, 1973.

Scarola, Jack V. "Chronology of the Nativity Era," Pages 61-84 in *Chronos, Kairos, Christos II: Chronological, Nativity, and Religious Studies in Memory of Ray Summers.* Edited by E. Jerry Vardaman. Macon, GA: Mercer University, 1998.

Schenker, Adrian. "The Biblical Legislation on the Release of Slaves: The Road from Exodus to Leviticus," *JSOT* 78 (1998): 23–41.

Schürer, Emil. *A History of the Jewish People in the Time of Jesus Christ.* 5 vols. New York: Scribner's, 1896; reprint, rev. G. Vermes and F. Millar, eds. 3 vols. in 4; Edinburgh: T. and T. Clark, 1973–1987.

Schwartz, Daniel R. "On Quirinius, John the Baptist, the Benedictus, Melchizedek, Qumran and Ephesus." Pages 635–646 in *Mémorial Jean Carmignac: études Qumrâniennes.* Edited by Florentino García Martínez and Emile Peuch. Paris: Gabalda, 1988.

_____. *Agrippa I:The Last King of Judea.* (Tübingen: J. C. B. Mohr [Paul Siebeck]), 1990.

_____. "On Some Papyri and Josephus' Sources and Chronology for the Persian Period." *JSJ* 21 (1990): 175–199.

_____. "The End of the Line: Paul in the Canonical Book of Acts," Pages 3–24 in *Paul and the Legacies of Paul*. Edited by William S. Babcock. Dallas: Southern Methodist University, 1900.

_____. "Joseph ben Illem and the Date of Herod's Death," Pages 157–166 in *Studies in the Jewish Background of Christianity*. Tübingen: J. C. B. Mohr (Paul Siebeck), 1992.

Segal, Judah Ben-Zion. "Intercalation and the Hebrew Bible," *VT* 7 (1957): 250–307.

Shea, William H. "Daniel 3: Extra-Biblical Texts and the Convocation on the Plain of Dura." *AUSS* 20 (1982): 29–52.

_____. "Nabonidus, Belshazzar, and the Book of Daniel: An Update." *AUSS* 20 (1982): 133–149.

_____. "Esther and History." *CJ* 13 (1987): 234–248.

_____. "A Review of the Biblical Evidence for the Use of the Fall-to-Fall Calendar." *Journal of the Adventist Theological Society* 12 (2001): 152–163.

_____. "The Date of the Exodus," Pages 236–255 in *Giving the Sense: Understanding and Using Old Testament Historical Texts*. Edited by David M. Howard, Jr. and Michael A. Grisanti. Grand Rapids: Kregel, 2003.

Shepherd, Massey Hamilton. "Are Both the Synoptics and John Correct About the Date of Jesus' Death?" *JBL* 80 (1961): 123–132.

Skehan, Patrick William. "Date of the Last Supper." *CBQ* 20 (1958): 192–199.

Slingerland, H. Dixon. "Acts 18:1–17 and Luedemann's Pauline Chronology." *JBL* 109 (1990): 686–690.

_____. "Acts 18:1–18, the Gallio Inscription, and Absolute Pauline Chronology." *JBL* 110 (1991): 439–449.

Smallwood, E. Mary. *The Jews under Roman Rule: From Pompey to Diocletian*. SJLA 20. Leiden: Brill, 1976.

Smith, Barry D. "The Chronology of the Last Supper." *WTJ* 53 no. 1991 (1991): 29–45.

Smith, D. Howard. "Concerning the Duration of the Ministry of Jesus." *ExpTim* 76 (1965): 114–116.

Smith, Mark D. "Of Jesus and Quirinius." *CBQ* 62 (2000): 278–293.

Smith, Walter C. "The Chronology of Acts and the Epistles." *London Quarterly and Holborn Review* 179 (1954): 270–276.

Snaith, Norman. "The Date of Ezra's Arrival in Jerusalem," *ZAW* 51 (1951): 53–66.

Söding, Thomas. "Zur Chronologie Der Paulinischen Briefe: Ein Diskussionsvorschlag." *BN* 56 (1991): 31–59.

Soggin, J. Alberto. "Ein Ausserbiblisches Zeugnig Für Die Chronologie Des Jehôaš/Jô'aš, König Von Israel." *VT* 20 (1970): 366–368.

Spitta, Friedrich. "Die Chronologische Notizen und die Hymnen in Lc 1 U. 2," *ZNW* 7 (1906): 281–317.

Stein, Robert H. "The Relationship of Galatians 2:1–10 and Acts 15:1–35: Two Neglected Arguments," *JETS* 17 (1974): 239–242.

Steiner, Richard C. "Bishlam's Archival Search Report in Nehemiah's Archive: Multiple Introductions and Reverse Chronological Order as Clues to the Origin of the Aramaic Letters in Ezra 4–6," *JBL* 125 (2006): 641–685.

Steinmann, Andrew E. "The Chronology of 2 Kings 15—18." *JETS* 30 (1987): 391–397.

_____. "אחד as an Ordinal Number and the Meaning of Genesis 1:5." *JETS* 45 (2002): 577–584.

_____. "The Mysterious Numbers of the Book of Judges." *JETS* 48 (2005): 491–500.

_____. "A Chronological Note: The Return of the Exiles under Sheshbazzar and Zerubbabel (Ezra 1–2)." *JETS* 51 (2008): 513–522.

_____. *Daniel.* Concordia Commentary. St. Louis: Concordia, 2008.

_____. "When Did Herod the Great Reign?" *NovT* 51 (2009): 1–29.

_____. *Ezra and Nehemiah.* Concordia Commentary. St. Louis: Concordia, 2010.

Stewart, John. "The Dates of the Nativity and the Crucifixion of Our Lord: A New Discovery." *EvQ* 4 (1932): 290–315.

Stigers, Harold G. "The Interphased Chronology of Jotham, Ahaz, Hezekiah and Hoshea." *Bulletin of the Evangelical Theological Society* 9 (1966): 81–90.

_____. "Biblical and Archaeological Data Bearing on the Late Date of the Exodus." *Near East Archaeological Society Bulletin* ns 30 (1988): 5–26.

Story, Cullen I. K. "The Chronology of Holy Week." *BSac* 97 (1940): 63–80.

_____. "The Bearing of Old Testament Terminology on the Johannine Chronology of the Final Passover of Jesus." *NovT* 31 (1989): 316–324.

Strand, Kenneth A. "Thiele's Biblical Chronology as a Corrective for Extrabiblical Dates." *AUSS* 34 (1996): 295–317.

Strange, John. "Joram, King of Israel and Judah." *VT* 25 (1975): 191–201.

Stroes, H. R. "Does the Day Begin in the Evening or Morning." *VT* 16 (1966): 460–475.

Suggs, M. Jack. "Concerning the Date of Paul's Macedonian Ministry." *NovT* 4 (1960): 60–68.

Tadmor, Hayim. "Chronology of the Last Kings of Judah." *JNES* 15 (1956): 226–230.

_____. "The Campaigns of Sargon II of Assur: A Chronological-Historical Study." *JCS* 12 (1958): 22–40.

_____. "The Campaigns of Sargon II of Assur: A Chronological-Historical Study." *JCS* 12 (1958): 77–100.

_____. *The Inscriptions of Tiglath-Pileser III, King of Assyria.* Jerusalem: Israel Academy of Sciences and Humanities, 1994.

Taylor, N. H. "The Composition and Chronology of Second Corinthians." *JSNT* 44 (1991): 67–87.

Tetley, M. Christine, *The Reconstructed Chronology of the Divided Kingdom.* Winona Lake: Eisenbrauns, 2005.

Thiele, Edwin R. "The Chronology of the Kings of Judah and Israel," *JNES* 3 (1944): 137–186

_____. "Comparison of the Chronological Data of Israel and Judah." *VT* 4 (1954): 185–195.

_____. "The Synchronisms of the Hebrew Kings—a Re-Evaluation." *AUSS* 1 (1963): 121–138.

_____. "The Synchronisms of the Hebrew Kings—a Re-Evaluation." *AUSS* 2 (1964): 120–137.

_____. "Pekah to Hezekiah and the Azariah and Hezekiah Synchronisms." *VT* 16 (1966): 83–107.

_____. "Coregencies and Overlapping Reigns among the Hebrew Kings." *JBL* 93 (1974): 174–200.

_____. "Additional Chronological Note on 'Yaw, Son of 'Omri'." *BASOR* 222 (1976): 19–23.

_____. *The Mysterious Numbers of the Hebrew Kings.* Second Ed. Grand Rapids: Eerdmans, 1965.

_____. *The Mysterious Numbers of the Hebrew Kings.* New Rev. Ed. Grand Rapids: Zondervan, 1983.

Thiering, Barbara E. "The Three and a Half Years of Elijah." *NovT* 23 (1981): 41–55.

Torrey, Charles Cutler. "The Date of the Crucifixion According to the Fourth Gospel." *JBL* 50 (1931): 227–241.

Toussaint, Stanley D. "Chronological Problem of Galatians 2:1–10." *BSac* 120 (1963): 334–340.

Trebilco, P. "Itineraries, Travel Plans, Journeys, Apostolic Parousia." Pages 446–456 in *Dictionary of Paul and His Letters.* Edited by Gerald F. Hawthorne and Raplh P. Martin. Downers Grove: InterVarsity, 1993.

Tuland, Carl G. "Ezra-Nehemiah or Nehemiah-Ezra: An Investigation into the Validity of the Van Hoonacker Theory." *AUSS* 12 (1974): 47–62.

Tyson, Joseph B. "Jesus and Herod Antipas." JBL 79 (1960): 239–246.

Van der Kooij, Arie. "On the Ending of the Book of 1 Esdras." Pages 37–49 in *7th Congress of the International Organization for Septuagint and Cognate Studies*. Atlanta: Scholars, 1991.

Van Siclen, Charles Cornell. "The Accession Date of Amenhotep III and the Jubilee." *JNES* 32 (1973): 290–300.

VanderKam, James, *From Joshua to Caiaphas: High Priests after the Exile*. Minneapolis: Fortress, 2004.

Vardaman, "Jesus' Life: A New Chronology," Pages 55–82 in *Chronos, Kairos, Christos: Nativity and Chronological Studies Presented to Jack Finegan*. Edited by Jerry Vardaman and Edwin M. Yamauchi. Winona Lake, IN: Eisenbrauns, 1989.

Vernes, Maurice. *Précis d'histoire juive depuis les origines jusqu'a l'époque persane*. Paris: Hachette, 1889.

Wacholder, Ben Zion. "Calendar of Sabbatical Cycles During the Second Temple and the Early Rabbinic Period." *HUCA* 44 (1973): 153–196.

_____. "Chronomessianism: The Timing of Messianic Movements and the Calendar of Sabbatical Cycles." *HUCA* 46 (1975): 201–218.

_____. "The Calendar of the Sabbath Years During the Second Temple Era: A Response." *HUCA* 54 (1983): 123–133.

Wacholder, Ben Zion and Sholom Wacholder. "Patterns of Biblical Dates and Qumran's Calendar: The Fallacy of Jaubert's Hypothesis." *HUCA* 66 (1995): 1–40.

Walker, Norman. "Concerning the Jaubertian Chronology of the Passion." *NovT* 3 (1959): 317–320.

_____. "'After Three Days'." *NovT* 4 (1960): 261–262.

_____. "Pauses in the Passion Story and Their Significance for Chronology." *NovT* 6 (1963): 16–19.

_____. "Yet Another Look at the Passion Chronology." *NovT* 6 (1963): 286–289.

Wallace, Daniel B. *Greek Grammar Beyond the Basics*. Grand Rapids: Zondervan, 1996.

Walther, James A. "The Chronology of Passion Week." *JBL* 77 (1958): 116–122.

Waltke, Bruce K. "Palestinian Artifactual Evidence Supporting the Early Date of the Exodus." *BSac* 129 (1972): 33–47.

_____. "The Date of the Conquest." *WTJ* 52 (1990): 181–200.

Warner, Seán M. "Dating of the Period of the Judges." *VT* 28 (1978): 455–463.

Washburn, David L. "The Chronology of Judges: Another Look." *BSac* 147 (1990): 414–425.

Weber, Wm. "Der Census des Quirinius nach Josephus," *ZNW* 10 (1909): 307–319.

Weisberg, David B. *Texts from the Time of Nebuchadnezzar*. New Haven: Yale University, 1980.

Wellhausen, Julius. *Prolegomena to the History of Israel: with a Reprint of the Article "Israel" from the Encyclopedia Britannica*. Atlanta: Scholars, 1994.

Wenham, David. "Piecing Together Paul's Life: A Review Article." *EvQ* 68 (1996): 47–58.

Whibley, Leonard, *A Companion to Greek Studies.*Third ed. Cambridge: Cambridge University, 1916.

Whitley, Charles Francis. "The Term Seventy Years Captivity." *VT* 4 (1954): 60–72.

_____. "'Thirtieth' Year in Ezekiel 1:1." *VT* 9 (1959): 326–330.

_____. "Date of Jeremiah's Call." *VT* 14 (1964): 467–483.

_____. "Carchemish and Jeremiah." *ZAW* 80 (1968): 38–49.

Wifall, Walter R. "Chronology of the Divided Monarchy of Israel." *ZAW* 80 (1968): 319–337.

Williams, Charles Stephan Conway. "The Date of Luke-Acts." *ExpTim* 64 (1953): 283–284.

Williamson, H. G. M. *Ezra, Nehemiah*. WBC 15. Waco: Word, 1985.

Winger, Michael. "When Did the Women Visit the Tomb?" *NTS* 40 (1994): 284–288.

Winkle, Ross E. "Jeremiah's Seventy Years for Babylon, Re-Assessment: Pt 2, the Historical Data." *AUSS* 25 (1987): 289–299.

Wiseman, Donald J., *Chronicles of the Chaldean Kings (626–556 B.C.) in the British Museum.* London: Trustees of the British Museum, 1956.

————. *Nebuchadrezzar and Babylon.* Oxford: Oxford University Press, 1985.

Wood, Bryant G. "Did the Israelites Conquer Jericho? A New Look at the Archaeological Evidence." *BAR* 16, no. 2 (1990): 44–58.

————. "Dating Jericho's Destruction: Bienkowski Is Wrong on All Counts." *BAR* 16, no. 5 (1990): 45–49, 68, 69.

————. "From Ramesses to Shiloh: Archaeological Discoveries Bearing on the Exodus–Judges Period," Pages 256–282 in *Giving the Sense: Understanding and Using Old Testament Historical Texts.* Edited by David M. Howard, Jr. and Michael A. Grisanti. Grand Rapids: Kregel, 2003.

————. "The Rise and Fall of the 13th-Century Exodus-Conquest Theory." *JETS* 48 (2005): 475–489.

————. "The Biblical Date for the Exodus Is 1446 BC: A Response to James Hoffmeier." *JETS* 50 (2007): 249–258.

————. "The Search for Joshua's Ai," Pages 205–240 in *Critical Issues in Early Israelite History.* Edited by Richard S. Hess, Gerald A. Klingbeil, and Paul J. Ray, Jr. Winona Lake, IN: Eisenbrauns, 2008.

Wright, Christopher J. H. "What Happened Every Seven Years in Israel: Old Testament Sabbatical Institutions for Land, Debts and Slaves." *EvQ* 56 (1984): 129–138; 193–201.

————. *God's People in God's Land: Family, Land, and Property in the Old Testament.* Grand Rapids: Eerdmans, 1990.

Yamauchi, Edwin. "The Reverse Order of Ezra/Nehemiah Reconsidered," *Them* 5 (1980): 7–13.

————. *Persia and the Bible.* Grand Rapids: Baker, 1996.

York, Anthony D. "Ezekiel I: Inaugural and Restoration Visions?" *VT* 27 (1977): 82–98.

Young, Rodger C. "When Did Solomon Die?" *JETS* 46 (2003): 589–603.

_____. "When Did Jerusalem Fall?" *JETS* 47 (2004): 21–38.

_____. "When Was Samaria Captured? The Need for Precision in Biblical Chronologies." *JETS* 47 (2004): 577–595.

_____. "Tables of Reign Lengths from the Hebrew Court Recorders." *JETS* 48 (2005): 225–248.

_____. "Ezekiel 40:1 as a Corrective for Seven Wrong Ideas in Biblical Interpretation." *AUSS* 44 no. 2 (2006): 265–283.

_____. "*Seder Olam* and the Sabbaticals Associated with the Two Destructions of Jerusalem. Part 1." *JBQ* ns 34 (2006): 173–179.

_____. "*Seder Olam* and the Sabbaticals Associated with the Two Destructions of Jerusalem. Part 2." *JBQ* 34 (2006): 252–259.

_____. "The Talmud's Two Jubilees and Their Relevance to the Date of the Exodus." *WTJ* 68 (2006): 71–83.

_____. "Inductive and Deductive Methods as Applied to OT Chronology." *MSJ* 18 (2007): 99–116.

_____. "Three Verifications of Thiele's Date for the Beginning of the Divided Kingdom." *AUSS* 45 (2007): 163–189.

_____. "Evidence for Inerrancy from a Second Unexpected Source: The Jubilee and Sabbatical Cycles." *Bible and Spade* 21 (2008): 109–122.

_____. "Evidence for Inerrancy from an Unexpected Source: OT Chronology." *Bible and Spade* 21 (2008): 54–64.

_____. "The Parian Marble and Other Surprises from Chronologist V. Coucke," *AUSS* 48 (2010): 225–249.

Younger, K. Lawson, Jr. "Neo-Assyrian Inscriptions: Shalmaneser III (2.113)," Pages 261–270 in *Scripture in Context II: Monumental Inscriptions from the Biblical World.* Edited by William W. Hallo. Leiden: Brill, 2000.

Zahn, Theodor "Die Syrische Statthalterschaft und die Schatzung des Quirinius," *NKZ* 4 (1893): 633–654.

Zawadzki, Stefan. "The First Year of Nabopolassar's Rule According to the Babylonian Chronicle BM 25127: A Reinterpretation of the Text and Its Consequences." *JCS* 41 (1989): 57–64.

Zeitlin, Solomon. "The Date of the Crucifixion According to the Fourth Gospel." *JBL* 51 (1932): 263–271.

_____. "Dates of the Birth and the Crucifixion of Jesus: The Crucifixion, a Libelous Accusation against the Jews." *JQR* ns 55 (1964): 1–22.

_____. "Duration of Jesus' Ministry." *JQR* ns 55 (1965): 181–200.

_____. "Paul's Journeys to Jerusalem." *JQR* 57 (1967): 171–178.

Zuckermann, Benedict. *A Treatise of the Sabbatical Cycle and the Jubilee: A Contribution to the Archaeology and Chronology of the Time Anterior and Subsequent to the Captivity Accompanied by a Table of Sabbatical Years.* Trans. A. Löwy. London: Chronological Institute, 1866.

GLOSSARY

Ab—Fifth month in the Israelite solilunar calendar; began in late July or early August each year.

Accession Year—The year in which a king assumed the throne.

Accession Year Reckoning—Method of numbering a king's years that does not count his first partial (accession) year.

Adar—Twelfth month in the Israelite solilunar calendar; began in late February or early March each year.

Adar II—Occasional intercalated (thirteenth) month in the Israelite solilunar calendar; added in some years to align the first month of the following year with the beginning of spring.

Aviv—First month in the Israelite solilunar calendar; began in late March or early April each year; after the Babylonian exile called *Nisan*.

Bul—Eighth month in the Israelite solilunar calendar; began in late October or early November each year; after the Babylonian exile called *Marcheshvan* or *Heshvan*.

Coregency—A period when a king reigns with his son also reigning as king; coregencies were used to ensure an orderly transition of the throne.

Elul—Sixth month in the Israelite solilunar calendar; began in late August or early September each year.

Ethanim—Seventh month in the Israelite solilunar calendar; began in late September or early October each year; after the Babylonian exile called *Tishri*.

Gregorian calendar—Modern calendar in use today; originally decreed by Pope Gregory XIII for use starting in 1582; a modification of the Julian calendar that differs from it only in that intercalary days are not added to the calendar in years that are divisible by 100 but not divisible by 400.

Intercalary—Added to the calendar between months; ancient solilunar calendars added intercalary months; the modern Gregorian calendar adds an intercalary day every leap year; intercalation is used to keep the calendar aligned with the seasons.

Jubilee Year—A year occurring every forty-ninth year (i.e., every seventh Sabbatical Year) in which any land purchased from an Israelite was to be returned to its original owner or his heirs; began in the month of Tishri; legislated at Lev 25:8–19.

Julian calendar—Calendar decreed by Julius Caesar for the Roman Empire. An intercalary day is added to the end of February in every year divisible by four.

Iyyar—Second month in the Israelite solilunar calendar; began in late April or early May each year; before the Babylonian exile called *Ziv*.

Kislev—Ninth month in the Israelite solilunar calendar; began in late November or early December each year.

Lunar month—the period in which the moon goes through all its phases from New Moon to the next New Moon; approximately 29½ days.

Marcheshvan—Eighth month in the Israelite solilunar calendar; sometimes shortened to *Heshvan*; began in late October or early November each year; before the Babylonian exile called *Bul*.

Nisan—First month in the Israelite solilunar calendar; began in late March or early April each year; before the Babylonian exile called *Aviv*.

Non-accession Year Reckoning—Method of numbering a king's years that counts his first partial (accession) year as his first year. This method counts this year twice—once for the previous king and once for the new king.

Sabbatical Year—A year occurring every seventh year; began in the month of Tishri; during Sabbatical Years the land was to lie fallow and no crops were to be harvested; legislated for Israel at Exod 23:10–11; Lev 25:1–6; Deut 15:1–3.

Shebat—Eleventh month in the Israelite solilunar calendar; began in late January or early February each year.

Sivan—Third month in the Israelite solilunar calendar; began in late May or early June each year.

Solilunar calendar—A calendar with twelve lunar months alternating between 29 and 30 days. A intercalary thirteenth month is added when needed to align the year with a solar year (i.e., about 365¼ days).

Tammuz—Fourth month in the Israelite solilunar calendar; began in late June or early July each year.

Tebeth—Tenth month in the Israelite solilunar calendar; began in late December or early January each year.

Tishri—Seventh month in the Israelite solilunar calendar; began in late September or early October each year; before the Babylonian exile called *Ethanim*.

Ziv—Second month in the Israelite solilunar calendar; began in late April or early May each year; after the Babylonian exile called *Iyyar*.

INDEX OF SCRIPTURE
AND OTHER ANCIENT LITERATURE

20:2	335	25:15–22	339
20:3a	335	25:23–26:32	339
20:3b–6	336	27:1–2	340
20:6	277	27:3	340
20:7	10	27:4	339
20:7–15	336	27:4–6	340
20:16	336	27:5–6	339
20:17–38	336	27:7	339
21:1	337	27:7–10	340
21:2–7	337	27:9	339
21:8–14	337	27:11–13	340
21:10	337	27:27	340
21:15	308	27:33	340
21:15–16	337	28:1	340
21:15–17	309	28:7	340
21:15–27	306	28:8–10	340
21:17–23:20	337	28:11	340
21:27	337	28:13	7
21:38	337	28:14	340
22:30	337	28:15–16	340
23:12	337	28:17	341
23:12–15	337	28:23–29	341
23:12–22	340	**Romans**	
23:23	10, 295, 337	1:1–6	2
23:26	337	1:8–15	335
23:31–35	337	5:6	5
24:1–21	338	8:28	4
24:17	313	15	336
24:22–23	338	15:24	341
24:24–25	338	15:25	307, 308
24:27	338	15:28	341
25:1–5	339	16	336
25:3	340	16:3	335
25:6–12	339		
25:13–14	339		

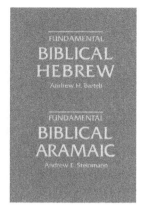

Fundamental Biblical Hebrew
Andrew H. Bartelt

Fundamental Biblical Aramaic
Andrew E. Steinmann

Introductory textbook provides a solid overview of Hebrew and Aramaic grammar and vocabulary in separate grammars bound together for a complete approach to the languages of the Old Testament. The authors address grammar, vocabulary, morphology, and syntax. Includes translation and reading exercises, paradigm charts, a Hebrew-English and Aramaic-English dictionary, and more. (P) 399 pages. Hardback.

53-1120LBR **978-0-7586-0528-3**

Workbook and Supplementary Exercises
For Fundamental Biblical Hebrew and Fundamental Biblical Aramaic
Andrew H. Bartelt and Andrew E. Steinmann

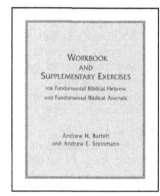

Replicates the exercises from the textbook, providing more space for writing out the answers to the exercises and taking notes. Also provides supplementary exercises and additional translation and vocabulary material for both the Hebrew and Aramaic lessons, as well as chapter summaries. (P) 294 pages. Spiral-bound paperback.

53-1129LBR **978-0-7586-0690-7**

www.cph.org • 1-800-325-3040

Concordia
Publishing House

Concordia Hebrew Reader: Ruth

John R. Wilch

". . . a fine new learning aid for intermediate Hebrew students . . . textual notes focus on the meaning of difficult phrases and the interpretation of unusual syntactical features . . ."
—Stephen Burnett, University of Nebraska–Lincoln

Based on the popular Concordia Commentary series, this Hebrew reader provides the text from Biblia Hebraica Stuttgartensia coupled with a literal translation that indicates Hebrew line breaks. In addition, students will find references to more than 20 advanced reference tools and nearly 100 exegetical studies, plus a complete works cited list. (P) 206 pages. Paperback.

53-1174LBR   **978-0-7586-2617-2**

Intermediate Biblical Hebrew

Andrew E. Steinmann

"Well organized and indexed for easy reference. The charts are easy to understand and will be especially helpful to visual learners."
—Robert B. Chisholm Jr., Dallas Theological Seminary

Bridges the learner from the first year of Hebrew into thoughtful reading and deeper study of the biblical text. Includes diagrams; practice exercises; glosses for Hebrew words appearing fewer than one hundred times in the Old Testament; definitions of linguistic and grammatical terms; select, annotated bibliography; topical and scriptural indexes. (P) 270 pages. Paperback.

53-1170LBR   **978-0-7586-2516-8**

The Concordia Commentary Series

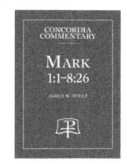

"I have a great deal of respect for this series. It takes serious regard of the biblical text in its original language, and deals with both textual difficulties and theology—an impressive feat at a time when many commentaries are trying to avoid difficult details."—David Instone-Brewer, University of Cambridge

"Pastors and scholars alike will find plenty of helpful insights . . . in the series as a whole."—Robert B. Chisholm Jr., *Bibliotheca Sacra*

"One of the best commentary series currently available for those seeking an exposition of the biblical text that balances the academic with the pastor."—David W. Jones, *Faith and Mission*, Southeastern Baptist Theological Seminary

Contributors to the Concordia Commentary series provide greater clarity and understanding of the divine intent of the text of Holy Scripture. Each volume is based on the Hebrew, Aramaic, or Greek with sensitivity to the rich treasury of language, imagery, and themes found throughout the broader biblical canon. Further light is shed on text from archaeology, history, and extrabiblical literature. This landmark work from Lutheran scholars will cover all the canonical books of the Hebrew Scriptures and the Greek New Testament. Two new volumes are released each year.

OLD TESTAMENT		NEW TESTAMENT	
Leviticus	*John W. Kleinig*	Matthew 1:1–11:1	*Jeffrey A. Gibbs*
Joshua	*Adolph L. Harstad*	Matthew 11:2–20:34	*Jeffrey A. Gibbs*
Ruth	*John R. Wilch*	Mark 1:1–8:26	*James W. Voelz*
Ezra and Nehemiah	*Andrew E. Steinmann*	Luke 1:1–9:50	*Arthur A. Just Jr.*
Proverbs	*Andrew E. Steinmann*	Luke 9:51–24:53	*Arthur A. Just Jr.*
Ecclesiastes	*James Bollhagen*	John 1:1–7:1	*William C. Weinrich*
The Song of Songs	*Christopher W. Mitchell*	Romans 1–8	*Michael P. Middendorf*
Isaiah 40–55	*R. Reed Lessing*	1 Corinthians	*Gregory J. Lockwood*
Isaiah 56–66	*R. Reed Lessing*	Galatians	*A. Andrew Das*
Ezekiel 1–20	*Horace D. Hummel*	Ephesians	*Thomas M. Winger*
Ezekiel 21–48	*Horace D. Hummel*	Colossians	*Paul E. Deterding*
Daniel	*Andrew E. Steinmann*	Philemon	*John G. Nordling*
Amos	*R. Reed Lessing*	2 Peter and Jude	*Curtis P. Giese*
Jonah	*R. Reed Lessing*	1–3 John	*Bruce G. Schuchard*
		Revelation	*Louis A. Brighton*

Concordia
Publishing House

www.cph.org/commentary • 1-800-325-3040

Peer Reviewed

Concordia Publishing House

Similar to the peer review or "refereed" process used to publish professional and academic journals, the Peer Review process is designed to enable authors to publish book manuscripts through Concordia Publishing House. The Peer Review process is well-suited for smaller projects and textbook publication.

We aim to provide quality resources for congregations, church workers, seminaries, universities, and colleges. Our books are faithful to the Holy Scriptures and the Lutheran Confessions, promoting the rich theological heritage of the historic, creedal Church. Concordia Publishing House (CPH) is the publishing arm of The Lutheran Church—Missouri Synod. We develop, produce, and distribute (1) resources that support pastoral and congregational ministry, and (2) scholarly and professional books in exegetical, historical, dogmatic, and practical theology.

For more information, visit:
www.cph.org/PeerReview.

CPSIA information can be obtained
at www.ICGtesting.com
Printed in the USA
LVOW03*0916050418

572355LV00004B/22/P